Retracing a Winter's Journey

Retracing a Winter's Journey

Schubert's *Winterreise*

Susan Youens

Cornell University Press

Ithaca and London

International Standard Book Number 0-8014-2599-9
Library of Congress Catalog Card Number 91-55234
Printed in the United States of America
Librarians: Library of Congress cataloging information appears on the last page of the book.

In memory of my teacher and dearest friend,
Paul Amadeus Pisk

Contents

Illustrations

[ix]

Preface

Franz Schubert's *Winterreise* has been a magnet for musicians and writers on music since its creation in 1827. Recent years have seen the publication of a new edition of the song cycle by Walther Dürr for the Neue Schubert-Ausgabe, as well as the new facsimile edition from Dover Publications of the autograph manuscript in the Pierpont Morgan Library. Arnold Feil, in his monograph on the two cycles Schubert set from Wilhelm Müller's poems (*Die schöne Müllerin* had appeared four years earlier), has pointed out many previously unremarked features of the songs, and Cecilia Baumann and others have continued the efforts of earlier literary scholars to redress Müller's battered reputation as a second-rate poet. Cultural historians such as Paul Robinson, the music theorist David Lewin, and musicologists such as Anthony Newcomb, Robert Winter, and Kurt von Fischer have examined aspects of the cycle ranging from single songs to questions of tonal-dramatic unity, paper and chronology, and the literary context of the work. Recordings and performances of *Winterreise*, one of the best known and most challenging of all song cycles, continue to proliferate. More than 150 years after its birth, Schubert's eighty-ninth published opus still compels the fascination due a masterpiece.

No one questions the musical stature of *Winterreise*, but the poetry that inspired the music, describing the narrator's soul-searching winter wanderings, has not often been so favorably judged. Wilhelm Müller has had a bad press in this century, although an occasional voice is raised to argue the contrary, and several new editions of selected poems, including *Die Winterreise*, have been published recently, further evidence of critical reevaluation of a poet acclaimed throughout the nineteenth century. It is surely time for musicians to rediscover what Schubert, who was customarily discriminating in his choice of poetry to set, found so powerful in this verse and why he again chose Müller's work for a major song cycle. Müller, I believe, was more skillful at his craft and more original in his treatment of conventional themes than is commonly recognized today. The supposed naiveté of his poetry, for which condescending critics condemn him, is deceptive. A close examination reveals a felicitous choice of simple words and skillfully deployed changes of poetic rhythm to underscore shifts of tone, address, or focus. When Müller obsessively repeats key words in "Letzte Hoffnung" to depict acute anxiety or when a change of meter marks the transition from external awareness to inner reflection, he proves that he is, after all, a true poet, one who chose words precisely to achieve the greatest allusive richness by the most economical means.

Müller's avowals of creative spontaneity notwithstanding, his aesthetic of poetry was conscious and calculated. The resultant text of *Die Winterreise* is a deliberately paradoxical fusion of folklike forms and unfolklike content. In his articles on poetry and his reviews of other poets, Müller stated his dislike of complex poetic syntax and his preference for simplicity of expression in order best to convey the immediacy of emotional life. The inward experiences he portrays in this cycle, however, are not simple. His wanderer, after his beloved forsakes him, embarks on a solitary journey into the depths of his being and there conducts a lengthy process of self-questioning. His attempts to understand his alienation from humanity are periodically interrupted by surges of emotional current and by increasingly urgent longings for a death that is always denied him. Tone and technique throughout this cycle are consistent with the pretense that there are no listeners, no one present but the wanderer himself. In order to trace what the poet Novalis called "the path inward" (*der Weg nach Innen*), Müller does not invent a third-person narrator or any other speaker for this monodrama in twenty-four episodes. When the poet omits didactic explanations and answers to the wanderer's questions, he admits us into a fictive consciousness and its mysteries. The result is a richer, more complex text than some have supposed.

It is my desire to demonstrate both that the poetry of this cycle has considerable merit and that Schubert paid it the homage of close reading when he converted the poems into songs. Every aspect of his setting, from considerations of the cycle as a whole to the compositional choices for each individual song, reflects his attention to Müller's nuances of meaning. Even where Schubert on occasion alters the poet's words for better melodic sound, he does so in evident awareness of the effect on the listener's understanding of the text— he was an excellent editor. His wanderer is different from Müller's because musical, an interpretation and a dramatic reading *in music* of Müller's creation; but despite this inevitable difference, rather than overwhelming the poetry, riding roughshod over it, Schubert's compositional choices underscore the protagonist's psychological complexity. The "closeness" of words and music is not an ideal often perfectly attained in song settings, including Schubert's lieder; music competes with text, and overwhelms and contradicts it more often than not. But even a cursory examination of any of the songs in this cycle makes apparent Schubert's close reading of the poetry and his desire to enhance rather than obliterate it. *Winterreise*, D. 911, is not great music superimposed on mediocre words. Instead, the cycle arises from a cultural context of contemporary literary ideals given new expression in Müller's verse and Schubert's music, and that context should be brought to bear on matters of interpretation.

Accordingly, I have begun the first chapter, "Genesis and Sources," with a brief biographical study of Wilhelm Müller, famous in his own day as something other than "the poet of the Schubert song cycles," and with an account of the poetic sources for the cycle. Although the tale of Schubert's setting is familiar to many, I have included it here because the complicated genesis of the work has a direct bearing on questions of order and structure. Throughout the book and especially in the first chapter, my interpretation relies heavily on cultural history and on public reception of the work. Reading the earliest reviews, for example, not only tells us how certain critics understood the work in its own day but should also help to impel a reexamination of later opinions, especially the supposed worthlessness of Müller's poems. The second chapter, "The Texts of *Winterreise*," is an argument for an altered understanding of Müller's protagonist and his fate, while Chapter 3, "The Music of *Winterreise*," is an overview of Schubert's cycle, including consideration of the song forms, tonalities, melodic style, the writing for piano, meters, tempi, and the like, aimed to demonstrate the particular nature of this cycle. "Liederkreis" or "song cycle" is a Protean term, one that different composers have defined variously. Schubert's lengthy Müller cycles (longer by far than the average song cycle of the era) are constituted of self-sufficient lieder; before examining the individual songs, I have asked what the cycle as a whole is like.

To this point, the format of the book is conventional, but such treatment is not feasible for the second part, which examines the songs in order. Each small essay on the individual songs opens with Schubert's piano introduction and a few textual phrases, his German text (I have modernized the spelling), and my prose translation. Then I generally begin by examining aspects of the poetry not included in the second chapter and end with aspects of Schubert's setting not discussed in the third chapter, but I have not forced the entries into a rigid format. Rather, I have paid attention to a host of matters, from singularities of poetic and musical form to details of prosody and musical rhythm, and have permitted myself frequent digressions into reception, past history, literary antecedents and descendants, biography, folklore, even art history, when they are appropriate to the song at hand. For example, the magic of "Der Lindenbaum," one of the climactic songs in the first half of the cycle, is heightened all the more when one understands the antiquity of the linden-tree image in German poetry and its symbolic associations with love and beneficent Nature.

Sometimes I also discuss aspects of the compositional process for particular songs as evident in the autograph manuscript and engraver's fair copy. The use of sketches in analysis is a contentious topic these days, but the autograph manuscript of the first twelve songs, with its mixture of "working papers" and fair copies, is one of the most revealing of all Schubert manuscripts, and I find it fascinating to observe the progression by clearly defined stages from an initial idea to the printed version. A thorough accounting of the numerous revisions belongs properly to the critical notes of an edition, not to prose, and yet certain instances compel attention for the light they shed on the formal structure, text-music relationships, or the compositional history of a particular song, and I have discussed those passages in the essays. The recent appearance of a new facsimile edition of the autograph manuscript makes it possible for any interested music lover to observe Schubert's work on one of his greatest compositions. "They [the songs in *Winterreise*] have cost me more effort than any of my other songs," he told his friends, and the effort is visible on paper for all to see.

With each generation, people retrace Müller's and Schubert's winter journey anew, seeking to understand more deeply a work they love and interpreting it within their own historical, psychological, and cultural context, whatever the claims to objectivity. I will disavow from the start any such claims: this book is an interpretation, but one I hope will be of service to other musicians, scholars, and music lovers who find *Winterreise* as compelling as I do.

I owe a great debt of gratitude to the people and institutions who have so generously helped me with this project since its inception in 1984. For the past seven years, I have spent each summer in Cambridge, Massachusetts, where the librarians of the Eda Kuhn Loeb Music Library and Widener Library at Harvard University were unstinting with their assistance; I am especially grateful to Millard Irion at the Music Library. The scholars and librarians at the Vienna Stadt- und Landesbibliothek, in particular, Ernst Hilmar, Eric Partsch, and Johann Ziegler, have been unfailingly helpful, and the International Franz Schubert Institute at that library generates a stream of publications, lectures, concerts, colloquia, and newsletters of invaluable aid to Schubertians worldwide.

It was at the Stadt- und Landesbibliothek that I was able to study the engraver's copy of *Winterreise*, the first edition of the cycle, Conradin Kreutzer's setting of "Die Post," and many of the most important secondary sources required for this book. J. Rigbie Turner of the Pierpont Morgan Library allowed me to examine the autograph manuscript for many hours in the course of several visits to New York; he and Mark Stevens of Dover Publications, Inc., were subsequently my patient and extremely helpful editors in the preparation of a facsimile edition of the manuscript *Franz Schubert, Winterreise: The Autograph Score*, The Pierpont Morgan Library Music Manuscript Reprint Series (New York, 1989). I am grateful to Dover for permission to use material from my introduction, in particular, the four illustrations regarding the folio structure of the manuscript, in Chapter 1 of this book.

I thank Walther Dürr of the Neue Schubert-Ausgabe for sending me the unpublished typescript notes to his edition of *Winterreise* for the NSA (4th series: Lieder, vols. 4a and 4b [Kassel, 1979]) and both Professor Dürr and Bärenreiter-Verlag for graciously granting me permission to use the edition as the source for the incipits that introduce the discussion of each song, as well as for Examples 7–14, 15B, and 16–22B (Urtext der NSA, Heft 2 Winterreise, BA 7002, © Bärenreiter-Verlag, Kassel). I am grateful to the Vienna Stadt- und Landesbibliothek for permission to reproduce parts of Kreutzer's "Die Post" from the musical *Beylage* to the *Wiener Zeitschrift* (MC 55231). For permission to reprint the music in Example 36 from Johannes Brahms, *Kanons für Frauenstimmen*, Op. 113, I thank the music-publishing firm of C. F. Peters.

The section titled "Signposts in *Winterreise*" in Chapter 3 is taken from my article "*Wegweiser* in *Winterreise*" in *Journal of Musicology* 5, no. 3 (Summer 1987), 357–79, with permission from the University of California Press Journals, © 1987 by the Regents of the University of California. Another article, "Retracing a Winter's Journey: Reflections on Schubert's *Winterreise*" in *19th-Century Music* 9, no. 2 (Fall 1985), 128–35, forms the basis for both the title of the present book and the

second chapter, although I have greatly altered my former conclusions. Writing this book has been a journey in itself and one that took
me far from the starting point.

Doubleday, a division of Bantam, Doubleday, Dell Publishing
Group, Inc., has given permission to quote a portion of the poem
"Under der linden" by Walther von der Vogelweide from *German and
Italian Lyrics of the Middle Ages*, translated by Frederick Goldin (Anchor
Books, 1973). Brae Korin in Chicago provided me with the English
translation of the lines from Wilhelm Müller's "Die Griechen an die
Freunde ihres Alterthums" in Chapter 1 and has discussed the re-
finements of Müller's style with me on several occasions.

I am grateful to the Institute for Scholarship in the Liberal Arts at
the University of Notre Dame for their financial support of a research
trip to Vienna in 1985 and a summer grant for study in Vienna in
1989. Holly Bailey, Marilyn Sale, Carol Betsch, and everyone associated with Cornell University Press have patiently nursed me
through all the minutiae involved in completing and producing a
book. Most of all, I thank my friends and colleagues Mimi Segal Daitz
of City College, New York; Ethan Haimo of the University of Notre
Dame; and Roger Parker of Cornell University for reading the manuscript at each stage along the way and giving me the benefit of
many suggestions. Any merit in this work is due largely to their
contributions.

The Viennese-born composer, musicologist, critic, and teacher Paul
Amadeus Pisk, who suggested that I write this book and who then
sustained me through all the trials familiar to any author, died on 12
January 1990 after a long and remarkable life. Although he did not
live to see *Retracing a Winter's Journey* reach press, he had read and
corrected it many times and knew before his death that it would be
dedicated to him. Indeed, everything I have written has been in tribute to the most inspiring teacher and dearest friend I will ever have.

SUSAN YOUENS

Notre Dame, Indiana

PART I

THE POET AND
THE COMPOSER

CHAPTER 1

Genesis and Sources

Schubert's song cycle *Winterreise*, D. 911, is one of the most famous representatives of the genre, the beauty and power of its twenty-four songs widely acknowledged. Most twentieth-century writers on music, however, have scorned the poems by Wilhelm Müller which Schubert chose for the cycle, although some critics in the last century and literary scholars both then and now have believed otherwise. Song begins with a composer's responses to a poet's words, and Schubert responded to these words with some of his best and most intense music. Those who characterize Müller's text as second-rate verse that happened to inspire a great composer ignore, I believe, the genuine virtues of the poetic cycle and Müller's original use of then-current literary themes. A closer look at both the poet and his poetry reveals much to admire.

In fact, Müller conceived much of his verse as poetry for music. Shortly after his twenty-first birthday in 1815, he wrote in his diary: "I can neither play nor sing, yet when I write verses, I sing and play after all. If I could produce the melodies, my songs would be more pleasing than they are now. But courage! perhaps there is a kindred spirit somewhere who will hear the tunes behind the words and give them back to me."[1] A few years later, when the composer Bernhard Josef Klein (1793–1832) published his settings of six poems by Müller (including "Trock'ne Blumen" from *Die schöne Müllerin*) in 1822, the poet wrote in a letter of thanks, "For indeed my songs lead but half a life, a paper existence of black-and-white, until music breathes life into them, or at least calls it forth and awakens it if it is already dormant in them."[2] Elsewhere, he wrote that the "dormant melodies"

---

[1] *Diary and Letters of Wilhelm Müller*, ed. Philip Schuyler Allen and James Taft Hatfield (Chicago, 1903), 5.
[2] See Carl Koch, *Bernhard Klein (1793–1832): Sein Leben und seine Werke* (Leipzig, 1902), 34–35, for a lengthy quotation from the letter in the original German. Shorter passages

exist, he believed, in one ideal embodiment: "Strictly speaking, for every melody there is only one text, for every text only one melody. Naturally I am speaking here of the best in each art. Mediocrity has everywhere a wide range."[3] Some would argue that Müller's desire for musical setting was a defense against his realization that his poems were insubstantial as literary creations, but his interest both in folk song and art song is known fact. His musical friends and other composers beyond his circle of acquaintances obliged his desire for song composition,[4] but Müller never knew that his true kindred spirit

---

from the letter are also cited in English translation in Cecilia Baumann, *Wilhelm Müller— The Poet of the Schubert Song Cycles: His Life and Works* (University Park, Pa., 1981), 60, and Otto Erich Deutsch, ed., *Schubert: A Documentary Biography*, trans. Eric Blom (London, 1947; rpt. 1977), 436–37. In the continuation of this letter, Müller sends Klein a selection of his *Trinklieder*, or drinking songs, and asks whether the composer might compose four-voice compositions for the singing club (*Liedertafel*) started by his friend, the older Berlin composer Ludwig Berger (1777–1839). He also apologizes for not being able to say more in praise of Klein's settings and pleads his ignorance of musical matters, this despite his musician friends' attempts to initiate him into the mysteries of text-setting, declamation, and the like. Berger set early versions of five of Müller's poems later included in the poet's cycle *Die schöne Müllerin* in his *Gesänge aus einem gesellschaftlichen Liederspiele "Die schöne Müllerin,"* Op. 11 (Berlin, [1818]).

Composers at this time often extracted individual poems or small groups of poems from a cycle and set them singly; Müller, who accepted the practice, did not object to Klein's choice of a single work from the twenty-five poems in his complete *Die schöne Müllerin* cycle (Schubert omitted the prologue, epilogue, and three poems from the body of the narrative). It is a curious coincidence that Klein employs a repeated-note ostinato in an inner voice for his setting of "Trock'ne Blumen," and Schubert in 1823 does likewise, with greater skill and to greater effect, in "Die liebe Farbe" from the same poetic source.

[3]Cited in Aloys Joseph Becker, *Die Kunstanschauung Wilhelm Müllers: Ein Beitrag zum Verständnis und zur Würdigung seiner künstlerischen Persönlichkeit* (Borna-Leipzig, 1908), 9.

[4]Richard Paul Koepke, "Wilhelm Müllers Dichtung und ihre musikalische Komposition" (Ph.D. diss., Northwestern University, 1924), gives an incomplete list of 241 settings. The list is taken largely from Ernst Challier's *Grosser Lieder-Katalog* (Berlin, 1885) and includes seventeen songs by Heinrich Marschner, a setting of "Ungeduld" by Ludwig Spohr, five songs from *Die schöne Müllerin* set by Ludwig Berger, the first six poems of *Die Winterreise* set by Theodore Derège as his Op. 2 (Leipzig, [1838?]), and other songs by many *Kleinmeister* such as Friedrich Curschmann, Otto Tiehsinn, and A. F. Wustrow. Other settings are listed in Ferdinand Sieber, *Handbuch des deutschen Liederschatzes: Ein Catalog von 10,000 auserlesenen nach dem Stimmumfange systematisch geordneten Liedern, nebst einer reichen Auswahl von Duetten und Terzetten* (Berlin, 1875). In a letter of 1821, Müller told a friend that various composers, including Karl Maria von Weber, Albert Methfessel, and Friedrich Schneider, had already set poems from his first anthology to music (see Baumann, *Wilhelm Müller*, 60).

One collaboration with a composer apparently cost Müller considerable effort. The critic Ludwig Rellstab wrote in *Ludwig Berger, ein Denkmal* (Berlin, 1846, p. 112) that Berger hounded Müller unmercifully for alterations to the five poems Berger set from *Die schöne Müllerin.*

(*gleichgestimmte Seele*, a beautifully apposite term) was a younger Viennese contemporary. Perhaps strangely, there is no evidence that Müller ever encountered Schubert's 1823 cycle *Die schöne Müllerin*, D. 795, or that Schubert ever heard the news of young Müller's death on the night of 30 September 1827. Schubert had just returned from a vacation in Graz and was probably completing the last of his compositional labors on *Winterreise* when the poet for whom he had such a great affinity died. Ironically, Müller might not have approved entirely of Schubert's setting, had he lived to hear it. Despite his veneration of music and his desire for musical settings of his own works, he believed that the two arts, poetry and music, should remain distinct in certain respects and not encroach upon each other's boundaries. In particular, he disliked word-painting in music and "musical" onomatopoeia in poetry, practices he compared to painting or coloring a marble statue. Yet he approved of Klein's songs, and Klein, although he was not a particularly adventurous composer, took pains to interpret his chosen texts in music, to attempt matching musical gesture to poetic sentiment or image. Whether Schubert's far richer musical means would have received a similarly favorable response is something we shall never know.

Johann Ludwig Wilhelm Müller was born in 1794 in Dessau, at that time a quiet little town just north of Leipzig, and was the only surviving child of a tailor, Christian Leopold Müller (1752–1820), and his wife, Marie Leopoldine Cellarius Müller (1752–1808). His parents' cottage at 53 Steinstraße was only a few steps from the Mulde River, along whose banks the city was founded. In his charming memoirs, *Auld Lang Syne*, Müller's son, the distinguished Oxford scholar Friedrich Max Müller, named for the hero in Karl Maria von Weber's *Freischütz*, describes Dessau—"a small German town in an oasis of oak trees where the Elbe and the Mulde meet"—as it looked when he was a boy:

It was a curious town, with one long street running through it, the Cavalierstraße, very broad, with pavements on each side. But the street had to be weeded from time to time, there being too little traffic to keep the grass from growing up between the chinks of the stones. The houses had generally one storey only; those of two or three storeys were mostly buildings erected by the Duke of Anhalt-Dessau for his friends and higher officials. Many houses were mere cottages, consisting of a ground floor and a high roof. Almost every house had a small mysterious looking-glass fastened outside the window in which the dwellers within could watch and discuss an approaching visitor long before he or she came within speaking distance. . . . All this is changed now.[5]

Several of the images in *Die Winterreise* seem like evocations of Dessau, its one-story cottages with their high peaked roofs the perfect perches for crows in winter ("Rückblick"). Wilhelm Müller's memories of boyhood strolls on the banks of the Mulde could be one source for a wanderer who walks alongside a river in "Erstarrung" and "Auf dem Fluße" and remembers when he did so in the past. The wanderer's evident feeling for trees and greenery could have originated in lifetime impressions of an oasis in the riverside plain, and it is possible to imagine the tears in "Wasserflut" flowing down the Cavalierstraße in Dessau. Despite his interest in Greek and Italian folk poetry, Müller believed that the best German poetry was rooted in native soil, that poets should not seek models for their own verse in Persian, Oriental, Nordic, or other cultures. He would later base his second novella, *Debora*, written in 1826, in part on his own experiences—the principal character is a young, headstrong German medical student named Arthur, whose childhood resembles Müller's and who accompanies an elderly marquis to Italy, just as the twenty-three-year-old Müller traveled with a Baron von Sack to the land "wo die Citronen blüh'n" on the way to Greece, beginning in August 1817.[6] The landscapes and villages of *Die Winterreise* suggest, in their immediacy and wealth of detail, painting from life.

The young Müller's studies in philology, history, and literature at the University of Berlin in 1812–1813 were sponsored by Duke Leopold Friedrich of Anhalt-Dessau, who in 1820 gave the twenty-six-year-old writer a post as ducal librarian and in 1824 appointed him privy councillor (*Hofrat*). As such, he became eligible to take part in court society; the honor notwithstanding, Müller did not ever think highly of the aristocracy. His university stay was interrupted after one year by the War of Liberation in 1813, the Prussian war against Napoleon's armies in retreat from the disastrous Russian campaign; on 10 February 1813 the newspapers published an appeal from the king for army volunteers, and Müller joined the ranks two weeks later. Of his

[5]Friedrich Max Müller, *Auld Lang Syne* (New York, 1898), 5.
[6]Cecilia Baumann, in *Wilhelm Müller*, 105, points out that there has been speculation as to whether the love of the young Christian Arthur for a beautiful young Jewish woman named Debora could possibly have been a reflection of personal experience. One can say with greater certainty that the Arthur who reads Lord Byron's *Childe Harold* reflects Müller's own interest in the English writer, that both Arthur and Müller lived in the Via Sistina in Rome, and that Müller's fascination with Italian customs and folk poetry are elements of the novella.

wartime experiences we know only that he fought in four battles with the French at Lützen, Bautzen, Haynau, and Kulm and escaped injury. After a brief stay in Brussels, where he had an affair with a woman we know only as Thérèse, he returned to Berlin in late November 1814. The episode, according to Müller's own report, caused his father much concern and apparently ended badly. The chastened youth a year later characterized the affair in his diary for 1815 as "a time of sensuality and freethinking that held me in its chains all too long."[7] When Müller wrote those words, he was once again in Berlin and in love, but this was an idealized love for a different sort of woman, the seventeen-year-old Luise Hensel (1798–1876). A gifted poet, she was the sister of Müller's artist friend Wilhelm Hensel and was courted as well by the great Romantic writer Clemens Brentano and the Berlin composer Ludwig Berger. She never married, and after her conversion to Catholicism in December 1818 devoted her life to religious good works and spiritual poetry.[8] Two years earlier, when Müller was recording his love for her in his diary, she was preoccupied with Brentano's passionate suit for her hand, recurring religious crises, and grief over her elder sister's death on 23 December 1816. Although she probably knew of Müller's feelings for her and may even have encouraged them somewhat, she did not respond in kind.

Between January 1815 and August 1817, Müller resumed his studies at the university and then departed for two years of travel in Austria and Italy. From the evidence of the semiautobiographical novella *Debora*, his professors may have recommended the restless youth, unable to settle down to disciplined work in any field of study, as a traveling companion for Baron von Sack in order to remove him from his dilettante's life in Berlin. On his return to Dessau in January 1819, he wrote the delightful *Rom, Römer und Römerinnen* (Rome, Roman men, and Roman women) about his experiences in that city[9] and then launched a sixfold career as town and ducal librarian, teacher, editor, translator, critic, and poet. The limitations of his duties conflicted

[7]*Diary and Letters of Wilhelm Müller*, 4.
[8]See Hans Rupprich, *Brentano, Luise Hensel und Ludwig von Gerlach* (Vienna, 1927); Hubert Schiel, *Clemens Brentano und Luise Hensel* (Frankfurt, 1956); and Frank Spiecker, *Luise Hensel als Dichterin* (Evanston, Ill., 1936). Luise Hensel's letters were published in Paderborn in 1878, none before 1823 and none to Müller.
[9]Müller's Roman travelogue, *Rom, Römer, Römerinnen: Eine Sammlung vertrauter Briefe aus Rom und Albano*, 2 vols. (Berlin, 1820), has been reprinted twice in the present century: *Rom, Römer und Römerinnen: Eines deutschen Dichters Italienbuch aus den Tagen der Romantik*, ed. Christel Matthias Schröder (Bremen, 1956), and in an edition by Wulf Kirsten (Berlin, 1978). Müller wrote, not a conventional Italian travel guide of the time emphasizing classical art, but a description of ordinary life and customs, and the book established Müller as a writer to watch. See Baumann, *Wilhelm Müller*, 98–101.

with his creative ambitions and his innate restlessness; by June 1820 he was already chafing against the boundaries of his existence: "Although my situation is certainly not unpleasant and my occupation as a librarian not in opposition to my studies, rest does not agree with me; I sit as if on burning coals and cannot feel at home," he wrote.[10] He was to feel "nicht heimisch" (not at home, by extension, not at peace) for the duration of his brief life, and wandering is the foremost theme of his prose fiction and his poetry.

Despite this restlessness, there is nothing at all in Müller's life or the lives of those closest to him that can be linked directly to the experiences he invents in *Die Winterreise*; those looking for immediate bonds between life and art are doomed to disappointment. In fact, 1821, the year in which he wrote the first twelve poems of the cycle, was also the year in which he married the twenty-one-year-old Adelheid von Basedow (1800–1883), to whom he had become engaged in November of the preceding year and who shared his interest in music: she played the piano and was an accomplished contralto singer. Adelheid was the granddaughter of Johann Bernhard Basedow, an important reformer of public education in Germany, and a daughter of one of the leading families in Dessau, and the marriage, although a love match, was therefore an advantageous one for a poor tailor's son. The couple had two children, a daughter, Auguste (1822–68), and a son, Friedrich Max (1823–1900), and from the evidence of Müller's letters to Adelheid, the marriage was a remarkably secure and happy one. So, largely, was Müller's entire short life. Despite his problems with the censors, a bitter feud in 1823 with his immediate superior in the Dessau school system (Müller, who was apparently an excellent if unorthodox teacher, won a fight with the pedantic Christian Friedrich Stadelmann), and the hypochondria that darkened the last year of his life, he seems to have led, on the whole, an untroubled existence, filled with friends, family, music, writing, and travel to appease his Wanderlust. To cite only a few of the most notable events, he visited Dresden in 1823 and there heard the famous bass Eduard Devrient sing Ludwig Berger's *Gesänge aus einem gesellschaftlichen Liederspiele "Die schöne Müllerin,"* Op. 11, composed in late 1816–early 1817 and published in 1818. In July 1824, Adelheid Müller was one of the soloists in a festival held in Quedlinburg to commemorate the hundredth anniversary of the poet Friedrich Klopstock's birth. In 1826, Müller became director of the court theater in Dessau

---

[10]*Diary and Letters of Wilhelm Müller*, 97. Also cited in Frieder Reininghaus, *Schubert und das Wirtshaus: Musik unter Metternich*, 2d ed. (Berlin, 1980), 204.

and in 1827 fulfilled a desire he had harbored since he was a young man: to make a "pilgrimage to the hoard of the Nibelungen"[11] by traveling down the Rhine River from 31 July to 25 September. Five days after his return from the Rhine expedition he died in his sleep, according to his widow and his first biographer Gustav Schwab, of a sudden heart attack. The rumors of political skullduggery at the ducal court and poisoning have never been proven, and it is likely that he died of natural causes.

Müller was a prolific writer whose works reflect the interests of many German intellectuals and poets in the second and third decades of the century: medieval German literature, folk poetry, Italian travel lore, Homeric studies, opera and drama criticism, contemporary English and German poetry, and philhellenism. Like many in post-Napoleonic Europe, Müller's frustrated liberal ideals found a convenient vent in the cause of Greek independence from the Ottoman Empire. His allegiance to the Greek cause began in 1817, when he met the editors of the nationalist Greek literary newspaper *Hermes Logios* in Vienna, an allegiance spurred on by Metternich's support of the Turks, by Müller's philological studies and Homeric research, and by his championship of Lord Byron, the most famous philhellene of all.

Criticism of governmental oppression could not be directed openly at the Prussian government without incurring official punishment. Consequently, German calls to rekindle the flames of Greek democracy were often veiled gestures of domestic political protest as well, gestures that aroused the censor's wrath. Müller's frequent brushes with the government's powerful censorship bureaucracy began as early as 1816, when he and five friends from the War of Liberation published a poetic anthology titled *Die Bundesblüthen*, just after the Prussian monarchy had forbidden all mention of "secret societies" in print. The offending references to "freedom" and "the league" in the dedicatory poem[12] were actually rather innocuous (when Müller asked the censor if the king himself had not enjoined his subjects to fight for freedom three years earlier, the censor replied, "Yes, but that was

---

[11]Wilhelm Müller, *Wilhelm Müllers Rheinreise von 1827 sowie Gedichte und Briefe*, ed. Paul Wahl (Dessau, 1931), 73.

[12]*Die Bundesblüthen* (Berlin, 1816) were written by Müller, Wilhelm Hensel (a better artist than poet), Graf Friedrich von Kalckreuth, Graf Georg von Blankensee, and Wilhelm von Studnitz. The volume was published without the offending prefatory poem, which is cited in Baumann, *Wilhelm Müller*, 46, and Reininghaus, *Schubert und das Wirtshaus*, 202. Reininghaus also reproduces in facsimile on page 210 the beginning of Müller's article "Denkfreiheit" (Freedom of thought) for the *Allgemeine deutsche Real-Enzyklopädie für die gebildeten Stände* (Leipzig, 1827).

then!"); however, Müller's later poetry and prose, with its stinging critiques of a repressive political order, were not so inoffensive. *Urania für 1822*, the *Taschenbuch* whose succeeding edition contained the first twelve poems of *Die Winterreise*, was placed under interdiction by the censor: in other words, Schubert's source was a banned publication. But the poet was no martyr. Müller continued to write politically subversive poetry, the subversion both covert and overt and railed against the censors' intrusions in letters to the liberal Leipzig publisher Friedrich Arnold Brockhaus (from December 1819 until his death, Müller was closely associated with the prestigious firm of Brockhaus), but he was also capable of accommodation where his bread-and-butter prose, even his poetry, was concerned.[13]

Müller's fame throughout the nineteenth century was based in large part on the forty-seven *Griechenlieder* (Greek songs), published in six pamphlets between 1821 and 1824 and ending in 1826 with four poems on the fall of Missolonghi, the event that also inspired Eugène Delacroix's famous painting *Greece Expiring on the Ruins of Missolonghi* (1827). Unlike the modern Greeks, Byron, Müller, and much of the liberal West viewed the conflict as a way to revive "the glory that was Greece" and to exalt freedom of speech from within societies notoriously inimical to free expression of political ideas. Like many other philhellenic poems, Müller's first Greek song is a "recruiting speech,"

---

[13]In September 1821, Brockhaus was informed that *Urania* had been stigmatized with the "Damnatur," meaning that it was prohibited for sale in Austria and that the Viennese censor Joseph Schreyvogel, a famous dramatic critic, had objected to a passage in Müller's essay "Kritik Lord Byron als Dichter" in the same issue with the first twelve poems of *Die Winterreise*. The passage that aroused Schreyvogel's anger was actually a footnote written by Brockhaus himself in which the publisher sought to explain Byron's political views in language that was a direct stab at Metternich's tyrannical hold on the reins of government. As the Austrian censors also banned all but four of Brockhaus's other publications and sent their negative findings to the Prussian censors in Berlin as well, Brockhaus worked frantically to have the interdiction repealed. The prohibition of *Urania* was finally revoked in November 1822, more than a year after its publication and the same month in which Brockhaus, worn out by lawsuits and battles with the censors, became critically ill; he died the next year. See Paul Martin Bretscher, "The History and Cultural Significance of the *Taschenbuch Urania*" (Ph.D. diss., University of Chicago, 1936), 26–30, and Heinrich Hubert Houben, *Der gefesselte Biedermeier* (Leipzig, 1924), 218–24.

In his letters to Brockhaus, Müller often speaks of the censors, especially with regard to his politically subversive Greek songs. See Heinrich Lohre, ed., *Wilhelm Müller als Kritiker und Erzähler: Ein Lebensbild mit Briefen an F. A. Brockhaus* (Leipzig, 1927). In a letter of 4 January 1823 (Lohre, 179), Müller hopes that publication of the first volume has not caused the firm any trouble with the censorship bureau and assures Brockhaus that the second volume contains nothing controversial. On 15 January 1823 he writes of his fears that new and more stringent regulations might impede publication of his latest philhellenic poems and urges printing before the new laws go into effect (Lohre, 181). See Reininghaus, *Schubert und das Wirtshaus*, 204–10.

an exhortation by the spirits of antiquity to the classically educated
European populace whose veneration of ancient Greece had been
newly spurred by the archeological discoveries of the late eighteenth-
century and the neoclassical revival.

Die Griechen an die Freunde ihres Alterthums

Sie haben viel geschrieben, gesungen und gesagt,
Gepriesen und bewundert, beneidet und beklagt.
Die Namen unsrer Väter, sie sind von schönem Klang,
Sie passen allen Völkern in ihren Lobgesang;
Und wer erglühen wollte für Freiheit, Ehr' und Ruhm,
Der holte sich das Feuer aus unserm Alterthum,
Das Feuer, welches schlummernd in Aschenhaufen ruht,
Die einst getrunken haben hellenisch Heldenblut.[14]

(The Greeks to the friends of her antiquity: Much have they written,
sung, and told, praised and admired, envied and lamented. The names
of our ancestors, they have a beautiful sound, fitting for all peoples in
their songs of praise. And whoever would be aflame for freedom, honor,
and glory might catch fire from our antiquity, the fire that rests dormant
in the pile of ashes which once drank the blood of Hellenic heroes.)

Müller's philhellenism led him swiftly to the far more famous philhellene George Gordon Lord Byron, whose works Müller did much
to disseminate in Germany. "The German Byron" came to admire—
he did not at first—Byron's poetry and wrote a biographical study of
the English poet, a monograph on his works, a lengthy poetic eulogy
on his death, and a review of Byron literature, early and important
manifestations of Byron's literary influence in Germany.[15]

[14]Wilhelm Müller, *Gedichte: Vollständige kritische Ausgabe*, ed. James Taft Hatfield (Berlin, 1906; rpt. New York, 1973), 183. The translation here is Brae Korin's. Other re-
cruitment appeals in the Greek songs are "Die Griechen an den östreichischen
Beobachter" and "Die Ruinen von Athen an England" (The Greeks to the Austrian
observer and The ruins of Athens to England). In the final poem, "Hellas und die
Welt" (Greece and the world), of his *Neueste Lieder der Griechen* (Newest Greek songs)
of 1824, Müller encloses the poem at its beginning and ending with the couplet "Ohne
die Freiheit, was wärest du, Hellas? / Ohne dich, Hellas, was wäre die Welt?" (What
would you be, Greece, without freedom? Without you, Greece, what would the world
be?). See ibid., 223.
[15]Wilhelm Müller, "Lord Byron—Literarische Charakteristik mit kleinen Proben, en-
glischen und deutschen," in *Urania für 1822*, 205–47; and "Lord Byron's Don Juan"
and "Leichenrede auf Lord Byron, gehalten von Spiridion Trikupi, gedruckt auf Befehl
der griechischen Regierung," both in the *Literarisches Konversationsblatt* for 1824. Schubert did not set any of Byron's poems; either he did not encounter German translations
of Byron's poetry or did not find them to his taste. German translations did appear
during Metternich's rule, despite the horror of certain Prussian censors at so scandalous

Müller's livelihood came largely from his prose, in particular, reviews of the burgeoning Italian travel lore and translation. He was
an excellent translator: Goethe may well have known Christopher
Marlowe's *Tragicall Historie of Doctor Faustus* in Müller's German rendering. His interest in medieval literature led to the publication in
1816 of fifty poems from the Manesse Codex, complete with contemporary musical settings by Theodore Gade; to the youthful uncom-
pleted romance on the life of the troubadour Jaufré Rudel; and to
later studies of the *Nibelungenlied*. Folk poetry and philhellenism com-
bine in his translations of the neo-Greek folk songs collected and
published by the Frenchman Claude Fauriel (1772–1844) in 1824–1825.
Müller also edited ten volumes of seventeenth-century German poetry
for the *Bibliothek deutscher Dichter des siebzehnten Jahrhunderts*, wrote
over 450 articles for the *Allgemeine Enzyklopädie der Wissenschaften und
Künste*, and tried his hand at drama, in which he was influenced by
the unlikely combination of Andreas Gryphius and William Shakespeare ("Herr Peter Sequenz: Oder die Komödie zu Rumpelskir-
che").[16] The complete list of works, although not as prodigious as the
Schubert catalogue, is nevertheless long and impressive for such a
short life.

A pencil sketch of Müller drawn by Wilhelm Hensel on 8 December
1822 shows a slender, refined young man (Illus. 1). The image seems
modeled both from life and from the early nineteenth-century view
of the artist as an introverted, moody creature, his arms folded as if
to ward off any encroachment by the philistine world. (Delacroix's
portraits of Fryderyk Chopin and George Sand, Caspar David Friedrich's self-portraits, and Joseph Severn's depictions of Percy Bysshe
Shelley and John Keats are all characterized by a similar reserve, the
stance and withdrawn expression hallmarks of the Romantic artist.)

---

a poet. The numerous German settings of his "Poems for Music," including those by
Felix Mendelssohn, Carl Loewe, and Robert Schumann, began to appear only in the
years after Schubert's death.
    [16]Wilhelm Müller and Oskar Ludwig Bernhard Wolff, eds., *Egeria: Raccolta di poesie
Italiane populari*, begun by Wilhelm Müller, completed and published by O. L. B. Wolff
(Leipzig, 1829). The translation of Marlowe's tragedy was published as *Doktor Faustus:
Tragödie von Christopher Marlowe*, translated from the English by Wilhelm Müller, with
a foreword by Ludwig Achim von Arnim (Berlin, 1818). See Otto Heller, *Faust and
Faustus: A Study of Goethe's Relation to Marlowe* (St. Louis, Mo., 1931). Müller's other
translations include *Blumenlese aus den Minnesingern: Erste Sammlung* (Berlin, 1816).
There was never a second volume. The Greek folk songs, *Neugriechische Volksliedern*,
were collected and edited by Claude Charles Fauriel, translated and with commentary
by Wilhelm Müller (Leipzig, 1825). Müller proposed the editorship of a series of seventeenth-century poets, including Martin Opitz, Andreas Gryphius, Paul Gerhardt,
Angelus Silesius, and others, to Brockhaus in the summer of 1820, and the first of ten
volumes appeared in 1822.

1. Wilhelm Müller, as sketched by Wilhelm Hensel in 1822.
From Müller, *Gedichte*, ed. James Taft Hatfield (Berlin, 1906).

In Hensel's drawing, the carefully tied silk stock, extended and be-
ringed index finger, high forehead, and large, intense eyes are
in keeping with the doubtless idealized image of a creative soul
and confirm the Romantic writer Friedrich de la Motte-Fouqué's description of the artist as a sensitive young man in his twenties: "His
countenance bloomed in its first youth, and an almost feminine em-
barrassment colored the transparent skin of his cheeks with red that
quickly waxed and waned. In his eyes gleamed the pride of the budding poet; a full garland of blond, half-combed hair adorned his high

2. Wilhelm Müller, the "German Byron," engraving by Johann Schröter.
By permission of the British Museum.

forehead."[17] A copper etching of Müller by Johann Schröter for the
frontispiece to volume five of the *Allgemeine Enzyklopädie* depicts the
"German Byron" grown older (Illus. 2), no longer quite so slender.
In place of the former close-fitting garb and silk scarf, Müller, by then
a near-compulsive traveler, wears a many-caped greatcoat whose di-
agonal folds radiating outward from his shoulders form an exact compositional parallel to the area of light behind the poet's head. Only

[17]Cited in Wilhelm Müller, *Vermischte Schriften*, ed. Gustav Schwab, vol. 1 (Leipzig,
1830), xxvi, and in Madeleine Haefeli-Rasi, *Wilhelm Müller: "Die schöne Müllerin."* Eine
*Interpretation als Beitrag zum Thema STILWANDEL im Übergang von der Spätromantik zum
Realismus* (Zurich, 1970), 9.

the appearance is Byronic, however. The English poet's foremost German proponent led an undramatic life; Wanderlust, philhellenism, and an early death (from dissimilar causes) are the only similarities. Much of Müller's lyric poetry is contained in two companion volumes, the first with the imposing title *Siebenundsiebzig Gedichte aus den hinterlassenen Papieren eines reisenden Waldhornisten* (Seventy-seven poems from the posthumous papers of a traveling horn player), published in October 1820 (dated 1821) in Dessau by Christian G. Ackermann. Müller offered the second volume of his collected poems to Heinrich Brockhaus, who had succeeded his father as head of the firm, but his proposal was rejected, to his disappointment. The letters say nothing of reasons for the rejection, and one wonders if the political content of two sections of the book, the *Tafellieder für Liedertafeln* (Songs for choral societies) and a group of several hundred epigrams, might have been a cause. Many of these drinking songs and epigrams are satirical political commentary, spiked with the poet's acidulous views of the Prussian regime ("Der neue Demagoge," "Schlechte Zeiten, guter Wein," "Geist der Zeit und Geist des Weins"), and no censor could have missed their message. This second volume, *Gedichte aus den hinterlassenen Papieren eines reisenden Waldhornisten II: Lieder des Lebens und der Liebe* (Songs of life and love), was published by Ackermann in 1824 and dedicated to Karl Maria von Weber, "the master of German song." The poetry in both collections is grouped in sets and cycles, diverse in subject matter and uneven in quality. *Die Winterreise* is the second group in the 1824 volume, following, in marked contrast, the *Tafellieder für Liedertafeln*. The other poetic cycles in the volume include landscape poems and rustic genre pictures (the *Ländliche Lieder* and the *Frühlingskranz aus dem Plauenschen Grunde bei Dresden*, the latter among Müller's best works), a sonnet cycle on the months of the year, the *Devisen zu Bonbons*, named after the mottos and vignettes on candies for a sweetheart, and many *Wanderlieder*. Most of the sets in both volumes are nonnarrative, unified by a theme or motif rather than by a plot. *Die schöne Müllerin* and *Die Winterreise* are both exceptions to Müller's usual practice.

Müller's poetic personae are largely conventional figures, familiar from folk poetry and the poems of his contemporaries: hunters, millers, drinkers galore, night watchmen, shepherds, fishermen, apprentices, sailors, and maidens in love. *Die Winterreise* is his most original treatment of a favorite topos of the time: wanderers on quests of many kinds, impelled by a curse or spell, by longings for redemption or a homeland, by the search for experience, vocation, or love. The pronounced streak of restlessness evident in Müller's inability to choose one preferred field of study and in his frequent travels is manifested as well in his attraction to this central Romantic theme, whether he pays it homage without post-Romantic subversion or revises the theme en route to Realism. In the poem "Grosse Wanderschaft" (The great journey), Müller insistently repeats the refrain "Wandern, wandern"—he had already used a similar refrain, "Das Wandern, das Wandern," in the first poem of the cycle *Die schöne Müllerin*—throughout a poem that continues on nonstop, without division into stanzas:

> Wandern, wandern!
> Gestern dort und heute hier;
> Morgen, wohin ziehen wir?
> Wandern, wandern!
> Wißt ihr wohl das Losungswort,
> Das die Welt treibt fort und fort?
> Wandern, wandern!
> Sehet Sonne, Mond und Sterne,
> Wie die wandern all' so gerne!
> Wandern, wandern!
> Auch die Erde macht sich auf
> Alle Jahr zum frischen Lauf.
> Wandern, wandern!
> Ei, so laß das Sitzen sein,
> Mensch, du muß doch hinterdrein![18]
> [thirty-four lines follow]

(Wandering, wandering! Yesterday there and today here: where will we go in the morning? Wandering, wandering! Do you know the word that drives the world ever onward? Wandering, wandering! See the sun, moon, and stars, how gladly they all wander! Wandering, wandering! The earth too journeys boldly forth throughout the year. Wandering, wandering! So cease your sedentary ways—Man, you must go forth!)

"Grosse Wanderschaft" is a lighthearted paean (although with disturbing undercurrents of compulsion) to changing amours as often as one changes locations, but other incarnations of the theme are less frothy. In a tale published in 1819, "Die drei Könige, aber nicht die heiligen" (The three kings, but not the Magi), his kings do not follow the star to Bethlehem but instead travel restlessly, like the Wandering

---

[18]Wilhelm Müller, *Gedichte aus den hinterlassenen Papieren eines reisenden Waldhornisten*, 2d ed. (Dessau, 1826), 67–69. The poem is the first in the section titled *Reiselieder* (Songs of journeying) and is a poetic announcement of the principal theme of that section.

Jew, throughout the world.[19] The Wandering Jew himself appears in close proximity to *Die Winterreise* in "Der ewige Jude" from *Waldhornisten II*:

> Ich wandre sonder Rast und Ruh',
> Mein Weg führt keinem Ziele zu;
> Fremd bin ich in jedwedem Land,
> Und überall doch wohlbekannt.

(I journey on without rest and peace; my path leads to no goal. A stranger am I in every land and yet everywhere I am well known.)[20]

The wanderer in *Die Winterreise* is not a legendary figure, but like all of Müller's wanderers he is impelled to go forth into the world not by Romantic *Sehnsucht* (the longing within the spirit for that which is unattainable and unknown), but for other, darker reasons: *Wanderlust* ("delight in wandering," or the compulsion to travel) undergoes a sea change in the hands of the latecomer Müller. In his use of a familiar subject—a journey undertaken in sorrow, Müller's accomplishment is akin to that of Caspar David Friedrich, who painted the moonlit graveyards and hermit-inhabited ruins popular in his day but did so to unique and haunting effect. The North German Pietistic strain that suffuses Friedrich's images and the painter's distinctive mysticism are not to be found in Müller's verse, but both the painter and the poet used the clichés of their era to original ends.

Die Winterreise exemplifies many aspects of Müller's aesthetics as defined in his critical writings and reviews of other men's verse. In his opinion, "naturalness, truth, and simplicity" were requisite for poetic beauty, unlike the complex forms and baroque word play he condemned in the works of Friedrich Rückert, Count August von Platen-Hallermünde, and others. Verbosity and grandiose rhetoric, he believed, deformed the truth of feeling, always concomitant with simplicity. Craft should be hidden, rather than overtly displayed, and the reader should always be more aware of the emotional life captured in the poetry than its fabricator's skill in manipulating complex

---

[19]"Die drei Könige, aber nicht die heiligen, oder: Kommt Zeit, kommt Rath" was first published in *Der Gesellschafter, oder Blätter für Geist und Herz* for 1819.

[20]Wilhelm Müller, *Die Winterreise und andere Gedichte*, ed. Hans-Rüdiger Schwab (Frankfurt am Main, 1986), 133. Echoes of *Die Winterreise* abound in "Der ewige Jude." The initial line recalls "Der Wegweiser," the words "Fremd bin ich" are the wanderer's first phrase in the winter journey, and the phrase "Ob meinem Haupte rauscht kein Blatt" in a subsequent stanza is reminiscent of "Letzte Hoffnung."

rhythms and structures.[21] Poetic forms should mimic Nature in their organic development from the poet's inmost nature and native language, hence his distaste for orientalizing poetry and forms borrowed from other cultures and nationalities. (Presumably, Müller would have made an exception for his own Italianate *Ständchen in Ritornellen*.) Cultural copies, however dexterous and refined, were *made* rather than *created* from within. Beauty of sound in verse was for Müller divisible into two classes, absolute and relative, with a vote in favor of the latter. Absolute beauty of sound is word-music, a "klingende-singende" quality he considered to be endemic in Spanish and Italian poetry; in true German verse, beauty of sound should originate in the accord between form and content.

The simplicity and expressivity Müller sought was best exemplified in folk poetry and in art verse modeled on the essence of folk song, not merely its forms and stock characters but its inner dynamics. It was fashionable in his day to write folklike poetry, but Müller did so more knowledgeably and successfully than most because he went beyond superficial imitations. He had harsh words for the legion of poets who failed to understand what he considered was the essential nature of folk poetry: the immediacy of its influence on life, its direct relation to experience ("Die eigentümliche Natur des Volksliedes ist die Unmittelbarkeit seiner Wirkung auf das Leben").[22] Genre pictures of peasants, hunters, and village maids were only the exterior trappings of folk verse; its true nature resides in the intrinsic elements of poetry—vocabulary, syntax, form, meter, rhyme and rhythm—chosen and arranged for their directness of expression. The task is more difficult than it might seem because it necessitates the removal, as much as possible, of the poet's perceived presence from the reader's consciousness. The more one is aware of a mediating mind outside the poem itself and the more one notices artful poetic technique, the less truly folklike the poem is.

Nineteenth-century writers lauded Müller's sophisticated understanding of folk poetry and his ability to reproduce its essence in original verse, to write poetry that "resounds from a full heart, like

[21]In a review, "Östliche Rosen von Friedrich Rückert: Drei Lesen. Leipzig 1822," in the *Literarisches Konversationsblatt* of 1822, no. 15, Müller criticizes the poet's orientalizing poetry as "high-flown, baroque, neck-breaking, stupefying—but neither beautiful nor true." The article—a diatribe in which Müller, a harsh critic, is at his most severe—was reprinted in *Vermischte Schriften*, 5:290–313; the quotation above appears on page 299.

[22]Wilhelm Müller, "Ueber die neueste lyrische Poesie der Deutschen: Ludwig Uhland und Justinus Kerner," in *Hermes* (1827), 94–129; reprinted in Müller, *Vermischte Schriften*, 4:95–162. The quotation appears on page 105.

a true folk song," as one critic wrote in 1820.[23] The younger and greater poet Heinrich Heine praised Müller for his emulation of German folk song; in his essay "The Romantic School," he wrote that Müller "understood more profoundly the spirit of the old song forms and thus did not need to imitate them in externals."[24] The story of Müller's influence on Heine is a familiar one: the younger poet, dissatisfied with the complexities of his *Romanzen und Balladen*, found the model for a new manner in Müller's *Waldhornisten-Gedichte I* and acknowledged the influence in a letter of homage written to Müller in 1826.

I confess to you openly that my Intermezzo meter [the poems of the *Lyrisches Intermezzo* in the *Buch der Lieder*] possesses not merely accidental similarity to your own accustomed meter, but probably owes its most secret rhythm to your songs—those dear Müller-songs which I came to know at the very time when I wrote the Intermezzo. At a very early age I let German folk song exercise its influence upon me. Later on, when I studied at Bonn, August Schlegel opened many metrical secrets to me, but I believe it was in your songs that I found what I looked for—pure tone and true simplicity. How pure and clear your songs are, and they are all true folk songs. In my poems, on the contrary, only the form is to a certain extent popular, while the thoughts belong to our conventional society. . . . Through the study of your seventy-seven poems, it became clear to me for the first time how from the forms of our old still-existing folk songs new forms may be taken which are quite as popular, though one need not imitate the unevenness and awkwardness of the old language. In the second volume of your poems, the form seemed to me even purer and transparently clear. But why say so much about the form? What I wish to tell you is that, with the exception of Goethe, there is no lyric poet whom I admire as much as you.[25]

Heine is careful to define the exact nature of the influence and to differentiate his poetry from Müller's, but the praise and gratitude were genuine, for the moment—Heine would not later rank Müller and Goethe in such close proximity. But even after Heine had renounced Romantic song poetry, including Müller's ambiguous style of Romanticism, he still had kind words for Müller. In his "Reise von München nach Genua" (Journey from Munich to Genoa), Heine sin-

[23]Cited in Baumann, *Wilhelm Müller*, 38, and F. Max Müller, *Auld Lang Syne*, 49.
[24]Heinrich Heine, "The Romantic School," trans. Helen Mustard, in *The Romantic School and Other Essays*, ed. Jost Hermand and Robert C. Holub (New York, 1985), 121.
[25]Heinrich Heine, *Briefe*, ed. Friedrich Hirth, vol. 1 (Mainz, 1950), 269–70; also F. Max Müller, *Auld Lang Syne*, 58, and Reininghaus, *Schubert und das Wirtshaus*, 210–12. See also Nigel Reeves, "The Art of Simplicity: Heinrich Heine and Wilhelm Müller," *Oxford German Studies* 5 (1970), 48–66.

gled out Müller's *Rom, Römer und Römerinnen* as the best of the vast German travel lore on Italy and lamented the poet's early death.[26] From his self-imposed Parisian exile, Heine was capable of coruscating nastiness on the subject of things German, but Müller was largely exempt from his sarcasm.

Other writers point out Müller's gift for precise and lively depictions of Nature and the way in which the poet delineates the transactions between the human soul and Nature. Friedrich Max Müller, in the introduction to his edition of his father's poetry and in his reminiscences, speaks of the special feeling for Nature evident in many of the poems.[27] Henry Wadsworth Longfellow, an enthusiastic proponent of his German contemporary, also praised Müller for the same quality. In *Hyperion: A Romance*, the Baron of Hohenfels says to the young protagonist Paul Flemming

> I am persuaded that, in order fully to understand and feel the popular poetry of Germany, one must be familiar with the German landscape. Many sweet little poems are the outbreaks of momentary feelings— words to which the song of birds, the rustling of leaves, and the gurgle of cool waters form the appropriate music. . . . He [Müller] has written a great many pretty songs, in which the momentary, indefinite longings and impulses of the soul of man find an expression. He calls them the songs of a Wandering Hornplayer. There is one among them much to our present purpose. He expresses in it the feeling of unrest and desire of motion, which the sight and sound of running waters often produce in us. It is entitled, "Whither?" ["Wohin?"] and is worth repeating to you.[28]

He does not mention *Die Winterreise*, which can hardly be described as a series of "sweet little songs," but there, as elsewhere in Müller's poetry, the protagonist seeks his reflection in the surrounding landscape. More than in the tale of the miller lad and his unrequited love for "die schöne Müllerin," the passionate self-observation in *Die Winterreise* is intertwined with observation of the external world—aspects of the landscape and the towns catch the wanderer's eye and impel wonderment about who he really is and why he acts as he does. The

[26]Heinrich Heine, *Werke*, vol. 2: *Reisebilder, Erzählende Prosa, Aufsätze*, ed. Wolfgang Preisendanz, 4 vols. (Frankfurt am Main, 1968), 287.
[27]Wilhelm Müller, *Gedichte*, ed. F. Max Müller (Leipzig, 1868), vii–viii.
[28]Henry Wadsworth Longfellow, *Hyperion: A Romance* (Philadelphia, n.d.), bk. 2, chap. 7, "Mill Wheels and Other Wheels," 120–22. Müller's influence on Longfellow is discussed in Baumann, *Wilhelm Müller*, 124–25. See also James Taft Hatfield, "Longfellow, Transmitter of German Culture," in *Four Lectures* (Evanston, Ill., 1936), 41–55, 95–108.

progression is one from outward to inward reference, in which impressions of the self are either corroborated or questioned in Nature's mirror. The relationship between Nature and the mind perceiving Nature in the winter journey is actually more complex than Longfellow's words of praise might indicate. Ruskin would later define the pathetic fallacy as the result of morbidity which distorts the "plain and leafy fact" through the curved glass of poetic ego, although great poets validly resort to the fallacy out of awareness of the origins of strong feeling.[29] For Müller's wanderer, however, the "plain and leafy fact" entails such loneliness that he endows objects in Nature with human significance in his search for meaning. Both the human soul and Nature are mysteries to him and therefore analogous.

The Textual Sources

The poetic cycle was first published in three stages. On 16 January 1822, Müller sent the first twelve poems of Die Winterreise to Friedrich Brockhaus in Leipzig, saying only, "You now receive my poetry for Urania 1823,"[30] before going on to other matters. Nowhere else in the correspondence is there reference to the cycle. The "Wanderlieder von Wilhelm Müller. Die Winterreise. In 12 Liedern" were published in Urania: Taschenbuch auf das Jahr 1823, pages 207–22.[31] It was this source that Schubert evidently discovered in late 1826 or early 1827, as the order corresponds exactly to Part I of his setting. In March

[29]John Ruskin, "Of the Pathetic Fallacy" in Modern Painters, vol. 5 of The Works of John Ruskin, ed. E. T. Cook and Alexander Wedderburn (London, 1904), 201–20. One of Ruskin's examples, a comparison of a passage from Dante's Inferno with Coleridge's "Christabel," is of interest here for its similarity to Müller's "Letzte Hoffnung." Ruskin writes, "Thus, when Dante describes the spirits falling from the bank of Acheron 'as dead leaves flutter from a bough,' he gives the most perfect image possible of their utter lightness, feebleness, passiveness, and scattering agony of despair, without, however, for an instant losing his own clear perception that these are souls, and those are leaves; he makes no confusion of one with the other. But when Coleridge speaks of 'The one red leaf, the last of its clan, That dances as often as dance it can,' he has a morbid, that is to say, a so far false, idea about the leaf; he fancies a life in it, and will, which there are not; confuses its powerlessness with choice, its fading death with merriment, and the wind that shakes it with music." In Müller's "Letzte Hoffnung," the wanderer invests what he believes to be the last vestiges of hope in the fate of the last leaf on a tree. The device resembles the pathetic fallacy but is not to be confused with it because the leaf is not represented as possessing an independent existence.
[30]Lohre, Wilhelm Müller als Kritiker und Erzähler, 157.
[31]See Paul Martin Bretscher, "The History and Cultural Significance of the Taschenbuch Urania" (Ph.D. diss., University of Chicago, 1936).

1823, ten additional poems were published in Karl Schall and Karl von Holtei's *Deutsche Blätter für Poesie, Litteratur, Kunst und Theatre*.[32] The complete poetic cycle, with the addition of "Die Post" and "Täuschung," appeared on pages 75–108 of the *Waldhornisten II* in 1824. In this final version, the source for Schubert's *Fortsetzung* (Continuation, or Part II), Müller changed the order of the poems as follows (the number in Schubert's ordering appears in parentheses after the title):

Gute Nacht (1)	Im Dorfe (17)
Die Wetterfahne (2)	Der stürmische Morgen (18)
Gefror'ne Tränen (3)	Täuschung (19)
Erstarrung (4)	Der Wegweiser (20)
Der Lindenbaum (5)	Das Wirtshaus (21)
Die Post (13)	[Das] Irrlicht (9)
Wasserflut (6)	Rast (10)
Auf dem Fluße (7)	Die Nebensonnen (23)
Rückblick (8)	Frühlingstraum (11)
Der greise Kopf (14)	Einsamkeit (12)
Die Krähe (15)	Mut (22)
Letzte Hoffnung (16)	Der Leiermann (24)

The poetic cycle "grew" organically in stages, with each new section published as the compositional process continued, and was put in order only at the end. Müller evidently conceived the first stage, the *Urania* poems, as a complete work "in 12. Liedern"; exactly when and why he decided to extend the winter journey is unknown. Since the wanderer at the end of the *Urania* cycle is in much the same condition as at the beginning of the tale, if more exhausted and melancholy, Müller perhaps wanted to go beyond the null and void of "Einsamkeit" to a more conclusive ending, a resolution in death or epiphany, peace or madness. He may also have wished to provide answers to the wanderer's search for self-understanding. The insight in the twelfth poem—that the wanderer, rejecting other people, is "happier" alone and in the midst of winter storms—does not constitute understanding of why he feels and acts that way. The ten poems published in the *Deutsche Blätter* bring the protagonist to a crossroads and revelation, while the addition of "Die Post" and

---

[32]The Schall and von Holtei *Taschenbuch* appeared in Breslau, 13–14 March 1823. The ten new poems were, in order, "Der greise Kopf," "Letzte Hoffnung," "Die Krähe," "Im Dorfe," "Der stürmische Morgen," "Die Nebensonnen," "Der Wegweiser," "Das Wirtshaus," "Mut," and "Der Leiermann."

"Täuschung" at the last stage amplifies important themes already established.

Why Müller changed the ordering at the final stage is anyone's guess. He might have attempted duplication of the same unifying procedure he had used earlier in *Die schöne Müllerin*. There, poems are grouped in pairs or trios by leitmotifs, repeated words and images: the little blue flowers ("Morgengruß," "Des Müllers Blumen," and "Tränenregen"), the green lute-ribbon ("Pause" and "Mit dem grünen Lautenbande"), and the hunter's green garments ("Die liebe Farbe" and "Die böse Farbe"). "Halt!" and "Danksagung an den Bach" are paired by a phrase linking the adjacent poems ("War es also gemeint?"). Müller could not reproduce precisely the same kind of connectives in the later cycle because the wanderer does not remain in one place, and the images change from scene to scene. He does, however, bring closer together those poems with the same key words and images. "Die Post," "Wasserflut," and "Auf dem Fluße," all with references to the sweetheart's house or village, are grouped together in the *Waldhornisten II*. "Irrlicht" was perhaps moved from its former position as the ninth poem in *Urania für 1823* to the eighteenth in the final version because it shares with the seventeenth poem, "Das Wirtshaus," the themes of death and the grave—the wanderer who is denied death in "Das Wirtshaus" attempts to console himself at the end of "Das Irrlicht" by declaring that every sorrow eventually reaches the grave. Certainly the most striking aspect of the final ordering is Müller's placement of what were originally nos. 9–12 in *Urania* ("Das Irrlicht," "Rast," "Frühlingstraum," and "Einsamkeit") much later in the *Waldhornisten II* ordering. Because the cycle traces thought processes and emotional states of being rather than a conventional narrative of actions and reactions, it seems likely that Müller was searching for the completion and ideal order of his multimovement composition with each addition and reshuffling of the poems, arriving finally at the version in his second anthology. As we shall see, Schubert does not duplicate Müller's ordering, and opinions differ about which is preferable.

Evidently, the critical eye and the dissatisfaction that impelled the poet to reorder and revise *Die Winterreise* were typical, despite his desire to write rapidly and spontaneously, as if seized by a Romantic muse and filled to overflowing with poems. In *Rom, Römer, und Römerinnen*, he writes of being an "improvisator" from whom poems and streams of words flow without lengthy labors.[33] Earlier, Müller had

[33]Müller, *Rom, Römer, Römerinnen*, 1:234.

written in his diary for 9 October 1815 that his best poems germinated within his mind, were completed and refined there, then written down very quickly and without alteration,[34] but it would seem that the fantasy in *Rom, Römer und Römerinnen* was the exception rather than the rule. Later, Müller would admit to Heinrich Brockhaus, "I am very scrupulous about matters of style and count syllables anxiously."[35] All of the details of poetic craft discussed in future pages were, it would seem, the product of painstaking effort.

The Genesis of the Musical Setting

In his 1858 "Reflections and Notes on My Friendship with Franz Schubert," Joseph Spaun romantically maintained that the feverish composition of such melancholy songs hastened the composer's early death.[36] The assertion belongs to the Romantic mythology of genius destroyed by the intensity of its own artistic fire, and the labors on *Winterreise* have no place on a coroner's certificate as a contributory cause of death, although several of Schubert's friends later attested to the composer's troubled mood in 1827. The dramatist Eduard Bauernfeld, at times an unreliable witness, later wrote of two occasions during the summer of 1827 when Schubert expressed great anger and despair about the future, once when the two were out walking together and the composer spoke bitterly of becoming a beggarmusician, like Goethe's Harper in *Wilhelm Meister*, and again when Schubert supposedly lost his temper with two musicians at a café outside Vienna.[37] The poet Johann Mayrhofer, in his 1829 "Recollections of Franz Schubert," wrote of *Winterreise*: "He [Schubert] had been long and seriously ill, had gone through disheartening experiences, and life had shed its rosy color; winter had come for him. The poet's irony, rooted in despair, appealed to him: he expressed it in

[34]*Diary and Letters of Wilhelm Müller*, 6.
[35]Quoted in Lohre, *Wilhelm Müller als Kritiker*, 274.
[36]In Otto Erich Deutsch, ed., *Schubert: Memoirs by His Friends*, trans. Rosamund Ney and John Nowell (London, 1958), 139. "There is no doubt in my mind that the state of excitement in which he composed his most beautiful songs, and especially his *Winterreise*, contributed to his early death." See also Deutsch, ed., *Schubert: Die Erinnerungen seiner Freunde* (Leipzig, 1957), 162.
[37]See Bauernfeld, "Some Notes on Franz Schubert," in Deutsch, *Memoirs*, 236–37, and Deutsch, *Die Erinnerungen*, 270–71, for the reference to Goethe's Harper. See Deutsch, *Memoirs*, 231–33, and Deutsch, *Die Erinnerungen*, 264–65, also Reininghaus, *Schubert und das Wirtshaus*, 13–15, for Schubert's supposed tirade at Grinzing.

cutting tones. I was painfully moved."[38] Mayrhofer and Schubert were no longer close friends in 1827, but Schubert undeniably had reason to feel bleak in the last years of his life. The venereal disease for which he was hospitalized in 1823 had ruined his health, and he knew it:

> Imagine a man whose health will never be right again, and who in sheer despair over this ever makes things worse and worse, instead of better; imagine a man, I say, whose most brilliant hopes have perished, to whom the felicity of love and friendship have nothing to offer but pain at best, whom enthusiasm (at least of the stimulating kind) for all things beautiful threatens to forsake, and I ask you, is he not a miserable, unhappy being?—"My peace is gone, my heart is heavy, I shall find it never and nevermore" [lines from Goethe's *Faust, Part I*, which Schubert had set as "Gretchen am Spinnrade," D. 118], I may well sing every day now, for each night, on retiring to bed, I hope I may not wake again, and each morning but recalls yesterday's grief.[39]

Schubert wrote the above letter to his friend Leopold Kupelwieser in March 1824, and neither his health nor his youthful optimism had been restored by 1827. If Maynard Solomon's speculations are correct (and they are certainly credible), the passage is truly dark in its under- and overtones of despairing self-awareness: Solomon has suggested that Schubert was a homosexual, one furthermore with a preference for adolescents and younger men, whose promiscuity led to disease and early death.[40] Great artists can and do empathize with aspects of the human condition not their own, but one need not subscribe to naive notions of art imitating life to see that Schubert might have felt an affinity with a cycle about a protagonist possessed of despair, a self-declared social outcast.

According to Schubert's friend Franz von Schober, Schubert discovered the cycle in Schober's library.[41] Schober and Schubert shared lodgings during the autumn of 1826, after which Schubert lived alone from the end of 1826 until February of 1827, when he once again moved in with Schober at "The Blue Hedgehog." Schober does not say when the discovery was made or which of the two sources Schubert found in the "small library"—*Urania* or the *Waldhornisten* poems.

[38]In Deutsch, *Schubert: A Documentary Biography*, 863, and Deutsch, *Die Erinnerungen*, 20.
[39]Letter of 31 March 1824 in Deutsch, *Schubert: A Documentary Biography*, 339.
[40]Maynard Solomon, "Franz Schubert and the Peacocks of Benvenuto Cellini," *19th-Century Music* 12 (Spring 1989), 193–206.
[41]See Heinrich Kreißle von Hellborn, *Franz Schubert* (Vienna, 1865), 482, and Deutsch, *Die Erinnerungen*, 235.

The autograph manuscript is dated February 1827, but that date appears on a fair copy of the first song, a copy that surely postdates the
beginning of his work on the cycle. It is quite possible that Schubert
found the Leipzig periodical *Urania*, either at Schober's or elsewhere,
in late fall or winter of 1826, rather than in early 1827.

Fritz von Hartmann, one of a pair of brothers (Franz was the other)
who belonged to the Schubert circle in the composer's last years,
wrote in his diary for 4 March 1827 about an unveiling of new works
that the composer wished to perform for his friends; unaccountably,
Schubert did not appear for the soirée he himself had arranged. The
"new compositions" of which Hartmann writes could well be Part I
of the cycle, especially since the diarist refers to Moritz von Schwind's
substitution of "earlier *songs* [italics mine]" for the promised new
works. The implication is that those new compositions were also
songs, that the prospective listeners might have been told that much—
and no more—before the planned première.

> We went to Schober's where we met Spaun, Schwind, [the dramatist
> Eduard] Bauernfeld, and [the portraitist Joseph von] Kriehuber with his
> wife and sister-in-law (the "Flower of the Land") because Schubert, who
> is Schober's lodger, had invited us to hear some new compositions of
> his. Everybody was assembled, but friend Schubert did not come. At
> last Schwind undertook to sing several of Schubert's earlier songs, which
> enchanted us. At half past nine we all went to the "Castle of Eisenstadt,"
> where Schubert too arrived soon after us and won all hearts by his
> amiable simplicity, although he had deceived our hopes by his artist's
> negligence.[42]

Schubert's unreliability in social matters was well known to his
friends, but his failure to appear for a gathering he himself had arranged was unusual.[43] Hartmann does not say whether Schubert offered an explanation or identified the new works unheard that
evening. Schubert's other compositions from late 1826 and early 1827
are of far less import than *Winterreise*: the variations in C major for
two pianos on a theme from Louis-Joseph-Ferdinand Hérold's opera
Marie, Op. 82; two arias on Italian texts by Metastasio, D. 902, nos.

---

[42]In Deutsch, *Schubert: A Documentary Biography*, 613.
[43]Ernst Hilmar, *Franz Schubert in seiner Zeit* (Vienna, 1985), 23–31, has pointed out
that the documentary evidence does not confirm the legend of the *Schubertiaden*—a
term whose origins are unknown—as primarily musical gatherings with Schubert at
the center. The March 1827 soirée would seem the exception that proves the rule.
Schubert called his friends together for the purpose of hearing his new music, but
when he did not appear, they carried on without him.

1 and 2; and lieder to texts by Bauernfeld and Schober ("Der Vater mit dem Kind," D. 906, to a text by Bauernfeld, "Jägers Liebeslied," D. 909, and "Schiffers Scheidelied," D. 910, both to texts by Schober). It seems unlikely that he would have hesitated about playing any of these works for his friends, would indeed have wanted Bauernfeld and Schober to hear the songs born of their poetry. Is it possible that Schubert's plans for the informal performance of his "completed" work in March could have been overturned by his discovery of the *Waldhornisten* poems in Schober's library and his subsequent realization that the cycle was not, in fact, complete? It is an intriguing speculation, if entirely unfounded; we shall almost certainly never know the full story.

Some time later, Schubert *did* perform the cycle for his friends, but we do not know when. Joseph Spaun, who described the occasion in his 1858 reminiscences, was a reliable witness, but the account comes long after the event itself.

> For some time Schubert appeared very upset and melancholy. When I asked him what was troubling him, he would say only, "Soon you will hear and understand." One day he said to me, "Come over tò Schober's today, and I will sing you a cycle of horrifying [*schauerlicher*] songs. I am anxious to know what you will say about them. They have cost me more effort than any of my other songs." So he sang the entire *Winterreise* through to us in a voice full of emotion. We were utterly dumbfounded by the mournful, gloomy tone of these songs, and Schober said that only one, "Der Lindenbaum," had appealed to him. To this Schubert replied, "I like these songs more than all the rest, and you will come to like them as well."[44]

Spaun does not mention any dates. By the time of his reminiscences, the words "the entire *Winterreise*" suggest just that, the entire cycle, not Part I alone and therefore a date sometime in the autumn of 1827, although John Reed questions whether Schubert could have kept the first twelve songs from his friends for such a long time.[45] Could the occasion Spaun records, he asks, have occurred after the March soirée, during the late spring or early summer when Schubert was still lodging with Schober and with reference only to Part I? Spaun refers only to himself and Schober as listeners; the artist Schwind, who left Vienna for Munich in August and who might, with his greater musical sensitivity, have responded differently, is not mentioned. Spaun

---

[44]In Deutsch, *Memoirs*, 137–38, and Deutsch, *Die Erinnerungen*, 160–61.
[45]John Reed, *Schubert: The Final Years* (New York, 1972), 124–25, 130.

shortly came to appreciate the cycle when the initial shock gave way to greater familiarity and the composer's death had invested his late works with funereal poignancy. In his 1829 eulogy "On Franz Schubert," he wrote: "More moving than anything, however, are the songs published under the title of *Winterreise.* They are the last of Schubert's larger works [sic!] but well worthy of closing such labor. No one, surely, could play, sing or hear without being shaken to the depths by the songs contained in this work: 'Gute Nacht,' 'Gefror'ne Tränen,' 'Der Lindenbaum,' 'Irrlicht,' 'Die Post,' 'Die Krähe,' 'Das Wirtshaus,' and a number of others."[46]

The chronological mysteries, already evident, multiply rapidly throughout the compositional history. We do not know when Schubert discovered the complete poetic cycle, although he was evidently engaged in work on Part II during the summer of 1827, as the sketches of "Mut" and "Die Nebensonnen" can tentatively be dated from late summer of that year. Whenever he made the discovery of Müller's winter journey extended to its full length, he evidently realized that he could not duplicate Müller's final ordering without disrupting the musical structure already created. Therefore he simply set the remaining poems in order, beginning with "Die Post," although he reverses the order of "Mut" and "Die Nebensonnen."[47] We do not know when Schubert delivered the autograph manuscript of the first twelve songs to the publisher, Beethoven's friend Tobias Haslinger,

---

[46]In Deutsch, *Schubert: A Documentary Biography,* 874.

[47]Most commentators, where they express an opinion on the matter, prefer Müller's order. A. Craig Bell, *The Songs of Schubert* (London, 1964), 94, writes: "A study of the two, in fact, shows that from a dramatic point of view Müller's [order] is to be preferred, and that Schubert lost by the unfortunate accident of picking up a mutilated version." In a recording on the English label Hyperion A66111 (1983), David Wilson-Johnson, baritone, and David Owen Norris, pianist, perform the cycle in Müller's order. I have argued in "*Winterreise:* In the Right Order," *Soundings,* no. 13 (Summer 1985), 41–50, that Schubert's order is to be preferred. To cite only two examples, the eleventh and twelfth songs in *Urania* and therefore in Schubert, "Frühlingstraum" and "Einsamkeit," are the twenty-first and twenty-second poems in the *Waldhornisten II.* The two poems are poetically linked by the motifs of loneliness and exhaustion. When the wanderer is awakened from the dream in "Frühlingstraum" a second time, he bitterly says, "Now I sit here all alone"; when he resumes the journey in "Einsamkeit," he is exhausted, having been twice jolted from sleep by the ravens' and cocks' screeching. His realizations in "Einsamkeit" are a consequence of the interrupted dream: he is, he discovers, not happy but "less miserable" in the midst of a winter storm and alone because his unhappiness is incompatible with balmy breezes and the presence of other people. "Frühlingstraum" seems to belong most logically in the first half, clustered together with all the other poignant reminiscences of the sweetheart who left him to marry a rich man, while the realization in "Einsamkeit" should precede "Der Wegweiser," in which the wanderer wonders *why* he shuns other people.

whether before or after the discovery of Müller's complete cycle. Presumably, Haslinger made the decision to proceed with publication of the first half, that is, to bring out the cycle in two stages rather than wait to publish the entire work but there are no extant documents to change speculation into fact. Because the autograph manuscript of Part I is difficult to read in many places, an engraver's copy had to be prepared, a copy received and approved by the Central Book Censorship Office on 24 October 1827, but we know neither the copyist nor the exact circumstances. It seems likely, however, from the manuscript evidence of the engraver's copy that the copyist and Schubert worked in tandem during the month of October.

The autograph manuscript of Part II is a fair copy and was not delivered to Haslinger until the end of September 1828, almost one year after its completion in October 1827 and over eight months after the publication of Part I in January 1828. Schubert wrote to a friend, Johann Baptist Jenger, on 25 September 1828 to say, "I have already [!] handed the second part of the 'Winter Journey' to Haslinger."[48] Five witnesses—Bauernfeld, Spaun, Haslinger, Schindler, and Schubert's brother Ferdinand—attest that Schubert corrected the proofs of Part II after he took to his bed in Ferdinand's apartment on Kettenbrückengasse with his last illness, either on the eleventh of November (Spaun and Bauernfeld) or on the fourteenth (Ferdinand).[49] The corrected proofs are no longer extant.

A further subject for speculation in the complicated history of this work is the possible influence of a contemporary song cycle Schubert discovered eight or nine years before composing *Winterreise*. He had perhaps found a prior model for aspects of his second Müller cycle

---

[48]In Deutsch, *Schubert: A Documentary Biography*, 807. Johann Baptist Jenger (1792–1856) was an amateur pianist who accompanied the first performance of Schubert's "Nachthelle," D. 892, on 25 January 1827. Franz Lachner's tale to Sir George Grove of delivering six songs from Part II to Haslinger and receiving only six gulden for them is surely inaccurate, although we do not know what payment Schubert received for either half of the cycle. See Grove, *Dictionary of Music and Musicians*, vol. 3 (London, 1882), 352, also Deutsch, *Memoirs*, 267, and Deutsch, *Die Erinnungen*, 306.

[49]Deutsch, *Schubert: A Documentary Biography*, from Spaun's account, 879: "The few lucid intervals he still devoted to the correction of the second part of the 'Winter Journey.' " See also ibid., from Bauernfeld's obituary, 893: "He nevertheless still made use of a few better moments to correct the proofs of the second part of the 'Winter Journey.' " According to the composer's brother Ferdinand, in the Leipzig *Neue Zeitschrift für Musik*, 23 April–3 May 1839, "It was 14 November when he became bedridden, although he sat up for a few hours each day and still corrected the second part of the 'Winter Journey,' " in ibid., 920. According to Tobias Haslinger in the *Wiener Zeitung* for 30 December 1828 (Deutsch, *Die Erinnerungen*, 449–50), the correction of the proofs for Part II was "die letzten Federstriche."

in the *Neun Wander-Lieder von* [Ludwig] *Uhland*, Op. 34,[50] by Conradin Kreutzer (1780–1849), the German-born *Kapellmeister* of the Vienna Kärntnertor-Theater from 1822 to 1827 and the composer of the operatic successes *Das Nachtlager in Granada* and *Der Verschwender*. Even before the Schubert-Kreutzer connection, Müller, who knew Uhland personally, seems to have borrowed poetic images and themes from the famous older poet, especially Uhland's sixth poem, "Winterreise," for his own lengthier winter journey; the links to Kreutzer's Uhland settings are thus twofold (the texts and translations for Uhland's cycle are given in the Appendix). One finds in Uhland the depiction of Nature as motionless and frozen, similar to Müller's "Auf dem Fluße"; the darkened world/sun (Uhland's line "Die Sonne scheint so trübe" in "Winterreise" becomes Müller's "Nun ist die Welt so trübe" in "Gute Nacht"); the antinomy of heat and cold, ice and fire; the frozen heart; and the sole protagonist's deserted pathways and aimless straying: these are all elements that recur in Müller. The words "Die kalten Winde tosen" from Uhland's "Nachtreise" become Müller's line "Die kalten Winde bliesen" in "Der Lindenbaum"; the withered, falling leaves, also in "Nachtreise," reappear invested with symbolic meaning in Müller's "Letzte Hoffnung"; and the inn and the apple tree of Uhland's "Einkehr" are transformed into Müller's cemetery/inn and linden trees. The sun's light extinguished by the death of love in "Nachtreise" becomes the wanderer's wish in "Die Nebensonnen" that the sun would vanish and leave him in darkness, while the "Morgenlied" sung loudly to combat anxiety—Uhland's wanderer is also a singer-poet—becomes Müller's "Mut." Luise Eitel Peake has even suggested that Müller may have intended some of the poems in *Die Winterreise* as a parody of Uhland and Kreutzer, a way of providing his musical friends in Dessau with other words for Kreutzer's melodies.[51]

Of all the similarities between the two poetic cycles, one looms largest: before the creation of Müller's tragic figure, Uhland's wanderer undertakes a *psychological* journey in the form of a lyrical monodrama. This view would explain the seeming inconsistency of a character who speaks of his sweetheart as dead and buried in her

---

[50]The cycle was published in Augsburg by Gombart in 1818.
[51]See Luise Eitel Peake, "Kreutzer's *Wanderlieder*: The Other *Winterreise*," *Musical Quarterly* 65 (1979), 83–102. The discussion of parody is found on 99–100, where Peake writes that the poetic rhythms of "Gute Nacht" could be a parody of the second Uhland song, "Scheiden und Meiden"; "Erstarrung" a parody of "Winterreise"; "Rast" of the third Uhland song, "In der Ferne"; and "Rückblick" of the seventh song, "Abreise."

grave in the fifth song, "Nachtreise," but who wishes to return to her in the final song, "Heimkehr." It is his *love* for her ("Mein Lieb zu Grab' getragen"), not the sweetheart herself, that has, for a time, died and is resurrected at the end as a consequence of his inner peregrinations. The loss of love as emotional death, not the physical death of a person, is made explicit in the sixth song "Winterreise," when the monologist declares that love is extinguished, joy no longer possible ("Erloschen ist die Liebe, / Die Lust kann nicht bestehn"). Similarly, the town he leaves in the seventh song, "Abreise," is a state of being or existential condition more than a place on a fictional map. Müller, however, uses his borrowed themes differently, transforming them into tragedy; the two journeys originate from different causes and conclude with diametrically opposed endings. Uhland's wanderer leaves his sweetheart at the behest of an incomprehensible compulsion and parts from her with kisses and embraces. He has not been jilted, and his journey ends, not in tragic self-division but in reconciliation and return; his is a prototype of the Romantic circular quest that leads "immer nach Hause," back to its beginnings.[52] Not so Müller's tragedy.

Schubert knew and admired Kreutzer's cycle. Spaun twice told the following anecdote of his friend's reaction to the *Wander-Lieder* shortly after their publication: "We once found him playing through Kreutzer's *Wanderlieder*, which had just appeared. One of his friends [Anselm Hüttenbrenner] said 'Leave that stuff alone and sing us a few of your songs instead,' to which he replied tersely, 'But you are unjust; the

---

Müller "Gute Nacht"	*Uhland / Kreutzer* "Scheiden und Meiden"
Fremd bin ich eingezogen, Fremd zieh' ich wieder aus.	So soll ich dich nun meiden, Du meines Lebens Lust!
"Erstarrung" Ich such' im Schnee vergebens Nach ihrer Tritte Spur...	"Winterreise" Bei diesem kalten Wehen, Sind alle Straßen leer...
"Rast" Nun merk' ich erst, wie müd' ich bin, Da ich zur Ruh' mich lege...	"In der Ferne" Will ruhen unter den Bäumen hier Die Vöglein hör' ich so gerne...

See also Annaliese Landau, *Das einstimmige Kunstlied Conradin Kreutzers und seine Stellung zum zeitgenössischen Lied in Schwaben* (Leipzig, 1930), and Barbara Turchin, "The Nineteenth-Century *Wanderlieder* Cycle," *Journal of Musicology* 5 (Fall 1987), 498–525.

[52] This famous phrase comes from Novalis's fairy tale *Heinrich von Ofterdingen*, a poetic pilgrimage exemplary of Romantic circular quests. See M. H. Abrams, *Natural Supernaturalism: Tradition and Revolution in Romantic Literature* (New York, 1971), 249–52, for a discussion of optimistic and pessimistic journeys as an important Romantic topos.

songs are very beautiful, and I wish I had written them.' "[53] One can sympathize both with Hüttenbrenner and Schubert. Kreutzer's music is more conservative than Schubert's in every way, although he is capable of an occasional striking chromatic detail, of voice-leading with an unusual harmonic goal, of sensitive musical prosody and word-painting that is less pedestrian than most. The deceptive motion at the culmination of the phrase "bleibt auch das Herze kalt" (my heart also stays cold) in "Winterreise" is one example of Kreutzer at his most vivid (Ex. 1), although nothing in the cycle approaches the

Example 1.   Kreutzer's "Winterreise," mm. 50–58

power of Schubert's "Letzte Hoffnung" or "Auf dem Fluße." But if the *Neun Wander-Lieder* are not as musically profound as Schubert's cycle, one can nevertheless find Kreutzer's influence in matters both small and large. Even the tempo marking "In mässig geschwinder Bewegung" (In moderately rapid motion) for Kreutzer's first song, "Lebewohl," seems the precursor for the indication "Mässig, in gehender Bewegung" for "Gute Nacht" in the autograph manuscript. The arpeggiated unison figure at the beginning of "Nachtreise" could be a source for the introduction to "Die Wetterfahne," and the soft but agitated triplet figuration that follows is kin to the accompaniment

[53]Deutsch, *Memoirs*, 135, also 27 (Spaun's obituary for Schubert). In the obituary, Spaun writes, "Once, when he was playing the *Wanderlieder* by Kreutzer, and one of his friends expressed himself disparagingly about them, he replied quite quietly: 'I wish I had written them.' "

Example 2.   Kreutzer's "Nachtreise," mm. 1–10

figuration in "Erstarrung" (Ex. 2), although Schubert allies the broken-chordal patterns with an important melodic line in the bass, unlike Kreutzer. The contrast in Kreutzer's "Nachtreise" of driven, obsessive motion in the unhappy present (G minor) with memories of a happier past in parallel major ("Oft hab' ich diesen Weg gemacht, / Wann goldner Sonnenschein gelacht, / Bei lauer Lüfte kosen") foreshadows "Rückblick" (Ex. 3), and the tremolando octaves at the end seem a

Example 3.   Kreutzer's "Nachtreise," mm. 28–42

precursor of the ending of "Auf dem Fluße." The tonal succession in both cycles is open-ended, and the same general associations of keys with poetic themes occur in both: G minor and D minor for tragedy, F major for the hospitality of the apple tree or inn, and E major with beneficent Nature. But if Kreutzer provided the mold, Schubert then proceeded to break it with a work in every way greater. "I wish I had written them," he said in 1818 or 1819 (?); almost a decade later, he would set to music the verses Müller may well have written out of a similar response to Uhland's achievement.

The Sources of Schubert's Setting

The principal sources consist of seven handwritten manuscripts and the first editions of Part I and Part II. Those sources do not tell the whole story: we can infer from the extant manuscripts the existence of others, now lost. But despite our awareness of missing sources, the existing manuscripts are revealing and fascinating documents, especially the autograph manuscript of Part I.[54] Tales of Schubert's compositional facility abound in his friends' reminiscences[55] and can be verified from many manuscripts, including Part I; he evidently wrote the first versions of the twelve songs in Part I at great speed. Nevertheless, the effort of which Schubert spoke to his friends is also apparent in the large number of revisions and emendations, unusual only in the number, not in the fact of their existence. Schubert had a lifelong habit of revising and rewriting his songs in his concern to achieve the best possible musical realization of the words: even a cursory perusal of the Deutsch Schubert catalogue reveals two, three, or more versions of many of his songs.

The autograph manuscript of Part I contains a wealth of information about Schubert's compositional process and working methods—mute but eloquent verification of the unusual effort this work cost its com-

[54]See Franz Schubert, *Winterreise: The Autograph Score*, a facsimile published by Dover as part of the Pierpont Morgan Library Music Manuscript Reprint Series (New York, 1989). The manuscript in the Mary Flagler Cary Music Collection of the Pierpont Morgan Library is catalogued as LPhA 1134, Cary Catalogue no. 191, a manuscript formerly owned by the publisher Tobias Haslinger, and then by Haslinger's widow, Carl Meinert, Siegfried Ochs, and Louis Ochs.

[55]Spaun, in his "On Schubert" of 1829, writes, "Schubert's speed in composition was extraordinary, and the fact that the reading and composition of Goethe's 'Erlkönig' was the work of one single afternoon may serve as an illustration of this" (see Deutsch, *Memoirs*, 21).

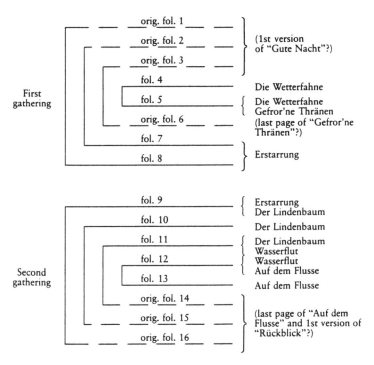

3. The two original gatherings of *Winterreise*, Part I
   (missing pages indicated by broken lines)

poser. The manuscript, with its heading "Winterreise von Wilh. Müller" and the signature "Frz. Schubert Wien," is dated "Febr. 1827" in the upper-right-hand corner of fır, the first page of "Gute Nacht," but that song is a fair copy that was certainly preceded by an earlier version, now lost. It is intriguing to speculate that Schubert's unusual efforts may well have begun right at the beginning with "Gute Nacht." The autograph of Part I is a mixture of first versions, or "working papers," and fair copies, and includes a total of seven marginal stubs or tongues that show where leaves were cut from the two original regular gatherings of four bifolia (eight leaves) each, gatherings which now form incomplete internal subgroupings within the manuscript (Illus. 3). Schubert apparently began the composition of *Winterreise* with these two gatherings, of which only the innermost bifolium (fols. 4 and 5) remains in its entirety from the first gathering. When he had completed the first versions of songs 4–8 (the end of "Erstarrung," "Der Lindenbaum," "Wasserflut," "Auf dem Fluße,"

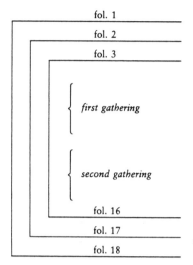

4. The two gatherings with
three wraparound bifolia

and "Rückblick") in one continuous process on the second gathering, he realized that he had run out of paper and therefore wrapped three additional bifolia around the two filled gatherings (Illus. 4). In all likelihood, he left the first three folios blank while he continued with the first version of "Irrlicht" on folios 16 and 17r, "Rast," and "Frühlingstraum." Having run out of paper once again, he took a single bifolium (fols. 19 and 20) and worked on it separately, not wrapping it around the existing gatherings. He composed the remainder of "Frühlingstraum" on folio 19 and began "Einsamkeit" on folio 20, but encountered compositional difficulties with the latter. Dissatisfied with everything he had written on folio 20v, he vigorously crossed out the page and tipped in an additional leaf, folio 21, for the continuation of "Einsamkeit" (Illus. 5).

At some unknown time (or times), Schubert returned to the manuscript to replace entire songs or portions of songs with fair copies, for what reasons we do not know. The leaves cut out of the manuscript have been lost, and there is no way to ascertain whether he substantively revised the first versions or simply copied what was contained on the original pages in a neater, more legible hand. In other words,

fol. 19

fol. 20

fol. 21   5. The final gathering of Part I

Schubert seems to have composed Part I as a swift, albeit difficult, march through "working versions" of songs 1–12 in order, before recopying (after further reworking?) the entirety of "Gute Nacht" and "Rückblick," as well as portions of "Gefror'ne Tränen" and "Auf dem Fluße" (Illus. 6). "Rückblick" was speculatively the last addition to this fascinatingly complex manuscript, as it is written in part on a tipped-in leaf whose paper is different from that of the rest of the manuscript; furthermore, the handwriting is neater and more compact and the format different from that used for all the other songs in Part I (only three staves for each system rather than his customary four, without the usual blank staff between the voice and piano parts). The effort of which Schubert spoke is apparent not only in the revisions but in the omissions and replacements as well, the invisible as well as the visible.

For those songs that are not fair copies (most of Part I), the autograph manuscript reveals a compositional process in at least two stages. The initial stage, varying in degrees of completion, is written in a light brown ink, while the completion and revisions are notated in a distinctly darker, clearer ink. Most commonly, Schubert would set down the entire vocal line, the piano introductions, occasionally all or part of the accompanimental interludes, and mnemonic aids at stage 1. He would then return to the song sometime later to fill in the remainder of the accompaniment, to make numerous revisions, and to add such refinements of detail as articulation markings: virtually all indications for tempi, dynamics, slurs, staccato markings, and the like belong to stage 2. Stage 1 also includes revisions made "on the spot," but not nearly so many as at stage 2. Frequently, he would notate just enough of the piano accompaniment after the vocal entrance to serve as a mnemonic aid when he returned to the work at stage 2; the result is often a complicated interweaving of stage 1 and stage 2 inks in the piano parts.

This autograph is a glimpse into the composer's workshop: many pages of Part I look like a battle zone, with the composer finally triumphant over most of his momentary obstacles.[56] The revisions include changes of key shortly after Schubert began work on a song,

---

[56]At least one scholar feels that the cross-relation between D-natural and D-sharp in m. 63 of "Auf dem Fluße" is the result of Schubert's abandoning a compositional problem caused by a series of revisions between the autograph manuscript and the first edition. (The double-dottings one finds here in the autograph, for example, disappear by the time of the engraver's copy.) See Julian Armitage-Smith, "Schubert's *Winterreise*, Part I: The Sources of the Musical Text," *Musical Quarterly* 60 (January 1974), 20–36, and my essay on "Auf dem Fluße" in Part II of this book.

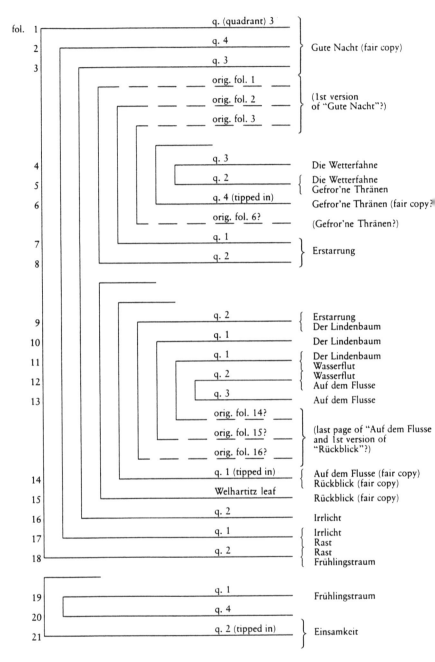

6. The gathering structure of Part I (missing pages indicated by broken lines)

the addition of piano interludes and sequential repetitions, excised passages, alterations of the vocal line, and changes to previous rhythmic patterns—ample evidence of Schubert's scrupulousness regarding detail. For example, in "Auf dem Fluße," Schubert did not devise the brief excursion into D-sharp minor at mm. 9–11 until after he had written the vocal line for those measures in G-flat; before completing the cadence in m. 12, he returned to the start of the phrase "Wie still bist du geworden" and altered the line. In "Frühlings-traum," he began by notating the right-hand part for the four-measure introduction in the key of G major, then changed the tonality to A major before writing the vocal line. At stage 2, he decided to add a piano introduction to the C section (mm. 27–43, the setting of the third and sixth stanzas of the twofold ABC–ABC stanzaic structure) and wrote the additional measures on a hand-drawn extension of the staves into the right-hand margin; similarly, the sequential repetition of the question "Was fragen sie nach meinen Schmerzen?" in "Die Wetterfahne" was an inspiration at stage 2 and also required hand-drawn extensions of two staff systems. In "Rast," he experimented at stage 1 with alternative versions of the bold, arpeggiated vocal line at m. 30, then altered the melodic contour at stage 2, crossing out the lower version (Ex. 4). (In the engraver's copy, he again revised the

Example 4.   "Rast," mm. 30–31

Der   Sturm   half   fort   mich   weh - en

line to place the highest pitch at the start of the second beat, remedying the vocally awkward leap in the earlier conception.) "Die Wetterfahne" especially is a case study in compositional trial and error, and it is fascinating to compare the first conception of a phrase or passage with the revisions he deemed necessary on the spot or shortly thereafter. To cite only one example, he originally conceived the words "[So hätt' er nimmer] suchen wollen / Im Haus ein treues Frauenbild" as an ascent to the emphasized verb "suchen," followed by a cadential tonicization of D minor. In the revised version, it is the word "nimmer" that receives an even greater emphasis than "suchen," a compositional choice more evocative of bitterness and anger than the original setting (Ex. 5). The downward turn for the words "Haus" and "treu - [es]" is less indicative of angry disturbance than the rising gestures, the higher pitches on weaker beats greatly

Example 5.   "Die Wetterfahne," mm. 17–20, autograph ms.

increasing the rhythmic-melodic tension of the cadence. The entirety of stanza 2 of "Die Wetterfahne" is remarkable for jagged melodic drama of this kind, well worth the effort required to achieve it. And there are many more such revisions: every "working version" in Part I is filled with emendations.

Three of the songs in Part I were transposed into lower keys before publication. At the beginning of the D-minor "Rast," Schubert wrote, "NB ist ins [aus?] C moll zu schreiben" (*Nota bene*: this is to be written in C minor), the only directive for transposition in Schubert's hand to be found in either Part I or Part II. When the engraver's copy of Part I was prepared, however, both "Wasserflut" and "Einsamkeit" were transposed, "Wasserflut" from F-sharp minor to E minor and "Einsamkeit" from the original D minor to B minor. In the manuscript of Part II, the brief red-penciled notes "in G-mol" for "Mut" (originally composed in A minor) and "in A-mol" for "Der Leiermann" (composed in B minor) are written in Haslinger's hand. All five are downward transpositions and were perhaps requested by the publisher to avoid instances of high A in the vocal line. Haslinger may well have been the first of many to ask, "For what voice was this cycle written?"—not a tenor (although some tenors have recently performed and recorded the work), but not a typical baritone either, since there are many passages too high for most baritones. Schubert's customary vocal tessitura was quite high, and publishers aware of the effects of difficult music on sales had perhaps asked the composer for downward transpositions of earlier songs. Actually, neither "Einsamkeit" nor "Der Leiermann" in its original key includes high A in the vocal part, but their instances of high F, F-sharp, and G would have been uncomfortable for most baritones, especially the final phrase of the last song. Confronted with the necessity of lower transpositions, Schubert made the best of his circumstances. The transpositions of "Rast" and "Einsamkeit" open up the formerly closed circle of Part I for the continuation of the journey, while the transposition of "Wasserflut" consolidates the tonal trio in E major–E minor ("Der Lindenbaum," "Wasserflut," "Auf dem Fluße") at the core of the first half.

The setting of "Mut" in G minor clarifies the motivic connection with "Der Wegweiser," also in G minor, and produces a new tonal link between "Mut" and "Der stürmische Morgen": in both songs, stormy weather is set in the subsidiary key of B-flat major. The transposition of "Der Leiermann" from B minor to A minor makes of "Die Neben-sonnen" (in A major) and "Der Leiermann" a tonal pair, an extended ending to the cycle.

The engraver's copy for Part I is at present in the collection of the Vienna Stadt- und Landesbibliothek, Music Division, and was closely corrected by Schubert himself. Five different hands are evident in the thirty-two folios (sixty-four pages): an unknown hand for the title page, the principal copyist, yet another copyist for the eighth song only ("Rückblick"), Haslinger, and Schubert. It seems probable that the fair copy of "Rückblick" was added after the preparation of songs 1–7 and 9–12, the implication being that Schubert did not complete composition of the song until that time, possibly after the remainder of Part I was delivered to Haslinger. The title page reads "Winterreise / von Wilh. Müller / in Musik gesetzt / von / Franz Schubert / A[nn]o 1827" and bears as well the censor's mark, "Excudatur / vom Kk Centbuch RevisAmte / Wien d.24te Oktober 1827 / Schodl." On folio 1v at the top of the page, Haslinger added the penciled notation, "NB: Joh. Schönwalder belieben den Stich so einzurichten, dass jedes [!] Nuṁer sich allein abdrucken läßt.—Haslinger" (Joh[ann] Schön-walder thinks it proper to arrange the engraving so that each number is printed separately); he also indicated at the beginning of "Früh-lingstraum" on f29r, "Beide Strophen ausstechen" (Engrave both strophes). Schubert had written the song in strophic format in the autograph manuscript, and the copyist had followed his lead. Messrs. Schönwalder and Schwarz ("Schwarz soll dieses Lied [Rast] in C-moll schreiben"—"Schwarz should write this song in C minor") are un-known quantities.

Either the copyist and composer worked in close collaboration with each other or the copyist had access to other sources that postdate the autograph manuscript, since passages that differ markedly from the autograph appear in the engraver's copy with no trace of correc-tion—the first supposition seems far more likely. The leap upward to the high F-sharp in m. 45 of "Rast," the culmination of the arching melodic line in mm. 30 and 35 of the same song, the change of tempo for "Auf dem Fluße" from *mässig* to *langsam* (a greater contrast with "Rückblick" to follow and a more suitable tempo for the reflective temper of the poem) are novelties that appear for the first time in the engraver's copy. Elsewhere in the manuscript Schubert himself made substantive musical revisions, the principal fascination of this important source. On folio 5 verso, the copyist notated the rising chromatic line—a melodic cliché for rising tension and terror, one that Schubert uses sparingly in *Winterreise*—for the words "Er hätt' es eher bemerken sollen / Des Hauses aufgestecktes Schild" from "Die Wetterfahne" as he found it in the autograph manuscript (Ex. 6). Schubert neatly crossed out the phrase with his customary cros-

Example 6.   "Die Wetterfahne," mm. 15–16, autograph ms.

shatching, partially enclosed by a boxlike outline, and substituted the melodic line as we know it now. The skeletal foundation of rising chromaticism is embellished with higher pitches on weak beats after the manner of his setting of the previous words "Sie pfiff' den armen [Flüchtling aus]" and "so hätt' er [nimmer suchen wollen]"—the revision is an inspired conception, no longer formulaic. The entire engraver's copy attests to a continued process of revision and refinement beyond the autograph.

The autograph of Part II is not a "working paper" but a fair copy on sixteen folios (two double-sheet gatherings) with the heading:

> Okt. 1827 Frz. Schubert
> Wien
> / Fortsetzung der Winterreise: /
> von Wilhelm Müller.

The "O" of "Oktober" was corrected from an "S"—for September? Was the copy perhaps begun in the early days of October, when such a mistake would be most likely? Schubert customarily dated his manuscripts from the beginning of composition, but the sketches for "Mut" and "Die Nebensonnen" predate this fair copy. Schubert took pains to make the manuscript, evidently an engraver's copy, more legible than the autograph of Part I. The note heads are rounded so that the pitches can be easily read, and even the thickest harmonies are clearly notated. Particularly in passages such as the chromatic introduction to "Der stürmische Morgen," Schubert's concern with the clarity of his hand is evident. Since Part II was published separately, the songs are numbered 1 through 12, not 13 through 24.

There were obviously earlier sources for Part II which are now lost, with only two exceptions. A first version of "Mut," now in a private collection in Vienna, is datable to sometime in the summer of 1827, and the first version of "Die Nebensonnen" (Vienna, Gesellschaft der Musikfreunde, A 235) can be dated between July and September 1827. Was "Die Nebensonnen" perhaps first composed while Schubert was on vacation in Graz September 2–28? According to the philosopher Ernst Freiherr von Feuchtersleben, in a letter to a doctor named Romeo Seligmann in autumn 1827, Schubert returned from Graz "full of enthusiasm [begeistert] but richer by only two songs,"[57] "Heimliches Lieben," D. 922, and "Eine altschottische Ballade," D. 923. Feuchtersleben does not mention the "Grätzer Walzer" and "Grätzer Galopp," and Schubert might not have mentioned the continuing work on *Winterreise*. The first versions of "Mut" and "Die Nebensonnen" are remarkably sure, with no revisions, although "Mut" in the autograph fair copy for Haslinger was lengthened by the addition of varied phrase repetitions and an extended conclusion.

Anton Schindler, intermittently Beethoven's factotum, played at least a minor role in Schubert's last years, although perhaps not as much as he later claimed. His Vienna diary is lost, and suspicions about his veracity are exacerbated by the known forgeries and mendacities in his Beethoven reminiscences. The loss of the diary is regrettable, however questionable a witness he might be, because he later spoke of a close relationship with Schubert during the summer of 1827, when Schubert was working on Part II of *Winterreise*: "The success that rewarded my efforts to give Beethoven, though already on his deathbed, the opportunity of getting to know and appreciate Schubert's talent from the right angle, which previously had always been prevented by mean-natured individuals [to whom was he referring?], earned me Schubert's gratitude and especially close friendship. As a result of this, I frequently had the pleasure, in the summer of 1827, of seeing him at my home, 'unbuttoned' *à la Beethoven*."[58] Neither Schubert nor his friends mention an association with Schindler, nor does Beethoven's leechlike associate speak of *Winterreise*. He does state that three of the songs to texts by Ludwig Rellstab later published in *Schwanengesang* were composed that summer in 1827, a full year earlier than their supposed date of composition in August

---

[57]In Deutsch, *Schubert: A Documentary Biography*, 673.
[58]In Deutsch, *Memoirs*, 319, and Deutsch, *Die Erinnerungen*, 367.

1828 (although the dating of the Heine songs is debatable).[59] According to a letter from Schubert's friend Joseph Hüttenbrenner to Ferdinand Luib in May 1861, both Schindler and Beethoven's nephew stated that Schubert had Beethoven's permission to dedicate the four-hand *Variations on a French Song*, Op. 10, to Beethoven and that the older composer played through it "almost daily" for a time.[60] From the evidence of an enigmatic note in Beethoven's conversation book from Spring 1824, Schindler apparently knew something of Schubert's brief disagreement with Weber over *Euryanthe*.[61] On 11 October 1828, Schindler wrote to Schubert from Pest with the intention of organizing a private concert there of Schubert's vocal works. In the letter, he directs "my dear, good friend Schubert" to obtain letters from noble houses in Vienna to various [unnamed] noble houses in Pest and bring them with him: "You need only deposit your fat carcass here and accompany whatever is performed."[62] The tone certainly bespeaks familiarity, but there is no evidence of a reply, and Schubert did not make the trip. Schindler wrote repeatedly in later years about his association with Schubert but never expanded the 1857 "Recollections of Franz Schubert" in the *Niederrheinische Musik-Zeitung für Kunstfreunde und Künstler* (Cologne, 7 and 14 March) into the projected full-scale biography.[63]

After both composers had died, Schindler wrote in the Vienna *Allgemeine Theaterzeitung* for 3 May 1831 of his efforts to distract the

---

[59]The dating of the Heine songs is discussed both in Richard Kramer, "Schubert's Heine," *19th-Century Music* 8 (Spring 1985), 219–25, and, more briefly, in John Reed, *The Schubert Song Companion* (Manchester, U.K., 1985), 259. One of Schubert's friends, the singer Karl von Schönstein (to whom *Die schöne Müllerin* was dedicated), stated in 1875 that the Heine songs were written long before August 1828.

[60]In Deutsch, *Schubert: A Documentary Biography*, 221–22, and Alexander Wheelock Thayer, *Life of Beethoven*, rev. and ed. Elliot Forbes (Princeton, N.J., 1967), 805–6. Thayer cites Joseph Hüttenbrenner's testimony that Schubert visited Beethoven in order to present the variations personally. Beethoven was not at home, and Schubert entrusted the work to a housemaid or manservant and never spoke to Beethoven. This account contradicts Schindler's that Schubert spoke with Beethoven and "fared badly," "losing control of himself" when Beethoven pointed out a mistake in harmony. See Deutsch, *Memoirs*, 325. The relations between Schubert and Beethoven, including Schindler's role as intermediary, are discussed in Maynard Solomon, "Schubert and Beethoven," *19th-Century Music* 3 (November 1979), 114–25.

[61]Schindler, in Deutsch, *Schubert: A Documentary Biography*, 341: "Best one! Do not trouble in the least about me in the matter of the quarrel with M. Weber. Schubert and I have the right man in front of us."

[62]Ibid., 814–17.

[63]Schindler first wrote some recollections of Schubert on 3 May 1831 in the "Musikalische Nachrichten," a supplement of the Vienna *Allgemeine Theaterzeitung*. For the later "Erinnerungen an Franz Schubert" in the *Niederrheinische Musik-Zeitung*, Schindler relied in part on notes written in 1841 by Ferdinand Schubert.

dying Beethoven from his condition by giving him, in February 1827, some sixty Schubert songs in manuscript. We have only Schindler's word for Beethoven's supposed ignorance of Schubert's lieder: Schindler writes that the older master knew "hardly five songs" before this date and was astonished to discover that the young composer had written over five hundred lieder (the true figure is over six hundred). Even more than the number, Schindler continued, Beethoven marveled at their content and spent days studying such works as "Grenzen der Menschheit," "Die Allmacht," "Die junge Nonne," "Viola," and *Die schöne Müllerin*.[64] Deutsch believed that Beethoven might have seen part of the Schindler Lieder Album in Lund; this manuscript in Schindler's hand, however, contains only twenty-six songs, not sixty, and its eight fascicles are variously dated between 1825 and 1829, the last fascicle copied after the deaths of both Beethoven and Schubert. A note in the manuscript could possibly explain the lost songs, unless Schindler simply exaggerated the number of Schubert lieder shown to Beethoven; Schindler apparently lent the manuscripts to someone in 1830 and did not receive them back again until 27 November 1851, to his marked displeasure.[65] Perhaps the mysterious borrower retained other fascicles, now lost, including "Die Allmacht," "Die junge Nonne," and *Die schöne Müllerin*, mentioned in Schindler's anecdote but not to be found in the Lund manuscripts. Two songs from *Winterreise* are included, "Im Dorfe" on folios 49r–50v and "Die Post" on folios 50v–52v.

The Initial Critical Reception of *Winterreise*

The history of *Winterreise* in performance begins with the program for the "Seventh Evening Entertainment of the Philharmonic Society" of Vienna on 10 January 1828, when the tenor Ludwig Tietze sang "Gute Nacht"[66] (the practice of extracting individual songs for performance continued until well into the present century). Four days

---

[64]Thayer, *Life of Beethoven*, 1043–44. According to Anselm Hüttenbrenner in 1858: "This I know as an absolute fact, that Professor Schindler, Schubert and I visited Beethoven at his sickbed about a week before he died. Schindler announced us both and asked Beethoven which of us he wanted to see first; whereupon he said that Schubert should come in first." See Deutsch, *Memoirs*, 66.

[65]Siegfried Mühlhauser, *Die Handschriften und Varia der Schubertiana-Sammlung Taussig in der Universitätsbibliothek Lund* (Wilhelmshaven, 1981), 57–59. The album was formerly owned by Otto Taussig of Malmo and is now ms. H39 in the Schubertiana-Sammlung of the Universitätsbibliothek Lund.

[66]In Deutsch, *Schubert: A Documentary Biography*, 709.

later, the publication of Part I was announced in the *Wiener Zeitung* with the promise of more songs to follow:

> This cycle of songs, the first part of which is herewith submitted to the art-loving public, and whose second half will follow as soon as possible, is the latest product of the mind of a composer who is justly esteemed for his treatment of numerous poems, and who here provides anew the powers he possesses in this direction particularly. Any poet may congratulate himself who is so well understood by his composer, understood alike with warm feeling and with daring imagination, and indeed only thus has his dead letter called into active life by all-powerful sound.[67]

One should not read too much into an advertisement, but the expression of Müller's own belief—a common one at the time—that "dead letters" require music and the designation of Schubert as primarily a song composer are striking. In at least three contemporary reviews, Schubert is described as an "indefatigable song composer," words slightly tinged with condescension.[68]

The few early reviews of Part I are interesting for what they reveal about attitudes at the time toward song composition. The announcement in the *Wiener Zeitschrift für Kunst* for 7 June 1828 of "glorious songs by the most noble of poets" consists of little more than a brief and general characterization of each song,[69] although the hyperbolic assessment of Müller is noteworthy in light of his subsequent fall from critics' grace. Three other reviews are more substantive, running the gamut from wholehearted praise to qualified approval to caustic near dismissal. The reviewer for the *Theaterzeitung*, 29 March 1828, lauds Schubert unreservedly for the composer's understanding of the poetry and his ability to transmute the verse into beautifully effective musical forms and gestures. The writing style is of the era, with its "premonitions of the infinite" and the "rosy radiance" evoked by Schubert's music, but within the purple prose is a largely astute assessment of the cycle. In particular, he points out the relationship

---

[67]In ibid., 710–11.
[68]In the Berlin *Allgemeine Musikalische Zeitung* for 21 December 1825, a critic wrote, "The young composer Schubert continues indefatigably to write songs. His first fruits, especially the 'Erl-King,' found a public, which, however, seems to be gradually diminishing. Diabelli has also published a Mass from his pen. At ballads he is better" (see Deutsch, *Schubert: A Documentary Biography*, 474). The critic for the "Foreign Musical Report, Vienna," in the London *Harmonicon* for April 1826 repeats much the same opinion (see ibid., 518). In the Leipzig *Allgemeine Musikalische Zeitung* for 4 April 1827, the critic writes, "The indefatigable song composer Schubert has again had two new vocal pieces performed at the Society's weekly evening entertainments, viz., 'Der zürnenden Diane' and 'Lied des gefangenen Jägers' " (see ibid., 607).
[69]In Deutsch, *Schubert: A Documentary Biography*, 782–83.

between external and internal worlds in the cycle and acknowledges, if somewhat obliquely, its psychological and natural realism and the boldness of Schubert's music:

To draw attention to anything well carried out is the most agreeable business a lover of art can serve. We thus very gladly speak of the work under notice, which does honor to its origin from the point of view of the poet, the composer, and the publisher. Müller is naive, sentimental and sets against outward nature a parallel of some passionate soul-state, which takes its colour and significance from the former. Schubert has understood his poet with the kind of genius that is his own. His music is as naive as the poet's expression; the emotions contained in the poems are as deeply reflected in his own feelings, and these are brought out in sound that none can sing or hear them without being touched to the heart. Schubert's mind shows a bold sweep everywhere, whereby he carries everyone away with him who approaches, and he takes them through the immeasurable depth of the human heart into the far distance, where premonitions of the infinite dawn upon them longingly in a rosy radiance, but where at the same time the shuddering bliss of an inexpressible presentiment is accompanied by the gentle pain of the constraining present which hems in the boundaries of human existence. Herein lies the nature of German romantic being and art, and in this sense Schubert is a German composer through and through, who does honour to our fatherland and our time. It is this spirit that is breathed by the present songs; it expresses itself through them even where the subject seems to point to entirely different paths; and in this logical establishment of harmony between outward and inward things lies the chief merit of both poets, the speaking and the singing one. An analysis of technical beauties cannot be attempted in this journal, which is not devoted to theory, but to draw attention to the viewpoint from which this beautiful and noble work may be most feelingly and fully enjoyed is an urgent necessity at this time of day, the more so since it has become almost a craze to submit only to material impressions in music.[70]

Another paragraph of enthusiastic praise follows, with the reviewer repeating in different words and at greater length that Schubert goes beyond the mere imitation of sounds to make the listener aware of "higher things in these impressions," an explicit complaint about the fashion for onomatopoeia of a lower order than Schubert's.

A review of songs by Theodor Fröhlich, Ferdinand Stegmayer, Johann Spech, K. E. Hering, and Schubert in the Berlin *Allgemeine Musikalische Zeitung* for 25 June 1828 is caustic in tone and grudging of praise, typical of reviews in that city, according to Deutsch.[71] The

[70]Ibid., 758–59.
[71]Ibid., 786.

writer mentions Schubert's "more widespread reputation" and concedes that he is gifted, but objects to the fad for cycles and the "glut in song composition," especially the "dozens and dozens" of love poems and lieder about wayfarers, millers, spring, and orientalizing subjects. "Schubert has talent, shows originality here and there, and would do even better work were it not for the fatal 89 [the opus number]. . . . However, there must be goods in bales too, and Müller and Schubert may be recommended!" Another reviewer also objected to cycles, but on different grounds. According to the writer for the *Allgemeine Musikzeitung* in Munich, the songs in *Winterreise* were not true German song. Cycles, he declares, are difficult to compose because each song is an individual entity that must "live its own life" and yet be part of a larger whole; in his opinion, Schubert was not successful in reconciling the two imperatives, although he finds "individual blossoms in the garland" worthy. More fundamentally, he finds cycles antithetical to the nature of song composition. A deeply moved heart, he says, overflows just long enough to leave behind a miniature work; he implicitly excludes from the ethos of song composition the craftsmanship required to fashion larger works. He saw more to praise in the poetry than in the music, declaring Müller's poems to be ideal material for songs because they have "nothing didactic, historical, or reflective" about them. "Love and tears" are the perfect subjects, he declares, for German song.[72]

Whether in approval or disapproval, reviewers remarked in *Winterreise*, as they had in the composer's earlier lieder, Schubert's rich harmonic language and the detailed—according to some critics, labored and excessive—treatment of the text. (The legend of Schubert's "obscurity" in Viennese musical life, especially with regard to his vocal works, has been disproved by Otto Biba and others.[73] Although the posthumous publication and long-delayed first performances of his instrumental works explain an incomplete and unbalanced assessment of the composer by his contemporaries, it is nonetheless clear that critics recognized Schubert's originality during his life and

---

[72]In ibid., 795.
[73]Otto Biba, "Schubert's Position in Viennese Musical Life," *19th-Century Music* 3 (November 1979), 106–13. Biba points out that once Schubert was admitted to the Gesellschaft der Musikfreunde in 1825 as an alternate, his music was second in popularity only to that of Rossini—delightful irony—on the society's concert programs; that the most famous instrumental soloists of the day regularly performed Schubert's works; that Diabelli paid Schubert high fees for his songs; that the numerous manuscript and album copies of his works reflect the composer's renown; and that Schubert's skill as a composer of dance music led one reviewer to place him with Joseph Lanner and Johann Strauss, Sr.

paid it both negative and positive tribute.) The critic for the Vienna *Allgemeine musikalische Anzeiger* of 1829, while he hailed Schubert for his unique gifts, all the more praiseworthy "in our sickly, imitation-prone times," also remarked what he considered the excessive attention to text-painting details. Somewhat inconsistently, he notes that Schubert often makes of the musical text interpretation something stronger and more profound than Müller's poetry. He singles out "Der Lindenbaum," "Wasserflut," "Rückblick," "Einsamkeit," "Die Krähe," "Letzte Hoffnung," "Der Wegweiser," "Mut," and "Der Leiermann" as "more or less successful" and reserves his highest praise for "Gute Nacht" and "Die Post."[74] The redoubtable C. W. Fink, critic for the Leipzig *Allgemeine musikalische Zeitung* for 1829 (Nr. 40), however, could hear *only* excess and accuses the public of an inordinate love of striking modulations, rhythmic jerkiness, and overly weighty accompaniments to uninteresting melodies. Schubert's reputation as a song composer of great originality was exaggerated and unmerited, in his opinion, the songs not true songs but paintings. In his particular discontent with *Winterreise* (he found *Schwanengesang* much more to his liking), he singles out several lieder for harsh words: "Auf dem Fluße" for its plethora of sudden modulations, "Frühlingstraum" for a melodic line at times too conventional and elsewhere too labored, "Die Wetterfahne" for onomatopoeia weightier than a small-scale song could bear, and so on.[75] Anarchy threatens at every turn where there is such an "overflow of originality," he felt. The Romantic cult of originality was by no means everyone's cup of tea.

It is an interesting commentary on contemporary tastes that several of the critics and listeners in Schubert's day particularly liked the few tearful songs and therefore characterized the cycle as more lachrymose than it really is. The wanderer weeps only four times in the course of twenty-four songs (in "Gefror'ne Tränen," "Erstarrung," "Wasserflut," and "Letzte Hoffnung"); the realization that the cycle is a remarkably dry-eyed work for a series of laments is an important clue to the nature of *Winterreise*.

[74]In Herbert Biehle, *Schuberts Lieder in Kritik und Literatur* (Berlin, 1928), 7.
[75]In ibid., 9.

CHAPTER 2

The Texts of *Winterreise*

Marie von Pratobevera, later the sister-in-law of Schubert's first biographer, Heinrich Kreißle von Hellborn, wrote in a letter shortly after the publication of *Winterreise*, Part I, that the cycle consisted of "laments over a sweetheart's unfaithfulness . . . a companion-piece to the 'Maid of the Mill' songs, by the same poet and nearly identical in content."[1] Part II had not yet appeared, and she could not have known what would follow after the twelfth song, but later writers who knew the entire work either saw little more than dated love laments or else fell into a trap arising from Müller's original trans- formation of a conventional subject. The poet adopts as his own a frequent Romantic theme—a journey by an isolated, alienated pro- tagonist—with a tragic finale in madness or death, but the discrep- ancies from convention compel us to take a closer look in order properly to account for Müller's permutations. This sustained "outcry of scorched sensibility"[2] goes far beyond grief over a sweetheart's infidelity to fundamental questions about the meaning of existence, questions couched in the deceptively naive folklike forms Müller pre- ferred. What is the relationship between the self and a world without God? What is illusion and what is reality? Where can one find meaning and purpose in a world where dissociation rules? When hope cannot be invested in spiritual institutions or in human bonds, the wanderer in "Letzte Hoffnung" even pins his displaced desire for meaning on a leaf, in whose fragility and inevitable downfall he finds his own image. Like himself, the leaf is detached from its tenuous moorings

[1]In Deutsch, *Schubert; A Documentary Biography*, 716–17. Marie Elisabeth von Prato- bevera (born 1804) was the eldest daughter of Karl Josef von Pratobevera, vice-president of the supreme court of appeals and the criminal court in Lower Austria. Schubert wrote the melodrama "Abschied von der Erde" for her brother Adolf. She had three sisters who were also musical: Louise, Franziska ("Fanni," who sang Schubert's songs "like a nightingale"), and Bertha, later Kreißle von Hellborn's wife (see ibid., 708).
[2]The term is Richard Capell's, in *Schubert's Songs*, 2d ed. (New York, 1957), 231.

by a force too strong to resist and falls to earth, with which it will merge in dissolution. The sorrow over lost love of which Marie von Pratobevera speaks does not end there but leads the wanderer to question the world and his own being with remarkable persistence. What he discovers in the course of his wintry inner voyage is more subtle (and more deserving of accolades for its creator) than some have previously thought.

Die Winterreise and Monodrama

Müller's originality is first evident in an element of *Die Winterreise* often criticized: its lack of a clearly defined plot, such as one finds in *Die schöne Müllerin*.[3] The earlier work began life as a *Liederspiel*, or song play, for a Berlin salon, and retains elements of drama in its final form as a sequence of lyric poems. It has a cast of characters, and vignettes in which people speak to the miller lad and to one another, come and go like the dramatis personae in a play. Although everything—actions, reactions, the presentation of other characters, what others say—is conveyed by a single speaker, the context is that of a small social world. *Die Winterreise*, however, is a monodrama, a predecessor of Expressionist interior monologues. In such works as Marie Pappenheim's and Arnold Schoenberg's *Erwartung*, a single character investigates the labyrinth of her or his own psyche in search of self-knowledge, escape, or surcease from pain, a flight inward into the hothouse of imagination rather than outward into the real world.[4] The later monodramas have their roots in Romantic soul-searching and in the late eighteenth- and nineteenth-century fascination with

[3]Helen Meredith Mustard, in *The Lyric Cycle in German Literature* (New York, 1946), 88, states that after the first four poems "the following poems ramble from place to place, from theme to theme, as aimlessly as the hero himself. . . . The apparent lack of purpose in the arrangement of the poems, the absence of any inner links whatsoever among them [!], and the fact that Müller made no significant changes or additions in the final version, all show that we have to do here with an entirely different principle from that which determined the form of *Die schöne Müllerin*." Mustard is of the opinion that Müller never again attained the formal perfection he achieved in the miller cycle.

[4]In Marie Pappenheim's text for *Erwartung*, the unnamed woman, also jilted by her lover, disintegrates psychically under the pressure of her loss, since she has invested all meaning in him. The resemblances to Müller's cycle are striking: the woman laments her solitude, sees life as an endless horror, declares her inability to go further, wonders what so disturbs her, forces herself to continue onward, finds analogies to her state of being in the nocturnal surroundings, wonders where the path is, speaks of singing in order to save herself (he will hear her then), and ends by crying out, "Ich suchte" (I searched).

lunacy, genius, outcasts, and the inner life of creatures *in extremis,* exiled to the outskirts of a prosaic society that drives them mad by denying their claims on creation. Alienated wanderers who shun the camaraderie of others on their aimless route to extinction are a commonplace of German Romantic poetry, the polar opposite of the wayfarers whose optimistic quests end in reconciliation, and Müller would have known both types from many sources. Georg Philipp Schmidt's wanderer in "Des Fremdlings Abendlied" (The stranger's evening song), which Schubert set to music under the title "Der Wanderer" (The wanderer) in October 1816 (D. 489, 493), is only one of numerous predecessors to Müller's winter wayfarer:

> Die Sonne dünkt mich matt und kalt,
> Die Blüte welk, das Leben alt,
> Und was sie reden, tauber Schall,
> Ich bin ein Fremdling überall.[5]

(The sun seems cold and weary to me, the flowers withered, life old and spent, and what you tell me, hollow sound, is that I am everywhere a stranger.)

The sterile landscape is the parallel in Nature to a soul similarly without life and warmth. In Müller's cycle, the wanderer refers to a former context of other people (the mother and the sweetheart), but the focus on the introspective speaker is unwavering, and the various stages of the journey are generated by conflicts within the wanderer's mind, not by the actions of others. This is a fundamental polarity between the two Müller-Schubert cycles: the unreflective miller lad reacts impulsively to the external world, without making any effort to understand cause and effect in himself or in others. The winter wanderer, however, probes his psychic wounds in a search for meaning conducted against the backdrop of a pervasive fear of meaninglessness.

Monodrama in *Die Winterreise* differs from traditional lyric monologue, and the differences define the special nature of Müller's achievement in this cycle. In both genres, the poet invents a fictional speaker who uses the first-person address that customarily signifies the poet himself, but dramatic monologues usually contain three distinct presences, the term "monologue" notwithstanding: the speaker, an implied auditor, and the poet himself, his own world view and

[5]Georg Philipp Schmidt [Schmidt von Lübeck], *Lieder,* 2d ed., ed. H. Schumacher (Altona, 1826), 76.

ethical judgments frequently apparent between the lines.[6] When a Suliot maiden or the spirits of Greek antiquity speak in Müller's *Griechenlieder*, one is aware both of an audience (potential European recruits for the Greek liberation forces) to whom the poem is addressed and the poet's controlling mind. In Robert Browning's monologues, among the most artful specimens of the genre, there is often an ironic discrepancy between the speaker's view of himself and a larger judgment that Browning implies and the reader must develop from hints in the poem. Browning's lyric monologues are more subtle in their multiple presences than Müller's simpler specimens, but the principle is the same.

Müller in *Die Winterreise*, however, deliberately excludes both the implied presence of an auditor and as much awareness of the poet's control as possible. There is no relativity of perception—whatever we know, we know entirely from the wanderer's point of view, the context thus more claustrophobic than in monologue. Neither Müller's own gregarious personality nor any world view identifiable as his intrudes on his wanderer's mind. There are no auditors, no implied or actual listeners from within the poem to hear his tale, no one in whom he may confide each incident along the way. Throughout the cycle, the wanderer talks to himself as if entirely alone, inducting the reader-spy directly into his mental processes with no narrator, no intermediary present. The feint is established from the beginning: the journey is born of an inner compulsion, a directive from within to forge his own path alone in the snow, and continues with questions and flashes of insight about who he is and why he acts as he does. In the geography of the psyche, a consciousness shocked into awareness of alienation probes for information of the unmapped regions within. The poet thus places the reader in the role of an eavesdropper who hears, at great length, things never intended to be heard. We know as we read that we are not actually spying unseen on private travail, but Müller succeeds in creating that possibility as a considerable claim on our emotions and imagination.

Müller's avowal of the forms of folk poetry assumes new significance in the context of monodrama in twenty-four lyric stages. Müller wanted his poetry to speak directly to the heart, without the intervening obstacles of either apparent poetic artifice (hence, folklike forms) or other voices from within the poetry, such as a narrator or

---

[6]See Alan Sinfield, *Dramatic Monologue* (London, 1977); K. E. Faas, "Dramatischer Monolog und Dramatisch-Monologische Versdichtung," *Anglia* 87 (1969), 338–66; and A. Dwight Culler, "Monodrama and Dramatic Monologue," *Publications of the Modern Language Association* 40 (1975), 366–85.

the poet himself (hence, monodrama). Even the most colloquial monologues are constructs invented and molded by the poet, but Müller
wanted to obliterate awareness of that invention as much as possible
by means of what he called *Eintönigkeit* as opposed to the *Vieltönigkeit*,
or variety, of such poets as Goethe. *Eintönigkeit* literally means "monotony," but Müller uses the word in a different sense, conjunct with
his ideals of simplicity and directness. He explains the contrasting
poetic modes with a musical analogy: the sound of a single instrument
compared to the rich and diverse sounds possible from a full orches-
tra. We ask of a single instrument, he says, only that it span the full
range from high to low, in varying tempi and changing dynamics
from softest to loudest; thus, within its limitations we find the full
beauty of its nature, the complete revelation of its capacities.[7] The
one instrument in *Die Winterreise* is the wanderer's voice, his consciousness alone, expressed in forms and rhythms largely derived
from folk poetry. The octave-plus-quatrain of "Im Dorfe" and the
single ten-line stanza of "Täuschung" are the only exceptions to the
roll call of quatrains throughout most of the cycle; the reflections
expressed in those scenes required, and received, a different formal
order. Müller's success in giving his wanderer the desired immediacy
of expression, in hiding himself from view behind the poetic persona,
is ironically evident in assessments of his (the poet's) naiveté.
　　The wanderer's reflections are couched as a succession of poems
for another reason as well, intrinsic to the cycle and exemplary of
Müller's belief that content and form are intertwined. Elevated rhetoric and intricate forms he deemed unsuitable because their evident
air of contrivance would betray too openly the poet's controlling hand
and would be at variance with the desired impression of immediacy,
but why a succession of lyric poems? The journey culminates in the
wanderer's attempt to overwhelm sorrow by means of music ("Mut")
and the vision of a beggar-musician who embodies the protagonist's
worst fears of the future ("Der Leiermann"). The monologist is a poet-
singer, and songs have been his means of expression all along, before
he comes to understand that music entails his isolation and is now
the sole inadequate weapon he has left against the miseries of the
mind. He has "sung" his reminiscences and questions throughout
the entire journey, without understanding the significance of what
he does until near the end. "And yet when I write poetry, I sing and
play after all," Müller wrote; despite the poet's ostensible absence
from the monodrama, his own desire to be a musician and his belief

---

[7]Cited in Becker, *Die Kunstanschauung Wilhelm Müllers*, 46–47.

in poetry-for-music are elements of a character otherwise distinct from himself, a character whose principal quest is for self-understanding.

The Winter Journey as an Inward Voyage

Müller is one of many nineteenth-century writers who obeyed Novalis's injunction to follow the *Weg nach Innen*, the path inward or an interior quest for self-knowledge. From the beginning, Müller tells the reader explicitly that the journey is a solitary exploration of one being's inner life. The wanderer states in "Gute Nacht," the first song, that his journey is uncharted and without plan; he does not know where he must go or how long the journey will take, and he must travel alone, with only his moon-cast shadow for companionship. This lack of plan determines a crucial factor of the entire poetic sequence: the wanderer's ignorance of what is to come and therefore the poet's care to exclude his own knowledge of futurity from the poems. (There is reason to speculate that Müller himself discovered the later sequence of events and the ending of the work well into its composition.) From the beginning, the wanderer reveals his philosophical bent when he briefly discourses on the nature of God and love in "Gute Nacht"—God, in whom the wanderer does not truly believe, exists only as a malevolent force who has created the inherently fickle properties of love—and thereafter when he dissects his own emotions. In particular, he fears the death of feeling as a consequence of the death of love. In the third poem, "Gefror'ne Tränen," the wanderer discovers that he has wept and does not know why: were his former sweetheart the sole cause of his tears, he would surely recognize more clearly the origins of his grief. Furthermore, he questions the disparity between the inner experience of grief as something fiery, a Vesuvius-like pressure chamber within, and its tepid outward manifestation. What is the mystery of emotional experience in the translation from inchoate inwardness to external behavior, and why is there such disparity between the two? Again, in "Auf dem Fluße," he asks himself whether the frozen river with, perhaps, a rushing torrent beneath the surface resembles his heart, the images of ice and rushing water a recurrent motif of the first half of the cycle (in Schubert's ordering).

It is ironic that a poet described as "simple and naive" should have created a figure whom people interpret in so many different ways. Writers have placed the wanderer along a spectrum that ranges from

a whining, slightly contemptible jilted lover to an atheist, a secular
Christ-figure whose journey parallels the Stations of the Cross, and
an alienated Everyman who eventually goes insane and dies.[8] Capell
complained that Müller did little more than sketch the outline of an
enigmatic and unhappy man: "We do not truly know [him], though
we hear the tale of his soliloquy from the ironical farewell, through
storms of reproaches, regrets, and plaints, to the final fancies of the
unhinged mind. We guess at a character more mature, more introspective and egotistic than the young miller. But we could see the
miller. Here only an outline is visible of the form that goes off staggering into the snowstorm."[9] The "storms of reproaches, regrets, and
plaints" are more revealing than Capell supposes. Beyond self-pity,
the wanderer subjects both actions and emotions to psychic self-
dissection decades before Freud's scientific framework for such in-
vestigations. His solitude is not only the anguished withdrawal of a
rejected lover but a necessary laboratory for existential research. To
no one else and in no one's company can he ask, "Why am I estranged
from life as others live it?" Even his obsessive dwelling on memories

[8]H. Lowen Marshall, "Symbolism in Schubert's *Winterreise*," *Studies in Romanticism*
12 (1973), 607–32, states that Müller's cycle is mediocre poetry, having to do with no
more than the "downfall of a young man after a great disappointment . . . little more
than the description of a rather weak individual pining after a lost love" (603). Klaus
Günther Just, in "Wilhelm Müllers Liederzyklen *Die schöne Müllerin* und *Die Winterreise*," *Zeitschrift für deutsche Philologie* 83 (1964), 452–71, reprinted in *Übergänge: Probleme
und Gestalten der Literatur* (Bern, 1966), 133–52, writes that the cycle is a tragic, secular
Passion story in twenty-four stations. Alan Cottrell, *Wilhelm Müller's Lyrical Song-Cycles:
Interpretations and Texts* (Chapel Hill, N.C., 1970), gives a more psychological interpretation: "The wanderer alienates himself more and more from the world by withdrawing
into his own being and asserting this being with fierce determination. . . . The longed-
for death, which is not granted the miserable man, asserts itself gradually as a death
of the soul, in the form of increasing alienation and despair. The danger of utter
psychological isolation, of a freezing-up of the soul, gradually becomes stark reality
and drives the wanderer into the contemplation of an old age devoid of any spiritual
warmth and meaning whatever. The picture of old age is the logical outcome of a one-
sided psychological state incapable of transcending the narrower limits of ego-
centeredness" (66–67). Cecilia Baumann, *Wilhelm Müller*, 67–68, sees in *Die Winterreise*
an earlier prototype of the stages of death and dying described by Elisabeth Kübler-
Ross in her *On Death and Dying* (New York, 1969). Hans Brandenburg, "*Die Winterreise*
als Dichtung: Eine Ehrenrettung für Wilhelm Müller," *Aurora* 18 (1958), 57–62, praises
Müller for his ingenious variations on the theme of an "eternal winter of the heart."
Elisabeth McKay, "Schubert's *Winterreise* Reconsidered," *Music Review* 38 (1977), 94–
100, believes, contrary to prior interpretations, that the wanderer neither goes mad
nor withdraws into total alienation but rather finds renewed hope and contact with
another human being at the end of the cycle. Paul Robinson, in *Opera and Ideas: From
Mozart to Strauss* (Ithaca, 1986), 58–102, writes that the theme of the cycle is the wanderer's inability to escape from life, "his imprisonment in a world of misery" (85), that
the wanderer is one of the great Romantic depressives and a philosopher *manqué* who
goes mad in the end.
[9]Capell, *Schubert's Songs*, 231.

of the past, the compulsion to repeat and relive his pain, is invoked as an instrument in the quest for self-knowledge and originates with the awareness of the inmost self as a foreigner, an entity whose ways are a mystery to him. If he seems shadowy, it is because we learn very little about his appearance and past history. Of his inner life, we learn much more.

The paucity of external description is the result of Müller's chosen medium, the compound of lyric poetry and monodrama. Since the wanderer speaks to himself, and there is no narrator to supply information the wanderer omits, we are never told his name, or any other name, what he looks like, his birthplace, occupation, upbringing, or personal history; there is no one else around to divulge background information. Furthermore, time in *Winterreise* is inner time, not the temporal ordering of a clock or calendar but a poetically crafted simulation of ontological thought processes. Müller's feint is that the sequence of twenty-four poems is being composed en route; this is surely a major determinant of the cycle's musicality, since music reorders chronological, measured time in a manner roughly analogous to the temporal flow of subjective experience. The objective measurement of time in *Winterreise* is seldom important and is given in a few instances only as punctuation and counterpoint to the more pervasive psychological time. Six months or so pass between the Maytime love affair and the start of the journey, but elsewhere, we never know how much time or distance passes from one song to the next or within one song. At the end of "Der Lindenbaum," how far is he from the spot where his hat blew off and he "did not turn back"? "Many hours," he says, have passed since the moment of decision in the winter storm, but how many? Days? Weeks? A sequence of day-night-next morning can be inferred from the succession of "Rast," "Frühlingstraum," and "Einsamkeit" in *Urania*, but the chronology is only implied, and Müller changed the ordering in the *Waldhornisten II*. One guesses that the "stormy morning" follows the nocturnal scene of "Im Dorfe," but once again Müller says nothing to verify the inference. When and where, even what, are largely unknown. The greatest unknown, of course, is the signpost at the crossroads in "Der Wegweiser." The wanderer believes himself alone and unheard: why should he read aloud what he can see all too clearly? He states to himself only that aspect which most horrifies him—that no one can return. Müller could not have made more clear the interiority of the cycle, nor could he have better exemplified the central problem of poetry that pretends to have no audience.

First impressions and first words are important: the wanderer begins by saying that he came to this place a stranger and departs still a stranger ("Fremd bin ich eingezogen, / Fremd zieh' ich wieder aus"). At the start of the journey, he implies that he was a wanderer before he came to the town, a wayfarer who is once again unsuccessful in his quest for a place of belonging. Müller was fond of antitheses, and the antithetical phrase "A stranger I arrived, / A stranger I depart" is characteristic. The wanderer's recognition that he is a stranger is further emphasized by the reversal of the poetic meter in those first two lines, before we even know what the principal meter is to be. "Fremd" constitutes a monosyllabic foot unto itself, preceding the regular trochees that follow it and the iambs in the remainder of the poem. From the beginning, the wanderer is obsessed with his sense of estrangement from the world and from himself, the loss of his sweetheart bitter confirmation of his isolation. When "the maiden spoke of love, the mother even of marriage" ("Gute Nacht"), he could believe himself no longer a stranger. When he is jilted, he loses more than the love of a single person: he loses the sense of belonging somewhere and the hope that human bonds are possible for him. Before he bids farewell to the strangely shadowy sweetheart, he says, "Why should I linger here any longer and be driven out?" With her loss, he becomes so conscious of his alienation from everyone, not just her, that he fears being forced away from the town like a pariah and meets that fear with defiance.

Illusions and Reality

The wanderer's capacity for strong feeling is obvious, but he is not passive prey to waves of emotion. He is analytically minded and a realist, prone to philosophical reflection. He believes in facing facts— the simplicity of the first two lines does not come from indulgence in self-pity. His clear-sighted perceptions of his wretched condition cannot be alleviated by dreams or fantasies because he has no faith in their relevance to waking life; for him the polarity between the two is absolute. The return to solitude and alienation after a brief respite in dreams or fancies is a wrenching experience. In "Frühlingstraum," the short-lived dream idyll of green meadows and reciprocated love is followed by a heightened awareness of cold and loneliness when he awakes, and eventually he renounces all dreams as not worth the price he must pay for them in waking misery. Even his dreams in "Frühlingstraum" are remarkably realistic, undreamlike, with nothing surrealistic, disjunct, or bizarre. There is no encoded symbolism, nothing condensed or disguised; rather, it is a near-exact repetition of the wanderer's idealized memories in "Rückblick" of flowers, green fields, birdsong, a beloved woman, and a warm, brightly lit house, "unreal" only in its perfection, in the absence of all dissonance and pain.

The refusal of ciphered expression in the wanderer's dreams and fantasies is part of the wanderer's denial of any possibility of transcendance, whether through mysticism, allegory, symbolism, enchantment, magic, God, regression to childhood, or any of the myriad ways in which personal experience is seen as belonging to a larger order. The fairy-tale, supernatural elements that Müller knew from the poems and tales of Ludwig Uhland, Friedrich de la Motte-Fouqué, Ludwig Tieck, E. T. A. Hoffmann, and many others are entirely excluded. When the wanderer speaks to the river, the crow, the barking dogs, the snow, no one expects them to reply, as animals and inanimate objects might do in fairy tales. The voices that beckon "Come here to me, companion" in "Der Lindenbaum" emanate from within his own mind, and he knows it; in his characteristically simple, precise diction, he says that the rustling leaves seem *as if* calling to him (*"als riefen sie mir zu"*). The winter landscape is unlike the indeterminate vistas that stretch unendingly about the central characters in works by Joseph von Eichendorff and Tieck. The elderly Goethe once said that the Germans would wake up one day and find that they had done nothing for thirty years but transcend; his condemnations stemmed from a hard-won belief in the real world as the source for universal symbols of beauty and meaning. But the wanderer, lacking certainty about anything, seeks in each image taken from Nature a new confirmation of his existence, without success. *Die Winterreise* is not a work about atheism, but it is crucial that the wanderer cannot appeal to a higher power for consolation and does not invoke an afterlife to follow the death he longs for throughout the second half of the cycle—the death he envisages is extinction. Müller is careful to establish his character's lack of faith at the beginning of the cycle when the wanderer in "Gute Nacht" bitterly mocks God as the ill-intentioned creator of false love.

The wanderer condemns illusions but in his despair is unable to resist them. Müller twice uses the metaphor of the will-o'-the-wisp or illusory light that leads his questing voyager astray, into an abyss of the spirit in "Irrlicht" and to near madness in "Täuschung." The wanderer knows in both instances that the flickering light is an illusion, but he follows it anyway. Since both reality and illusion are unbearable conditions, it is no wonder that he vacillates between them for much of the journey. In "Irrlicht," the wanderer can console himself only with the thought that all paths lead to a destination and all sorrows eventually end. The motif of streams flowing into the sea, or individual lives merging into a watery cosmos of death and dissolution, at the end of "Irrlicht" is a familiar image, and Müller could have known it from Schmidt von Lübeck's "Des Fremdlings Abendlied," cited earlier:

> Ob die Bächlein voll und leer
> Auf der Höh' beginnen,
> Müßen unten doch ins Meer
> Allesamt verrinnen.
>
> Wandre, wandre stumm entlang
> Die verlassnen Stiege
> Bis nach Sonnen-Untergang
> Stirbt die Eintagsfliege.[10]

(Though the little streams, both full and empty, begin in the heights, they must all flow together and be submerged in the ocean.
Wander, wander mutely along the deserted paths until the fleeting day dies with the sunset.)

When the wanderer next conjures up a will-o'-the-wisp in Part II, he can no longer envision future resolution in oblivion. He has attempted to renounce illusions but discovers how difficult it is to do so when reality has nothing hopeful to offer. As he passes through a village at night in "Im Dorfe," he reflects on the useless dreams and illusions of the sleeping townspeople and declares himself finished with all dreams. Well in advance of Freud, he recognizes that dreams are wish fulfillments; the sleeping mind devises satisfactions unattainable in reality, fantasy-deceptions incompatible with waking life. The night in the village is followed by a defiant song on a stormy morning ("Der stürmische Morgen"), but the fierce exultation of the moment does not last because there is nothing to replace the dreams he has renounced. In his despair, he dances after another will-o'-the-wisp in a state of near insanity, even though he knows its promise of light and warmth is only a delusion ("Täuschung"). With characteristic strength of will, he abruptly breaks off the exercise in folly. Müller uses the rhetorical device of *aposiopesis*—an abrupt halt before

---

[10]Schmidt von Lübeck, *Lieder*, 141.

the completion of a statement—to mark the point where illusion is rejected and realism resumes its full hegemony.

> Ach, wer wie ich so elend ist,
> Gibt gern sich hin der bunten List,
> Die hinter Eis und Nacht und Graus
> Ihm weist ein helles, warmes Haus,
> Und eine liebe Seele drin—
> Nur Täuschung ist für mich Gewinn!

(Ah! one as wretched as I am gladly surrenders to the beguiling gleam that reveals to him, beyond ice and night and horror, a bright, warm house.)

Wrenching himself away from impossibility, the wanderer refuses to complete the fantasy, to follow "the beguiling gleam." Müller's choice of a single ten-line stanza within a cycle dominated by quatrain forms reflects the successive courtship and denial of madness. The first two rhyming couplets, linked by the interior repetition "Ich folg' . . . ich folg' " (I follow), are followed immediately by a misery at odds with the repeated word "gern" (gladly). The fantasy is not contained within the couplet boundaries but spills over into a fifth line, as if control were beginning to disintegrate. The title is tragic irony. For the wanderer, love and the shelter of human bonds are an illusion, while "reality" is the denial that love exists. But this is a denial he knows to be personal rather than universal ("Nur Täuschung ist *für mich* Gewinn!"). His will-o'-the-wisp is someone else's real happiness.

The necessity for illusions when existence is void of meaning, the human longing to cling to them even in the dreadful consciousness that they are illusions—this is Müller's version of a Mephistophelean Hell on earth. "Kein Weg! . . . Bist du bereit? . . . Von Einsamkeiten wirst umhergetrieben. / Hast du Begriff von Öd' und Einsamkeit?" (No path! . . . Are you ready? . . . You will wander about aimlessly in your solitude . . . Have you any concept of desolation and loneliness?), the devil asks Faust. Müller's wanderer is not ready and, in despair, conjures up will-o'-the-wisps to follow, surely the most apt metaphor for illusions that lead one astray.

By the end, he even understands his past love to have been illusion. In "Die Nebensonnen," he sees an atmospheric illusion that recalls the memory of his sweetheart for the last time (he has not spoken of her since "Die Post"), a link between the beginning of the journey and its conclusion. Like the short-lived light of the two illusory suns in the sky, her eyes shone on him only briefly and then vanished. Now he recognizes that she was not meant for him, although the realization saddens him so much that he wishes for total darkness. The obsession with lost love, banished and replaced by the desire for death in the second half of the song cycle, returns for a final summation.

Madness, Mourning, and Death

At the end, the wanderer sees the vision of a hurdy-gurdy player, a solitary beggar, and asks, "Will you grind your hurdy-gurdy to my songs?" The elderly beggar is his *Doppelgänger*, the self divided, the image of what he will become and a projection of his worst nightmares of the future. He is a reincarnation of Goethe's Harper, whom Schubert had feared he himself might become (if Bauernfeld's reminiscences are to be believed), and the closing complement to the *Mondenschatten* companion in "Gute Nacht." The eerie figure is indeed another moon-cast shadow who neither speaks nor listens but only grinds out music so obsessive and elemental as to be deprived of all possibility of transcendence. The solitude is total: there is not even the human presence of "pious hands" dispensing charity to a pitiable outcast, as in Goethe's Harper poems, or a belief in cruel gods who cause unvolitional sin. The wanderer who asserts his innocence of wrongdoing in "Der Wegweiser" ("Habe ja doch nichts begangen / Daß ich Menschen sollte scheun"—"I have done no wrong that I should shun people) cannot even postulate unknowable cosmic causes for his misery.

In most readings, the journey is seen as culminating in death or madness: one writer even purports to find clinical evidence of schizophrenia in "Der Leiermann."[11] Solitary madmen, their minds unmoored by demons that science and reason had failed to eradicate, were favorite characters in the art and literature of the time, but the wanderer's "insanity" is distinct from the paranoia, mental fragmentation, manic behavior, or grandiosity of the mind in shards. The alienation evident in "Gute Nacht" is heightened in "Der Leiermann" when the wanderer projects his vision of an unbearable old age onto the landscape and, desperate for companionship, begs the *Doppel-*

---

[11]See Günther Baum, "Das Problem der *Winterreise*," *Neue Zeitschrift für Musik* 111 (December 1950), 643–44.

gänger phantom for its company. Notably, Müller's language does not change at the end: the tone, syntax, vocabulary, images, and atmosphere, indeed, all of the verbal resources, of the last few poems are unaltered from the beginning, when the wanderer is incontestably sane, if depressed to the depths of his being. The "soulscape" or landscape of the psyche at the cycle's end—an unnamed town, a pack of dogs, snow and ice—seem, deceptively, to have come full circle back to the beginning of the winter journey.

Readers familiar with Freud's "Mourning and Melancholia" might find in Müller's *Die Winterreise* a poetic version of the process Freud describes in his short essay.[12] Mourning begins with an exclusive devotion to the labor of grief, with loss of interest in the outside world and a turning away from anything not connected with thoughts of the lost love. Reality tells the mourner that the beloved no longer exists and the attachment to the loved person, ideal, country, or cause must be withdrawn so that life may continue. The mourner inevitably rebels and carries out the commands of reality only little by little over an extended period of time, immersing himself in memories he is reluctant to relinquish for fear of losing the beloved irrevocably. The wavering motion of a step forward into continued life, followed by a step backward into memory, is beautifully portrayed in Part I of Schubert's *Winterreise*—the wanderer attempts to bury his love in the seventh song," Auf dem Fluße," carving an icy tombstone as a memorial, but then flees back into reminiscence with "Rückblick" just after. Even earlier, the wanderer realizes in the fourth song, "Erstarrung," that without a tangible souvenir of his sweetheart he will inevitably forget her when the pain of lost love is over. As yet unwilling to relinquish his memories of her, however painful, he searches frantically for traces of her footsteps in the snow, for the green grass and flowers that bloomed in this place when they were in love, but gives up when he understands that the search is futile. Successful mourning concludes with the self becoming free of its former total preoccupation with loss, but where melancholia is a factor, as it is in Müller's cycle, the process is more difficult and prone to failure. From the start of the journey, the wanderer believes himself severed from all human bonds by an invisible "mark of Cain," some mysterious element that compels him to remain apart from the world. His heroic attempts to comply with the demands of reality are dashed on the rocks of a more pathological narcissism, an obsession with the self as different and victimized. Even when the loss is finally accepted as inevitable and relinquished,

[12]Sigmund Freud, "Mourning and Melancholia," in *The Standard Edition of the Complete Psychological Works of Sigmund Freud*, ed. James Strachey, vol. 14 (London, 1953), 243.

the wanderer has nothing in life that he considers a source of hope, of a bearable future.

Unable to understand until nearly the end of the cycle why he is an exile from life, the wanderer in Part II longs for death, after memory has loosed its hold on him. The cycle has as one essential theme the difficulty of dying when one wishes, or the tenacity of life, all the more marked when unwanted. And yet the wanderer only once contemplates anything akin to suicide, significantly not by his own hand but as an accessory to natural death. That incident in the fifth poem, "Der Lindenbaum," is one of the climactic turning points in the cycle. Until this time, the wanderer has remained in the sweetheart's town and is now finally able to leave. But his journey is slowed and almost stopped by the temptation to end his journey here, to stand still, immersed in memory until he dies in the winter storm. Not yet as devoid of hope as he becomes later in the cycle, he chooses instead—without knowing why—to continue on his journey, or life, although the siren voices from within that murmur of rest and peace in death still haunt him. No matter how fervently and repeatedly he wishes for death later in the journey, it is denied him. The Rip van Winkle illusion of miraculous old age and the consequent hope for imminent death in "Der greise Kopf," the persistent hopes for death in "Die Krähe" and "Das Wirtshaus," are remarkable in part because the wanderer never mentions any means by which to die. Omitting any imagined agency of death, he leaps to the stark vision of his own corpse as prey for carrion birds in "Die Krähe." His lack of hope and his soul sickness should, he feels, entitle him to death, but tragically, it does not.

Music and Musicians in *Die Winterreise*

When the wanderer conjures up a mirror image of himself in "Der Leiermann," the fact that his *Doppelgänger* is a musician (of sorts) cannot be dismissed as genre painting but must be understood as crucial. The twinship between the wanderer and the hurdy-gurdy player is obvious: both are outcasts, "outside the town" (outside society), poor and alone, with only their music, such as it is, as scant consolation for the horrors of their condition. The hurdy-gurdy is literally the instrument of obsession and the symbol of a futile existence: all by himself, the beggar musician continues, with stiff, lifeless fingers, to play the hurdy-gurdy of his life. There is no pity, horror, or judgment in Müller's minimal words, but rather a remarkably objective tone, every detail of the scene noted with chilling exactitude. The myriad descriptive details in "Der Leiermann" hinge on one crucial point: that the old musician continues to play his instrument despite the cold, the dogs, and the lack of an audience. "Und er läßt es gehen, / Alles wie es will" (And he lets everything go on, as it will): in that vague, undefined "es" (it) is contained the entire powerlessness of the old man and the wanderer, the twin figures of a divided consciousness. Music reduced to its most elemental state is all that is left to the wanderer when his hopes for human bonds, even his persistent hopes for death, are no more. There can be no hope for change; the music is always the same, and the beggar's plate is always empty, simple symbols—but effective ones—for life as emptiness and futile repetition. The poem is a bitter twist on the truth that extremities of pain and grief can be sublimated in art, a notion that Heine both mocks and celebrates when he writes, "Aus meinen großen Schmerzen / Mach' ich die kleinen Lieder" (Out of my great sorrows I make small songs). But one cannot really say that when the wanderer sees the elderly beggar and hears his minimal, grim music that such obsessional strains as those his alter ego grinds out beyond the town are effective sublimations, are anything more than the sole companion and the sole means of survival remaining to him. "Der Leiermann" tragically epitomizes a human reality: finding an audience has much to do with how one keeps going, in life and art, even when the only audience possible is a projection of nightmare fears about misery's continuation into a wretched old age.

Interpreting the road in "Der Wegweiser" and the hurdy-gurdy player as symbols of death is an obvious and attractive theory, but a problematic one. The phrase "from which no one returned" at the end of "Der Wegweiser" and the solemnity of that moment, the awestruck stillness of recognition, are powerful arguments for a vision of death, but only if one considers the poem out of context. If the wanderer really sees his death, what then is the meaning of "Das Wirtshaus," which follows right after, both in Müller's final ordering and in Schubert? There, the wanderer's destined path ("mein Weg") brings him to a cemetery, where, once again, he hopes for refuge in death and, once again, his wish is denied. No other events intervene between his discovery of the road "from which no one returned" and the death denied in "Das Wirtshaus." The discovery of the metaphorical road-within-the-mind in "Der Wegweiser" and the possessive reference to "my path" in "Das Wirtshaus" link the two poems together. Unless one imputes confusion of purpose to the poet, other readings of the road and the elderly beggar must be sought. The iconographic tradition of the Dance of Death, Death as a musician, resonates within the figure of the hurdy-gurdy player interpreted as a messenger of death. The figure of Death in Hans Holbein's *Simulachres & historiees faces de la mort* of 1538 heralds his announcement, welcome or unwelcome, with music: he beats gleefully on a tabor slung about the skeletal pelvic girdle as the Lady meets her unwanted end; plays the vielle as Adam and Eve are driven out of paradise to their eventual deaths, as the Duchess retires to sleep, never to arise; blows the trumpet to signify his final victory over all mankind; and appears with a psaltery slung around his neck as he gently leads a careworn Old Man into the open grave.[13] In later centuries, Death is most often a violinist, but in earlier centuries, he plays every sort of instrument, including the hurdy-gurdy—the deaths of a master astrologer in Nikolaus Manuel's fresco at the Dominikerkirche in Bern and the village mayor at the Basel Predigerkloster are accompanied by that instrument.[14] But Müller had models for his vagabond musicians closer at hand. In the wake of the Napoleonic Wars, the highways of Europe teemed with beggars, the creations of a toppled empire. If Müller, a youthful veteran of the Prussian War of Liberation, was unfamiliar with the artistic tradition, he had certainly seen beggar musicians in real life playing the archetypal beggar's instrument for the scant pence of survival. Schubert too would have known the numerous organ grinders in Vienna (the *Werkelmänner*) who plied their trade from house to house, at the gates of the city, and on promenades, droning out popular music-hall melodies.[15]

Ultimately, a rejection of the iconographic tradition of *der Tod Spielmann*, or Death as a musician, must be based on internal evidence from the cycle. The moment of inner vision seems fated; "mein Weg" has brought the wanderer to a recognition scene, or grim epiphany. The spectacle of a consciousness so painfully divided in "Der Leiermann" is preceded by the earlier revelation at the symbolic crossroad in "Der Wegweiser." That crossroad is perhaps best interpreted in accord with a familiar Romantic theme, less venerable than the meta-

[13]Hans Holbein the Younger, *The Dance of Death: A Complete Facsimile of the Original 1538 Edition of "Les Simulachres & historiees faces de la mort,"* intro. Werner L. Gundersheimer (New York, 1971).

[14]See Reinhold Hammerstein, *Tanz und Musik des Todes: Die mittelalterlichen Totentänze und ihr Nachleben* (Bern and Munich, 1980), plates 348 and 349.

[15]See Robert Waissenberger, "The Biedermeier Mentality," in *Vienna in the Biedermeier Era,* ed. Robert Waissenberger (New York, 1986), 70.

phor of death as a road from which no traveler returns, but more consistent with the facts of the winter journey: the *Künstlerberufung*, or an artist's discovery of his calling. Once more, Müller alters Romantic conventions in his treatment of the theme. Musicians, poets, and artists typically appear in Romantic prose and poetry as unique beings who follow the demands of a consuming creative force rather than the dictates of society and convention, which they spurn.[16] The singer in Novalis's *Heinrich von Ofterdingen* is an "extraordinary stranger," Anselmus in E. T. A. Hoffmann's "Der goldene Topf" is taken for a madman when he is in the throes of a vision, and Kapellmeister Kreisler, whom Müller greatly admired,[17] is one of the most eccentric of all fictional musicians. The moment when these odd, possessed creatures realize their destiny and accept its dictates of difference from ordinary humanity is a privileged one; *Heinrich von Ofterdingen* is essentially a protracted *Künstlerberufung*, the tale of development of a man with a poetic nature to a practicing poet in full command of his powers. For Müller's wanderer, the signpost at the crossroads is a revelation of destiny: not the death he has desired so fervently but continued life, furthermore, life as a musician, a singer-poet irrevocably set apart from society and condemned to an existence without the "beloved soul" for whom he longs. If the vision of the path destined for him is interpreted in this way, the wanderer's despair in "Das Wirtshaus" acquires new meaning. He has yearned, first, for reciprocated love and domesticity and then for a nihilistic death, not an artist's lonely existence. The recognition that he is forever beyond the realm of "bright, happy life" is unbearable, and it calls forth once again the desire for death.

When Death turns him away at the graveyard, the wanderer tries to drown out the inner voice of lamentation with loud, merry song in "Mut," but the artificial cheer ends in defiance. "If there is no God on earth, we ourselves are gods," he sings. In a world without gods and therefore without cosmic order, men must create a real and significant world for themselves; only fools lament what cannot be changed. But the paradox of attempted affirmation from negation and creation from denial is not something the wanderer can sustain; no

[16]See George C. Schoolfield, *The Figure of the Musician in German Literature* (Chapel Hill, N.C., 1956).
[17]See *Diary and Letters of Wilhelm Müller*, entry for 8 October 1815, 5: "You odd Kapellmeister Kreisler! People have told me that you must have been a demon. But I understand better than those who allege they know you. If I were as good as I would like to be, I would strike an exchange for your eternal blessedness!" The passionate advocacy, the direct address to a fictional character, are striking (Müller was twenty-one at the time).

sooner does he proclaim "Will kein Gott auf Erden sein, / Sind wir selber Götter!" as "fact" than he falls silent, and the poem ends, the echo of hollow words ringing in the silence. It is not the first clause he cannot truly believe, but the second, its falsity betrayed in his choice of words. To what massed, corporate "we" does the wanderer claim alliance? Other poet-singers whose songs will constitute the new created order? Perhaps, but he cannot believe it, and the bravura moment quickly evaporates.

The attempt is valiant, but the reasoning is false and does not work because his grief is real. When he tries to deny the lamentation in his heart, he denies a part of himself and cannot sustain the enormous effort it takes to do so. Müller's omission of definite articles and the pronoun "ich" in the second verse of "Mut,"

> Höre nicht, was es mir sagt,
> Habe keine Ohren.
> Fühle nicht, was es mir klagt,
> Klagen ist für Toren.

(I do not hear what it says to me—I have no ears. I do not feel what it laments—lamenting is for fools.)

bespeaks both unnatural resolution—the compression of a clenched fist—and denial. The wanderer divides himself into an inner being who grieves and who therefore acts upon the stoic, rational self, determined to win mastery by rejection. Unlike "Die Post," in which the wanderer virtually hammers his heart for the knowledge only it can provide, here the heart becomes an inimical force whose intrinsic connection with himself he tries to deny. Within the extreme economies of the poetic parallelisms, the negations of the stoic self outweigh the messages from the heart, addressed as "it" rather than "thou." What it says, he dare not expound, because of the "foolishness" (danger) of giving such thoughts house room. Even Nature must be barred from consciousness, except as a force to be overcome, a denial unlike his customary attention to what lies around him. The images through which he conducted self-inquiry throughout the entire cycle he here denies as incompatible with new necessity; the winter landscape is still the mirror of his heart, but he now perceives both as hostile. The assignment of godlike powers to his new-found art, the attempted use of song to vanquish despair, do not work. Not surprisingly, the defiant resolution evaporates in the next song, "Die

song, "Die Nebensonnen"; heartfelt sorrow is indeed stronger than
the will to repress it.

Throughout most of the cycle, the wanderer echoes unknowingly
the Romantic artist's perception of himself as beyond the bounds of
society, he and the world in a relationship of inexplicable misunder-
standing, but the bereaved consciousness of alienation *precedes* the
knowledge that he is a musician. He is not, however, a Romantic
musician, neither a Titan-genius nor Hoffmannesque eccentric, but a
humbler creature without divine gifts or grandiose aspirations. Post-
Romantic musicians tend to be amateur performers rather than great
composers or mad Svengali guides for doomed sopranos. In his swaying motion and his concentration on the music to the exclusion of all
else, the hurdy-gurdy player is close kin to Franz Grillparzer's protagonist Jakob in the novella *Der arme Spielmann* (The poor minstrel):
"Bald and bareheaded he stood there, after the manner of such folk,
his hat as a collecting box on the ground in front of him, and thus
he labored at an old and decrepit violin and marked the beat by raising
and lowering one foot in accord with the general swaying of his entire
stooped body.... He was entirely immersed in his labors: his lips
twitched, his eyes were fixed on the sheet of music before him—yes
indeed, a sheet of music!"[18] He can neither play from memory nor
improvise. Personal and artistic failure are combined in a single tragic
figure, whose fixation on his music is solipsism in sound. The aber-
rant, unmeasured music he plays is both the single enduring value
of his life and that which seals his isolation from other human beings.[19]
In "Der Leiermann" as in *Der arme Spielmann*, musical quality—com-

[18]Franz Grillparzer, *Der arme Spielmann*, in *Sämtliche Werke*, vol. 3, ed. Peter Frank
and Karl Pörnbacher (Munich, 1964), 149.

[19]Gordon Birrell, "Time, Timelessness, and Music in Grillparzer's *Spielmann*," in
Grillparzer's 'Der arme Spielmann': New Directions in Criticism, ed. Clifford Albrecht Bernd
(Columbia, S.C., 1988), 234. There are significant differences, however, between Grillparzer's fiddler and Müller's wanderer. Grillparzer's Jakob believes fervently in the
benevolence of God and the accessibility of divine harmony even in a corrupt world.
Nor is he mysteriously compelled to shun people, like the wanderer. Even though
Jakob draws boundary lines in chalk to protect himself from too much contact with
the disorderly and materialistic world around him, he nevertheless goes out each day
to earn his daily bread with his music as a kind of musical missionary work. Müller's
wanderer is not thus armored in faith, and the music he hears at the end of the cycle
is not symbolic of divine timelessness and purity. See also Barbara Lindsey, "Music
in *Der arme Spielmann* with Special Consideration to the Elements of the Sacred and
Profane," in ibid., 273–86; David J. Levin, "The Tone of Truth? Music as Counter-
Discourse in *Der arme Spielmann*," in ibid., 287–99; and Peter Schäublin, "Das Musi-
zieren des armen Spielmanns: Zu Grillparzers musikalischer Zeichensprache," in
Sprachkunst 3 (1972), 31–55.

plexity, greatness, even accuracy of execution—is of no matter. Müller here denies a Romantic credo: that music has the power to lift a person out of the solitary confinement of the ego into the elective trust of other human beings (Schiller's "eines Freundes Freund zu sein"), that music's alliance with spiritual spheres can free one from the prison house of the self and bring one into communion with God and with other human beings similarly moved. That music can rescind the axiom of solitude is easily understood if the agency is manifestly sublime, a late Beethoven quartet or a Mozart mass, but the music the wanderer hears at the end of the winter journey is reduced to such skeletal dimensions that emotional transport is unimaginable. Music in its most elemental state—*laute Leere,* or "sounding nothingness"—is all he has. The privileged Romantic status of music as the queen of the arts is still evident in the wanderer's numbed, desperate grasp on it alone as the focal point of existence, but music is no longer either a means of transcendence or a way to communicate with another living being. Indeed, it heightens his isolation.

Biographical parallels are notoriously unreliable, but the fact that Müller's best-known characters, the miller lad in *Die schöne Müllerin* and the wanderer, are poet-musicians seems like wish fulfillment coming from a man who said, "I can neither sing nor play, but when I write poetry, then I both sing and play." Müller, who took great delight in Hoffmann's works, would have known the older writer's dialogues between fictional musicians and poets in "Kreislers musikalisch-poetischer Klub," "Der Dichter und der Komponist," and elsewhere; the above quotation from his diary is addressed to Hoffmann's Kapellmeister Kreisler. But the theme is not developed as if it were truly integral to either work: of all the ambiguities in *Die Winterreise,* this is surely one of the most puzzling. In both cycles, there are only a few reticent hints that the protagonists "sing and play." Neither one mentions music until late in the work: we discover that the miller lad plays the lute only in "Pause," when he hangs his hitherto-unmentioned instrument on the wall and says that his heart is too full to sing any longer. The wanderer says nothing about songs and singing until "Mut" and only once thereafter, at the end of the entire cycle. His sense of alienation and the enigma of the crossroads are comprehensible within the Romantic contexts of the artist-as-outsider and the transformative power of music, but one would wish the themes to be less subliminal. The disturbing suppression of all but a few hints here and there of what may lie at the heart of the journey is possibly explainable as a dual phenomenon, Müller's known desire for musicianship and the speculative defense against that desire. Perhaps he invents a compulsion to sing as the core of his protagonist's anguished existence in revenge on the muse of music for passing him by; perhaps the depth of the wanderer's anguish is all the more clear because music is a curse rather than consolation. Psychological explanations, however, cannot supply what is incompletely presented in the work itself.

The power of music is foreshadowed, again very elliptically, in "Die Post," the sixth poem in Müller's final ordering and the exact midpoint of Schubert's setting. The wanderer hears the posthorn, the signal for the imminent arrival of a mail coach, and his heart leaps at the sound, for no apparent reason. He knows that there is no letter for him, and yet he is irresistibly drawn to the horn fanfares. The coach, he tells us, comes from the town where "I once had a sweetheart," and therefore the strange attraction must originate in his memories of her, but the explanation clearly seems unsatisfactory, and he abandons the inquiry without an answer. There is a striking qualitative difference between his heart-felt response to the horn calls and the diffident, vaguely worded question he asks himself at the end of the poem, as if gingerly testing his hypothesis ("Willst wohl einmal hinübersehn, / Und fragen, wie es dort mag gehn, / Mein Herz?"— "Would you like to peer out someday and ask how things are there, my heart?"). The antecedent of "es" is unclear; the wording is remarkably vague, even incomprehensible. For a protagonist who usually speaks so clearly, such hedging is both atypical and revealing. What if the wanderer's heart, not his faculties of reason and understanding, were responding to the music itself? The fanfares are announcements: for the rest of the world, they tell of the arrival of letters or travelers, but for the wanderer, they speak, although he cannot yet understand their import, of the power of music, the most humble music. Not until the end of the cycle is there an answer to the central question of the poem, "Was drängst du denn so wunderlich, mein Herz?" (Why, then, do you surge so strangely, my heart?")

In E.T.A. Hoffmann's works, fellow musicians, *true* musicians, recognize one another instinctively and without words. "Secret bonds" (*geheime Beziehungen*) unite them in mutual experience, as when the narrator in the tale "Ritter Gluck" (Chevalier Gluck) says, on first seeing the ghostly composer (the young Schubert particularly revered Gluck): "I had never seen a face, a figure, which made such an impression on me so quickly."[20] The bond the wanderer feels with the hurdy-gurdy player is also, in a more universal context, an extreme statement

---

[20]E. T. A. Hoffmann, *Hoffmanns Werke*, vol. 1, ed. Gerhard Schneider (Berlin, 1979), 4.

of the absolute necessity for human bonds. Where they do not exist, the mind will project them onto the external world in a *Doppelgänger* mirror of itself. Müller clothes the grim discovery at the end in music, for Romantic writers and their inheritors the elite of all the arts, but the references to music elsewhere in the cycle are muted. Perhaps it is better so—the work might not have such profound significance if the meaning was applicable only to a privileged few. The wanderer in *Die Winterreise* undergoes experiences, pursued with great intensity, which are familiar to many, not just creative artists: the pain of isolation; the stages of grief, mourning, and recognition of what one ultimately understands could not be otherwise; the confrontations with life's inevitable harshness and the winter of the spirit; and the quest, whether successful or unsuccessful, for self-understanding. But the wanderer's *Künstlerberufung* is "An die Musik" in an embittered minor mode. Those people, including Schubert's friends, who suggested that Schubert saw in the cycle parallels to his own wintry condition may have spoken fairly, up to a point; the composer who knew that his own hopes of love and life had been blasted by syphilis could perhaps (all in the realm of speculation) have seen some of his own fears projected in Müller's words, rather as the wanderer sees his wretched state reflected in the hurdy-gurdy player. But unlike the wanderer, the composer could be consoled by music, at least in part— "I like these songs better than all the rest, and someday you will too."

CHAPTER 3

The Music of *Winterreise*

Winterreise is one of Schubert's largest and most profound compositions, its length (not, of course, the sole index of profundity) equivalent to that of many operas. Its tragic subject elicited from Schubert a deeper response to existential questions and greater musical complexity than did the *Deutsche Messe*, also composed in 1827; Schubert, uninspired by liturgical contexts for composition, was inspired to the highest degree by this secular poetry, with its poeticized philosophy of existential torment. Here, Schubert's operatic ambitions, hampered in their proper sphere by bad libretti and dramaturgical flaws, could be transferred to the genre that he above all others ruled, and the result is one of the greatest works of its kind. Mapping the musical topography of the winter journey reveals diversity ascendant over unity, and yet the cycle, like the grim landscape, is not without its consistent, recurring elements. To see and hear *Winterreise* as a whole before we invoke the wealth of particularities in each song, before we trace each episode along the way, seems the best approach to music of such richness.

Each of the twenty-four songs is both a self-sufficient entity, capable of extraction from the whole, and part of a larger musical whole, whose many stages numbered more than those of most song cycles of the era. Recent criticism decries the search for unifying elements in multimovement works, difficult in any case with respect to *Winterreise*. Earlier, Alfred Einstein went so far as to equate the lack of cyclical relationships with Schubert's conscious or unconscious wish to be different from Beethoven, whose *An die ferne Geliebte* is "fused into a musical and psychological whole . . . by means of the unifying accompaniment and the return to the beginning."[1] More recent writers,

[1] Alfred Einstein, *Music in the Romantic Era* (New York, 1947), 98. Brigitte Massin's statement in *Franz Schubert* (Paris, 1977), 1162, that "cyclical intent does not seem evident in the architecture of the twenty-four songs taken together" is typical.

[73]

such as John Reed, find unity to be "largely a matter of tonality and *Bewegung* (motion)."[2] It is not possible to force *Winterreise* into a procrustean bed of cyclical processes; this is not a tightly unified work in the organicist model according to which ideas stated at the beginning germinate and become an unfolding structure, each musical unit proceeding from what came before, but neither are its songs devoid of all relationships among one another. Both aspects—the refusal of cyclic structure and the motivic, tonal, and other relationships—can be explained with reference to the poetic text. Schubert avoids almost all temptation to call up reminiscences of previous melodies, a device, Capell suggests, which here would have spelt self-consciousness: "In the active life of the sentiment there are no recurrences, and no hour is like another."[3] Nor would the linking devices of a work such as Beethoven's *An die ferne Geliebte*, Op. 98, have been appropriate for a protagonist who believes, until near the end, that his journey is haphazard and without goal. Unlike Ignaz Jeitteles's and Beethoven's poetic persona, the wanderer does not survey the landscape of the past from a hillside perch, a vantage point from which memory can lead to summation and resolution. The declaration in "Gute Nacht" that the wanderer must forge his own path shortly gives way to the sense that he does no more than stray aimlessly from place to place. Only with the discovery of "my path" late in the journey does the wanderer realize that a cruel destiny—his inner nature—has worked purposefully to conduct him there and beyond. Reminiscences of previous melodies or entire sections of earlier songs would have contradicted the wanderer's feelings of futility, his perceived lack of direction. Furthermore, at the end the wanderer neither dies nor ceases his journey, and this open-ended conclusion of the tale proscribes a closed tonal circle as well as musical recollection.[4]

But if readily apparent cyclic return is ruled out by the poetic subject, more subterranean recurrence is not. As the wanderer in "Gute Nacht" describes his forthcoming journey, he is accompanied by groupings of non-legato repeated pitches and chords, an apt musical symbol for the journey: each chord or unharmonized pitch is a "footstep" in a figure that can be extended, transposed, and reharmonized, changing context and form as the journey progresses. It was not, however, until Schubert came to compose Part II that he brings back the earlier journeying figure in a conscious reminiscence, most notably

[2]Reed, *The Schubert Song Companion*, 443.
[3]Capell, *Schubert's Songs*, 232.
[4]The thorny problem of tonal structure across an entire cycle has provoked heated controversy, in part because general principles cannot be applied to the multiplicity of different cyclic designs. The debate has so far centered largely on Schumann's piano

in "Der Wegweiser" when the wanderer once again speaks of his journey. Elsewhere in Part II as well, brief instances of the figure recur as musical emblems of the journey, their placement implying a text-derived significance. Other small and equally nonlyrical motives link adjacent songs in Part I. The result does not approach either the pervasive thematic development in Richard Wagner's works from the *Ring* onward or the readily apparent reminiscences in cyclical structures, but it does demonstrate Schubert's attention to dramatic consistency in a work made up of so many individual pieces.

Schubert's music has other constants as well, the sounding analogues to Müller's grimly consistent poetic world. The numerous off-beat accents are a rhythmic mannerism of the composer which he turned to text-interpretive use in these songs and others—registers of mental turmoil, of stumbling footsteps and straying. One finds them clustered toward the end of *Die schöne Müllerin* when the rustic idyll becomes tragedy, and they are virtually omnipresent in *Winterreise*, a work devoid of any happiness or even tranquillity. When Schubert includes three *fp* weak-beat accents in the first six measures of the cycle (the piano introduction to "Gute Nacht"), the first two accents made even more emphatic by dissonance, he establishes a precedent for the remainder of the work. Furthermore, although Schubert did not devise a tonal scheme with close key relationships from song to song throughout the cycle after the manner of Beethoven and Schumann, he clearly associated particular tonalities with particular dramatic themes, such as A major for the dance songs about illusions of light and love ("Frühlingstraum," "Täuschung," "Die Nebensonnen"), C minor for the paired death wishes in "Der greise Kopf" and "Die Krähe" and its relative major E-flat for the songs on either side of the pair ("Die Post" and "Letzte Hoffnung"), B minor for the most intense mournfulness, and others. Where transpositions

---

cycles and song cycles. To cite only a few of the viewpoints put forward by theorists: David Neumeyer, in "Organic Structure and the Song Cycle: Another Look at Schumann's *Dichterliebe*," *Music Theory Spectrum* 4 (1982), 95–96, proposes that dramatic or narrative principles deriving from the text are determinants of structure coequal with tonal considerations in song cycles, and Patrick McCreless, in "Song Order in the Song Cycle: Schumann's *Liederkreis*, Op. 39," *Music Analysis* 5 (1986), 5–28, writes of "cross reference," or the close resemblance of material across movements, as another element of cyclic organization. Earlier, Arthur Komar attempted to prove a coherent succession of keys with respect to a single tonic by means of Schenkerian deep middleground structure. See Komar, "The Music of *Dichterliebe*: The Whole and Its Parts," in Schumann, *Dichterliebe*, Norton Critical Score, ed. Arthur Komar (New York, 1971), 63–94, and Peter Kaminsky, "Principles of Formal Structure in Schumann's Early Piano Cycles," *Music Theory Spectrum* 11 (Fall 1989), 207–25. *Winterreise* poses knotty problems in each of the above categories because of the singularity of its narrative design and tonal-harmonic structure.

were forced upon him, he chose new keys that reinforce the dramatic associations elsewhere in the cycle or repeat harmonic gestures from earlier songs: the new key of B minor for "Einsamkeit," with the emphasized Neapolitan in the final stanza, recalls "Irrlicht," similarly in B minor and similarly with a dramatic Neapolitan-to-tonic contrast in the final stanza. If this is not the most rigorous of architectural plans for a cycle, neither is it aimless or inconsistent.

In this chapter I discuss the song forms, general characteristics of the vocal part, the harmonic language, the writing for the piano, aspects of rhythm and meter (both poetic and musical), the dramatic associations of particular keys in the cycle, dynamics, and motivic links between adjacent and nonadjacent songs. The genesis of the cycle in two halves, in particular, the presumptive fact that Schubert had no knowledge of the additional twelve poems when he composed Part I, interestingly complicates the consideration of overall structure, of the musical atmosphere generated by the work as a whole. The composition of Part II required of Schubert both the continuation of the musical world defined in Part I and travels beyond "Einsamkeit" to a state of mind even more dreadful than the bleak isolation of that song, an evolution evident in the differences between Parts I and II. Those differences cannot sensibly be attributed to the probable lapse of a few months' time between the composition of each half, but rather to Schubert's perception of change in the wanderer who makes his way to the crossroads and the encounter with the hurdy-gurdy player. Although elements of both the poetry and music recur or remain similarly constituted throughout the cycle, for example, the similarities between the *mises-en-scène* of "Gute Nacht" at the beginning of the cycle and "Der Leiermann" at its end, *Winterreise* is nonetheless largely a linear progression into deepening bleakness. Closed structures, perceptible architecture, cyclical return—these would all be indicative of assured endings, but the wanderer's life/journey continues beyond what we hear, beyond the self-division and glacial restrictions of "Der Leiermann." Interior drama of this sort, in which so much remains the same and yet so much changes, is here given music that likewise registers both change from one moment to the next and a continuing anguished sensibility.

The Song Forms in *Winterreise*

Both of Schubert's large cycles are defined in part by the predominance of particular song-forms—the fact that nineteenth-century cycles are so individual in their structures is exemplified by the differences between these two works from the same composer and the same poet. Compared to *Die schöne Müllerin*, the small number of strict strophic songs in *Winterreise* is striking. The first Müller cycle begins and ends with strophic songs, each with five stanzas, an appropriate framework for a composition that includes seven strict strophic songs. The musical stanzas themselves are not simple (even a brief glance at "Morgengruß" proves the contrary), but the miller lad's closeness to his roots in folk poetry, his naiveté and fixity of purpose, or single-minded obsession with a single thought in many vignettes of the drama, lend themselves to expression in repeated musical stanzas. In *Winterreise*, however, emotional states and perceptions often change within the boundaries of individual songs; the wanderer at the end of the song is altered by the experiences either encountered in the course of singing the lied or remembered and recounted later. As a consequence, literal repetition of musical stanzas is only rarely congruent with Schubert's reading of the poetic content, and varied strophic forms are thus far more prevalent in *Winterreise* than strict strophic designs, beginning with the first song. "Gute Nacht" starts with two literally repeated strophes, but turns into varied strophic form at the third stanza, culminating in the sudden and exquisite turn to parallel major for the fourth and final stanza. Even "Rast" and "Die Post," which are both close to strict strophic form, include variations of detail, especially details of prosody, which necessitated writing out the second musical strophe. It seems only proper characterization that the analytically minded wanderer should reflect the varying nuances of poetic meaning even within the context of larger structural repetitions in the musical form.

Therefore difference reigns over similarity, and varied strophic form in "Gute Nacht" assumes a different shape than the varied strophic structures of "Der Lindenbaum," "Auf dem Fluße," "Der Wegweiser," or "Das Wirtshaus." For stanza 5 of "Der Lindenbaum," when the wanderer relives in memory the choice between life or death in the winter storm, Schubert's variation of elements from the previous strophes is so extensive as to constitute a true development section, an extended dominant to the tonic resolution that follows in the twofold setting of the final stanza. Varied strophic form assumes still another shape in "Auf dem Fluße," with its crescendo of increasing motion throughout the song, and yet another in the twentieth song, "Der Wegweiser," where the oblique reference in the third verse to other people impels a return to the music of the first verse. "Die andern Wand'rer" (the other wanderers) of stanza 1, unimpeded by the monologist's inexplicable urge to shun other people, can and do live in the cities of stanza 3. The twofold setting of the final stanza—Schubert's frequent practice in *Winterreise* and elsewhere in his songs—is the most far-reaching variation of all, foreshadowed in the piano interlude that follows the setting of stanza 2 but not dwelt upon at length until the wanderer sees the signpost within the crossroads of his mind. One notices that the varied strophic forms are clustered in Part I and become less prevalent in Part II, when the references to the lost sweetheart and the reminiscences of a happier past largely disappear from the cycle. This is one of the most telling indications of change between Part I and the Continuation, or Part II.

Where literal strophic form *does* occur in *Winterreise*, as in "Wasserflut" and "Frühlingstraum," the strophic disposition is unusual, determined in part by Schubert's reading of the poetic content. The ABC–ABC structure of "Frühlingstraum" mimics the doubled Dream–Rude awakening–Dream's aftermath pattern of the poetry, and the division of the repeated musical strophe in "Wasserflut" into halves emphasizes the contrast between misery in the minor mode and fantasy or imagination's realm in major mode. The bipartite form of the musical strophe in "Die Post" (A/stanza 1–B/stanza 2, repeated for stanzas 3 and 4) reflects Schubert's division of the poem into zones of startled emotional reaction to the posthorn fanfares and subsequent questions about what prompted such a strange response—the design thus loosely akin to the formal plan of "Wasserflut." But perhaps the most powerful instance of strict strophic design is found in the last song, "Der Leiermann." In the autograph manuscript of Part II, Schubert originally notated stanzas 1–4 in strophic format with the words of stanzas 3 and 4 written under that for stanzas 1 and 2; by the time of the engraver's fair copy, the decision was made to print both musical strophes in full, permitting a prosodic refinement in stanza 4 at the words "dreht, und seine Leier / Steht ihm nimmer still"—the only alteration. The strophic repetition measurably heightens the hypnotic intensity of the scene, especially given the minimal musical material of the song: here, monotony is made grimly powerful. Even so, the fifth and final stanza, in which the wanderer speaks to the *Doppelgänger* he has just described, is a variation.

Seven of the twenty-four songs, almost one-third of the cycle, are set in complex varieties of three-part form, five of those seven in Part II ("Erstarrung," "Rückblick," "Der greise Kopf," "Die Krähe," "Im Dorfe," "Der stürmische Morgen," "Täuschung"). Variation and change are the rules: in only one song, "Erstarrung," does the A section return musically unaltered, the literal repetition here a remarkable instance of music's capacity to question the surface of a text and to make overt the wanderer's psychological ambiguities. The seeming disjunction between musical form and poetic content reveals the wanderer's unwillingness truly to believe what he tells himself at the close of the poem; admitting harsh truth does not mean that one wants to accept it (see the essay on "Erstarrung"). In the remaining songs in three-part form, the music of the A section is lengthened, shortened, and / or infused with new musical material upon its return. For example, "Täuschung" and "Die Nebensonnen," both "dance songs" and both about illusions of light, also share one structural similarity, although within a different context and differently elaborated. In each, the recurring initial music is abbreviated for the same reason: the wanderer can no longer bear to think or speak of the matter at hand and brings the song to an abrupt close. The composer's artfulness is evident in the completion of the musical form despite the seeming proportional imbalance. In "Die Krähe," "Im Dorfe," and "Der stürmische Morgen," the first section returns enriched by a new musical element or a novel permutation of previous material, in each instance, the climax of the song: the plea to the crow to remain "faithful unto death" in "Die Krähe," the short-lived turn to B-flat major and the renunciation of dreams and dreamers alike in "Im Dorfe," and the hammered diminished seventh chords of "der Winter kalt und wild" at the end of "Der stürmische Morgen." The abbreviation of the returned A section in "Der stürmische Morgen" is differently predicated than the abbreviations in "Täuschung" and "Die Nebensonnen" to follow; the music of the initial vocal phrase ("Wie hat der Sturm zerrissen / Des Himmels graues Kleid!"), is omitted near the end, its greater degree of rhythmic and tonal balance no longer possible in the increasing agitation of the moment. In the eighth song, "Rückblick," the first A section tells of one memory, or "glance back," from the past, the B section still another memory farther back in time—Schubert dramatically depicts his wanderer ambushed by unlooked-for recollection. For the return of the A section, the music of both vignettes merges in the wayfarer's wistful desire to return to his sweetheart's house.

The rarities of *Winterreise* are Bar form (the traditional A A B[A] form familiar in German music from the medieval minnesong onward, consisting of two Stollen A and an Abgesang B) and through-composed form. The ninth song, "Irrlicht," is cast in a symmetrical Bar form that reflects the poetic content: the wanderer twice speaks of roaming aimlessly after a will-o'-the-wisp (the Stollen, verses 1 and 2), then reassures himself of an eventual end to his sorrows in the setting of the last verse (the Abgesang, with its traditional return to music from the Stollen at the end). In the sixteenth song, "Letzte Hoffnung," Müller traces an emotional crescendo that begins with *Angst* and progresses in a sequence through fear, increased panic, terror, and finally grief, a linear progression that makes three-part form or strophic format impossible. The three sections into which the song is divided, however, are each organized by internal repetitions and related to one another by the permutations of an intervallic cell established in the piano introduction. Neither through-composed form nor Bar form appears in *Die schöne Müllerin*, but then, the two wanderers inhabit different worlds, speak in different tones, and act in different ways. Although both are monologists whose unfolding inner lives are similarly divided into discrete lyric stages, their disparate natures are reflected in poetic content that elicited different musical structures from the composer.

The Vocal Part

Melodic reminiscence is not, as already discussed, a feature of *Winterreise*. Nevertheless, Schubert *does* create throughout the cycle a group of recurrent melodic types, similar in their configuration but not literally related, which delineate the wanderer's musical personality. As the scenes shift and the subjects change, Schubert's protagonist sings different melodic lines but in a manner analogous to "style" in speech; particular contours and inflections recur as musical emblems of individuality. I note four such contours:

1. Bold, wide-ranging, often triadic phrases, characterized by successive intervallic leaps
2. Declamatory melodic writing
3. Lyrical melodies evocative of folk song or hymnody
4. A subcategory of lyrical style characterized additionally by dance rhythms and grace-note ornamentation

Of these, the first is the most marked and the most frequent; the cycle begins and ends with vocal phrases of this type. Even in melodic lines where the range is not particularly large, the intervallic contours often have the boldness typical of the wider-spanning phrases, as in the setting of the lines "Nun ist die Welt so trübe, / Der Weg gehüllt in Schnee" from "Gute Nacht"; the range is only an octave, but Schubert traverses that octave span up and down three times within four measures. The crows who seem to hurl ice and snow at the wanderer in "Rückblick" do so to similar leaping-falling patterns, and the storm, both within and without, that impels the wanderer on his way in "Rast" assumes craggy melodic shapes evocative both of tempestuous energy and the difficulty of the path. Phrases spanning the intervals of a tenth, a twelfth, even a thirteenth in lines such as "jeder Strom wird's Meer gewinnen" from "Irrlicht," are a frequent occurrence; that penultimate phrase of "Irrlicht" is the symbol in sound of the great distance from stream to sea, life to death, despair to hope. The moments of greatest desperation are conveyed in this style, as when the wanderer falls to the ground in "Letzte Hoffnung" or pleads with the crow in "Die Krähe." ("Täuschung" is the exception. Here, Schubert conveys desperation through antinomy, or the play of opposites. Elsewhere intensity is overt, but in "Täuschung" despair breaks through the assumed lightness and gaiety—too obsessive to be true—in one touch of parallel minor, a single rising chromatic line, and the disturbance manifested in weak-beat accents.) Significantly, the last half of Part II, from "Täuschung" to the end, includes only a few examples of the craggier, wide-flung melodic style. The cries for rest and peace ("und suche Ruh', und suche Ruh' ") in "Der Wegweiser" (mm. 51–54), the defiance of "Der stürmische Morgen," and the heart-felt cry in the last line of the cycle, "Willst zu meinen Liedern / Deine Leier drehn?" (mm. 56–58) are so powerful in part because that particular melodic manner no longer prevails, as it did earlier.

Declamatory style in *Winterreise* is not recitative style derived from opera—Schubert bans any traces of operatic rhetoric from this drama differently conceived—but is instead defined by a single durational value repeated throughout a stanza or section, as in "Rückblick." There, Schubert stylizes the breathless, panic-stricken syllabification of someone in too much haste to give his words the inflections of more considered utterance or even to stop between lines. In the final stanza of "Der Wegweiser," the first stanza of "Die Krähe," and much of "Der Leiermann," the succession of eighth notes in the vocal part conveys, in its lack of rhythmic differentiation, the impression of an interiorized speech whose prosodic laws are distinct from those of direct address to the outside world, and yet each instance of a single rhythmic value predominating as the vocal tactus is distinct in character. The chanting on a single pitch at the end of "Der Wegweiser," the wanderer too awe-struck by what he sees to devise a "melody," differs from the swaying intervallic contours of "Der Leiermann," imitative of the old man's tread and tune, while the "floating" rhythms of stanza 1 of "Die Krähe"—a seamless flow of triplets in the piano, a quiet eighth-note tactus for the voice—contrast with the strong downbeats and dotted rhythms of stanza 2 and the final two lines. (The wanderer resorts briefly to chanting on a single pitch in "Die Nebensonnen" at the words "Ach, *meine Sonnen* seid Ihr nicht," again, the use of this kind of declamation to underscore statements of the greatest gravity in the cycle.) Schubert's prosody is, in *Winterreise* as elsewhere in his songs, characterized both by accuracy and interpretive freedom; passages such as these in which he overrides syntactical divisions or the inflections of heightened speech stem from a chosen poetic reading. Panic, awe, and finally the dissociated eeriness of the *Doppelgänger* vision at the end are brought to the fore in this unforgettable fashion.

The third and fourth styles are also infrequent. One finds lyrical melodies whose narrow range and symmetrical phrasing reflect folk song or hymnody, though transformed by the sophistications of art song, only in "Der Lindenbaum," "Das Wirtshaus," and "Die Nebensonnen." The traditional image of the linden tree in "Der Lindenbaum," evocative of love and Nature in German literature, impelled from Schubert an apotheosis of pseudo-folk-song-transformed-into-art-song that was then quickly assimilated into folk-song collections and anthologies of student songs (*Kommersbücher*). The refinements and nuances of late Schubertian lieder, whatever the link to folk tradition, made it necessary for the compilers to abbreviate and simplify the lied in order to convert it into popular or folk melody; typically, the fifth verse of the song and the stanzas in parallel minor are eliminated.[5] In "Das Wirtshaus," the wanderer sings what he hopes will be his own funeral hymn in a song whose secondary dominants and square-cut phrases recall chorales but without aping all of the conventions of hymnody. "Die Nebensonnen" is a sloweddown Ländler, an anticipation of the hurdy-gurdy player's imminent appearance to the strains of a mazurka pared to the bone; the secondbeat durational emphases in triple meter are a bond between the

[5]In the *Volksthümliche Lieder der Deutschen im 18. und 19. Jahrhundert: Nach Wort und Weise aus alten Drucken und Handschriften, sowie aus Volksmund zusammengebracht*, ed. Franz Magnus Böhme (Leipzig, 1895), 388, the fifth song in *Winterreise* appears as "Lindenbaum" (the definite article omitted) with the vocal melody of stanzas 1 and 2 in F major. The entire text is given. The song is also included as "Am Brunnen vor dem Thore" in *Deutsche Lieder: Klavierausgabe des Deutschen Kommersbuches: 621 Vaterlands-, Studenten und Volkslieder, sowie ein und zweistimmige Solo-Gesänge mit Klavierbegleitung* (Freiburg, 1906), 14. Typically, the music in parallel minor is omitted, and so is the music for stanza 5. The key is E-flat major; the piano introduction and postlude are both omitted; and the accompaniment is simplified.

songs. The musical constrictions that close in on the wanderer when the last flares of rebellion in "Mut" end are melodic and rhythmic in "Die Nebensonnen" (the narrow intervallic span of a fourth for many of the phrases and the first-beat dotted rhythmic pattern of dances and dance songs), harmonic and tonal in "Der Leiermann—there is neither a flesh-and-blood hurdy-gurdy player nor a true tonality in that last song. The fourth melodic style belongs only to the dream sections of "Frühlingstraum" (stanzas 1 and 4), "Täuschung," and the B section of "Im Dorfe," beginning with the words "Je nun, sie haben ihr Teil genossen" (mm. 19–26), all three melodies in $\frac{6}{8}$ meter and of medium span. Dreams and illusions, whether those of the wanderer or the sleeping villagers, have a ballroom lilt in *Winterreise*. Major mode and dance strains here radiate the most intense grief in this cycle, counter to their customary uses and associations.

Signposts in *Winterreise*

One of the fascinations of stalking reminiscence figures, or any figure to which a verbal meaning is assigned, in a vocal composition is that in doing so one proposes links between the words and music, despite the dangers of the exercise. The signifier and the signified are so designated by an interpreter, someone other than the composer, who may have intended no such thing and seldom uses the recurring figure as consistently as the interpreter might wish. Nevertheless, finding text-derived signification in the motivic and thematic patterns of a song cycle is one way of identifying the structural premises of a multipartite composition allied with words. Recurring figures are perceived as wedded to specific aspects of the text, functioning together with the words to explain or represent or express; the composer invents musical symbols for images from the external world, trajectories of action, even characterization. Advocates of "pure music" will complain that music is too often illegitimately linked to things extramusical and explained, often obscured, in terms other than its own, while others will justifiably invoke the dangers of motivic analysis. What, they ask, constitutes a motive, and how can one logically divorce a linear pattern and its subsequent transformations from their harmonic-tonal contexts? At the risk of incurring the displeasure of those who disavow the notion that poetic strategies impinge on compositional choices and those who reject all forms of motivic analysis, I propose that there is a recurring accompanimental motive with a significance derived from the text that can be found throughout *Winterreise*, although not in every song. The "journeying figure," which becomes emblematic of the central metaphor of Müller's poetic cycle, is hardly a major axis of the musical structure, but it *is* a link between self-sufficient songs, and its use in Part II seems deliberate rather than coincidental.

The role of memory in *Winterreise* is different from that in Beethoven's *An die ferne Geliebte* or Robert Schumann's *Frauenliebe und-Leben*, in which melodic reminiscence at the end "rounds out" the closed circle of the structure. When the music of "Seit ich ihn gesehen" returns at the end of Robert Schumann's Op. 48 cycle, it reincarnates memories that span the marriage and becomes its symbol and summation; remembrance engulfs the present, transforming it. The wanderer in *Winterreise* remembers events and images from his past throughout Part I (there are few reminiscences in Part II), but it is the present moment that is nearly always more important and to which he returns. Even the memory of the linden tree in "Der Lindenbaum" is significant for its new meaning in the present: the wanderer hears the remembered rustling of the linden leaves as thinly veiled enticement to die in the winter storm. Remembrance is more shaped by the moment than the moment by remembrance. Furthermore, by the time the wanderer sings "Der Lindenbaum," he already knows that memory is vulnerable to the passage of time. At the end of "Erstarrung," he states sadly that his sweetheart's image will vanish when his frozen heart thaws, when his grief for lost love is, inevitably, past. Where reminiscence is perceived from the beginning as subject to eventual obliteration by time, the cyclical recurrence of entire passages from earlier in the tale would have no place.

There *are*, however, small figures that link adjacent and nonadjacent songs. In particular, the grouping of four non-legato repeated pitches or chords which is the principal accompanimental figure in the first song, "Gute Nacht," thereafter recurs at intervals throughout the cycle, its signification acquiring greater definition and clarity with repetition in different contexts (Ex. 7).[6] The journeying motion of the

---

[6] There is a precursor of the journeying figure in one of Schubert's early songs. In mm. 20–24 of his setting of Ludwig Heinrich Christoph Hölty's poem "Klage an den Mond" (Lament to the moon), D. 436, composed in 1816, Schubert introduces a non-legato repeated-note figure in the piano at the point where the song turns from the F major in which it begins to the D minor in which it ends. The third and final stanza of the poem is the occasion for the turn to D minor and the appearance of the repeated note figure: "Bald, lieber Freund, / Ach, bald bescheint / Dein Silberschein / Den Leichenstein, / Der meine Asche birgt, / Des Jünglings Asche birgt!" (Soon, dear friend, ah, soon your silver light will shine on the tombstone that hides my ashes, that hides

Example 7.   "Gute Nacht," mm. 1–6

cycle begins as the wanderer envisions the journey he must take,
before he walks away from the sweetheart's house at the end of the
song and before he leaves the town in the fifth song, "Der Lindenbaum." Although the repeated pitches and chords and the stylized
funeral march pace suggest musical abstractions of footsteps (not,
however, in a true walking tempo), the figure is not onomatopoeic
but rather underscores the *idea* of the journey. It dominates the accompaniments to only two songs, "Gute Nacht" and the twentieth
song, "Der Wegweiser," in a direct link between the initial definition
of his journey and the revelation to which the journey has led him.
The introduction to "Der Wegweiser" is actually a compound both
of the journeying motive and the scalewise ascending third figure
from m. 16f of the first song (Ex. 8), which becomes an anacrusis to
the journeying figure. Elsewhere in the cycle, the wanderer's attention
is caught and captured by aspects of what he sees around him, sights
and sounds in which he finds the analogy to his own condition or a
spur to self-questioning; only in those two songs does the journey
itself engage his entire awareness and the journeying figure dominate
the song.

The figure appears only sporadically in Part I after "Gute Nacht"
and in contexts that make the assignment of a specific textual symbolism somewhat tenuous. A non-legato repeated pitch motive appears in the piano introduction and postlude to "Gefror'ne Tränen";
when the introduction becomes the accompaniment to stanza 1 of the
text, the non-legato figure sounds to the first of the wanderer's questions about why he acts as he does, "Ob es mir denn entgangen, /
Daß ich geweinet hab'?" The non-legato indications in m. 12 were
not added until the first edition, however, and may be no more than
a means of emphasizing the conjunction of a pedal note in the topmost
voice with motion in the bass line toward relative major. In "Auf dem

---

young man's ashes!). In three stanzas, the poetic speaker traces a progression from
happy past to grief-stricken present to anticipation of the grave. The theme of a journey
through time to death is similar to that the wanderer envisages in "Gute Nacht."

Example 8.   A. "Gute Nacht," mm. 16–19; B. "Der Wegweiser," mm. 1–5

Fluße," the piano interludes after each of the first two verses (mm. 13 and 22) foreshadow the accompaniment to the third and fourth stanzas of text, part of a rhythmic and dynamic crescendo of increasing weightiness beginning with the staccato figures of the first two verses, succeeded first by the non-legato articulation of the third and fourth verses, then by the legato slurs that first appear in m. 41 at the start of the last verse (Ex. 9). In "Irrlicht," the triplet sixteenth-

Example 9.   "Auf dem Fluße," mm. 21–23

note non-legato figures in m. 3 of the introduction and the four-note groupings of mm. 13 and 25 are one element in the textural contrasts that characterize the quixotic will-o'-the-wisp; where the figure accompanies the repeated assertion that finding a way out of the mountain abysses "Liegt nicht schwer mir in dem Sinn" (does not trouble my mind), it is as well another index of the truth behind the overt self-deception of the words, a corrective to the exaggerated bravado of the initial setting of those words (Ex. 10).

Example 10. "Irrlicht," mm. 12–16

In "Frühlingstraum," all signs of distress are banished from the idyllic dreams of springtime and reciprocated love in the first and fourth stanzas. All chromatic tension is absent, the offbeat accents that are one register of disturbance vanish, and a Mozartean clarity of texture prevails. Each time, when the wanderer is rudely awakened to reality by the cocks' crowing and the ravens that caw on the rooftop, dissonance and harsh accents mark the return to musical winter. Part of the reality to which he awakes is the journey, and, accordingly, the journeying figure reappears once again in the *Langsam* setting of stanzas 3 and 6, first, hidden in an inner voice at the beginning and then again, incomplete and in augmentation, in the bass at the end of the verse (Ex. 11). "Frühlingstraum" in the autograph manuscript

Example 11. "Frühlingstraum," mm. 27–31

has only a few of the articulation markings later added to the engraver's copy, but those few indications include the non-legato markings for the inner voice in the piano introduction to the third and sixth stanzas (mm. 27–28, 71–72). The journey itself is not the object of conscious thought in "Frühlingstraum," and the non-legato figure therefore appears in a covert and subtle guise, but its presence is significant. Refuge in an idyllic dream world is not possible, and the journey must continue, its continuation signaled from the moment the shock of awakening gives way to full consciousness. When the wanderer resumes his way, he is exhausted, overcome by despair, and walks "mit trägem Fuß" in "Einsamkeit," the journeying figure in the introduction divided between the right and left hands in a manner that suggests slow, dragging footsteps (Ex. 12). The non-

Example 12.   "Einsamkeit," mm. 1–5

legato markings of mm. 1–2 were written at stage 2 of the autograph manuscript; those in mm. 6–8 and mm. 11–12 were added to the engraver's copy, while the non-legato articulations in the piano post-lude (mm. 46–47) appeared only with the first edition. Whether the additional non-legato indications were inspired or influenced in any way by the more self-conscious use of the motive in Part II or whether this was no more than Schubert's usual "fine-tuning" for publication cannot be known.

As in Part I, the journeying motive appears infrequently in Part II, but when it does, it is as a sign, answer, or explanation, an instrumental subtext to the words in the vocal line. Throughout Part II the wanderer longs for his journey to end in death; when his repeated wishes are denied, the journey's continuation is, on rare and eloquent occasions, signaled by a musical symbol whose signification is by now unmistakable, as it is not in Part I. In "Die Krähe," the wanderer hopes that the crow circling overhead will soon claim him for its prey, but the postlude ends with a single statement of the journeying figure. Müller does not say that the bird flies on and that the wanderer, cheated of his desire, continues his travels ("Letzte Hoffnung" makes that clear), but Schubert does. If the non-legato figure is, in abstract musical terms, a way of emphasizing the bass descent to the low C, it is a manner of emphasis with a provenance from outside the lied, a closing gesture with a history that begins in the first measures of the cycle (Ex. 13).

Thereafter, until "Der Wegweiser," the motive appears only twice,

Example 13.   "Die Krähe," mm. 40–43

rhythmically altered in both instances. The figure at the midpoint of "Letzte Hoffnung" (mm. 22–24, "Zittr' ich, was ich zittern kann") returns varied in the postlude, the non-legato repeated chords / pitches of the earlier motive here combined with descending semitone voice-leading (a "sighing" figure) in the topmost voice (Ex. 14). The

Example 14.   "Letzte Hoffnung," mm. 42–47

non-legato articulation is reserved only for the postlude, a rhythmic *unicum* that "sums up" the transition from the staccato articulation throughout much of the song to the legato character of the last line: "Wein' auf meiner Hoffnung Grab." In the *contrafactum* "Täuschung," adapted from Troila's second-act aria in the opera *Alfonso und Estrella*, Schubert alters the non-legato markings of his source to bring back the journeying motive, rhythmically varied in $\frac{6}{8}$ meter. In the aria, each quarter-note and eighth-note figure is slurred as a separate entity with an accent on each quarter note through seven of the first nine measures, but in "Täuschung," the figures are regrouped into one-bar units (Ex. 15). The rhythmic pattern may seem simple at first, but a second glance (or first playing) reveals the actual complexity. The final eighth note of each measure is not an anacrusis to the next measure but rather belongs within the non-legato grouping of the measure in which it appears. The entire measure becomes a larger anacrusis to what follows, in its turn impelling the repetition of the rhythmic unit throughout the song. The verb "folgen," stated twice

Example 15.   A. *Alfonso und Estrella*, act 2; B. "Täuschung," mm. 1–5

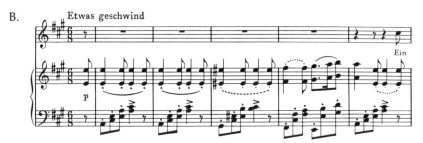

twice in the first verse, is borne out in the manner in which one measure "follows after" another.

The final instances of the journeying motive after "Der Wegweiser" are the most significant, literally so: they function, first, as an unspoken answer to a question and later as a subtext, with a force newly acquired from the extensive repetitions of the figure throughout "Der Wegweiser." In "Das Wirtshaus," the wanderer once again longs for death in the appropriate context of a cemetery; when he asks the innkeeper Death for a room, he is turned away, the refusal evident in the wanderer's disappointed rhetorical question, "O unbarmherz'-ge Schenke / Doch weisest du mich ab?" In Müller's poem, the unspoken, unwelcome answer "No" is implied in the gap between stanzas 3 and 4, but in Schubert's setting, the answer sounds in the accompaniment, just before the wanderer's grieving query (Ex. 16). The journeying figure, which here ends with the anticipation of an appoggiatura sighing figure, is a sign to wanderer and listener alike

Example 16.   "Das Wirtshaus," mm. 22–24

that the journey must continue. As in "Die Krähe," this is the only instance of the journeying figure in "Das Wirtshaus," although it is not the sole example of non-legato articulation in the song. The introduction (mm. 1 and 3), accompaniment (m. 8), interludes (mm. 10 and 16), and the postlude (m. 29) include the non-legato markings and mid-measure accents that have elsewhere in the cycle ("Rast" and "Einsamkeit") suggested the wanderer's weary footsteps.

The final instance of the journeying figure occurs in "Die Nebensonnen," as the wanderer reflects on the mock suns and their symbolic meaning for him. When he laments, "Ach, meine Sonnen seid ihr nicht!" the journeying figure appears for the last time in the accompaniment, elided with the last word of the phrase "nicht," as if to extend and underscore the negation. The wanderer began this journey because his sweetheart rejected him, and yet she was never meant for him because destiny (his inner nature) intended that he travel this road and no other. Schubert thus establishes a link between the lamentation in "Die Nebensonnen" and the journey's continuation at a point where the wanderer does not speak directly of the wandering impulse that has impelled him from the start (Ex. 17).

Example 17.   "Die Nebensonnen," mm. 16–19

Were it not for the obvious relationship between "Gute Nacht" and "Der Wegweiser," were not the isolated instances of the journeying figure in "Die Krähe," "Das Wirtshaus," and "Die Nebensonnen" so clearly an external reference, one could dismiss the occurrences of the non-legato figures as coincidence, but their cumulative significance seems undeniable. Only when one looks back is the meaning fully comprehensible, like the journey itself.

One other figure recurs almost as frequently as the journeying motive, but it is confined to the first half of the cycle; its disappearance from Part II is yet another barometer of change between the two halves. The "sighing motive," or descending semitone, with its traditional connotations of grief and mourning, first appears as an isolated motive in the accompaniment to "Gute Nacht," when the wanderer tells of happiness in the past ("Das Mädchen sprach von Liebe, / Die Mutter gar von Eh' "), then sighs and sings of his present misery. The figures, actually neighbor-note emphases on the supertonic and dominant pitches respectively, are derived from the first vocal phrase ("Fremd bin ich *eingezogen*") and appear in each stanza. When the wanderer tells himself in "Die Wetterfahne" that he should have known not to seek fidelity in the house with a weather vane, Schubert emphasizes the pitches A and D (mm. 19–20) in a manner similar to that in "Gute Nacht" (Ex. 18). The exclamations "Ei Tränen,

Example 18.   "Die Wetterfahne," mm. 18–21

meine Tränen" in "Gefror'ne Tränen" are set as semitone figures, while the rustling figuration in "Der Lindenbaum" culminates each time with the upper neighbor-note to the dominant (Ex. 19). The wanderer's footsteps in "Rast" ("Die Füße frugen nicht nach Rast, / Es war zu kalt zum Stehen") become accented ascending and descending semitone figures; the cocks crow in "Frühlingstraum" to dissonant, percussive harmonizations of sighing figures; and, after each puff of the mild breezes in "Einsamkeit," the semitone sighing figures reappear for the last time (Ex. 20). But in Part II the semitone

Example 19.   "Der Lindenbaum," mm. 25–28

Example 20.   "Einsamkeit," mm. 24–27

cell figures as separate entities vanish, even where exhaustion and melancholy are most evident, as in "Das Wirtshaus."

Other brief and equally plastic figures serve only to link two adjacent songs. Schubert in one instance thus brings to the fore an underlying connective, a subtle interior corridor from one stage of the journey to the next. In "Erstarrung," the wanderer desperately searches through the snow for a tangible souvenir of his lost sweetheart, for green grass, flowers, a trace of her footprints. He soon realizes that the search is futile, but the longing for the green river bank leads him, in the fifth song, to another green memory: the linden tree. He does not say in "Der Lindenbaum" that the frantic quest for something green and living in the winter desolation of "Erstarrung" has engendered the memory of the linden tree, but Schubert makes the connection apparent by means of related motivic figures. The triplet eighth-note figuration in the accompaniment throughout "Erstarrung" becomes the rustling figuration, onomatopoeia for the sound of the linden leaves, at the beginning of "Der Lindenbaum"

(Ex. 21). (The contrast between the C-minor tonality of "Erstarrung" and the E major of "Der Lindenbaum" signals a change of place within the wanderer's mind, the mediant relationship evocative of transport from present experience to the realm of memory.) In another example,

Example 21. A. "Erstarrung," mm. 106–9; B. "Der Lindenbaum," mm. 1–3

ascending octave figures in the right hand accompany the wanderer's recognition of his exhaustion in "Rast" ("Nun merk' ich erst, wie müd' ich bin," mm. 7–8), octave figures that recur in the Langsam sections of "Frühlingstraum" (stanzas 3 and 4) when the wanderer is abruptly woken and, exhausted, muses on the dream (Ex. 22).[7]

Figures such as these are far from being the only binding forces in *Winterreise*. They are too small for that, fractions of the whole, and

---

[7]John Reed, in *The Schubert Song Companion* 29, points to a predecessor in Schubert's song oeuvre for the octave figures at m. 27 of "Frühlingstraum." In "An den Mond in einer Herbstnacht" (To the moon on an autumn night), D. 614 (1818), composed to a text by Alois Schreiber (1763–1841), Schubert had earlier used a more embellished version of similar octave figures at mm. 83–87. The text for the passage is: "Du blickst auch auf die Stätte, / Wo meine Lieben ruhn, / Wo der Tau fällt auf ihr Grab, / Und die Gräser drüber wehn / In dem Abendhauche" (You [the moon] also gaze upon the place where my loved ones rest, where the dew falls on their graves, and the grass above waves in the evening breeze). Eight lines earlier, the poetic speaker says that the moon's light brings hope to the "silent sufferer, wandering all alone on the thorny path," and at the conclusion of the poem he anticipates the rest that he too will soon have in the grave. Whatever the mysterious operations in the mind that summon back and transform earlier fragments of music may be, one can readily understand the thematic links between the 1818 song and "Frühlingstraum."

Example 22.   A. "Rast," mm. 7–10; B. "Frühlingstraum," mm. 27–31

they operate so subtly that it is easy to miss them altogether. The relationship between "Gute Nacht" and "Der Wegweiser" is obvious, an unmistakable bridge spanning the two halves of the cycle, but the other instances are miniatures embedded within a large work. This is not, however, to deny their importance, which is in inverse proportion to their size. With the journeying figure in particular, an instrumental motive becomes the embodiment of the central textual metaphor. The succession of repeated pitches is both a neutral entity in its lack of iconic qualities and infinitely mutable in its transpositions, harmonizations, and changing contexts, but perhaps that is only appropriate to the thing symbolized.

The Tonal Drama

The tonal plan of *Winterreise* seems, in places, singularly *un*planned, "used to straying" and haphazard, like the journey itself. The subject of tonal order is further complicated by the transpositions of five songs between the autograph manuscript and the first edition, presumably at the request of the publisher to avoid instances of the high A for

the singer;[8] since it is known that Schubert often copied and transposed his songs, including songs extracted from *Die schöne Müllerin*,
for individual singers, would considerations of tonal architecture have
mattered to him?[9] I believe that the musical evidence supports the
possibility that Schubert did indeed conceive this cycle as a species
of drama in which tonalities are introduced and then recur with gen-
eralized associations derived from the text. All compositions lead a
"life on paper" and a "life in performance," subject to exigencies of
time, place, and individual musicians. Although Schubert sanctioned
transpositions for the sake of an individual performer, he still might
have conceived a tonal drama with certain consistent and therefore
unifying elements.

Tobias Haslinger was evidently not the first publisher to request
that Schubert transpose his songs to lower, more commercially viable
keys. Schubert's customary vocal tessitura is quite high, often with
few concessions to the untrained amateur voice, and publishers concerned about the commercial risks of selling technically challenging
music to the *Hausmusik* market may well have wanted the high vocal
lines lowered to a more comfortable register and the difficulties for
the pianist lessened. Many autograph manuscripts of Schubert's
songs have been lost, but among the extant autographs one finds
several examples of an initial higher tonality that was transposed
downward for publication, as in "Schäfers Klagelied," D. 121, Op. 3,
no. 1, transposed from E minor to C minor. Pity for the beleaguered
accompanist, as much as for the singer, may have impelled the transposition of Goethe's "Der Musensohn" from the original A-flat major
to G major; the full-textured chordal accompaniment is easier to ne-
gotiate in the second choice of key (G major is also one of Schubert's
"spring song" tonalities). The "third version with easier accompaniment" of "Erlkönig" is another example, although "easier" is a relative term in the circumstances: the reduction of the triplet chords to
duplet groupings in the right-hand part accompanying the elf
king's first blandishments is the only significant lightening of the
pianist's burden. In one of the manuscripts of "Die Rose," Op. 73,

[8]There was at one time a fair copy, now lost, of nos. 7–9 of *Die schöne Müllerin*
("Ungeduld," "Morgengruß," and "Des Müllers Blumen") in a private collection in
Vienna. All three songs were transposed to lower keys for the singer Karl von Schönstein; a note at the end of the ninth song said, "The accompaniment to this song can,
where convenient, be played an octave higher. Franz Schubert."

[9]Actually, there are no instances of high A in "Einsamkeit" and "Der Leiermann"
in their original tonalities, but the F-sharps and Gs would surely have been difficult
for most baritones, especially the ending of the last song. The leap from one register
to another remains challenging even in the lower transposition to E–F.

the song is transposed from the original G major to F major, with the vocal part notated in tenor clef and the text written in another hand; the transposed copy was evidently prepared for a specific singer.[10] Both Schubert's liking for a high vocal tessitura and his propensity for transposing songs are exemplified in an incident that happened during the composer's Graz holiday in September 1827, when a local music publisher, Johann Kienreich, requested copies of two songs to texts by Ernst Schulze, "Im Walde" and "Auf der Brücke." The fair copies that Schubert gave him for eventual publication in May 1828 were each placed in keys *higher* than those of the autograph manuscripts, "Im Walde" transposed to B-flat minor from G minor and "Auf der Brücke" from G major to A-flat major. The Graz scenario reverses the more common Viennese instances of downward transposition for publication; Kienreich would not have known the original tonalities and evidently did not request alteration of the scores given him.

Even if the transpositions in *Winterreise* were mandated by Haslinger to avoid uncomfortably high pitches for the singer, the new keys are in each case consistent with a loosely organized tonal plan whose rationale is largely dramatic. The compositional history prior to the transpositions bears this out, since the *Urania* texts were originally conceived as a closed circle, ending with the same keys as those established at the beginning; the D-minor–A-minor tonalities of "Gute Nacht" and "Die Wetterfahne" reappear at the end in the trio of "Rast" in D minor, "Frühlingstraum" in A major and A minor, and "Einsamkeit" in D minor (see the chart in Example 23 of the original tonalities, transpositions, and secondary keys). The transpositions of "Rast" and "Einsamkeit" "open up" the formerly closed structure, a change probably necessitated by Schubert's discovery that "Einsamkeit" was not the end of the tale. Furthermore, close tonal relationships *do* unite small groups within the cycle. The transposition of "Wasserflut" from F-sharp minor to E minor tonally consolidates the trio of memories and regrets at the center of Part I, and "Mut" in G minor makes clearer the motivic relationship between that song and "Der Wegweiser," whose ascending scalewise third figure (the anacrusis to the journeying motive) is the source for the principal cell figure in "Mut." Schubert might speculatively have conceived "Mut"

---

[10]"Die Rose," D. 745, Op. 73, composed in 1822 to a poem by Friedrich Schlegel from the poetic cycle *Abendröthe*, exists in two versions, the first in G major, the second in F major. The fair copy in the Wiener Stadt- und Landesbibliothek (MH 4180 / c) is written in the lower key of F major, with the vocal part in the tenor clef and the text added in another and unknown hand.

Example 23.   The tonal scheme of *Winterreise*

Part I

1. Gute Nacht	principal tonalities D minor, D major; cadences on F major, B♭ major, and G major
2. Die Wetterfahne	principal tonality A minor; cadences on D minor and A major
3. Gefror'ne Tränen	principal tonality F minor; cadence on A♭ major
4. Erstarrung	principal tonality C minor; subsidiary tonality A♭ major
5. Der Lindenbaum	principal tonalities E major, E minor
6. Wasserflut	original tonality F♯ minor; tonality of the final version E minor; subsidiary tonality G major
7. Auf dem Fluße	principal tonality E minor; subsidiary tonality E major; cadences on D♯ minor and F♯ minor
8. Rückblick	principal tonalities G minor, G major, G minor
9. Irrlicht	principal tonality B minor; cadences on D major and C major
10. Rast	original tonality D minor; tonality of final version C minor; cadences on E♭ major
11. Frühlingstraum	principal tonalities A major, A minor, A major
12. Einsamkeit	original tonality D minor; tonality of final version B minor

Part II

13. Die Post	principal tonality E♭ major; brief cadences on D♭ and G♭ major
14. Der greise Kopf	principal tonality C minor; cadences on G major and E♭ major
15. Die Krähe	principal tonality C minor; E♭ major briefly tonicized
16. Letzte Hoffnung	principal tonality E♭ major; much of song in E♭ minor indicated by accidentals
17. Im Dorfe	principal tonality D major; secondary tonality G major; reinforcement of B♭ major harmony in final section
18. Der stürmische Morgen	principal tonality D minor; secondary tonality B♭ major
19. Täuschung	principal tonality A major; brief allusion to A minor
20. Der Wegweiser	principal tonality G minor; secondary tonality G major; F minor briefly reinforced in A section
21. Das Wirtshaus	principal tonality F major; brief half-cadence on V of D minor; cadences on G minor, F major, A♭ major harmonies; and F- minor modal mixture
22. Mut	original tonality A minor; tonality of final version G minor; cadence on B♭ major
23. Die Nebensonnen	A major; brief references to A minor
24. Der Leiermann	original tonality B minor; tonality of final version A minor

and "Die Nebensonnen," both originally in A minor, as antitheses of energy and resignation, their common basis in grief signified by the shared tonic pitch and the antithetical moods by contrasting modes, but the tonal pairing of "Die Nebensonnen" and "Der Leiermann" is a better choice. The anticipation of the hurdy-gurdy player's appearance in the dance patterns of "Die Nebensonnen," the impression that the grief in the twenty-third song leads to the apparition in the last song, are strengthened by the tonal bond between the two.[11] It seems apparent from Schubert's song oeuvre that he did in fact associate particular tonalities with large and loosely defined poetic subjects, albeit with many exceptions. John Reed, in an appendix to *The Schubert Song Companion*, summarizes and lists the tonalities, poetic themes, and songs that exemplify these associations while warning against the dangers of pursuing the matter too far.[12] Schubert's "indefatigable zest for experiment," his willingness to transpose songs for friends and publishers, and the use of several tonalities within a single song make such codification risky, but neither is it entirely unjustified; Reed, for example, points to the dramatic masterpieces in D minor, including "Gute Nacht."[13] One notices in this regard that several tonalities important in *Die schöne Müllerin* appear only momentarily as subsidiary keys, never as principal tonalities, in the second Müller cycle, whose poet-musician differs in so many ways from the young lover of the earlier work: B-flat major (the key of "Das Wandern," "Pause," and "Mit dem grünen Lautenbande"), C major ("Morgengruß"), and G major ("Wohin?" and "Danksagung an den Bach"). Where those tonalities make brief appearances in *Winterreise*, they bring with them associations from elsewhere in the composer's song repertoire. Reed sees G major as "an essentially lyrical key,"

[11]The similarities may be mere coincidence, but I wonder whether the choice of A minor for the transposition of "Der Leiermann" might have been influenced by Beethoven's strophic lied, "Marmotte," the seventh song in the *Acht Gesänge und Lieder*, Op. 52, a poem from Goethe's play *Das Jahrmarksfest von Plundersweilern*. The song was published in 1805 but was almost certainly composed much earlier. Beethoven was taken to task by the critics for these songs, possibly early exercises in folk-song melody and strophic prosody. It is unlikely, as Beethoven's friend Ferdinand Ries once asserted, that the composer knew nothing of the arrangements for publication, but why he would have offered such trifles for sale is a mystery. Goethe wrote the satirical drama containing this song for amateur theatricals at Weimar in 1788. The title gives the show away: *Plunder* is trash or junk, and a *Weiler* is a hamlet. The bourdon drone, incomplete tonic-dominant simultaneities, A-minor tonality, and $\frac{6}{8}$ meter seem a foreshadowing of "Der Leiermann," but Schubert's song is far more complex. Although there is no mention of the Op. 52 lieder in the extant Schubert documentation, it seems likely that Schubert would have taken pains to know Beethoven's published song oeuvre.

[12]Reed, *The Schubert Song Companion*, App. II, 484–94.

[13]Schubert had earlier associated the key of D minor with an unhappy pilgrimage in search of lost love and death in his lovely but little-known strophic setting of Johann Georg Jacobi's poem "Die Perle" (The pearl), D. 466, composed in 1816. The poetic speaker is a man who in the month of May searches through the bushes, fields, and trees for a pearl (the allegorical symbol of true love). The final stanza reads: "Was mir gebricht, was ich verlor, / Was ich zum höchsten Gut erkor, / Ist Lieb' in treuem Herzen. / Vergebens wall' ich auf und ab; / Doch find' ich einst ein kühles Grab, / Das endet alle Schmerzen" (What I lack, what I have lost, what I counted as my dearest possession,

key," the tonality of springtime, love, and serenity, and it appears in *Winterreise* to evoke the remembered Maytime love in "Rückblick" (the B section), the sleepers' placid dream world in "Im Dorfe," and— very briefly—innocence of wrongdoing in "Der Wegweiser." Schubert began setting "Frühlingstraum" in this key but changed his mind after four bars and wrote the song in A major, the key, Reed says "that unlocked the quintessential Schubert"[14] and the tonality of those dance songs in the cycle in which illusions of light are the central image ("Täuschung" and "Die Nebensonnen"). C major as a secondary key in "Irrlicht" recalls previous connotations of sublimity in the cosmic order ("Die Allmacht"), of a grand inevitability in Nature's designs. The principal tonalities in *Winterreise* too have dramatic-poetic associations in earlier works, for example, D minor as the tonality of humanity's struggle with fate in its various manifestations ("Der Tod und das Mädchen," "Fahrt zum Hades," "Freiwilliges Versinken," and "Gretchen am Spinnrade"). The associations of E major with joy, nature, and innocence and of E minor with melancholia are affirmed in the internal trio at the center of Part I ("Der Lindenbaum," "Wasserflut," and "Auf dem Fluße"), as are the associations of C minor with the sinister side of nature, of F major with pastoral subjects and lullabies (sleep-in-death), and of A minor and B minor with mourning. One should not carry this Romantic *Affektenlehre* too far, as Schubert's love of experiment results in many permutations of these key connotations, but their influence on the choice of tonalities for the winter journey seems undeniable.

As in Part I, Part II also has its occasional subgroupings of songs thematically and tonally linked together, successions in which Schubert underscores similitude of subject and emotional climate, even cause-and-effect relationships. "Die Post" begins a miniature cycle-within-a-cycle about the renewal, denial, and seeming death of hope. Songs in E-flat major ("Die Post" and "Letzte Hoffnung"), a new principal tonality in the cycle, enclose paired songs in C minor about

---

is love from a faithful heart. In vain I wander here and there; but one day I will find a cool grave to end all my sorrow). Jacobi's poem is much simpler than Müller's *Die Winterreise*, but the themes are similar: longing for fidelity in love, once known but now lost; a pilgrimage; and an end to all sorrows in the grave. The incessant eighth-note motion in the right hand of Schubert's setting, especially the up-and-down arpeggiated figures, conveys wandering to and fro, and the quarter-note pulsations in the bass evoke a baroque walking bass (he marks the song "Schreitend," that is, striding or walking), the bass octaves even suggestive of a doubled continuo bass line.

[14]Reed, *The Schubert Song Companion*, 488.

illusions of imminent death ("Der greise Kopf" and "Die Krähe"), each with passages in the relative major key. The D major of the nocturnal village scene in "Im Dorfe" harks back to the D *minor* village scene of "Gute Nacht" and underscores, by its distance from the preceding tonality of E-flat, a very different mental state from the panic and grief of "Letzte Hoffnung." Schubert pairs "Im Dorfe" in D major with "Der stürmische Morgen" in D minor (both also include passages in the submediant key of B-flat major), the latter song beginning with a sequential figure for the piano in *major*—a tonal "corridor" between the two songs by which Schubert musically implies the casual relationship between the disdain for humanity in "Im Dorfe" and the fierce exultation in Nature's destructive power in "Der stürmische Morgen."

Even where the subgroupings and the notion of a tonal design seem to break down, as in the A-major–G-minor–F-major–G-minor–A-major succession of songs nineteen through twenty-three, Schubert on occasion establishes a referential link between the principal key of one song and the secondary tonalities of its neighbor as an appropriately subterranean bond between stages of the journey. When the wanderer in "Das Wirtshaus" (F major) sings "Auf einem Totenacker / Hat mich mein Weg gebracht," Schubert briefly cadences on G minor, the tonality of "mein Weg / meine Straße" discovered in "Der Wegweiser." Furthermore, the introduction of "Das Wirtshaus" ends with a half-cadence in the relative minor key preceding the dominant of F. The D minor—a solitary reference, without recurrence in the body of the song or in the postlude—can be understood in part as a symbolic invocation of the journey begun in "Gute Nacht," a journey he hopes will end here. Similarly, the C-*major* Neapolitan harmonies in the *Abgesang* of "Irrlicht" pave the way for the C-*minor* principal tonality of "Rast" in transposition, and the contrast of B minor–C major in "Irrlicht" reappears in "Einsamkeit." One should not make too much of these underground connectives, as they appear only occasionally, some as the result of subsequent transpositions, but their effect where they do occur is undeniable.

Even a cursory glance at the chart makes apparent the increased use of major tonalities as principal keys in Part II. Only "Der Lindenbaum" and "Frühlingstraum" in Part I are set in major keys, and "Frühlingstraum" actually dwells on minor tonalities for much of the song. In Part II, fully half of the twelve songs are composed in major keys, although the E-flat major of "Letzte Hoffnung" is the culmination of a tonal design largely in the parallel minor, with only premonitory glimpses of major before the final section. The difference in sound is not as striking as it appears to be on paper, since the ten lieder in minor keys in Part I include lengthy passages in contrasting major modes, while minor tonalities are prominent near the end of the cycle: three of the last five songs are set largely or entirely ("Der Leiermann") in minor. (It is notable that in *Die schöne Müllerin* the contrast of parallel modes appears only toward the end of the cycle as it shades into tragedy with nos. 15–19.) Nonetheless, the shift whereby major mode moves more to the fore in the second half of the cycle is another register of the wanderer's increasing alienation and misery en route to the final hallucinatory encounter in "Der Leiermann."

Furthermore, major mode is given an additional expressive function in the Continuation, one that transforms the expressive cliché in tonal music of minor mode/grief–major mode/tranquility, cheer, peacefulness. Even though Schubert calls on major mode for the realms of dream, imagination, illusion, and memory throughout the entire cycle—the memories in "Der Lindenbaum" and "Rückblick," the townspeople's dreams in "Im Dorfe," the illusory promises of the will-o'-the-wisp in "Täuschung," the spring dreams in "Frühlingstraum"—he also uses it in Part II for much that is neither idyllic, imaginary, nor remembered. Most remarkably, the brightness of parallel major appears at climatic moments as the wanderer, having recounted an episode in his *via dolorosa*, sums up the nature of the moment's particular anguish. When he laments at the end of "Der greise Kopf" that he has not yet grown old "auf dieser ganzen Reise," C major sounds more bitter, stronger, more despairing than minor; as in color theory, context alters and even determines perception. The E-flat-major key signature for "Letzte Hoffnung" appears only when the wanderer briefly reassures himself in stanza 1 that there are still many leaves left on the tree (the short-lived attempt to state a falsely optimistic "certainty" takes the form of a tonic cadential resolution, the colors of "manches bunte Blatt" or "many a colored leaf" given a tonal analogue in major) and at the end, when terror gives way to the certainty of grief. Even where the familiar contrast of unhappy present (minor mode) and idealized happier past (parallel major) recurs in Part II, Schubert varies the convention in wonderfully subtle ways, as in "Der Wegweiser." In this song, the wanderer sings of his rocky, snow-covered pathways, his current misery and isolation, in G minor, with a short-lived turn to parallel major when he protests at the beginning of stanza 3 that he is innocent of wrongdoing ("Habe ja doch nichts begangen, / Daß ich Menschen sollte scheun"). He has committed no crime in the past (some listeners will remember the G-major springtime of the central section of "Rückblick"), done nothing for which he should receive such punishment in the present. The contrast of parallel modes differs proportionally in Parts I and II as another reflection of change in the wanderer. In Part I, entire sections or stanzas in one mode are often followed by lengthy passages in the contrasting mode ("Gute Nacht," "Der Lindenbaum," "Auf dem Fluße," "Rückblick," and "Frühlingstraum,"—almost half of Part I). There is one exception when parallel major appears briefly near the end of "Die Wetterfahne" for the mock-triumphal/angry announcement that his sweetheart is now a "rich bride," but contrasts more sustained than this are common to the first half of the journey. Schubert seems, for only a moment, to continue the same kind of contrast—a lengthy section or passage in one mode, a balancing section in the parallel mode—in "Die Post" at the beginning of Part II, but the E-flat-minor harmonies last only for three measures before the music begins to move through the circle of fifths back to tonic major. Thereafter in Part II, brief, unstable passages or even single chords in the parallel mode replace the longer contrasting sections prevalent in Part I. When the wanderer no longer dwells on memories of the past, the lengthier contrasts between parallel modes disappear as well.

In sum, the tonal plan of *Winterreise* may not constitute the most rigorous of schemata, but neither is it devoid of all design. The cycle, however linear its progress, is more than a succession of musically independent songs; a subtle web of tonal connections and dramatic associations links groups of adjacent songs and even forms associative arches between widely separated songs, as when "Täuschung" brings back the dance rhythms and A-major tonality of the dream in "Frühlingstraum." Some performers, arguing the self-sufficiency of the songs and the lack of cyclic architecture, have restored Müller's final ordering to Schubert's composition. Certainly the associations of particular poetic themes with particular tonalities remain, no matter what the ordering, but one thereby loses the dramatic effect of the key succession as it was first published—the mediant relationship of B minor in "Einsamkeit" to the E-flat major of "Die Post," for example, which dramatizes the change from extreme melancholia in the former to renewed vitality prompted by sounds from the outside world. Hearing this cycle, it is impossible to imagine that Schubert did not take into account the way in which each change of tonal locale affects the listener and did not somehow calculate the analogy he created between the appearance of aimless straying and the subterranean purposefulness of tragic destiny—"meine Straße."

The Writing for Piano

Schubert did not seek to extend or even to use all the capabilities of the Viennese fortepianos for which he wrote, but if he was no Beethovenian innovator in that sense, his piano accompaniments do have a distinctive character, due in part to his characteristic multiple doublings of chord tones and the resulting full texture.[15] He does not exploit extremes of range as his great contemporary did, although he does use (sparingly) the lowest bass pitches available on the six-octave instrument. (The Walter *Tafelklavier* owned by the artist Wilhelm August Rieder and pictured in Rieder's famous portrait of the composer was a six-octave fortepiano.) Schubert had a marked preference for a rich piano sound that gravitates to the middle and lower registers, but even so, FF only appears in "Der stürmische Morgen" and the lowest available bass F-sharp in "Auf dem Fluße." Schubert is in general quite economical with the high register in *Winterreise*, using the more brilliant higher sounds only as special effects—the cocks' crowing in "Frühlingstraum" or the bravado assertiveness of "Mut." The highest pitch for the piano is found in "Mut" in its original key of A minor, and that pitch is c^3, far from the f^4 at the top of the contemporary instruments. Even "Die Krähe," with its stylized treble depiction of a bird flying overhead, descends to more accustomed lower levels and richer, fuller sounds, with Schubert's characteristic doublings of the third and fifth, by the end. It is not surprising that the storms in "Einsamkeit" sink to the low bass, rather than rise to heights of fury. Only the dream sections of "Frühlingstraum," removed from the real world of the cycle into a clear, Mozartean aether, and the first two stanzas of "Die Krähe" are notable for a lightening and thinning of the prevailing full textures.

The richness of the piano writing is punctuated on occasion by unison passages (*Die schöne Müllerin* has none) that serve, with a single exception, one of two functions: to represent the elemental force of

[15]The Leipzig critic Gottfried Fink complained in a review of Opp. 79–81 written in 1828 that Schubert "is inordinately addicted to giving too many notes to the pianoforte part, either at once or in succession" (see Deutsch, *Schubert: A Documentary Biography*, 718). One remembers Franz Joseph's complaint to Mozart about the superfluity of notes in *Die Entführung aus dem Serail*.

the winter winds in "Die Wetterfahne" and "Der stürmische Morgen" and to underscore certain of the starkest statements in the cycle by means of so austere a texture. Unharmonized melodic lines in late eighteenth-century operatic tradition heighten the dramatic tension of climactic moments in the drama (the Commendatore's final warning, "Il tempo più non v'è," to the unrepentant Don Giovanni), stripping away all distractions, any competing melodic strands or harmonic color so that the listener may hear important statements with the utmost clarity. Where ambiguity of harmonic or even tonal definition is joined to austerity of texture, the effect is especially powerful. Schubert had earlier spoofed the convention of dread spectral pronouncements in unison texture in his third setting of Friedrich Matthisson's "Der Geistertanz," D. 116; there, a company of ghosts comes forth at midnight to dance to the $\frac{6}{8}$ strains of diminished seventh harmonies—shades of the Wolf's Glen musical *diablerie* that would appear only a few years later—outlined in unison. Most of the unison passages in *Winterreise* are brief and serve to heighten profound thought ("in Gedanken stehn," mm. 11–13, of "Letzte Hoffnung"), grim realization ("Wie weit noch bis zur Bahre!" mm. 24–28 of "Der greise Kopf"), or self-questioning, as in "Gefror'ne Tränen" (an alternation between unison and harmonized textures in mm. 19–28) and "Der Wegweiser"("Treibt mich in die Wüstenei'n?" mm. 31–33). The absence of harmony, the austerity of sound, is perhaps a touch of word-painting for the barren wastelands in "Der Wegweiser," while the alternation between unharmonized, partially harmonized, and full chordal textures in "Irrlicht" is onomatopoeia for the flickering light of the will-o'-the-wisp. Unison writing in *Winterreise*, however, usually constitutes a renunciation of pictorialism. For the duration of those words and lines, the sounds of Nature are banished at the behest of a turning inward so concentrated as to banish all else. This is possibly one reason for the rarity, brevity, and power of the unison passages: it is not often that the wanderer, acutely aware of sights and sounds in the external world, blocks them from consciousness.

The typically Schubertian textures and keyboard style are especially apparent in the piano introductions and postludes that he customarily notated in full at the initial stage of composition. The importance of the opening instrumental passage in the establishment of the tonality, motivic and melodic material, and the atmosphere of each song is self-evident, but Schubert also took pains with the departure from each vignette in the journey and the closure of the musical structure. The postludes are most often either a varied restatement of the entire introduction (nos. 2, 3, 4, 5, 6, 9, 10, 15, and 22) or its recurrence in abbreviated form (nos. 12, 14, 17, 19, 21, 23, 24). The latter at times gives the impression that the wanderer leaves the scene more quickly than he entered it or that he refuses to allow particularly painful avenues of thought to become indulgence in despair. One notices that the more symmetrical instrumental frames belong largely to the first half of the cycle, the abbreviated postludes to the second half—another of the elements in Part II which speak of a wanderer altered by his experiences in the first half of the journey. Even where the conclusion in the piano most literally restates the introduction, one hears the returning passage differently, laden with associations both verbal and musical acquired in the course of the song. When the triplet sixteenth-note figuration from the beginning of "Der Lindenbaum" returns at the end, we now know what the rustling sounds signify and what they "say" to the wanderer; the hushed close of "Gefror'ne Tränen" has an altered resonance after the "heiß glühend" words of the last verse; and the transposition of the introduction an octave lower in the postlude of "Die Krähe" signifies the descent from hope to disappointment. Where the postludes are especially minimal or even nonexistent ("Rückblick" is the only instance of the latter), they are so in response to textual exigencies. The wanderer dreams of standing still in front of his sweetheart's house at the end of "Rückblick," and the music "stands still" as well, while the coach in "Die Post" vanishes from sight and sound, the posthorn no longer audible. Perhaps the very impossibility of the fantasy in "Rückblick" is signified in the cessation of the music once the wish is voiced. Similarly, the tentative proposal "Willst wohl einmal hinübersehn / Und fragen, wie es dort mag gehn, / Mein Herz?" at the end of "Die Post" strikes no answering chord from within his heart, and the music therefore ceases. There is no going back, and the wanderer knows it.

In "Gute Nacht" and "Der Wegweiser," the text explicitly bars musical recurrence at the end. The wanderer's very life changes between the beginning and end of "Der Wegweiser"; the introductory measures, the music that accompanies the query "Was vermeid' ich denn die Wege . . . ?" could not recur as the culmination of the vision at the crossroads. The few tonic chords at the end, traced through each inversion, have an elemental finality that seems the exact corollary to a vision that is both elemental—at the heart of existence—and final. At the end of "Gute Nacht," the wanderer's last words, "An dich hab' ich gedacht," continue to sound in the inner voice throughout the postlude: the eighth-note tactus of the journeying figure is combined here with the parting thoughts of the sweetheart.

But these are the exceptions: even in "Auf dem Fluße," the postlude ends with a return to the staccato chords of the introduction. The welling-up of passion invoked in the last stanza (the rushing waters beneath the frozen surface) ends, and the postlude returns to the chilled, barely moving sounds of the introduction.

Finally, it is the general rule that the piano introductions are restated, whether literally or varied, as the accompaniment to the first vocal phrase (nos. 1, 3, 4, 7, 9, 10, 11, 12, 14, 15, 17, 19, 20, 22, 23). In "Wasserflut" and "Der greise Kopf," the vocal line at the beginning is taken over and adapted from the melodic line of the introduction and the piano part reduced to accompanying harmonies; similarly in "Die Krähe," the vocal line comes from the introduction but is doubled an octave higher by the left hand part, a representation of the crow and the wanderer in tandem with each other—or so the wanderer interprets the bird's presence. When the wanderer speaks to the crow as an odd creature, distinct from himself (stanza 2), the vocal part is not doubled by the piano; furthermore, at the end of stanza 3, he loses hope that his companion is truly an omen of death, and the melodic unanimity of purpose vanishes. Where the introduction is not restated / varied when the body of the song begins, it is because Schubert creates a distinction between onomatopoeic description of a sound in the outside world and the wanderer's reaction to that sound. The fitful gusts of wind in "Die Wetterfahne" spring up between phrases and at the beginning and end, not as accompaniment to Müller's words. The rustling of the linden leaves in "Der Lindenbaum" leads to a memory and a meditation so intense that the impelling sounds themselves are momentarily banished from consciousness, while the posthorn fanfares precede but do not accompany the wanderer's words in "Die Post" (Kreutzer, who set this poem as an independent song, adopts a similar strategy.)

Winterreise is chamber music in which the pianist's part far surpasses the subordinate function implied in the word "accompaniment." Ultimately, what is most impressive about the writing for piano in this cycle is the pianist's role both in the enactment of the poetry and in music's inevitable antagonism to words. Music always insists on its identity as music, whatever representational and expressive text-setting duties it is assigned; here, this exigency of nineteenth-century song operates in agreement with the innermost substance of the poetry, not against it, because Müller's economical language implies more of psychological experience than is related directly. The wanderer grapples with mysteries of existence beyond his understanding; because music by its nature alludes to matters indefinable in words, Müller's calculated reticences invite fleshing-out in instrumental terms. Even the onomatopoeic passages for piano, suggestive of rustling linden leaves, barking dogs, post coaches, and storm winds, point beyond verbal images to realms where words cannot go and music can. After all, the cycle ends with the vision of the mute instrumentalist to whom only the most minimal of tones remain, a creature beyond the reach of language.

Accents

More than any other work by Schubert, *Winterreise* is permeated with offbeat or weak-beat accents, beginning with the second measure of "Gute Nacht" and continuing to the end. Such accents are a fre-quent hallmark of Schubert's compositions, but they are prominent to an extraordinary degree in this cycle and must be reckoned one of the foremost components of the *Winterreise* world. If they are the exception in *Die schöne Müllerin*, they are the rule here.

Weak-beat accents serve throughout the cycle as an index of dis-quiet, of emotional turmoil mirrored in rhythmic disturbance. To say that the numerous weak-beat accents are a musical mirror of the wanderer's despair is not to deny their function in purely musical terms, but it is remarkable that in those places where despair dis-appears momentarily, the offbeat accents also vanish. The dream sections in "Frühlingstraum" (stanzas 1 and 4) and the reminiscence of bygone happiness in the central section of "Rückblick" are free from the weak-beat accents so prominent elsewhere in both songs. In the latter song, the culmination of the wanderer's glance back at the City of Inconstancy in better times is the rueful, pained, and angry exclamation, "Da war's geschehn um dich, Gesell" (Then, my friend, you were done for): there, the weak-beat accents return in the ac-companiment beneath the word "da," foreshadowing the return of the canonic and cross-rhythmic complexities of the final stanza. When the wanderer reverts to the thought of present misery in stanza 3 of "Der Lindenbaum" ("Ich mußt' auch heute wandern / Vorbei in tiefer Nacht"), the offbeat accents absent from the setting of the first two stanzas are reinstated. The roads that other people take in "Der Weg-weiser" sound to a rhythmically untroubled and diatonic passage, but mention of his own hidden, rock-strewn paths elicits travel away from the tonic key, dissonance, and weak-beat accents. After the hushed utterances along the frozen river in stanzas 1 and 2 of "Auf dem Fluße," the action of carving his sweetheart's name into the icy rind impels both the recurrent rhythmic disquietude and increased rhythmic motion. The onomatopoeia of which the offbeat accents are so often a part is inseparable from the psychological portraiture in music; the cocks crowing and ravens screeching in "Frühlingstraum," the dogs barking and rattling their chains in "Im Dorfe," the breezes in "Einsamkeit," the leaves falling from the trees in "Letzte Hoffnung," and his own stumbling footsteps sound as extensions of a conflict-ridden consciousness. There is nothing weary about the rhythmic displacements to which the wanderer sings the words "Die Wolkenfetzen flattern / Umher in mattem Streit" (Tattered clouds flutter about in weary strife) in "Der stürmische Morgen"; recognizing strife as his element and condition, he exults in the forces that create similar turmoil on the canvas of the heavens. With each stage of the journey, Schubert insists on the rhythmic tension engendered by numerous weak-beat accents as the analogue to the wanderer's anguished inner inquisition.

Only three songs in *Winterreise* lack weak-beat accents. In one of those three, "Die Nebensonnen," the durational emphasis on the second beat of nearly every measure in $\frac{3}{4}$ meter anticipates the indicated second-beat accents in "Der Leiermann" just after. The dearth of offbeat accents in "Die Post" and "Die Krähe" is surely owing to the outward focus and central image in each of those poems, the coach and the crow. The posthorn fanfares and horses' hooves of "Die Post" are strongly metrical and regular; the mail coach, after all, belongs to the world of the "other wanderers," who know their destination and travel untroubled (or so the wanderer imagines), but that is not his world of tormented introspection and longing for death. In "Die Krähe," the wanderer looks upward at the bird who flies overhead, unimpeded either by ice and snow underfoot or human anguish; even the plea to the crow, "Krähe, laß mich endlich sehn / Treue bis zum Grabe!" remains within the parameters of his companion's rhythms. (There are, however, remarkable subtleties of phrasing across the bar line in the accompaniment to stanza 2 of "Die Krähe." The paucity of weak-beat accents does not mean that the song lacks metrical or rhythmic intricacies; rather, disturbance is manifested in the larger rhythms of the phrase structure.) Indeed, the intensity of his plea for death, a plea unclouded by mystery or ambiguity, is conveyed in part through a crescendo that culminates in *forte* and *forzando* accented downbeats. With "Letzte Hoffnung" immediately after, overt rhythmic turmoil returns in full force, the plethora of unsettling rhythmic devices all the more striking for the relative straightforwardness of "Die Krähe." When accents are placed, not only on weak beats—"In what meter?" one asks at the beginning of the song—but on greater dissonance rather than lesser dissonance or resolution, disquiet rules.

Tempi

Schubert's tempi reflect, as if on a seismograph, the changeable moods of the journey and the composer's concern for variety of pace. The moderate-to-more-swiftly-paced songs of Part I, for example, are clustered near the beginning, before the energy born of the wanderer's resolve to set out alone on an uncharted course is vitiated by the hardships and mental anguish of his seemingly aimless progress. Once he leaves the town in "Der Lindenbaum," the motion slows soon and dramatically. Fury, panic, and danger—his anger at the sweetheart and her parents in "Die Wetterfahne," the desperate search for greenery along the river bank in "Erstarrung," the menace of death in the winter storm in "Der Lindenbaum," the remembered flight in "Rückblick"—provide the impulsion for greater motion, but after "Rückblick," the motion slows down throughout the remainder of Part I. Only the idyllic waltz rhythms ("Etwas bewegt") and rude awakenings in "Fruhlingstraum" (the *schnell* tempi for stanzas 2 and 5), as well as the turbulent motion of remembered storms in "Einsamkeit," interrupt the depressed, plodding motion of the wanderer's reflections from "Irrlicht" through the end of Part I.

Schubert's Notations for Tempi

Part I

1. Gute Nacht. Mässig, in gehender Bewegung (Moderate, in walking tempo) [changed to "Mässig" in the first edition]
2. Die Wetterfahne. Ziemlich geschwind, unruhig (Moderately fast, restless) [changed to "Ziemlich geschwind"]
3. Gefror'ne Tränen. Nicht zu langsam (Not too slowly)
4. Erstarrung. Nicht zu geschwind (Not too swiftly) [changed to "Ziemlich schnell" (Moderately fast) in the first edition]
5. Der Lindenbaum. Mässig langsam [changed to "Mässig"]
6. Wasserflut. Langsam (Slow)
7. Auf dem Fluße. Mässig (Moderate) [changed to "Langsam" in the engraver's copy]

8. Rückblick. Nicht zu geschwind
9. Irrlicht. Langsam
10. Rast. Mässig
11. Frühlingstraum. Etwas bewegt (Somewhat lively) / Schnell (Fast) /
    Langsam
12. Einsamkeit. Langsam

Part II

13. Die Post. Etwas geschwind (Somewhat swiftly)
14. Der greise Kopf. Etwas langsam
15. Die Krähe. Etwas langsam
16. Letzte Hoffnung. Nicht zu geschwind
17. Im Dorfe. Etwas langsam
18. Der stürmische Morgen. Ziemlich geschwind, doch kräftig (Moderately fast, strongly)
19. Täuschung. Etwas geschwind
20. Der Wegweiser. Mässig
21. Das Wirtshaus. Sehr langsam (Very slow)
22. Mut. Ziemlich geschwind, kräftig
23. Die Nebensonnen. Nicht zu langsam
24. Der Leiermann. Etwas langsam

"Die Post" is perfectly placed to revitalize the cycle at the beginning of Part II by means of imitated sounds from the exterior world, beyond the claustrophobic confines of the wanderer's existential dilemma. The posthorn fanfares infuse the protagonist with renewed energy, and his journey for a brief time assumes the brisk pace of the mail coach. When the posthorn vignette gives way to repeated longings for death, the tempi are no longer quite so slow as at the end of Part I, perhaps because the wanderer no longer dwells on thoughts of the past, as he did in the first half of the cycle, perhaps because the wanderer finds omens of hope or desired death in objects in motion—the crow and falling leaves. Eight of the tempo markings in Part II include the qualifying designations "etwas," "nicht zu," or "ziemlich" (somewhat, not too, moderately), indications surely intended to counteract the inclination to perform certain songs too quickly ("Die Post," "Letzte Hoffnung," "Der stürmische Morgen," "Mut") and others too slowly ("Der greise Kopf," "Die Krähe," "Die Nebensonnen," and "Der Leiermann"). From "Der stürmische Morgen" (no. 18) to "Das Wirtshaus" (no. 21), the tempo of the cycle slows by degrees, beginning with one of the most wrought-up, tensely energetic lieder in the journey and decelerating to the slowest song of all, the only one marked *sehr langsam*. The funereal pace of "Das Wirts-haus" is succeeded by another of the rare instances of furious energy in the journey, "Mut": the greatest extremes of tempi, the most drastic contrast of motion and emotion, are found here. With the paired final songs, "Die Nebensonnen" and "Der Leiermann," the composition returns to its most characteristic motion, within the spectrum from *langsam* to *mässig*.

Dynamics

Winterreise is, appropriately for an interior monologue, very quiet, with long stretches of the cycle marked *piano* and *pianissimo*. Never-theless, the dynamic range is wider than that of *Die schöne Müllerin*, extending from *ppp* (the frozen hush of the river in "Auf dem Fluße") to *ffz* (the "cold, wild winter" in "Der stürmische Morgen"). Neither indication appears in the earlier Müller cycle, nor does one find in *Die schöne Müllerin* as many songs with abrupt dynamic contrasts. The swift changes from *forte* to *piano* and back again throughout "Die Wetterfahne," the cold winds that spring up so violently in the midst of "Der Lindenbaum," the crescendo from *ppp* to *forte* within four measures of "Auf dem Fluße," and the alternating levels of *piano* and *forte* in "Mut" are, like the numerous offbeat accents, indexes of dis-turbance. Louder dynamics, however are used only judiciously and briefly in *Winterreise*. All but three songs ("Die Wetterfahne," "Der stürmische Morgen," and "Mut") begin either *piano* or *pianissimo*, and in two of those instances, the wanderer's words after the piano in-troduction are characteristically soft. Only rarely are *forte* dynamics sustained throughout an entire section or series of phrases, as in the last stanza of "Auf dem Fluße"; even there, the stormy energies dis-sipate swiftly at the end in a return to the *pianissimo* dynamics and slower motion of the beginning. The only song that is loud-louder-loudest throughout is "Der stürmische Morgen," but the mood is both atypical and short-lived: this is the shortest lied in the cycle. "Mut" is similarly terse; defiance, throwing down the gauntlet to fate, exuberance, fury, are not characteristic of the wanderer, while more contemplative states are. The hush of winter and the quiet of introv-ersion dominate the journey, its drama seldom a matter of heightened decibel levels.

Poetic Rhythm and Musical Meter

Müller's poems for *Die Winterreise* are written mostly in simple meters and forms borrowed from folk poetry, iambic trimeters or tetrameters and trochaic tetrameters, with one instance of trochaic trimeters ("Der Leiermann"). In his desire for immediacy, Müller avoids the longer, more "learned" line lengths and rhythms of his sonorous *Griechenlieder* and writes nearly half of the poems in iambic trimeters with alternating feminine and masculine line endings, the so-called ballad stanza (nos. 1, 3, 4, 5, 7, 11, 18, 20, 21, 23). But, as Heine recognized in his letter of homage to Müller, it was not necessary to reproduce the linguistic roughness of folk poetry in order to seize its spirit for new uses. Müller, well read in poetic theory and familiar with the poetic experiments of his peers, consciously shaped his chosen simple forms in accord with aims of consistency and refinement foreign to anonymous folk balladeers. In *Die Winterreise*, poetic rhythm, as always in poetry, melds with meaning. The choice of trochees, less common in German verse than iambs, and short lines, three feet rather than four, for "Der Leiermann" is only one example, among the most striking, of the skillful calibration of rhythm, form, and poetic meaning in the cycle. The direct quality that results when each line begins on an accented syllable, the brevity of the lines, even the first-beat stresses on the connective "und" (underscoring the immediacy of the scene as the wanderer notices each successive detail of the old man's manner and appearance), all contribute to the power and impressive clarity of the poem, the sense that at this moment everything becomes clear.

Within his chosen and narrow boundaries / Müller was a master of metrical alterations, of rhythmic variations that reflect shifts in mood and tone, intensification, a moment of illumination, a change from narrative to direct speech, a new image or insight, or a question. Examples include the occasional appearance of spondaic feet within both iambic and trochaic meters, the spondees acting to slow down the tempo for moments of special gravity and intensity, and trisyllabic feet substituted for prevailing disyllabic feet (dactyls in the midst of trochees and anapests among iambs), lightening and enlivening the poetic rhythms ("Ich träum - te von bun - ten Blu - men" in "Frühlings-traum"). An iamb inverted and altered to a trochee—one seldom finds the reverse—is a jolt that accompanies a change of tone and meaning, a disturbance of thought manifested in rhythmic variation. When the near-insane wanderer dances off in the wake of a will-o'-the-wisp in

"Täuschung," then suddenly begins to lament, the waltzlike iambic rhythms of the beginning ("Ein Licht tanzt freundlich vor mir her, / Ich folg' ihm nach die Kreuz und Quer") change abruptly to a single spondee, followed by a dactyl culminating in a stressed syllable on "ich:" "Ach!/ wer wie ich/ so e - / lend ist." In "Gefror'ne Tränen," a change from the prevailing iambic trimeters to dactyls and trochees for the duration of a single line heightens the wanderer's question, "Ob es mir denn entgangen / [Daß ich geweinet hab'?]" the first of his analytical queries about the cause of his own actions. The anapestic foot at the start of the first line in "Die Post" sets in motion the brisk trotting pace of the poem ("Von der Stra - ße her/ ein Post - / horn klingt"); just after, Müller introduces a pyrrhic foot when the wanderer's heart leaps in response to the sound of the fanfares ("Was hat/ es, daß es / so hoch/ auf - springt"), the better to underscore a moment of special import by means of a rhythmic "rush" to the word "hoch." The alliteration of the two stressed syllables beginning with the aspirates "hat" and "hoch," and the s's of the pyrrhic foot are additional elements of intensification in the line.

Poetic rhythms are always subject to a sea change in musical setting, since metrical stresses in verse and meter in music are not alike, even though both are governed by a perceptible pulse and a patterning of stronger and weaker units of measurement. In most vocal settings, not only do the words last longer in time, unless the tempo is very quick, but the tactus is more regular and ordered than in speech. Even in the most strongly accentual languages, such as English and German, it is only certain types of ballads, dance songs, jingles, and comic poems that one would read in an insistently regular rhythm. Otherwise, in a sensitive reading whose inflections mirror shades of meaning and shifts of tone in the poem, the tactus fluctuates. To hear "Der Leiermann" read aloud in syllables of equal duration would be an unsettling experience, but Schubert sets each couplet of all but the last verse in precisely that fashion, in equal eighth notes—and Schubert surely intended little or no rubato. Furthermore, the meter in a musical setting is only partly conditioned by the poetic meter. In a cycle of twenty-four poems, considerations of metrical variety are more important to the composer than to the poet; if all nine poems in iambic trimeters shared the same metrical configuration in musical setting, there would be a real danger of tedium. Therefore Schubert set that same meter as $\frac{3}{4}$ in "Der Lindenbaum," as $\frac{4}{4}$ in "Erstarrung," as cut-time in "Gefror'ne Tränen," even as $\frac{6}{8}$ in "Frühlingstraum" to accommodate the anapaestic feet among the iambs. Throughout "Der Lindenbaum," Schubert dwells on the stressed second syllable of the first iamb and sets the second iamb in equal (shorter) note values and sometimes as a triplet eighth-note figure. This has the effect of placing a slight poignant emphasis on certain words and imbues the entire song with an elegaic quality from the beginning, from the first prolonged syllable on the dark vowel sound of *"Brunnen"*: "So *man*chen süßen Traum," "So *man*ches liebe Wort," "Ich *mußt'* auch heute wandern," "Komm *her* zu mir, Geselle / Hier *findst* du deine Ruh'."

For Müller's four poetic rhythms (iambic trimeters, iambic tetrameters, trochaic tetrameters, and trochaic trimeters), with iambs predominating, Schubert uses six time signatures, distributed throughout the cycle for maximum variety. Comparing the poetic and musical meters, one realizes that only twice does he pair songs in the same musical meter—"Der Lindenbaum" and "Wasserflut," "Die Nebensonnen" and "Der Leiermann," all four in $\frac{3}{4}$, and those paired songs do not share the same poetic meter.

1.	Gute Nacht	iambic 3	$\frac{2}{4}$
2.	Die Wetterfahne	iambic 4	$\frac{6}{8}$
3.	Gefror'ne Tränen	iambic 3	₵
4.	Erstarrung	iambic 3	**c**
5.	Der Lindenbaum	iambic 3	$\frac{3}{4}$
6.	Wasserflut	trochaic 4	$\frac{3}{4}$
7.	Auf dem Fluße	iambic 3	$\frac{2}{4}$
8.	Rückblick	iambic 4	$\frac{3}{4}$
9.	Irrlicht	trochaic 4	$\frac{3}{8}$
10.	Rast	iambic 3, 4	$\frac{2}{4}$
11.	Frühlingstraum	iambic 3	$\frac{6}{8}, \frac{2}{4}$
12.	Einsamkeit	iambic 3	$\frac{2}{4}$
13.	Die Post	iambic 4	$\frac{6}{8}$
14.	Der greise Kopf	iambic 4, 3	$\frac{3}{4}$
15.	Die Krähe	trochaic 4	$\frac{2}{4}$
16.	Letzte Hoffnung	trochaic 4	$\frac{3}{4}$
17.	Im Dorfe	iambic 4	$\frac{12}{8}$
18.	Der stürmische Morgen	iambic 3	**c**
19.	Täuschung	iambic 4	$\frac{6}{8}$
20.	Der Wegweiser	trochaic 4	$\frac{2}{4}$

21. Das Wirtshaus	iambic 3	$\mathbf{c}$
22. Mut	trochaic 3,	$\frac{3}{4}$
	4	
23. Die Nebensonnen	iambic 4	$\frac{3}{4}$
24. Der Leiermann	trochaic 3	$\frac{3}{4}$

The cycle is filled with special cases that represent a challenge to the prosodic capabilities of the composer, foremost among them the irregular poetic rhythms of "Im Dorfe." The complexities of tone are mirrored in the mixed meters throughout the poem. For example, the last line, "Was will ich unter den Schläfern säumen?" can be read as iambic tetrameters with one anapest, but it is more in accord with the poetic content to parse the line as beginning with spondees followed by a dactyl and two trochees. Schubert chose to set the poem in $\frac{12}{8}$—the only song in the cycle in that meter—to accommodate the longer lines and frequent metrical changes.

More complete consideration of the instances where Schubert altered Müller's rhythms properly belongs to the studies of the individual songs, along with much else. For each song, Schubert devised a self-sufficient structure filled with compositional choices that reveal his close reading of the text; his response to the unique atmosphere and nuances of each poem and the multiple felicities of his interpretive decisions deserve a closer accounting. In this chapter, I have argued that the cycle is a drama and, as such, has the cohesiveness of a musical play. The sum of the twenty-four songs is a clearly defined world in sound, its parameters established by such factors as the predominance of certain song forms, a dramatically determined succession of keys, and motivic recurrence. Nevertheless, it is Schubert's finesse in interpreting each poem that must surely strike anyone who hears and studies the cycle, and it is to the individual songs that we turn now.

P A R T I I

THE SONGS

1. Gute Nacht

Fremd bin ich eingezogen,
Fremd zieh' ich wieder aus.
Der Mai war mir gewogen
Mit manchem Blumenstrauß.
Das Mädchen sprach von Liebe,
Die Mutter gar von Eh'—
Nun ist die Welt so trübe,
Der Weg gehüllt in Schnee.

Ich kann zu meiner Reisen
Nicht wählen mit der Zeit:
Muß selbst den Weg mir weisen
In dieser Dunkelheit.

Es zieht ein Mondenschatten
Als mein Gefährte mit,
Und auf den weißen Matten
Such' ich des Wildes Tritt.

Was soll ich länger weilen,
Daß [Bis] man mich trieb' hinaus?
Laß irre Hunde heulen
Vor ihres Herren Haus!
Die Liebe liebt das Wandern—
Gott hat sie so gemacht—
Von Einem zu dem Andern—
Fein Liebchen, gute Nacht!

Will dich im Traum nicht stören,
Wär' Schad' um deine Ruh',
Sollst meinen Tritt nicht hören—
Sacht, sacht die Türe zu!
Schreib' im Vorübergehen
An's Tor dir[:] gute Nacht,
Damit du mögest sehen,
An dich hab' ich [Ich hab an dich] gedacht.[1]

Good Night

(A stranger I arrived, a stranger I depart. May blessed me with many flower garlands. The maiden spoke of love, her mother even of marriage—now the world is so desolate, the path veiled in snow.

I cannot choose the time for my journey; I must make my own way in this darkness. A moon-cast shadow is my companion, and I seek the wild animals' tracks in the white fields.

[1]The text given in each instance is Schubert's. Where Müller's poem in the *Waldhornisten II* differs from the song text, I have placed the poet's words and significant changes in punctuation in brackets. For example, Schubert inserts a colon before the words "gute Nacht" in the final stanza where Müller makes no articulation. Both the added punctuation and the accent on the first syllable of *"gu - te"* are the composer's way of indicating to the singer that he wishes an expressive emphasis at that point. There are no other textual changes of Schubert's devising in "Gute Nacht," but elsewhere he made numerous small emendations, mostly to improve the singability of the text.

In the *Waldhornisten II*, Müller changed one word of the first poem of the cycle from the first version in *Urania*. Originally, the second line of the third stanza began with the word "Daß," altered to "Bis" in the later version. Schubert either took no notice of the alteration or chose not to use it, perhaps because the /a/ vowel is more singable.

Why should I linger here any longer and be driven out? Let the stray dogs howl in front of their master's house! Love loves to wander—God made it so—from one to another. Beloved, good night! I will not disturb your dreams; it would be a shame to spoil your rest. You shall not hear my footsteps—softly, softly, the door is closed! Upon my departure, I write "Good night" on the gate, so that you might see that I thought of you.)

Müller was given to making numerous revisions of his poems, revisions one can trace throughout the extant sources. For example, he slightly altered the last four lines of "Gute Nacht" in the *Wald-hornisten II*:

> Ich schreibe nur im Gehen
> An's Thor noch gute Nacht,
> Damit du mögest sehen,
> Ich hab' an dich gedacht.[2]

(In leaving, I write only "Good night" on the gate, that you might see that I thought of you.)

In the later ending, Müller has the wanderer himself point out the simplicity and restraint of his parting message, with no harsh words, only the wish that she might have the rest and peace of which he is now bereft. In the earlier version (Schubert's text), the wanderer's leave-taking lacks the self-consciousness of the *Waldhornisten* revision. Both versions have their strengths. In the revised ending, attention is directed as much to the wanderer's analytical notice of his own actions as to the tender departing thoughts of the sweetheart, while the original closure places more of the outward focus on her, leaving the self-observation implicit.

The wanderer's words of farewell on the sweetheart's door could speculatively have originated in an episode from Müller's youth re-corded in his diary, the dangers of the biographical fallacy notwith-standing. For a time, he wrote faithfully in his journal, beginning with his twenty-first birthday on 7 October 1815, but the practice soon palled; there is nothing at all for the period from 23 May 1816 through 10 November of the same year, and the diary ends with an entry on 15 December 1816. During those fourteen months, the principal leit-motives are love and art, in particular, his love for the poet Luise Hensel (1798–1876), the sister of Müller's friend Wilhelm Hensel, an

---

[2]Müller, *Waldhornisten II*, 77–78.

artist and poet whose poems appear in Müller's *Die Bundesblüthen*. Müller's fervor is evident on every page: he dreads the thought that she might not, after all, return his love; reverently echoes her opinions; wishes he could rush off and study theology immediately because Luise has said he must become a theologian; worries about her health; brings her both his own poetry and works he encounters for the first time and particularly likes; records the rhapsodies of one in the grip of a Wertherish grand passion; and rejoices in his certainty that she at last returns his love, although the "certainty" was perhaps more wish-fulfillment than fact. Luise seems to have been aware of Müller's feelings for her, but her religious conflicts made it impossible for her to return his love. In her poem "Die Siebzehnjährige auf dem Balle" (The seventeen-year-old girl at the ball), a *memento mori* or reminder of death, the poetic persona tells her hapless suitor—probably Wilhelm Müller—that he loves only the transitory youthful beauty doomed to wither and die all too quickly.[3] Determined to find everything she did perfect but perturbed by the tone and content of her poems, Müller characterized them in his diary as "dark . . . without love, [filled with] a longing for the afterlife, lost hopes, weariness with life."[4]

Whatever the vicissitudes of love, the budding writer and literary critic never disappears. After an especially rhapsodic outpouring, he looks back over his words and finds them "unintelligible, extravagant, and occasionally commonplace," but he refuses to strike out what he has written because he is, he writes, too deeply moved for artful creation.[5] One thinks irresistibly of "Pause" from *Die schöne Müllerin* and the miller lad who says, "Ich kann nicht mehr singen, mein Herz ist zu voll / Weiß nicht, wie ich's in Reime zwingen soll" (I can no longer sing, my heart is too full; I do not know how I can constrain it in verse), all the more as Müller and Luise were among the chief participants in the *Liederspiel* (song play) "Rose, die Müllerin" created and performed at a Berlin literary salon in November and December 1816.[6] Müller would subsequently revise and augment his poems for the *Liederspiel* as the poetic cycle *Die schöne Müllerin* ("Pause" was among the poems added later, possibly in early to mid-1820), published in 1821 and set to music by Schubert in 1823.

---

[3]Luise Hensel, *Lieder von Luise Hensel*, ed. Hermann Cardauns (Regensburg, 1923), 46.
[4]*Diary and Letters of Wilhelm Müller*, 30 November 1815, 54.
[5]Ibid., 8 November 1815, 38.
[6]See my *Franz Schubert: Die schöne Müllerin*, forthcoming from Cambridge University Press, and my "Behind the Scenes: *Die schöne Müllerin* before Schubert," in *19th-Century Music* 15, no. 1 (Summer 1991), 3–22.

Müller often ends his diary entries with the words "Gute Nacht, Luise!" On 12 November 1815, five days after recording his self-assurances of her reciprocal love, he writes of going out that night to a house where he thought Luise was attending a ball and finding that all was dark and silent. Although he laughs at himself for a romantic fool, for the genre picture he had imagined of bright lights, beautifully dressed men and women, the sound of dance music, and, outside in the darkness, the unfortunate lover, the self-mockery is pained, and he ends with the words "Good night, my Luise . . . if only you had heard my sighing!"[7] On New Year's Eve, he writes of his hopes for a future shared with Luise and thanks God for rescuing him from "sensuality and unbelief" by means of pure love, but the hints of difference are already manifest. Both the diary and his dreams of marriage to Luise end with significantly brief entries for the Christmas season of 1816, entries in which much is left unsaid, perhaps because the events of that month were too painful for him to record in full. "I was at the Hensels for the holy evening. Luise gave me a songbook. Brentano was also there," he wrote.[8] Clemens Brentano (1778–1842) was indeed there, and what transpired between the great writer and Luise Hensel that Christmas put a halt to Müller's fantasies. Müller, a student of medieval literature, may have patterned his love for Luise after the model of courtly love in the Middle Ages, but Brentano's suit was less chivalric. Ultimately, Luise Hensel, the daughter of a Lutheran pastor, converted to Catholicism in 1818 and never married anyone. Whether or not Müller's youthful love for Luise and his nightly farewells to her in his diary for 1815–1816 had any bearing on the later poetic cycle is beyond determining, although he made use of his own experiences in life for other works, as we have seen in Chapter I.

For Müller's wayfarer, this newest journey is impelled by the experience of love in the recent past, so briefly recapitulated that the rawness of fresh grief is thereby apparent. He begins the cycle by recognizing that he is still a stranger, just as he was when he first came to the town, and that his dashed hopes for love have left him in darkness. For one spring season,[9] he had thought his life might

---

[7]*Diary and Letters of Wilhelm Müller*, 12 November 1815, 42–43.
[8]Ibid., 15 December 1816, 89.
[9]Müller had earlier contrasted Maytime love with winter's desolation in the *Ländlicher Reigen* (Countryside round dances) published in the *Waldhornisten I*. The little cycle of four poems alternates between a broken-hearted male "Schnitter" (harvester) and a cold-hearted female "Schnitterin" to whom men are fools and love a pastime. The male protagonist begins by announcing: "Ich hab' ein Herz verloren / Wohl in dem grünen Mai, / Und Keine will mir sagen, / Wo's nun geblieben sei" (I lost my heart in the

change, his wanderings and isolation supplanted by love for "the
maiden" whose mother (both mother and daughter are curiously
faceless creatures) "even spoke of marriage." Possibly he speaks of
the mother-daughter pair in this distancing manner as a shield against
pain, but the effect, reinforced by other similar references, is of archetypal figures: the Maiden, the Rich Bride, the Mother, "They" (the
sweetheart's parents). The successful suitor is never mentioned—the
wanderer's solipsism is apparent from the start in the lack of detailed
reference to other human beings. Beyond the desire of wounded
creatures for solitude, the wanderer is obsessed with difference rather
than common bonds of humanity; he sings of maidens, mothers, and
villagers as if they were separated from him by far more than distance,
social standing, or any other human parameter. Now the warmth and
love of that springtime past are gone, replaced by darkness, cold, and
isolation as the wanderer resolves to forge his own path for a solitary
journey of unknown duration and uncertain destination, his distress
over his bereft condition and his longing for companionship evident
in the image of the moon-shadow companion.

"Gute Nacht" is one of many poems in the cycle in which the
wanderer's emotions change from beginning to end, poems that each
constitute a miniature journey. After the realistic assessment of his
condition in the first two lines and the spare summation both of the
cause for his departure and the nature of what lies ahead, anger and
scorn, despairing sarcasm, even paranoia come to the surface in the
third verse. The wanderer's first question to himself in the cycle,
"Why should I linger here any longer and be driven out?" conveys
his sense of being a misfit, out of a place in a hostile society that he
fears will cast him out and to which he responds with defensive scorn.
The antecedent of "they" ("Daß *man* mich trieb' hinaus") is deliberately left unclear: the parents? the villagers? anyone, perhaps everyone, who can perceive that he is different? The wanderer's
exclamation "Laß irre Hunde heulen / Vor ihres Herren Haus!" (Let
the stray dogs howl in front of their master's house) is markedly
ambivalent, expressive both of angry dismissal and grief. He equates
people by implication with stray dogs, but those lines in the imperative can also be understood as a reference to himself, the rejected
lover who stands outside his sweetheart's house and speaks in such

---

green Maytime, and no one will tell me where it is now). He ends by saying: "Ich hab'
ein Herz begraben / Wohl im Dezemberschnee, / Und wenn das Eis zerrinnet, / So fällt
es in den See" (I buried my heart in December's snow, and when the ice melts, it will
fall into the sea). The motifs of ice-locked hearts and the envisioning of a future thaw
are also taken up again in *Die Winterreise*.

pain of the love now lost to him. The wanderer's scorn is heightened by Müller's adroit choice of words and use of sound, especially the sharp / *ee* / sounds, the breathy and emphatic / *h* / 's that occur at the same place within those two lines, and the hissing / *s* / 's of the lines "Laß irre Hunde heulen / Vor ihres Herren Haus!" It is with this change of mood and tone, from the austere narrative of the first two stanzas to greater overt feeling in the third verse, that Schubert begins to vary the musical strophe, the defiant upward turn of the melodic phrases a departure from the steep descending trajectory of the earlier phrases. The plummet downward in the first phrase, "Fremd bin ich eingezogen, Fremd zieh' ich wieder aus," is a powerful directional metaphor for disillusionment, one Schubert uses often in this cycle.

In "Gute Nacht," the terms of reference progress from the personal (the wanderer's recognition of alienation and the nature of his journey) to increasingly larger realms (the principal dramatis personae of his recent past, the townspeople, and finally the cosmic order itself) and back to the personal sphere at the end (the farewell words to the sweetheart[10]). Each stage of the progression, each change of subject, is contained in an eight-line stanza, broader than the quatrains predominant elsewhere in the cycle:

Stanza 1. The contrast of the past / springtime / love and the present / winter / isolation
Stanza 2. The nature of the journey that begins here
Stanza 3. Anger against the townspeople and against God, who created Love as inherently fickle
Stanza 4. The farewell to the sweetheart

In the last half of the third stanza, the wanderer assigns the cause of his grief to the cosmic order, to a God who cruelly designed an imperfect principle of love. Not just the sweetheart's affections but love itself is inconstant, by "divine" plan made to roam from one person to another without the capacity for fidelity. Luise Hensel, who was long departed from Müller's life by the time he wrote this cycle, would not have approved such aspersions on God as implicitly malicious, but the economical suggestion of a world view devoid of God's love

---

[10]The final line is one Müller had used earlier in the folklike poem "Thränen und Rosen" (Tears and roses) from the section titled *Musterkarte* (Pattern card, or sample card) in the *Waldhornisten I*. At the beginning, a lad picks a rose, throws it in his sweetheart's window, and asks if she is asleep or awake. She replies: "Ich habe nicht geschlafen, / Ich habe nicht gewacht, / Ich habe nur geträumet, / An dich hab' ich gedacht" (I have not slept; I have not awakened. I have only dreamed—I thought of you). Those same closing words become the farewell to lost love in "Gute Nacht." See Wilhelm Müller, *Waldhornisten I*, 2d ed., 144–46.

renders the bleak journey outlined in stanza 2 and traced throughout
the cycle even bleaker. Jacques Chailley suggests that the increasingly
anticlerical Schubert was attracted to the godlessness of Müller's text
(Schubert is known to have disagreed with his pious father on religious matters),[11] and the supposition is a plausible one, although
neither Romantic nihilism nor its opposite, Romantic mysticism, are
the wanderer's principal concerns. The lack of a benevolent deity in
the protagonist's cosmos is briefly but strongly established and then
taken for granted. In this respect, the cycle confirms Müller's place
in literary history. His works belong to a transitional zone between
late Romanticism and post-Romantic Realism, in which themes formerly examined in great depth are assumed without question. His
wanderer is not a Byronic atheist who probes his loss of faith but
seems instead to have lost all belief in a cosmic order a long time ago
and now no longer thinks about the matter. If he rails against the
cruelty of a misdirected universe on occasion, he nonetheless does
not seek to understand its mysteries or lament its workings as an
earlier bona fide Romantic would have done.

Instead, the wanderer is obsessed with the contrast between reality
and imagination. Müller's wording in the last stanza, when the wanderer speaks as if to the sweetheart, reveals a view of dreams as
privileged realms of happiness and escape from misery. Peace,
beauty, and goodness are accessible only in imagination, in the villagers' or the sweetheart's or his own dreams. It is surely the most
somber measure of the cycle's darkness that idyllic dreams are replaced at the end by divided consciousness, a retreat into imaginary
realms of beauty no longer possible. Schubert's understanding of this
crucial theme throughout the cycle is evident in one compositional
choice made and another rejected near the end of "Gute Nacht," after
the breathtaking turn to the parallel major tonality for the final stanza.
Another composer might have read the line "Wär' Schad' um deine
Ruh'" (It would be a shame to spoil your rest) as tinged with sarcasm
and the final message as heaping coals of fire on her head, especially
as the wanderer's anger against the perfidious sweetheart and her
parents breaks out just afterward, in "Die Wetterfahne." Schubert,
however, understood those words to be literally true. For the wanderer, dreams are too precious to transgress. The word "Ruh'"
changes meaning later in the cycle and becomes surcease in death,
but here it is an avenue to a dream world entirely free of reality's
sorrows. The wanderer's imagination is so vivid and his dreams such

compelling purifications of real life that he cannot bear the contrast with present misery and later renounces the products of imagination altogether.

The measured tread of the journey begins in the piano introduction, with its hollow perfect fifths in the left-hand part of mm. 1–2 which suggest a fateful, tragic atmosphere. Here, Schubert introduces several of the recurring musical elements of the cycle: the "journeying motive," the neighbor-note/semitone figures, and offbeat accents. The latter are all the more noticeable because of the constant eighth-note tactus throughout the song and the dissonant tone clusters—these are among the most acerbic dissonances in the entire winter journey. Hearing the start of this cycle, one can understand why Schubert's tonal and harmonic boldness was a byword in his own day. These dissonances, their great tension reminiscent of the cries "Mein Vater! Mein Vater!" in "Erlkönig," interrupt the successive tonic harmonies with jolts expressive of acute psychic discord. The tone cluster at the end of m. 2 can also be understood as a forcible restoration of metrical order. On the neutral tactus of the non-legato repeated chords in m. 1, requiring the addition of a melodic line before one can distinguish the meter, Schubert introduces a melody that conspicuously fails to clarify the matter. Rather, the tonic harmony is extended through the barline between m. 1 and 2, and the meter is set to rights only by means of an exaggeratedly brutal upbeat to the tonic resolution. Arnold Feil has pointed out that the melody for the right-hand part and for the singer enters after the seemingly incessant eighth-note motion that has already begun, the effect one of weary waiting for the upper voice to join in.[12] When it does, the instrumentally conceived melody and the journeying motion merge in acute discord, resolve, and then diverge once more into melody-and-accompaniment. It is perhaps not too fanciful to hear the first three measures of *Winterreise*, and particularly the dissonant tone cluster and its resolution, as symbolic of the wanderer's psychic condition, a fall into melancholia marked by extreme discord as he approaches the end of the descent.

The accented dissonances decrease in intensity throughout the introduction and finally disappear altogether. The dissonances and weak-beat accents are far less frequent in the texted phrases, perhaps because the wanderer attempts, for the most part successfully, to be objective about the loss just suffered and to bid his former sweetheart

[12] Arnold Feil, *Franz Schubert—Die schöne Müllerin, Winterreise*, trans. Ann C. Sherwin (Portland, Ore., 1988), 90.

a reticent, civilized, even tender farewell. Disquiet and grief, largely controlled when the wanderer speaks, assert their presence in the interludes when the words cease. In the autograph manuscript, Schubert places an accent on the dotted figure E–F–[D] in the bass of m. 28, stressing the penultimate harmony of the cadence at the words "Der Weg gehüllt *in* Schnee" (the path veiled in snow), as if the wanderer stumbles because he can no longer see clearly where he is going in so dark and turbulent a world. The initial melodic interval and the pitches F E are not only an important figure throughout this song but recur, although in different keys, in "Die Wetterfahne," in "Frühlingstraum," and at the end of the entire cycle in "Der Leiermann." The penultimate dissonant accent before the tonic resolution thus mimics the harsher dissonances of the introduction. With the first edition, Schubert eliminated the accent in m. 28, reserving the weak-beat disturbances only for the piano passages. Notably, throughout most of the texted phrases, the journeying figure in the accompaniment sounds in a higher register than the melodic line, as if Schubert were thereby both making apparent the inward nature of the wanderer's thoughts, the words contained inside the music, and calling quiet attention to the continual footsteps.

The world in which "the maiden spoke of love, the mother even of marriage" was altogether different from the winter wasteland the wanderer now inhabits. Schubert makes the contrast concrete with a short-lived passage in F major (not a true modulation but a contrast of mode and tonic), a melodic line that rises in depiction of the wanderer's once-ascendant hope, and a legato indication for the piano, unlike the non-legato figuration elsewhere in the song. Could the mirror-image relationship between the melodic line and the bass in mm. 16 and 22 at the words "Die Mutter gar von Eh'" be a musical symbol of marriage? Schubert may also have added the directive "ligato" (from *ligare*, to bind together) for these phrases in the engraver's fair copy as a similar subtle reference to marriage. But it is the musical symbolism of relative major and minor modes and of heights and depths in the melodic line which are most revealing of the contrast between past and present in stanza 1. When the wanderer twice states that "the maiden spoke of love, the mother even of marriage," not only does the melodic line for the first statement ascend but its repetition is transposed upward, both phrases in major mode. When he returns to D minor and repeats the statement "Now the world is so desolate, the path veiled in snow," the only difference between the two phrases is the descent back down to the depths of his present misery for the second cadence.

Throughout the cycle, Schubert is adept at suggesting in the piano interludes the preconscious stirrings of thought and emotion between Müller's stanzas, the wordless progression in the mind from one idea to the next. When the wanderer at the end of stanza 3 sarcastically says, "Beloved, good night!" (the adjective "fein" has connotations of daintiness and refinement—she is, we discover shortly, now rich), his thoughts return to her, however angrily, and to night and sleep. From there, it is but a short step to unlock the world of dreams, a realm he imagines as blessedly bright—the F-naturals from all those earlier dark, minor chords are now no more than two E-sharp passing tones buried in an inner voice. The semitone F E that is such an important compositional element in the song is now a whole-step, F-sharp E, and it is this transformation, even more than the change of mode, that seems so magical. Parallel major and the phrases in a G major not heard before in this song do indeed sound luminous, but the major mode of illusions, dreams, and imagination is always vulnerable to reality's dominance in *Winterreise*. D minor returns as the wanderer for the last time sings, "An dich hab' ich gedacht," the same cadence to which he earlier sang, "Fein Liebchen, gute Nacht." It was then that the wanderer first "thought of you" within the cold, dark climate of waking reality and it is that darkness to which he returns.

Schubert does not bring back the introduction as the postlude, although the eighth-note tactus continues to the end. What he makes wonderfully apparent in the postlude is the continuation of thought beyond the point where words cease. The bass on the first beat of m. 99, beneath the last syllable of text ("[ge] - *dacht*"), remains on the fifth of the tonic chord and only moves to root position D on the subsequent eighth note, not as an ending but as forward motion. The last words, "An dich hab' ich gedacht," echo in the inner voices of the postlude: the wanderer has not only thought of her, but continues to do so.

In his play "Candle in the Wind (The light which is in thee)," Aleksandr Solzhenitsyn uses references to and passages from "Gute Nacht" to lend still more tragic weight to the deathbed dénouement of the drama. In the final scene, the elderly music professor Maurice Craig, near death, orders his daughter Alda to play *Winterreise*:

MAURICE: Of all my relatives you are the only one to have music in your soul and it was you I wouldn't permit to study . . . Schubert. Get me the *Winterreise*. We'll play it together.

ALDA: Daddy! Something else! Not the *Winterreise!*
MAURICE: No, it must be the *Winterreise!* Hurry, or I'll never hear it again.
A winter journey . . . If Schubert didn't flinch at the age of thirty—what
do I have to be frightened of at the age of seventy? And what good is
life to someone who does not know how to live? . . . In the middle of
a snowstorm . . . a snowstorm. . . . Everyone is able to stay inside today,
but someone. . . .

(He then quotes the first quatrain of the second stanza of "Gute Nacht.")[13]

He and Alda begin to sing and play "Gute Nacht," but Maurice breaks
down and stops singing after the first couplet ("Fremd bin ich eingezogen, / Fremd zieh' ich wieder aus"), resuming the song only with
the third stanza. Alda alone sings and plays the last stanza as Maurice
dies, Müller's words of undisturbed dreams, parting, and a "good
night" given a tragic meaning not the poet's, except by symbolic
extension. The "place" from which we all depart, as alone as when
we first arrived, is life itself, the Maytime love the irrevocably vanished happiness of life, and the winter journey death. At the end of
the play, the melody of "Gute Nacht" is played by a single horn, the
instrument nineteenth - century poets and musicians had made evocative of nostalgia for the past. It is not a particularly subtle use of
Schubert's song (it is not meant to be subtle), but it is moving. Solzhenitsyn, with the freedom of fiction, posits a direct connection
between life and art, between Schubert's awareness of an early death
sentence imposed by disease and his setting of *Winterreise* as a fearless
confrontation of that fact—what Edward Cone has called the "cold
wind [that] seems to blow through even some of his sunniest or most
placid movements."[14]

[13]Aleksandr Solzhenitsyn, *Candle in the Wind*, trans. Keith Armes (Minneapolis,
Minn., 1960).
[14]Edward T. Cone, "Schubert's Promissory Note," in *Schubert: Critical and Analytical
Studies*, ed. Walter Frisch (Lincoln, Nebr., 1986), 28.

2. Die Wetterfahne

Der Wind spielt mit der Wetterfahne
Auf meines schönen Liebchens Haus:
Da dacht' ich schon in meinem Wahne,
Sie pfiff' den armen Flüchtling aus.

Er hätt' es eher [ehr] bemerken sollen
Des Hauses aufgestecktes Schild,
So hätt' er nimmer suchen wollen
Im Haus ein treues Frauenbild.

Der Wind spielt drinnen mit den Herzen,
Wie auf dem Dach, nur nicht so laut.

Was fragen sie nach meinen Schmerzen?
Ihr Kind ist eine reiche Braut.

The Weather Vane

(The wind plays with the weather vane on my beautiful sweetheart's house; in my delusion, I thought it whistled to mock the poor
fugitive.
He should have noticed it sooner: then he would never have sought
a faithful woman in that house.
Inside, the wind plays with hearts, just as it does on the roof, only
not so loudly. What do they care about my sorrow? Their child is a
rich bride.)

As the wanderer leaves his sweetheart's house, he looks back and
sees the weathervane spinning in the wind. In another instance of
the paranoia born of his sense of difference from others, he imagines
that it "whistled to mock the poor fugitive." The wanderer's very
identity now is as a "Flüchtling," a choice of word all the more powerful because of the third-person address. The wind that plays with
hearts, spinning them about like a weather vane, is emblematic of
inconstant love. A younger contemporary of Müller's, the great poet
Eduard Mörike, made the simile explicit in his "Lied vom Winde,"
later set to music by Hugo Wolf:

> Lieb' ist wie Wind,
> Rasch und lebendig,
>   Ruhet nie,
>   Ewig ist sie
> Aber nicht immer beständig.

(Love is like the wind, bold and lively, never resting. It is eternal but
never faithful.)

Müller does not identify the wind directly with the force of love but
leaves the reader to draw the obvious inference. Both are powerful
and cruel forces of Nature, uncontrollable and unpredictable, who
toy with the objects in their path and with human hearts without care
for the misery they inflict. In both stanzas 1 and 2, the wanderer
admonishes his former self in the third person, saying that "he"
should have realized that the weathervane was a sign of inconstancy.
The conscious division into different selves, the embittered present

self reprimanding the younger and more trusting self, is a distant foreshadowing of the unvolitional rupture at the end of the cycle when the wanderer is no longer aware that the "other" he addresses is himself.

In a revealing choice of word, the wanderer in stanza 2 speaks of the *image* of female fidelity rather than "a faithful woman" (the existing translations often omit the meaningful reference to a picture or image). Beyond the need for a sound to rhyme with "Schild," the word *Frauenbild* suggests an image, not reality. The use of third-person address seems a method of self-protective distancing—"the poor fugitive" has experienced this, not "me," but the distress and pain are all his ("in *meinem* Wahne," "nach *meinem* Schmerzen") and belong to the present moment. The psychological strategem by which the wanderer finds an outlet for his rage, a cause for his pain, and yet spares his former sweetheart is the climax and closure of the poem. He has already implied in "Gute Nacht" that his sweetheart's marital fate was in her parents' hands, since it was the mother who "even spoke of marriage" and who evidently retracted her words when a wealthier prospect came along, but the refusal to castigate the beloved directly is notable.

Müller orders the phrase structure and poetic rhythm to suggest the wind's rapid motion, a tempo quicker than that of "Gute Nacht." The odd-numbered lines of both the first and second stanzas end with an unaccented syllable, followed by the unaccented initial syllable of the iambic foot at the start of the even-numbered lines, usually a continuation of the same clause (stanza 1, lines three and four are an exception).

> Der Wind spielt mit der Wet - ter - fah - ne
> Auf mei - nes schö - nen Lieb - chens Haus.

The effect is one of increased haste and breathlessness at mid-couplet, heightened by Müller's substitution of anapests for iambs in the second verse, quickening the pace still further.

> Er hätt' es eh - er be - mer - ken sol - len
> Des Hau - ses auf - ge - steck - tes Schild.

Only once, in the second line of the last stanza, does Müller slow down the rapid poetic rhythms for the statement that Love toys with human hearts more quietly than the wind that spins the weather vane: "Wie auf dem Dach, [caesural break] nur nicht so laut" (as on the roof top, but not so loudly). This is the only line in the poem divided into symmetrical halves in this fashion, the poet slowing the poetic rhythms that we might attend to the quietude within. The line itself pauses as if poised on the roof top. Schubert, attentive to poetic detail, indicates fermatas not only at the word "Dach" but also the rest that follows the words "nur nicht so laut," unlike the predecessor to this phrase ending in m. 9. In the brief silence, his wanderer hears the pain within his heart and bursts out in a protest marked "laut" (loud). If the havoc wreaked within is quiet because internal, his aggrieved questions are not so hushed.

Iambs are most often set to music in duple meter, but Schubert transforms the iambic tetrameters of "Die Wetterfahne" into $\frac{6}{8}$ or compound meter, the better to elide the feminine endings of the odd-numbered lines with the unaccented syllable at the start of the succeeding line. The stronger or accented syllables of the iambic feet are set either as quarter notes or two slurred eighth notes; in the passage from the feminine line endings to the subsequent iamb, the accented syllable appears properly on a strong beat, either beat one or four, but has only an eighth-note duration and is followed by the two subsequent unaccented, weaker syllables. In m. 11, Schubert varies the pattern by quickening the pace, compressing part of the line into three sixteenth notes ("Da dacht' ich schon *in meinem* Wahne"), rushing through the possessive adjective in haste to greater emphasis on the noun "Wahne." The same rhythmic pattern recurs to similar effect in mm. 30–31, 40–41, and 42–43 at the question "Was fragen sie nach meinen Schmerzen?"—the crucial word "Schmerzen" (sorrows) emphasized in the same way. Only twice does he lengthen an accented syllable beyond the duration of a quarter note: at the word "Dach," by means of a fermata, and at the end of the vocal part (m. 45), where the singer prolongs the first syllable of the adjective "*rei* - che" for nearly an entire measure. Because Schubert replaces Müller's self-pity with wild, angry energy, the quarter-note–eighth-note patterns common to $\frac{6}{8}$ meter are strongly emphasized, but the prosodic nuances are, here as elsewhere in the cycle, finely calculated.

In "Die Wetterfahne," the wanderer once again finds images in Nature for his inner emotional state, images Schubert seizes with obvious relish. Fitful gusts of wind spring up and quickly die down between each phrase, and creaking, rattling, sighing figures accompany the singer's words as well. But if "the song is more outward-looking than the poem," in John Reed's apt phrase,[1] more than mere

[1]Reed, *The Schubert Song Companion*, 445.

onomatopoeia is at work. The first icy blast in the piano introduction introduces the motivically important pitches F and E (F as the upper neighbor to E) from "Gute Nacht," which are subsequently restated as the apex of the ascent traced in the first vocal phrase (mm. 8–9) and in stanza 2 (mm. 17–19) and as the source of the semitone figures in stanza 3 ("Was fragen sie nach meinen Schmerzen?"). The wintry forcefulness of the song's climate is evident first and foremost in the unison writing: nowhere else in the cycle does one find an entire introduction, complete phrases, and the instrumental interludes thus unharmonized, nor are there precedents in earlier songs by Schubert or anyone else. Schubert uses unison texture not only to tell of the wind's icy energy but as a way of underscoring Müller's poetic analogy between the wind-and-the-weathervane, love-and-hearts. Each time the wanderer speaks of the wind and its effects ("The wind plays with the weathervane . . . the wind plays with hearts"), he does so to an extended unison phrase whose frequent changes of direction up-and-down are word-painting for the spinning weathervane. After the unison introduction and first phrase, the wanderer's subsequent imaginings and emotional reactions are then "fleshed-out" harmonically in the subsequent phrases. Especially in the twofold setting of the third stanza, one hears a progressively thickening texture in the accompaniment, from the icy austerity of its unison beginnings to the full chordal harmonies beneath the words "eine reiche Braut." Schubert has his wanderer then repeat the entire last stanza with details varied for greater intensity, including the contrast of unison and fuller textures. The stanza does not begin with unison passages; rather, the combination of the wanderer's vocal line and the wind's trilled sighing sounds in mm. 35–36 outline a diminished seventh chord heard earlier, and the unison texture is deferred until the half-cadence in mm. 37–38. There, in response to Müller's word "drinnen" (within), Schubert sinks the piano part an octave lower than before.

In Schubert's reading, the second stanza is fraught, not with the self-pity others might find there, but with tensions he expresses as an increasingly rapid rise in the bass and as a series of ascending sequences; the tonal jolt upward in mm. 41–42 is especially shocking in its violent unconventionality. The intensity barely controlled by the wanderer's third-person address grows ever greater throughout this self-admonition after the fact and culminates with the wind whistling him away yet again at the end of the stanza, higher, more shrill and derisive than before. In their final form, after the emendations one can trace through the sources, mm. 15–22 are remarkable for the jagged, unlyrical quality of the vocal writing, the extraordinary embodiment of acute psychic tension well worth the effort required to achieve it. This bitter self-reproach is tonally unsettled for most of its length, and its ultimate point of arrival, the cadence on D minor for the words "Im Haus ein treues Frauenbild," is a short-lived recollection of the tonality of "Gute Nacht" just before. The poetic link between the scenario of the first song and the words "house" and "faithful woman's image" is obvious and prompted from Schubert a brief reminiscence of the earlier tonality, proof if any were needed of Schubert's conception of tonalities as conveying dramatic meaning.

But what is perhaps most remarkable is the principal means of melodic emphasis throughout the stanza. The wind that whistled the poor fugitive away at the end of the first stanza now tosses the words of stanza 2 about, spinning them up and down even more forcefully than it had spun the weather vane in stanza 1. Schubert stresses each of the accented syllables in the second verse not only by means of the usual downbeat emphases and by dissonant appoggiaturas on the fourth beat in $\frac{6}{8}$, but by a prosodic masterstroke. More exaggeratedly than in mm. 12–13 at the words "Sie pfiff' den armen Flüchtling aus," a syllable introduced on a strong beat leaps to a higher pitch on the next (weak) beat, the emphasis all the greater when the ascending interval is as large as a tritone, perfect fifth, or minor sixth. Schubert uses the potent combination of higher pitches and weak beats in the vocal line only sparingly in *Winterreise* and never again at such length. Another composer, less enamored of music for a winter wind than Schubert, might have seen more pathos in these same words, rather than the storm-tossed intervals, rising tension, and barely suppressed anger of this music, the wonderfully ingenious result of his struggles with the text. The music at the end of stanza 1 is further developed in stanza 2, while the rising chromatic sequences of stanza 2 lead in turn to the rising chromatic sequences in stanza 3—a chain link of compositional relationships extending throughout the lied and one that cost Schubert considerable effort to create.

The chain receives yet another new link in the twofold setting of the last verse. Müller virtually compels the composer to bring back the first phrase of stanza 1 for the beginning of stanza 3, but the former whistling wind will no longer serve for the "rich bride" at the poem's end. Once again, Müller's self-pity becomes Schubert's expressions of anger. When the wanderer cries out, "What do they care about my sorrow?" Schubert brings back the rhythmic pattern in the piano and the chordal punctuation of mm. 11–12 ("Da dacht' ich schon in meinem Wahne"), reharmonizing the F E neighboring pitches from those earlier measures. The "Wahne" from before has returned. The D-flat neighboring tones in the vocal line are then enharmonically respelled as the C-sharps in the cadence on A major for the words "eine reiche Braut," all the more emphatic for the rattling burst of sixteenth notes that drive to the cadence. Her good fortune is his sorrow: the D-flat that belongs to the world of the wanderer's sorrow becomes the C-sharp and the full, rich chords that signify the former sweetheart's bridal wealth. Here, the contrast of parallel major and minor modes, the latter immediately reinstated, repeats the signification of the twin modes in "Gute Nacht." The wanderer imagines the former sweetheart's life and prospects as bright, rich, and full, in contrast with his own darkness, but the return of the icy wind in the postlude dispels both the rich textures and major mode. When the wind dies away for the last time, Schubert indicates a fermata over the final rests of the measure, a dramatic gesture found nowhere else in the cycle and one that stems from m. 38. The wind no longer plays with the weather vane outside but has once again moved inside and buffets his heart in the silence at the end of "Die Wetterfahne."

3. Gefror'ne Tränen

Gefror'ne Tropfen fallen
Von meinen Wangen ab:
Ob es [Und ist's] mir denn entgangen
Daß ich geweinet hab'?

Ei Tränen, meine Tränen,
Und seid ihr gar so lau,
Daß ihr erstarrt zu Eise,
Wie kühler Morgentau?

Und dringt doch aus der Quelle
Der Brust so glühend heiß,
Als wolltet ihr zerschmelzen
Des ganzen Winters Eis.

[138]

Frozen Tears

(Frozen drops fall from my cheeks: have I then not noticed that I
have been weeping?
Tears, my tears, and are you so tepid that you turn to ice, like the
cool morning dew?
And yet you well forth from your source within my heart, as fiery
hot as if you would melt all the winter's ice!)

Müller's detractors have traditionally found fault with "Gefror'ne
Tränen" for its supposed triteness and improbability; castigating the
unfortunate image of the rolling ice tears is among the first lines of
attack on the poet. The poem is actually a psychologically acute portrayal of the mechanisms of grief and alienation, beginning with lamentation so deep-seated that the mourner weeps before he is aware
of doing so. From the analytically inclined wanderer, the phenomenon impels an uneasy probing of his alienated state and questions
about the mystery of his emotional being. "Gefror'ne Tränen" is the
first poem in the cycle with no reference to the prehistory of the
journey, the first poem that consists entirely of emotional analysis.
The rejection in love has opened up deeper fissures through which
the molten lava of these tears is forced, only to freeze on contact with
the icy air as if no hotter than morning dew. The Petrarchan polarity
of fire and ice is a poetic vehicle, frozen tears being a physical impossibility, by which the protagonist questions the intensity of his
emotions as well as their source, for the first but not the last time. A
similar opposition of unseen tumultuous motion whose very existence
the wanderer doubts and a frozen outward surface reappears in "Auf
dem Fluße," in which the wanderer's fears of emotional catatonia are
more strongly marked than before and all the more a matter for anxiety. Here, he asserts an interior cauldron sufficient to melt an entire
winter's ice, the exaggeration indicative of doubt, but then wonders
why the manifestation of such grief should be little different in temperature and intensity from the frozen waste that surrounds him.
When Schubert locates the flood of fiery tears in a G-flat-major tonality
distant from the F-minor reality of the scene, when he reestablishes
both F minor and the frigid atmosphere of the beginning in the postlude, he confirms the wanderer's implicit fear of frozen desolation.
Like the speaker in Goethe's "Wonne der Wehmut," who also addresses his tears ("Trocknet nicht, trocknet nicht, / Tränen der ewigen
Liebe," or "Do not dry up, tears of eternal love"), Müller's wanderer

knows that weeping is a sign of life and longs for tears' fiery affirmation of humanity, but unlike Goethe he doubts his capacity for passionate emotion. Melancholy, *Angst*, depression, and resignation are not Vesuvian in temperature, and he knows it.

In stanza 1, the wanderer first states an observed fact and then asks a question. Schubert sets the two different modes of self-address as contrasting but closely related tonal regions of F minor (the stark statement that "Frozen drops fall from my cheeks") and A-flat major (the subsequent question). The motivic and harmonic sameness, however, bespeak relationship more strongly than difference. Both key areas in stanza 1 are markedly static and harmonically restricted; the sameness of the rolling ice drops and the simplicity of the wanderer's factual observation find their concomitants in the reiterated tonic and dominant triads in F minor. And yet the mystery of the event and the unease it occasions are registered in the unharmonized pitches and in the weak-beat accents. Only the transition from the F-minor statement to the A-flat-major question moves, if not very far, to an area similarly mired within limited boundaries, the harmonies little richer, the voice-leading cautious and restricted in range. Both the factual comment and the ensuing question are simple, self-evident, but the mystery of unknowing that surrounds both is of the kind that does not permit movement for the moment. With nothing to go on, no avenue for exploration, no answer in sight, the tonality is not given any fuller definition than this treadmill iteration of the most basic chords of each key. The foreign tones in the single measure of transition from minor to relative major, however, are later powerfully reinterpreted, and the D-flat pivot tone becomes, unforgettably, the bass throughout the Neapolitan tonal area in stanza 3. The *Terzensteigerung* (repetition a third higher, a common means of musical intensification) to which the wanderer repeats the perplexing words "Daß ich geweinet hab'?" ends on the same C (nontonic closure to convey a questioning tone) that is so strongly emphasized throughout the F-minor statement at the beginning of both introduction and stanza.

The harmonic treadmill is so effective that the copyist for the engraver's manuscript amusingly became caught up in it. (That "treadmill" is rhythmic as well, the self-perpetuating circularity heightened by the recurrent weak-beat accents.) In the transition for the piano from stanza 1 to stanza 2, the wanderer continues, but without words, to reiterate " . . . geweinet hab'? geweinet hab'?" The redoubled weak-beat accents of mm. 17–18 reinforce the sense of obsession, of harping on a question or musical figure in search of an answer. The copyist, even more obsessively than Schubert's wanderer, repeated the A-flat-major cadential figure beyond the point where Schubert began the passage downward, and the proofreading composer neatly boxed in the superfluous measure and crossed it out. One wonders if he was struck by this slightly comic homage to the power of his compositional choices in the first stanza.

Where Schubert's wanderer is most reflective, when he is most struck by the mysteries of his existence, he speaks in unison texture. The descent traced in the piano just before the second stanza, merging with it, seems the musical parallel to sinking into depths of thought, the harmonization pared away as the downward motion nears its goal. Schubert throughout stanza 2 dramatizes the dominant poles of both of the preceding tonalities by isolating and emphasizing the fifth and (flatted) sixth scale degrees in a development stemming from the half-cadence at the end of the introduction (mm. 6–7). In the alternation between the unharmonized semitone figures and their harmonized continuation, Schubert also creates a musical analogue for the polarity between different states of being, that is, frozen tears—the unharmonized pitches—and the tepid, liquid dew. The ascent throughout stanza 2 back to the register of stanza 1, a reversal of the descending motion in the introduction and first piano interlude, leads to further reiterations of the "question music" in A-flat major from the first stanza. The rising motion could as well be a musical metaphor for the process given words in stanza 3, the wanderer's tears rising from inward depths to their changed outward manifestation. (It is a striking property of the transitions between both stanzas 1 and 2 and stanzas 2 and 3 that they merge into the vocal line. The singer's words join a musical progression already en route, as if pre-conscious thoughts expressed by the piano eventually become articulation in text and vocal melody.) Only the questioning tonality and figure from stanza 1 return at the beginning of stanza 3; there is no need to repeat the initial observation "Frozen drops fall from my cheeks." In the twofold setting of the last stanza, the tonic key F minor is reserved for the culmination of the stanza, not its inception.

In each stanza, with each successive attempt to probe the enigma first expressed in stanza 1, Schubert reshapes anew the element of contrast between inner and outer manifestations of emotion which so puzzles the wanderer. With each formulation, the matter becomes more intense, an outgrowth of the preceding elements but newly heightened as the wanderer's frustration and tension increase. The contrast of frozen tears and cool dew in the second stanza becomes the far more dramatic contrast between fire and "all the winter's ice" in the final verse. The rhythmic and motivic fixations remain constant throughout, however, as if the wanderer hoped to force understanding by sheer repetition of the dactyls, second-beat accents, and motivic patterns to which he first asks the question "Have I then not noticed that I have been weeping?" It is no wonder that the composition of stanzas 2 and 3 evidently cost Schubert some difficulty, requiring an interleaved fair copy in the autograph manuscript of the music for those stanzas. How, one wonders, did he first imagine the Vesuvian eruption of burning-hot tears in the vanished first version?

In the final stanza, the wanderer proclaims that his fiery grief is capable of melting an entire winter's accumulation of ice and snow even though there is no outward evidence of such passionate emotion. Schubert has him make the assertion twice, with internal text repetitions that further extend a statement the wanderer wants, but does not know, to be true. Significantly, it is at the verb "wollten" ("would," to wish, to want) that the music swerves suddenly to a diminished-seventh chord. The exaggeration of the longed-for emotion, its violent effects, and possibly its distance from reality are all conveyed in a phrase that is a later extension of the D-flat–C pitches from the piano introduction and the beginning of stanza 2. When Schubert has the wanderer in mm. 37–39 swerve so suddenly from the G-flat–D-flat chords to F minor by means of the same German sixth chord he used in m. 22 ("... meine Tränen, / Und seid ihr gar so lau") and then repeat the words "des ganzen Winters Eis," he makes tragically plain exactly what ice the wanderer wishes to melt: the frozen tears of stanza 1 that contain "all the winter's ice" of the wanderer's desolation. But in Schubert's reading, the wanderer seems to doubt that this is possible. Refusing resolution to tonic in m. 39, he swerves suddenly back to A-flat major by means of the same diminished chord that was the pivot chord in the sudden turn to the short-lived D-flat pedal and repeats the entire stanza, culminating in a powerful new cadence. After the chromatic disturbance of the G-flats just before, the extension upward to high G-natural invests the last vocal phrase, which yet again stresses the semitone F E from the two preceding songs, with a power wonderfully disproportionate to the economy of the gesture.

When Schubert brings back the introduction almost unchanged as the postlude, he does more than reaffirm tonic and provide a classical frame for the song. None of the wanderer's variations on a question has been answered, and the frozen tears in F minor still impel the brief "questioning" motion to A-flat in the postlude, but the song ends with a refusal to pursue the matter any further. The more he has investigated the mystery, the greater it becomes, the polarity between inward grief and outer grief all the stronger. In the end, left with a still-inexplicable enigma, he closes the book on the subject and leaves it unsolved.

4. Erstarrung

Ich such' im Schnee vergebens
Nach ihrer Tritte Spur,
Wo sie an meinem Arme
Durchstrich die grüne Flur.

[144]

Ich will den Boden küssen,
Durchdringen Eis und Schnee
Mit meinen heißen Tränen,
Bis ich die Erde seh'.

Wo find' ich eine Blüte,
Wo find' ich grünes Gras?
Die Blumen sind erstorben,
Der Rasen sieht so blaß.

Soll denn kein Angedenken
Ich nehmen mit von hier?
Wenn meine Schmerzen schweigen,
Wer sagt mir dann von ihr?

Mein Herz ist wie erstorben [erfroren]
Kalt starrt ihr Bild darin:
Schmiltzt je das Herz mir wieder,
Fließt auch ihr [das] Bild dahin.

Numbness

(I search in vain through the snow, looking for traces of her footsteps where she used to walk through the green meadows, arm in arm with me.

I will kiss the ground, my hot tears piercing the ice and snow, until I see the earth.

Where shall I find a flower? Where shall I find green grass? The flowers are dead; the grass looks so pale.

Shall I then take no keepsake from here? When my sorrows are stilled, who will speak to me of her?

My heart seems dead, her image frozen within. If my heart ever melts again, her image too will melt away.)

The frozen/fiery polarity of hot tears melting the ice and snow in "Gefror'ne Tränen," a German descendant of the Petrarchan conceit "il cor in ghiaccio e'n foco" (the heart in frost and fire), recurs in the next song. There is an implied cause-and-effect relationship between the two poems as well, the wanderer's panic-stricken search in "Erstarrung" for souvenirs of his sweetheart impelled by his doubts in "Gefror'ne Tränen." He has already begun to fear that his heart is frozen, without the capacity for great grief; without a tangible memento, an object of some kind, he fears that he will forget her very image when the last pangs of lost love and hope end. Now he weeps with a purpose. The burning tears are to be instruments of a futile search, the means by which to melt the ice and snow so that he may find a trace of past times with her, flowers or the green grass of the banks where they once walked together, something that will impel remembrance in the future. The extravagance of his actions and intent briefly masks their futility, although he is unable to sustain such melodramatic gestures for long. Because of the wanderer's characteristic self-awareness, the poem has a fine psychological complexity at its core. The wanderer knows, even as he searches desperately through the snow, that his actions are pointless ("Ich such'... vergebens"), but he is impelled to look nonetheless. With the third stanza, reason resumes command, and the wanderer admits that he cannot find what no longer exists. Poignantly, the admissions are at first couched in the form of questions, as if he were still hoping for an answer more to his liking than reality, but the final lines are declarative statements. The only souvenir that remains is her image locked within his frozen heart, and its rigidity is the only barrier against her final disappearance.

In the *Waldhornisten II*, Müller replaced the last two lines of stanza 1 with the following lines:

> Hier, wo wir oft gewandelt
> Selbander durch die Flur.

(Here, where we often went walking together in the meadow.)

When Schubert discovered the complete poetic cycle, he did not revise "Erstarrung" in accord with the poet's final choice of words. His previously composed melodic line would not have fit Müller's final text, especially the third line of the verse, with its marked caesura after the first word—stopping "here" for an instant and slowing momentarily the forward impetus of the poetic rhythm. As with Müller's other alterations to the *Urania* texts, both versions have their virtues. The *Waldhornisten* lines emphasize more strongly the sense of place, while the earlier version establishes motifs that recur in later poems. We recall the words "Wo sie an meinem Arme" when the wanderer plaintively asks, "Wann halt' ich mein Liebchen im Arm?" at the end of "Frühlingstraum," and the color green recurs in the "green meadows" of "Frühlingstraum," the fir tree in "Einsamkeit," and the green funeral wreath in "Das Wirtshaus." There are only a few touches of color in a cycle otherwise etched in black and white—black depression and endless stretches of white snow.

The introduction is an extraordinary beginning to an extraordinary song. The wanderer looks on the ground for keepsakes, so Schubert places an incessant, sweeping melody in the bass and a rapid broken-chordal pedal, its motion evocative of panic-stricken motion, in the right hand. The same two-bar figure in the bass is repeated over and over, transposed and varied, in apt representation of an *idée fixe*. Even the neighbor note and turning figures of which it is composed seem like searching motions on either side of their central pitches. The completion of the cadence at the end of the introduction is elided with the singer's entrance. In this search and this song, there are no breaks in the constant flow of instrumental sound and no separations between sections; one merges into the next, the end of one stanza is the beginning of its successor, and at the close of the entire song, the right-hand pedal has to run down, "spin its wheels" for a moment before it finally stops.

"Erstarrung" is the longest song of the cycle in length (109 bars), if not duration in actual performance. In the autograph manuscript, Schubert at first indicated the tempo "Nicht zu geschwind," atypically at stage 1, but altered it to "Ziemlich schnell" in the engraver's copy, the difference a matter of nuance; in both, the composer warns against the temptation to race through the lied. The length is due in large part to the insistent text repetitions, more than in any other song in the cycle—we hear each verse twice and certain phrases even more often. Musical and textual repetition throughout "Erstarrung" is the mirror of an obsessional state of mind, which seeks to deny love's loss by means of frenetic activity and by grasping at memories as if they had corporeal substance, as if they were real. In the beginning, the repetitions seem like a goad for the wanderer, a way to spur on the search. If he repeatedly invokes his actions aloud, he can prolong the futile quest, despite the realization that what he does is in vain, "vergebens." For example, when the wanderer in stanza 2 sings of tears piercing the snow so that he might see the ground, he is in fact unable to do so and therefore repeats the words he wishes would become reality. In music, this becomes deceptive motion and elision, leading to the repetition of the verse. It is only at the last moment, in Schubert's conception, that reality tells him that the ground is not visible, and so he plunges away in shock to continue the frantic questing motion. The cadence in mm. 33–34 ("die Erde seh") does not resolve to the expected tonic C minor, but instead progresses to a diminished seventh harmony, impelling the subsequent musical variation of the entire poetic stanza. That same diminished seventh chord then continues throughout six measures, perpetuating the leading tone that as yet refuses to resolve to C. (The C-sharp appoggiatura at the word "küssen" in m. 36 will shortly be enharmonically respelled as the pivotal D-flat in the turn to A-flat major in m. 46.) When the cadence to C minor is finally completed (m. 44), even though it is elided with the return of the piano introduction, the search cannot continue as before. The realization of impossibility occasions the turn to another tonality, emblematic of thoughts other than the *idée fixe* of his frantic quest.

The abrupt modulation to A-flat at the center of "Erstarrung" must be understood as the tonal emblem of the wanderer's capitulation to reason, his admission that what he seeks is an impossibility. Before the middle section, the recurring piano introduction is abbreviated and the new tonic brought in a measure early so that the voice enters on an existing harmony—the singer accedes to a truth the piano has already admitted. The submediant key is weaker in relation to tonic than the dominant tonality would be, especially since the complex counterplay of bass and soprano lines that at times merge, at times diverge, in stanzas 1 and 2 is gone. The melodic bass disappears, the wanderer no longer looking downward with such panic-stricken attention, and yet the incessant motion of the *idée fixe* continues unchecked. He cannot banish his wish to retain his lost love merely by stating that there is no keepsake to be found, however, and once again repetitions and elisions delay both cadence and full acceptance of the words. In mm. 54–55, Schubert approaches a cadential resolution on A-flat and once again swerves away ("blaß"), leading to the same diminished seventh that conveys the shock and surprise in mm. 52–53. The realization that the green fields are covered with snow is given expressive force in the chromatic harmonies and deceptive motion. Here in stanza 3, Schubert gives the contrast of major and minor modes a new signification. When the wanderer in stanza 1 invokes bygone times when he walked along the green banks arm in arm with his beloved, Schubert perpetuates the more familiar minor-major contrasts by turning briefly to E-flat major (mm. 20–23), but the setting of stanza 3 is another matter. Here, the deluded search takes place in minor mode, as the wanderer imagines in the bitter present that he can find remnants of a happier springtime past; the realization of futility, the displacement of deluded imagination by reason and reality, occur in major mode—not, however, parallel major or relative major.

In stanza 3, the text repetitions continue, this time to enact two different readings of the same words, one by the heart, one by the mind. It is these two forces that are in contention throughout "Erstarrung," and Schubert accords them each hegemony at different times. When the wanderer first asks the questions "Where shall I find a flower? Where shall I find green grass?" at the beginning of the central section (the setting of stanza 3) of this three-part form, they are a goad to spur reason's return, a form of self-chiding: "Where can I possibly expect to find flowers and green grass?" says the wanderer in this reading of those lines. When he repeats those same questions at the end of the section, he reverts to the C minor of the search for souvenirs, and the bass line becomes a separate entity once again as he looks back down at the ground. Here, the questions mean "*Where* can I find a flower? *Where* can I find green grass?"—the deluded desire to locate keepsakes revived yet again. The "answer" is the full-fledged return of the music of stanzas 1 and 2.

It seems at first a curious miscalculation on Schubert's part that he should repeat the music of the beginning, when the search for keepsakes is at its hottest and most deluded, to the text of the last two stanzas, in which the wanderer has ostensibly abandoned the vain hunt. The large-scale recapitulation is furthermore quite literal, almost note for note, even where the repeated music creates a seeming syntactical error in conjunction with the new text. In stanza 2, the lines "Durchdringen Eis und Schnee / Mit meinen heißen Tränen" are joined in a seamless melodic flow, but the corresponding lines of poetry in stanza 5 include a marked grammatical articulation ("Kalt starrt ihr Bild darin: / Schmilzt je das Herz mir wieder"). Repeating the vocal line for stanza 2, Schubert charges right through the poet's punctuation with no recognition of its divisive function at all. Only the extension of the last vocal cadence of the song is varied significantly from the ending of stanza 2. Such exact and lengthy repetition in a three-part song form is highly unusual in this cycle, especially where the poetic content seems to interdict such repetition. Schubert, however, understood that reason does not overcome desire immediately. The wanderer in stanzas 4 and 5 simultaneously realizes that there are no keepsakes to be found and yet still fervently longs for that which will keep his sweetheart alive and present for him.[1] In reason's war with the heart, he sings of rational understanding to the

[1]Both in the autograph manuscript and in the engraver's fair copy, Schubert sets the initial words of stanza 4, "Soll denn kein Angedenken," such that the E-flat at the apex of the crucial word "An - *ge* - *denk* - en," is anticipated. With the first edition, he reinstated the melodic line from the first stanza, but the extra emphasis on the word "keepsake, souvenir" in the earlier sources is telling.

music of irrational desire. A smaller detail of the final vocal cadence, varied from that of stanza 2, tells of the same conflict in microcosm. When the wanderer prolongs the word "dahin" in mm. 101–2, he briefly contradicts the sense of the phrase. "If my heart ever melts again, her image too will melt away," he sings while sustaining the word "dahin" as if to hold on to the image, before capitulating and completing the cadence.

"The heart has its reasons which Reason does not know," Pascal wrote, long before Müller's wanderer sang of the same phenomenon. Schubert, despite his nearly uncanny sympathy with his chosen poet, transgresses Müller's ending to make explicit the conflict between mind and heart. Where Müller implies that reason is in complete control by the poem's end, Schubert says No and continues the painful search for keepsakes. The music of stanza 1 and 2 is the only memento possible for the wanderer after the realization at the center of the song that no tangible souvenirs remain, and Schubert grants it to him.

5. Der Lindenbaum

Am Brunnen vor dem Tore,
Da steht ein Lindenbaum;
Ich träumt' in seinem Schatten
So manchen süssen Traum.

Ich schnitt in seine Rinde
So manches liebe Wort;
Es zog in Freud' und Leide
Zu ihm mich immer fort.

Ich mußt' auch heute wandern
Vorbei in tiefer Nacht,
Da hab' ich noch im Dunkel
Die Augen zugemacht.

Und seine Zweige rauschten,
Als riefen sie mir zu:
Komm' her zu mir, Geselle,
Hier findst du deine Ruh'!

Die kalten Winde bliesen
Mir grad' in's Angesicht,
Der Hut flog mir vom Kopfe,
Ich wendete mich nicht.

Nun bin ich manche Stunde
Entfernt von jenem Ort,
Und immer hör' ich's rauschen:
Du fändest Ruhe dort!

The Linden Tree

(By the well, before the gate, there stands a linden tree; I dreamt many a sweet dream in its shade.

I carved many a word of love in its bark; I was ever drawn to it in joy and sorrow.

Today, too, I had to pass by it in the dead of night; though in darkness, I shut my eyes.

And its branches rustled as if calling to me: "Come here to me, friend, here you will find rest!"

The cold wind blew straight into my face. My hat flew off my head;
I did not turn back.
Now I am many hours distant from that place; yet still I hear the
rustling: "There you would find rest!")

The wanderer's futile search in "Erstarrung" for a souvenir of his
past love, a flower or a fragment of the grassy bank, leads him to
another green memory: the linden tree that had been his refuge in
the past, the tree he had just that evening passed by on his way out
of the town. Even though it is dark when he begins to sing, he closes
his eyes, shutting out the winter night and replacing it with a different
darkness in which he can recall more clearly the remembered sound
of the linden leaves rustling. What he hears and how he responds
mark this as one of the most crucial episodes in the wanderer's
journey.
    Müller's text begins like a true folk poem, set in a place both specific
and yet unnamed and unknown: "By the well, before the gate, there
stands a linden tree." The choice of tree was calculated. The linden
has a long history in German literature as the traditional lovers' rendezvous and a symbol of all that is gentle and beneficent in Nature,
beginning with the songs of the thirteenth-century minnesingers.
Müller almost certainly knew one of the earliest poems about love
beneath the linden tree, the minnesong "Under der linden an der
heide" by Walther von der Vogelweide" (ca. 1170–1220) because it
was included in a collection of folk poems he knew, even though
minnesong is not folk poetry. Furthermore, Müller had published his
own modern German translations of minnesong in the *Blumenlese* of
1816. In Walther's poem, an example of so-called "niedere Minne"
("low" or "natural love") as opposed to "hohe Minne" or courtly
love, a maiden sings of the meadow grass that was her and her lover's
bed beneath the linden tree:

> Under der linden
> an der heide,
> dâ unser zweier bette was,
> dâ mugt ir vinden
> schône beide
> gebrochen bluomen unde gras.
> vor dem walde in einem tal,
> tandaradei,
> schône sanc diu nahtegal.

(Under the linden tree in the field, where we two had our bed, you
still can see lovely broken flowers and grass. On the edge of the woods
in a vale, tandaradei, sweetly sang the nightingale.)[1]

In an incident recorded in Müller's diary, he tells of meeting a young
man at a lending library in Berlin. The stranger was unable to find
either of the books he was seeking there, the famous Arnim-Brentano
anthology *Des Knaben Wunderhorn* and "Hagen's collection of folk-
songs."[2] The medievalist Friedrich von der Hagen, in collaboration
with another scholar of medieval Germanic and Nordic literature
named Gustav Büsching, had published a *Sammlung deutscher Volkslieder* in 1807 in which Walther's poem, titled "Minnelied" and translated into modern German, is included.[3] Müller lent the young man
his own copy of *Des Knaben Wunderhorn*; he says nothing further about
the Büsching-Hagen collection, but his casual reference would seem
to indicate close acquaintance with it. Müller would also have encountered the image of the linden tree in other collections of German
folk poetry which he refers to in his letters and critical essays, including Friedrich Nicolai's *Eyn feyner kleyner Almanach* (A fine little
almanac) of 1777–1778 and Johann Gottfried Herder's anthology *Stim-
men der Völker in Liedern* (Voices of the peoples in song) of 1778–1779.
The appearance of a linden tree invested with all of the prior associations from German literary history in Müller's original verse was
perhaps inevitable.

   Des Knaben Wunderhorn, which Müller certainly knew, includes several poems and ballads about lovers who meet under the linden tree
for either good or ill fortune in love. In the early sixteenth-century
poem "Wächter, hüt dich bass!" (Watchman, keep close guard!), a
young noblewoman goes to meet her lover at a place where the "cold
little brook" or "Brünnlein kalt" (an early forerunner of Müller's first
line, "Am Brunnen vor dem Thore") springs from a hollow stone and
a nightingale sings in the linden tree:

> Die Jungfrau, die war edel,
> Sie kam zum hohlen Stein,

[1]Frederick Goldin, *German and Italian Lyrics of the Middle Ages* (New York, 1973),
124–25.
[2]*Diary and Letters of Wilhelm Müller*, 31 October 1815, 28.
[3]Friedrich von der Hagen and Johann Gustav Büsching, eds., *Sammlung deutscher
Volkslieder* (Berlin, 1807), 84–85. The *Sammlung* also includes a tragic ballad "Die Linde"
(183–86), which ends with a grief-stricken count burying his beloved beneath the linden
tree where they used to meet.

Daraus da sprang ein Brünnlein kalt,
Auf grüner Linde drüber
Frau Nachtigall saß und sang.[4]

(The noble maiden came to the hollow rock from which flowed a cold
little brook. Lady Nightingale sat and sang overhead in the green linden
tree.)

Her lover does not appear; when she finds him dead, she kills herself.
The ending is not always so tragic, however; "Die Entführung" (The
abduction) seems like a direct descendant of Walther von der Vogelweide's thirteenth-century masterpiece.

Da der edel Ritter da unter die Linden kam,
Was fand er unter der Linden?
Ein Mägdlein, die war wohlgetan.
Ab zog er den Mantel sein,
Er warf ihn in das Gras.
Da lagen die zwei die lange Nacht
Bis an den lichten Tag.
Er halst, er küsst, er drücket
Sie lieblich an sein Leib:
"Du bist, auf meine Treue,
Das allerliebste Weib."[5]

(When the noble knight came to the linden tree, what did he find
under the tree? A maiden who was pleasing. He removed his cloak and
spread it on the grass. There the two lay together the entire night until
the break of day. He clasped her, he kissed her, he pressed her lovingly
to his body. "You are, by my faith, the most beautiful woman.")

The small ballad "Liebesprobe" (Love's ordeal), included both in *Des
Knaben Wunderhorn* and in Hagen's *Sammlung*, opens with the familiar
scene of two lovers beneath the linden tree:

Es sah eine Linde ins tiefe Tal,
War unten breit und oben schmal,

[4]Achim von Arnim and Clemens Brentano, eds., *Des Knaben Wunderhorn: Alte Deutsche
Lieder*, in Clemens Brentano, *Sämtliche Werke und Briefe*, vol. 7, ed. Heinz Rölleke (Stuttgart, 1976), 241–45.
[5]Ibid., 281–83.

Worunter zwei Verliebte saßen,
Vor Lieb' ihr Leid vergaßen.[6]

(Down in the valley, there was a linden tree, broad beneath and narrow
above, under which two lovers sat, their sorrow forgotten in love.)

When Müller begins his poem by placing a linden tree in an evocative
setting (wells and gates suggest symbolic meaning but without making any specific signification apparent), he is borrowing from poems
such as this.

Müller would also have encountered the venerable image in the
works of his contemporaries who, like him, were influenced by folk
song and medieval lyric verse. Ludwig Uhland (1787–1862) wrote a
ballad titled "Die Zauberlinde" (The enchanted linden),[7] and Friedrich
Rückert (1788–1866), a friend of Müller's in their youth, also wrote
poems with the traditional linden image, including the sonnet "Die
Linde"[8] and "Ich atmet' einen linden Duft" from the *Aprilsreiseblätter*,
set to music by Gustav Mahler in 1899. In this small poem, in which
the scent from a sprig of linden evokes tenderness for the absent
beloved, Rückert plays on the sound-sense associations of "lind"
(soft, gentle, sweet) and "die Linde" (the linden tree):

Ich atmet' einen linden Duft.
Im Zimmer stand ein Zweig der Linde,
Ein Angebinde von lieber Hand.
Wie lieblich war der Lindenduft,
Wie lieblich ist der Lindenduft,
Das Lindenreis brachst du gelinde!
Ich atme leis im Duft der Linde
Der Herzensfreundschaft linden Duft.[9]

(I breathe a gentle scent. In the room is a sprig of linden, a gift from
a beloved hand. How lovely was the linden scent, how lovely is the
linden scent. You gently broke the linden twig. In the linden's perfume,
I softly breathe the gentle scent of heart's friendship.)

[6]Ibid., 6:57–59.
[7]Ludwig Uhland, *Gedichte*, vol. 2 (Stuttgart, 1898), 281–82.
[8]Friedrich Rückert, *Gedichte*, vol. 2 (Frankfurt-am-Main, 1868), 300. In the final lines,
the linden itself speaks of its destiny as a place for lovers' rendezvous.
[9]Ibid., 337. Mahler altered the last line, abbreviating "Der Herzensfreundschaft linden
Duft" to "Der Liebe linden Duft."

Müller disapproved of Rückert's propensity for word play, for poetic artifice displayed rather than concealed, and yet this small, slight poem is a notable variation on the traditional literary motif. Rückert brings a single twig of linden indoors rather than depicting an entire tree set outside in Nature, and he thereby heightens the evocative power of the image. When he juxtaposes past and present ("lieblich *war*, lieblich *ist*"), he invokes as well the linden's sight and scent as the key to unlock specifically Germanic memories of love and poetry. Müller himself wrote two other poems about lovers and linden trees, one a folkish ballad titled "Die dürre Linde" (The withered linden), similar to "Liebesprobe" in its tale of lovers parting and the lad's promise to return to the beloved in springtime.

> "Bis unter den grünen Lindenbaum,
> Herzliebste, geh' mit mir!
> Und wenn er junge Blätter treibt,
> Kehr' ich zurück zu dir!"[10]

("Go with me, beloved, beneath the green linden tree! And when it buds, I will return to you!")

The motifs of a winter storm, falling leaves, May flowers, the linden tree on which the lovers' names are carved within the outline of a heart, and a grave would all recur later in *Die Winterreise*. But "Die Bäume" (The trees), one of the "Wanderlieder" in the *Waldhornisten II*, has even closer ties to the fifth poem of the winter journey: here, Müller praises all trees as welcome shelter for wanderers, especially the linden tree, evocative of home, peace, and love.[11] The sense of profound peace that the wanderer of "Die Bäume" finds in the shade of the linden tree, the comfort it offers, "better in darkness than in sunshine," are reiterations of themes more succinctly developed and to different ends in "Der Lindenbaum."

Neither Schubert nor Müller could have known the final item in this brief and incomplete catalogue of linden trees in German verse, but for Schubertians, it may well be among the most moving. The

---

[10]Wilhelm Müller, *Waldhornisten II*, from the "Wanderlieder," 145–46.
[11]From the third stanza: "Euch begrüß' ich auch, ihr Linden, / Mag euch gern auf Märkten finden, / Dicht und kugelrund belaubt. / In des Abends Feierstunde / Führt mich die gewöhnte Runde / Immer zu den Bäumen hin."

Austrian poet Johann Mayrhofer (1787–1836), who met Schubert in
1814 through the intermediary of Joseph Spaun, was among the most
important influences in the composer's life between 1817 and the end
of 1820, when an unexplained rift ended their formerly close relationship. Schubert's forty-seven songs to texts by Mayrhofer span the
decade from 1814 to 1824 and include some of his most beautiful
compositions, such as "Lied eines Schiffers an die Dioskuren," D.
360; "Auf der Donau," D. 553; "Erlafsee," D. 586; "Freiwilliges Versinken," D. 700; "Nachtviolen," D. 752; "Auflösung," D. 807; and
"Gondelfahrer," D. 808. The melancholiac Mayrhofer, who forged a
unique synthesis of neoclassic ideals with Romanticism in his often
powerful verse, clearly loved Schubert—his poems "An Franz" and
"Nachgefühl: An Fr. Schubert (19. November 1828)" are explicitly
addressed to his friend, while others are encoded memorials to that
love—and wrote comparatively little poetry after Schubert's early
death. He published only one poetic anthology during his lifetime,
in 1824; after Mayrhofer's suicide in 1836, the philosopher Ernst von
Feuchtersleben edited a second collection of his friend's works in 1843.
In that *Neue Sammlung* (New anthology) is a short poem in which the
poetic persona returns to the linden tree where he had earlier carved
his beloved's name and wonders whether he felt any presentiments
of future sorrow when he carved the "noble name"—he says no more
than this—in its bark.

Wiederseh'n

Vertrauter Ort, geliebte Linde!
Ich nahe und ich grüße euch.
Den holden Namen les' ich an der Rinde,
Mein wildes Herz, es wird noch einmal weich.

Als ich die unvergeß'nen Züge,
In's zarte Mark des Baumes schnitt,—
Ahnt' ich es wohl, daß ich nur eine Lüge
Verewigte, und meine Schmerzen mit?[12]

(Familiar place, beloved linden! I draw near and greet you. I read the
proud name carved in your bark, and my wild heart grows tender once
more.

[12]Johann Mayrhofer, *Gedichte von Johann Mayrhofer: Neue Sammlung*, ed. Ernst von
Feuchtersleben (Vienna, 1834), 64.

When I cut the unforgettable lines in the dear boundary of the tree,
did I foresee that I forever perpetuated a lie, and with it, my sorrow?)

Like Müller, Rückert, Uhland, and all the rest, Mayrhofer relies on
the reader's knowledge of the linden tree as the place where lovers
meet and Nature welcomes and shelters them. In the fifth song of *Winterreise*, the linden tree was a place of rendezvous and love in the past, although the wanderer who carved "many a word of love" in the tree's bark does not mention the faithless sweetheart at all. The murmuring sounds of the linden leaves—emblematic of Nature, love, homecoming, peace, youth, past happiness, all bound together in a single potent symbol—seem like voices that say to the wanderer, "Come here to me, friend, here you will find rest." Characteristically, he does not mistake the auditory memory for reality but says that the leaves rustle *as if* calling to him. Because the sound is so sweet, he becomes all the more aware of the cold and the darkness, the sting of the icy wind in his face. And yet, when his hat blows away in the storm, he does not turn back to retrieve it, but presses forward, refusing to heed the enticing voices in his mind.

The line "Ich wendete mich nicht" is the crux of the poem, a moment of great import in the winter journey. It is typical of Müller's deceptive simplicity that he has the wanderer say merely, "I did not turn back," encapsulating two decisions in a single phrase, the truly momentous choice cloaked within a seemingly trivial resolution. He neither goes back to find his hat nor does he heed the linden leaves' invitation, even though it is such a seductive offer that he continues to hear their voices calling him long after he is distant from that place. (There is an implicit gap both of time and distance, unknown but considerable, between stanzas 5 and 6 of "Der Lindenbaum.") The invitation is a beckoning to death. If the wanderer continues to stand there, listening raptly to the remembered sound in the midst of the winter storm, he will freeze and die. When he realizes his danger, he must decide whether to reject the "offer," which originates within himself, and live or succumb to the promise of rest and die. Müller had earlier written of the longing for death as dissolution into Nature, becoming one with Nature in a denial of human existence, in "Tränenregen" from *Die schöne Müllerin*, when the miller lad looks into the brook and sees the entire heavens reflected there. The youth fancies that the brook wants to draw him within its depths, a prophetic fancy, and hears it call to him, saying "Geselle, Geselle! mir nach."

Und in den Bach versunken
Der ganze Himmel schien
Und wollte mich mit hinunter
In seine Tiefe zieh'n.

Und über den Wolken und Sternen
Da rieselte munter der Bach,
Und rief mit Singen und Klingen:
Geselle, Geselle! mir nach.

(And the entire heavens appeared, sunken in the brook, and wished
to draw me into its depths.
And the brook rippled merrily over the clouds and stars and called
out with song and music: Companion, companion! follow me.)

Between "Tränenregen" and the next poem, "Mein!", the miller's
daughter becomes, if only briefly, the lad's sweetheart, and he begins
his song of rejoicing with the joyous command that the brook stop
its noise: "Bächlein, laß dein Rauschen sein." (Nature's invitations to
become one with it, to die, sound as rustling voices, whether water
or foliage, in Müller's two best-known cycles.) He wants all other
sounds to cease so that he might proclaim and all might hear that the
lovely miller maid is his, but surely there is also a dismissal for the
moment of the brook's invitation to submerge himself in its depths,
an invitation he accepts in his despair at the end of the cycle. But the
wanderer in *Die Winterreise* does not reveal why he chooses to live
and continue his journey, if he even knows why. Whatever chains
this unhappy man to life and refuses to grant him release in suicide
is withheld from knowledge here and throughout the cycle.

If Schubert spurned overt musical links between songs, he was not
averse, as we have already seen, to suggesting kinship between adjacent songs by rhythmic and motivic means. The eighth-note triplets
in the piano throughout "Erstarrung" are succeeded by the sixteenth-
note triplet figures in the piano introduction to "Der Lindenbaum,"
the slower tempo of the latter thus ensuring that the pace of the triplet
figuration in both songs is similar and that the listener hears them as
related. Furthermore, the cell figure—nothing more than a neighbor
note to tonic—with which both songs begin is another subtle connective, the briefest of "head motives." By means of these rhythmic
and motivic links, Schubert suggests musically what is only implied
in Müller's poetic sequence: that the sad realization in "Erstarrung"
of love's eventual obliteration from memory impels in reaction the

death wish in the next song. At the same time, he establishes the difference between the two episodes in terms of tonality, the E major of "Der Lindenbaum" distant from the C minor of "Erstarrung." The effect of the mediant tonal shift is magical, the sensation of sudden transport to another place in the mind brought about in the most economical way.

In Müller's poem, the wanderer begins to recount his memories without preamble, but not so Schubert. The lengthy piano introduction can be heard as the instrumental script for a sequence of events within the mind, a wordless process that leads to the articulation of memory in words. The wanderer first hears a rustling sound that arises unbidden to awareness in mm. 1–2, not consciously evoked. The ending of the brief phrase on a hollowed-out dominant chord from which the bass drops away, leaving only the unharmonized dominant pitch and its upper neighbor, is typically Schubertian in its aura of ambiguity and enigma, its implications left for explication later in the song. When the rustling resumes at a higher plane in m. 3, the wanderer is more fully aware of its presence, the figuration now extended and marked by the disquietude of further offbeat accents and chromatic inflections, in particular the B-sharps in the bass that will later become the C-natural neighbor to the dominant in the setting of stanza 5. The promise/threat of death later made explicit in the winter storm is already stated in the introduction but as yet without either the words to tell of its significance or development of its musical implications. The extension of the initial figure leads to a cadence whose block chords are the transition to Müller's words in stanza 1, a built-in ritardando as memory submerges the wanderer. The instrumental corridor that leads from the first faint rustlings of sound to the song proper culminates in echoing horn-call figures, evocative of wandering *Waldhornisten* in the German forests, by extension, of idealized Romantic memories of the past. Schubert's music thus traces the dawning awareness that precedes Müller's words, from the first stirrings of memory to agitated full consciousness, then a surrender to recollection of the past. The horn-call figures on the dominant herald the wanderer's arrival at the "well before the gate" where the linden tree stands. An entire drama within the mind transpires before a single word is sung.[13]

[13]The *Hörnerklang*, or the sound of distant horn calls summoning the protagonist away from where he is either into the unknown or into the recesses of memory, is a quintessentially Romantic image, even more endemic in the poetry of the period than linden trees. It was Schubert's marvelous invention to merge the musical motif of the horn call, an evocative wisp of sound issuing from ancient forests, with the linden tree

Where the words begin, so does one of the best-known melodies in the world. Thomas Mann in *The Magic Mountain* draws a distinction between the largely anonymous works of those who, in Müller's words, "know nothing of thorough-bass" and art song by trained composers, then lauds Schubert for having fused these two different kinds of music in this song. "Der Lindenbaum," he writes, is one of those rare lieder "which are folk-song and masterpiece together, and from the combination receive their peculiar stamp as spiritual epitomes. . . . We all know that the noble lied sounds rather differently when given as a concert-number from its rendition in the childish or the popular mouth."[14] No one would mistake the piano introduction for folk music, but the setting of stanzas 1 and 2 in particular was quickly assimilated into folk-song and student-song collections. The diatonic purity of this music, its symmetrical phrase structure (each line of poetry becomes a separate phrase of music), narrow vocal range, the frequent doubling of the vocal line in the accompaniment, and tessitura in the middle register, are all reminiscent of folk song, but with a difference. The perfection seems so effortless and uncontrived in its simplicity that one notices the accumulation of artful compositional choices only on second hearing. There are, for example, the instrumental interludes in doubled thirds (mm. 12–13, 16–17) that are elided with the beginning of the succeeding vocal phrase to create

---

as the image of beneficent Nature. This is not the first time he had done so: he had earlier used a horn-call figure very similar to the one in mm. 7–8 of "Der Lindenbaum" in a song about Nature as an idyllic refuge for those who seek peace. He found the text of his 1816 "Lied," D. 483, beginning "Ferne von der großen Stadt" (Far from the great city), in a poetic idyll titled "Der Sommerabend" (The summer evening) by the Viennese poet, novelist, and playwright Karoline Pichler (1769–1843), whose salon he would later frequent in 1821–1822. The poetic speaker at first prays, "O valley, which Nature has adorned with spring's abundance, receive me into your stillness," and then speaks in the second stanza of peace beneath the linden trees, "Freuden, die die Ruhe beut, / Will ich ungestört hier schmecken, / Hier, wo Bäume mich bedecken, / Und die Linde Duft verstreut, . . ." (Here I will enjoy undisturbed the joys that tranquillity offers; here, where trees cover me and the linden scatters its sweet scent"). Schubert writes horn-call figures in the first three measures of this strophic song, like "Der Lindenbaum," set in E major, and again in mm. 6–7. At the beginning of each stanza, the figure in the right hand alone, all the more delicately evocative because there is no bass in m. 2, functions as a musical corridor, an ingress into an enchanted world of perfect peace in the bosom of Nature. The "Lied" is an unpretentious hymnlike song (with an unmistakable allusion to Haydn's "Emperor's Hymn" in the closing measures and in the postlude), lacking the complexity and power of "Der Lindenbaum," but it does foreshadow in its own simpler way the later masterpiece.

    [14]Thomas Mann, *The Magic Mountain*, trans. H. T. Lowe-Porter (New York, 1927), 818.

a seamless flow from one perfectly symmetrical phrase to the next and the varied reappearance of the horn-call motif with its hollow fifth B F-sharp passing chord in mm. 12–13, a link with the half-cadence at the end of the introduction. The rustling figuration disappears from these two stanzas, since the wanderer has retreated farther back into his memories, out of range of the voices that rustle in the present. The unharmonized neighbor-note figure from m. 2 *does* reappear, however, in the piano interludes of stanza 2, after the C-sharp has been given a new context and meaning as the first expansion upward of the vocal compass ("So *man* - ches liebe Wort"). There is also the alternation in stanza 2 of contrary motion between the vocal line and the bass for the odd-numbered lines of text and the different treatment of the even-numbered lines, in which all of the voices move together in graphic depiction of the words "zu ihm mich immer fort." Unforgettably, the E in the topmost voice appears for the first time only at the end of the A section in m. 23, the denial of the tonic pitch in the upper octave until this point a wonderfully effective way of underscoring the linden tree's power of attraction ("Zu *ihm* mich immer fort").

As long as the wanderer remains immersed in his idyllic memories, the torment of his present existence recedes from awareness and the music reflects a rare unanimity of design, with the voice and piano in perfect concord. Such privileged moments of escape from reality are rare in this cycle, and they never last for more than a few moments before the present intrudes once again. It was Schubert's brilliant imaginative stroke to have the rustling voices from mm. 1–2 reappear in parallel minor just after the words "I was ever drawn to it in joy and sorrow" and without a break or rest. The wanderer's refuge in the past now draws him seamlessly into the present to deliver its promise of rest and peace. With the turn to parallel minor, the whole-tone figure in m. 2 becomes the semitone C-natural–B, and the placement of those pitches in the low bass of m. 28 is a premonition of the bass foundation for the winter storm in stanza 5. The implicit menace of the enigmatic semitone figure is not explained until then. With awareness of the present restored in stanza 3, the journeying motion resumes ("Today, too, I had to pass by it in the dead of night"), the triplet eighth-note figuration in the piano a driving force beneath the words, and the disquietude of weak-beat accents reappears in force. The accompaniment only occasionally doubles the vocal melody, unlike mm. 9–24, while the accents on the second beat of the measure in all but a few bars of stanzas 3 and 4 are once again registers of disquiet, the near-perfect peace of the first two stanzas gone. Even though the wanderer attempts to shut out the wintry desolation around him and submerge himself once more in the memory, he is only partly successful. The E-major tonality returns briefly (mm. 37–44), but the weak-beat accents and triplet eighths remain. What comes unbidden to memory cannot be recreated at will in its former perfection.

In major mode (the realm of imagination and dreams), the linden leaves promise the wayfarer rest and then fall silent, the piano's extension of the vocal cadence reaching back up to the E of "findst" in further emphasis. Schubert's care for the smallest of significant details is evident here in one miniscule aspect of that cadence. There is no cessation of sound between the memory of the linden tree in stanzas 1 and 2 and the return to present awareness in the piano introduction to stanza 3. But at the end of stanza 4, at the word "Ruh" in m. 44, Schubert writes the final tonic harmony on the third beat as an eighth note, not a quarter note as before in m. 24. There is a brief instant of silence that heightens the shock effect of m. 45f, and it is perhaps in that moment, the space of a single eighth-note rest, that the wanderer realizes what the linden's message truly means and, realizing, feels the full force of the storm in which he must make his choice.

With stanza 5, the rustling figuration banished from the accompaniment to previous stanzas—even where the wanderer sings "And its branches rustled as if calling to me"—returns and fills the entire stanza. This is both metamorphosis and unmasking, the rustling enticements revealed as "cold winds." The winter storm is a reharmonized variant of the linden leaves' rustling in minor, immediately recognizable as such. The meaning of the musical enigmas in the introduction and in mm. 26 and 28, the mysterious unharmonized endings to the rustling figuration, is at last made explicit. The entire fifth stanza is a development via harmonic expansion and rhythmic augmentation of the semitone figure C-natural–B. Here, the menace hinted in these small figures, the sense of things unspoken, blares forth with horrifying forcefulness. B major is not tonicized in this stanza; rather, there is a struggle for primacy between the two pitches and the chords built on them, with C and C major in the ascendancy at first. The power and tenacity of the C-major storminess is evident in the pedal that sounds throughout four measures (mm. 49–52) and is intensified by the alternation between a sustained bass pitch and repeated eighth notes. Not until the wanderer sings, "Ich wendete mich nicht" in mm. 52–53 do the C-naturals resolve to B and remain there. We hear an E-major tonic chord for the first time in this stanza at the word "nicht," as if to confirm the negation. The cold winds continue to blow, and the C-naturals do not disappear from the instrumental conclusion of the stanza, but that conclusion is firmly anchored on the low B.

The chromatic tempest leads back to the horn-call figures, the musical emblems of memory, as if to indicate that the decision in the winter storm belongs to the past and the linden has returned to its ancient forest. The horn calls in turn culminate in triple fermatas, a pause that symbolizes the time and distance the wanderer has journeyed away from the place where death first beckons him. But the rustling voices continue to haunt him, and he brings back the entirety of stanzas 1 and 2 for the twofold setting of the final stanza. The homorhythmic tranquillity of the earlier vignette is gone beyond recapturing, however. When Schubert places the triplet figures of the accompaniment in a higher register, *above* the voice, he emphasizes the journeying motion more strongly than before. Furthermore, unlike the second-beat accents in stanzas 3 and 4 where the anguish of the comparison between "then" and "now" is most acute, Schubert indicates a first-beat accent, stronger than the usual emphasis on the first beat in triple meter, for virtually every measure of stanza 5. These first-beat stresses underscore the regular motion of the journey onward and perhaps as well the strength of will that has brought him "many hours" from that place.

There is no mention in the extant Schubert documentation of Conradin Kreutzer's *Sechs Ländliche Lieder von Wilhelm Müller*, Op. 80, published by H. A. Probst in Leipzig in 1824, and therefore no way of knowing whether Schubert ever encountered the work, which includes settings of "Der Lindenbaum" and "Frühlingstraum" as the fourth and fifth songs respectively. We know that he respected Kreutzer as a composer and that he praised the *Neun Wanderlieder von Uhland*, Op. 34 (see Chapter 1). Kreutzer's compositions, however, do not surpass the bounds of songs intended for the numerous private circles of musical and literary amateurs in Germany and Austria; for all Mann's praise of Schubert's "Der Lindenbaum" as a transfigured folk song, at least in stanzas 1 and 2, one has only to compare a passage from Kreutzer's strophic setting in the same E-major tonality (Ex. 24) with Schubert's to realize the difference. There is nothing as taxing for either pianist or singer as Schubert's tempest in stanza 5— in fact, no tempest at all in Kreutzer—and no musical differentiation between the past and the present. Much of Müller's text, which has

Example 24.   Kreutzer's "Der Lindenbaum," from *Ländliche Lieder*, Op. 80

its own poetic reticences, is omitted from all musical mention in Kreutzer's lied, its dimensions far more modest than Schubert's.

Like the linden voices that haunt the wanderer, Schubert's setting has haunted later composers and writers. Over fifty years after Schubert's cycle, Gustav Mahler recomposed the tale of *Die Winterreise* through "Der Lindenbaum" in his first song cycle, *Lieder eines fahrenden Gesellen*, and changed the ending in accord with his own poetic and psychological imperatives. Mahler's cycle begins with a setting of a poem from *Des Knaben Wunderhorn* ("Wenn mein Schatz Hochzeit macht," which Mahler, in his characteristic fashion, altered) and continues with three of Mahler's own poems. His wayfarer's journey is, probably unconsciously, an abbreviation and inversion of certain key elements from the earlier cycle—instead of winter ice and snow, Mahler's favorite summer landscapes, for example. Most important, the ending is different. The fin-de-siècle jilted lover who sets out alone and at night in the fourth song, "Die zwei blauen Augen," travels only as far as "Der Lindenbaum." When he finds a linden tree by the side of the road, he falls asleep there, blissfully dreaming while the light-green blossoms of the linden "snowed down" upon him (the very choice of verb points to the source). In death, everything is transformed and becomes "good" once again, Müller-Schubert's earlier promise "Komm her zu mir, Geselle / Hier findst' du deine Ruh' " fulfilled.

> Auf der Straße steht ein Lindenbaum,
> Da hab' ich zum ersten Mal im Schlaf geruht!
> Unter dem Lindenbaum!
> Der hat seine Blüten über mich geschneit.
> Da wusst' ich nicht, wie das Leben tut
> War alles, alles wieder gut!
> Ach, alles wieder gut!
> Alles! Alles! Lieb' und Leid,
> Und Welt, und Traum!

(A linden tree stands by the road. There I rested in slumber for the first time! Beneath the linden tree! It snowed down its blossoms over me. There I knew nothing of what Life had done. Everything, everything was good again. Oh, everything once more good! Everything! Everything! Love and sorrow, and the world, and dreaming!)

The later composer grants his wayfaring alter ego fulfillment of the death wish (this is the first of the death lullabies or lullaby farewells that end several of Mahler's song cycles) that Müller's wanderer, made of sterner stuff, rejects. The speculative supposition of unconscious response, even challenge, to Schubert's *Winterreise* does not explain the genesis of Mahler's texts for the *Lieder eines fahrenden Gesellen*, but it seems a plausible link between Schubert's last song cycle and Mahler's first.

For Thomas Mann and his protagonist Hans Castorp in *The Magic Mountain*, "Der Lindenbaum" becomes the symbol of German tradition, of the German spirit itself, in its most beautiful/dangerous guise, a further extension and transformation of what the linden tree represents to Müller's wanderer. *The Magic Mountain* is a *Bildungsroman*, and Mann's creation Hans grows from sheltered immaturity in the symbolic confines of a tuberculosis sanitorium (a hothouse metaphor for an enclosed, confined world of humanity diseased in body and destined for death) to maturity and emergence into a larger world. That is the classical progression in earlier novels of this type, but Mann devises a gloomier modern metamorphosis of the Goethean model. His central figure discovers at the end of his "schooldays," not a universal but a German self, a nationalistic core insidiously compounded of high culture and popular or folk culture to which he responds with death-dealing fervor. Like all schoolboys, Hans has his "tutors," but his final spiritual teacher is music. Once he has learned of the "Fullness of Harmony," most powerfully evident to him in Aida's death scene and "Der Lindenbaum," he descends from the magic mountain in Switzerland to join the German army fighting World War I. At the end of the novel, he charges into battle singing "Der Lindenbaum," not even aware that he sings as he and the rest of the "three thousand feverish boys" run headlong into a storm of bullets, bayonets, and cannons, a tempest of a different sort than the "cold winds" of the song but just as deadly. The ultimate fascination of "Der Lindenbaum" for Hans, for all Germans, Mann suggests, lies in the Teutonic attraction to death, in the acculturated innate desire for extinction.

> To him the song meant a whole world, a world which he must have loved, else he could not have so desperately loved that which it represented and symbolized to him. We know what we are saying when we add—perhaps rather darkly—that he might have had a different fate if his temperament had been less accessible to the charms of the sphere of feeling, the general attitude, which the lied so profoundly, so mystically epitomized. . . .
> . . . But wherein lay Hans Castorp's conscientious and stock-taking misgiving, as to the ultimate propriety of his love for the enchanting lied and the world whose image it was? What was the world behind the song, which the motions of his conscience made to seem a world of forbidden love?
> It was death.
> What utter and explicit madness! That glorious song! An indisputable masterpiece, sprung from the profoundest and holiest depths of racial feeling; a precious possession, the archetype of the genuine; embodied loveliness. What vile detraction![15]

But Hans misunderstands the lied that so fascinates him; it is the omniscient narrator, not Hans Castorp, who identifies the source of the obsession with "Der Lindenbaum." Müller's poem indeed tells

[15]Mann, *The Magic Mountain*, 820.

of the seductive appeal of death cloaked in memory, tradition, and Nature, but his wanderer resists the temptation to die and elects life instead, not out of any resurgent optimism or indeed any reason he can express. Hans and the German people, in Mann's analysis, succumb to a massive death wish. The desire for death is all the more seductive, both for the winter wanderer and Hans, when it appears cloaked in beauty and speaks of home, tradition, peace, and the past. Yet Hans in the end misreads the voices in "Der Lindenbaum," ignoring whatever causes the wanderer to choose continued life and blindly following the directive, "Komm' her zu mir, Geselle!" to his death.

6. Wasserflut

Manche Trän' aus meinen Augen
Ist gefallen in den Schnee;
Seine kalten Flocken saugen
Durstig ein das heiße Weh.

Wenn [Wann] die Gräser sprossen wollen,
Weht daher ein lauer Wind,
Und das Eis zerspringt in Schollen,
Und der weiche Schnee zerrinnt.

Schnee, du weißt von meinem Sehnen;
Sag', wohin doch [Sag mir, wohin] geht dein Lauf?[1]

[1]Schubert surely altered this line to make it accord with his melodic design. "Wasserflut" is strophic, and the vocal line conceived to the words "Ist gefallen in den

Folge nach nur meinen Tränen,
Nimmt dich bald das Bächlein auf.

Wirst mit ihm die Stadt durchziehen,
Muntre Straßen ein und aus;
Fühlst du meine Tränen glühen,
Da ist meiner Liebsten Haus.

Flood

(Many a tear has fallen from my eyes into the snow; its cold flakes
thirstily absorb my burning grief.

When the grass is ready to grow, a mild breeze blows, and the ice
breaks into pieces, and the soft snow melts away.

Snow, you know my longing: tell me, where does your path go?
You have only to follow my tears and the brook will soon absorb you.

You'll flow through the town with it, in and out of merry streets.
When you feel my tears burning, that is my beloved's house.)

The polarity of hot and cold, "cold flakes" and "burning grief," is
a poetic leitmotiv already familiar from "Gefror'ne Tränen" and "Erstarrung." Once again, the wanderer insists that his sorrow still
speaks to him of his lost sweetheart and that his grief is not tepid,
but burning hot. The exaggerated phantasms of the imagination that
he concocts in "Wasserflut" are the products of the anxiety and fears
he has expressed earlier. Lest he forget and his heart freeze in the
emotional death he dreads, he will send his grief back to its source
for renewal. The stream of tears he has wept is, he implies, hot enough
to warm the earth and bring about the return of spring, that is, to
melt the ice and snow in his heart. The violent verbs "zerspringen"
and "zerrinnen" ("to explode, burst, fly to pieces," "to melt, disappear") tell how intense his fears are, so intense that he imagines
obliterating the ice within his heart as suddenly and completely as
possible. Displacing his anxiety about the directionless journey (this
is the first hint in the cycle of what will shortly become an obsession)
onto the anthropomorphized snow, he asks what its path might be.
When the snow feels the wanderer's tears glowing hotter than ever,

---

Schnee" fits badly with Müller's line "Sag mir, wohin geht dein Lauf," especially the
misaccentuation of "Wohin" on the first syllable.

it will know that both guide and follower have reached their destination.

The transposition of "Wasserflut" from F-sharp minor in the autograph manuscript to the E minor of the engraver's copy raises an interesting question with regard to the drama of key relationships in *Winterreise*. The E major of "Der Lindenbaum" and the F-sharp minor of "Wasserflut" in the autograph are tonally distant, but the transposition creates a close relationship between the two adjacent songs. In the first version, the wanderer in "Wasserflut" is indeed "many hours distant" from the tonal place where he sang those words in "Der Lindenbaum," but in the later version, the last chord of "Der Lindenbaum" and the first chord of "Wasserflut" are almost identical, with the only difference the lowered third degree of minor mode. The listener inevitably hears the right-hand triplet figures of "Wasserflut" as related to the arpeggiated figuration in the last stanza of "Der Lindenbaum."

Schubert set "Wasserflut" as a strophic binary song form, the music for stanzas 1 and 2 then repeated literally for stanzas 3 and 4. By dividing the song into halves in this manner, he makes apparent the contrast between misery in the minor mode (stanza 1) and fantasy in major mode. At the same time, he derives the latter from the former, just as the tears of the first verse give rise to the imagined future springtime of the second verse. Once more, Schubert suggests in the instrumental part the precise moment at which the wanderer's thoughts turn from one image or subject to the next in the space between Müller's stanzas. Not until after the words of the first verse, with its tears and fiery grief, does the modulation to relative major occur in the last measures of the piano interlude. One can imagine the excursions into fantasy which one finds in stanza 2 first occurring to Schubert's wanderer at the instant when the D-naturals belonging to G major appear in the bass of m. 17. The formal structure of "Wasserflut" was thus most likely suggested by the poetic content of the first two stanzas and applies less precisely to the third and fourth stanzas, although the fourth verse, like the second, is a creation of the wanderer's active imagination.

Much of the first half can be heard as an inspired exercise in wide-ranging but diatonic melodic lines, with only a single harmonic deviation from the most basic chords of the key. The piano part is less overtly pictorial, more neutral than that of other songs and does not call attention to itself as an entity independent of the vocal part. Rather, the falling motion of the tears as they flow down the wanderer's cheeks and drop to the ground, their winding course in fantasy back to the sweetheart's house, are properties of the vocal line, while the obsessively repeated rhythmic patterns of the slow chordal harmonies create a heavy, funereal atmosphere. As in "Gefror'ne Tränen," Schubert contrasts the leaden melancholy of the wanderer's grief with the assertion of passionate emotion by means of restriction to a few diatonic chords for the former and a chromatic event of great intensity for the latter. Müller ends the declarative statement at the close of stanza 1 with a period ("its cold flakes thirstily absorb my burning grief"), but Schubert both substitutes an exclamation mark indicative of greater passion and climaxes the first statement of those words with chromatic voice-leading to a diminished seventh chord. As Arnold Feil points out, Schubert does not resolve the diminished seventh harmony in any direction new to this song but instead follows it with a conventional cadence and descending motion in the vocal line. The effect is "of someone sinking down in exhaustion after writhing in pain."[2] The emotional turbulence generated by the "heisse Weh" is symbolized in music by the overthrow of the previous harmonic restrictions and by the ascent to so unstable a point of arrival, all the more dramatic for the dissonance created by the piano's arrival at the flatted second degree before the voice. The chromatic outburst, the shifting voices, the steep ascent, every aspect of the phrase were obviously composed with the first stanza in mind and accord only awkwardly with the line "nimmt dich bald das Bächlein auf" in stanza 3. The repetition of the music for stanza 1, however, brings with it such a strong reminiscence of the words "heisse Weh" that the later text is virtually obliterated by it.

The tonal stability of the first section (stanzas 1 and 2, mm. 5–18), only momentarily unseated by the chromatic disturbance of mm. 11–12, is followed in the second section (stanzas 2 and 4, mm. 19–32) by an extended cadential deferment in the major mode of imagination's realm. For the imagined scenarios of the second and fourth stanzas, Schubert reverses the order of diatonic stability/chromatic disturbance in the first section. In the latter half of the musical strophe, there is no resolution to tonicized G major in root position until the final line of poetry in mm. 25–26. Müller speaks in those stanzas of motion leading to a goal (the growing grass and warm breezes that melt the snow, the brook that bears the wanderer's tears to their destination), and the harmonic progression likewise begins in instability and culminates in a completed resolution to the "springtime" tonality of G major. (That same tonality is also associated with a return in imagi-

[2]Feil, *Franz Schubert*, 99.

nation to "meiner Liebsten Haus" in the eighth song, "Rückblick.")
This second section is a variation of the first, beginning with a reinterpretation of the "flowing tears" sequence of scalewise third figures in the final vocal phrase of stanza 1 and continuing with the
wide-ranging arpeggiated figures and rhythmic patterns of the first
half. At the end, the G-major tonality is then abruptly and forcefully
displaced by a cadence that reinstates the principal key and minor
mode. Refuge in the major mode emblematic of imagination's realm
seldom endures for long in Part I.

Schubert has his wanderer repeat the last line of each quatrain, the
emotional tone and interpretation of the line different upon repetition.
It is a truism that composers can in this way present different possible
"readings" of a text, but what is so compelling about this instance is
the fact that the second statement is clearly a reaction to the first.
Having made a statement, Schubert's wanderer feels compelled to
revise it, to alter its emotional temperature and degree of passion.
The first time he sings the words "Durstig ein das heiße Weh" (thirstily my burning grief) at the end of stanza 1, he emphasizes the
intensity of his anguish and the harmonic tension generated by that
misery. The second time, "heiße Weh" is transmuted into gentle tears
trickling down to the tonic pitch in the lower register and to cadential
resolution. That succession of ascending motion/anguish, followed
by descent/gentler melancholy, is then reversed in stanzas 2 and 4.
The first statement of the words "Und der weiche Schnee zerrinnt"
and "Da ist meiner Liebsten Haus" is far less stark than the reversion
to E minor and the vault upward in the second statement. In the first
stanza, the wanderer asserts great grief but cannot sustain such high
mercury readings and lapses into the weary, reflective melancholy
that is more his wont. At the end of the second and fourth stanzas,
however, he "rewrites" the temperate G-major cadences as if to proclaim yet again the fiery heat of "heiße Weh." If he states it often
enough, perhaps he can convince himself that his heart is still alive
and wracked with pain. But the piano postlude sinks back down to
the lower octave, and in the next song the wanderer seeks even more
desperately for assurance that his heart retains some capacity for life,
motion, and feeling.

Prosody is particularly difficult in strict strophic settings, since melodies and rhythms devised to fit the initial quatrain often do not
accord so well with the verses that follow. The marriage of compelling
melodic design with text inflection that is both correct and expressive
is in many ways easier to devise in formal structures without the
large-scale literal repetitions of strophic form. Schubert does not en-

tirely evade the problems of strophic prosody in "Wasserflut," but his extraordinary sensitivity in these matters is nevertheless very evident. For example, in the first line of Müller's trochaic tetrameters, "Manche Trän' aus meinen Augen" (Many tears from my eyes), the accented syllable of the initial trochee on the adjective "*Man* - che" is not as important as the noun "Trän' " it modifies. Schubert sets the adjective on the strong first beat as a rising triplet figure that leads to the crucial word "Trän' " on the highest pitch of the phrase. Even though "tears" occurs on the second, normally the weak, beat, it receives durational emphasis and pitch emphasis as a sustained high note. When that initial melodic phrase recurs for the third line of text, it is the adjective "cold" that receives the melodic/durational stress ("Seine *kal* - ten Flocken saugen"), the chill striking even deeper. In stanza 3, however, the arpeggiated ascent flows through the articulation of direct address, that is, the designation of a listener followed by words to that audience: "Schnee, du weißt...." Similarly, the successive falling fourths devised for the words "ist gefallen in den Schnee" override the comma between the single word of imperative address and the question that follows: "Sag, wohin doch geht dein Lauf?" But these are relatively minor matters where so much is so right. One might note in passing a particular prosodic gesture used earlier in the cycle: at the words "weiche Schnee" and "meiner Liebsten" in stanzas 2 and 4, Schubert places the higher pitch of a syllable assigned two notes on the weak half of the beat, just as he had done in "Die Wetterfahne" at the lines "Sie pfiff' den armen Flüchtling aus" and "Im Haus ein treues Frauenbild." There, as here, the controlled flight upward of words and intervallic figures at the apex of the phrase bespeaks great intensity of feeling.

7. Auf dem Fluße

Der du so lustig rauschtest,
Du heller, wilder Fluß,
Wie still bist du geworden,
Gibst keinen Scheidegruß.

Mit harter, starrer Rinde
Hast du dich überdeckt,
Liegst kalt und unbeweglich
Im Sande ausgestreckt.

In deine Decke grab' ich
Mit einem spitzen Stein

[176]

Den Namen meiner Liebsten
Und Stund' und Tag hinein:

Den Tag des ersten Grußes,
Den Tag, an dem ich ging,
Um Nam' und Zahlen windet
Sich ein zerbroch'ner Ring.

Mein Herz, in diesem Bache
Erkennst du nun dein Bild?
Ob's unter seiner Rinde
Wohl auch so reißend schwillt?

On the River

(You who used to ripple so happily, you clear, wild river, how still you have become: you give no parting greeting.

You have covered yourself with a hard, stiff crust. You lie cold and motionless, stretched out in the sand.

On your surface I carve the name of my beloved, the hour and the day, with a sharp stone:

The date of our first greeting, the date when I went away; a broken ring is entwined around the name and numbers.

My heart, in this brook do you now recognize your own image? Is it, beneath its crust, swelling near to bursting?)

Capell singles out this poem as a particularly telling example of Müller's faults as a poet. "The text contains some of Müller's rather unfortunate conceits, conceits so much below the music that non-German audiences perhaps have some compensation if they miss the words when Schubert is sung. The verses are about the graving of the jilt's name on the ice of the frozen river."[1] There is more to "Auf dem Fluße" than that, as shown by the recent and differing interpretations by David Lewin and Anthony Newcomb.[2] The "graving of the jilt's name" is not the childish gesture it might seem, but the attempt to carve a makeshift tombstone for his love, a memorial to the past cut in ice rather than stone. There is no indication in the

[1]Capell, *Schubert's Songs*, 234.
[2]See David Lewin, "'Auf dem Fluße': Image and Background in a Schubert Song" in *Schubert: Critical and Analytical Studies*, ed. Walter Frisch (Lincoln, Nebr., 1986), 126–52, and Anthony Newcomb, "Structure and Expression in a Schubert Song: *Noch einmal* 'Auf dem Fluße' *zu hören*," in ibid., 153–74.

poem that the wanderer's action is "idle" or "almost inadvertent," as Lewin proposes. If it is not the product of long and careful planning, it is nonetheless deliberate and the choice of inscriptions significant: her name and two dates, the day they first met and the date of his departure from the town. These are the birth-and-death dates of his love for her, and the mock-graveyard ritual is an affirmation of his own continued life and fate, no longer reckoned with hers. For the first time, the wanderer wants to bury his memories rather than dwell on them, to consign them to the grave where they belong. But mourning (if successful) is not a linear march forward into a new life, but rather a slow dance of "one step forward and two steps back" in which advances impel a regressive reaction. If the lost love is truly dead and buried, consigned to the past, will the present be lifeless and devoid of feeling? Does the passionate emotion the wanderer asserts beneath the chill of grief truly exist, or has he too died to all feeling? The doubts that first appear in "Gefror'ne Tränen" persist and impel renewed questions.

The conflicting analyses of "Auf dem Fluße" have begun with differing interpretations of Schubert's reading. From the musical evidence, how did Schubert understand the wanderer's final questions in the fifth stanza? The debate about poetic meaning has centered largely on that fifth and final stanza, the only verse that stands alone and unpaired. The first and second stanzas are linked by the wanderer's observation of the frozen, immobile river, the third and fourth stanzas by the action of carving the makeshift tombstone in the ice. With the final stanza, the wanderer turns from description (1, 2) and action (3, 4) to inward questions, querying his heart or his emotional self. The debate has focused on the interpretation of those two questions either as rhetorical, a way of imparting information asserted to be true (Newcomb), or open ended, a matter of genuine uncertainty and doubt (Lewin). Actually, both are correct, and it is a testament to Müller's fine tuning of psychological verities that such emotional ambiguities appear throughout Winterreise. The wanderer's doubts and his reactions to the "burial" of his love have impelled the comparison he proposes at the end of "Auf dem Fluße," but for the moment he believes the analogy to be true. Schubert's alteration of Müller's text from "Erkennst du nun dein Bild?" to "Erkennst du wohl dein Bild?" in the engraver's copy (the autograph manuscript preserves the poet's wording) can be cited, as Newcomb recognizes, in support of the rhetorical reading; in the removal of the time element and the added emphasis of the word "wohl," the wanderer implies that his heart should answer "Yes," with no qualifications. For the first edition, however, Schubert reverted to the poet's text. In terms of pure sonority, the multiple /u/ and /n/ sounds of "du nun dein" reinforce the flow of the sixteenth-note figures into the cadential phrase ending, but the wanderer's awareness of time in Müller's poem is what truly distinguishes the two versions of the fifth stanza. Implicit in the poet's use of the word "now" is the recognition that things will inevitably change, even though the wanderer wants to believe that the simile of the frozen surface over concealed torrential motion is apt for the moment. At the end of "Erstarrung," the wanderer has forecast a future thaw for his frozen heart, and Müller implies in "Auf dem Fluße" that the wanderer still expects a change in his condition at some later time. If recurring uncertainty has impelled the questions asked here, the wanderer nonetheless insists that the simile is true because he greatly desires that it be so.

The poem is written in iambic trimeters, but the first line consists of a dactyl and two trochees; the unruly motion of the river as it used to be is embodied in the bolder poetic rhythms of the initial line. Schubert, however, abjures Müller's contrast. His wanderer is struck more by the present glacial metamorphosis, by the stillness and silence. The introduction is characterized by minimal harmonic motion, tiptoeing around the tonic without going anywhere, and even more restricted melodic motion, the neutral pulse devoid of rhythmic variety as well. The vocal line too is fixed in place on the tonic harmony throughout its first four measures. The first motion in the piece occurs at the words "Wie still bist du geworden" (How still you have become), as if the transformation of the river to its frozen state takes place in the instant of that startling semitone shift downward from E minor to an unprepared-for D-sharp-minor chord.[3] Abrupt displacement to such a distant key was a radical compositional choice in 1827; not until the last quarter of the nineteenth century does one find the frequent and systematic use of similar semitone shifts. Newcomb points out, however, that even though the maneuver is "violent in its unconventionality," a modulatory register of the wanderer's shock at the metamorphosis, it is a very small and, significantly, downward motion.[4] With mm. 11–12, Schubert quickens the melodic motion, thus beginning a progressive increase in motion throughout the song.

[3]Schubert originally set the words "Wie still bist du geworden" as a nearly monotonic chant on A-sharp, the vocal line frozen in place except for the upbeat pitch B. At stage 2, he changed the final A-sharp ("ge - wor - *den*") to F-sharp, a small falling inflection to eliminate what would otherwise have been slight overemphasis on the final weak syllable of the word.
[4]Newcomb, "Structure and Expression in a Schubert Song," 157.

Here, the wanderer gives himself the parting greeting that the river has denied him, Schubert translating "Scheidegruss" as a cadence whose quickened rhythms and melodic motion evoke a wave of the hand. What Newcomb has called the "cheerful little inverted mordent," however, seems to me not a matter of perverse cheer but of a musical shudder or shivering emphasis on the adjective "*kei* - nen," "*no* parting greeting."

The setting of the second verse, in which the wanderer continues to describe the frozen river, is a repetition of the music for stanza 1, with only a few differences. The initial vocal phrase from mm. 5–6 now has a semitone neighbor-note figure at the word "Rinde" in yet another example of greater activity and motion as the song progresses. The singer emphasizes the crucial first syllable of "*un* - beweglich" by reaching up to the tonicized D-sharp and then prolonging it slightly, while the remainder of the word remains on the single pitch A-sharp, literally not moving from that note. But with the third and fourth verses, Schubert's wanderer already begins to enact musically the swelling, bursting passions he invokes in stanza 5. The tonality warms to major mode, the motion in the accompaniment quickens markedly, and the wanderer's vocal line becomes more lyrical, less cautious and hushed, reaching past the D-sharp apex in stanzas 1 and 2 to high E. The sixteenth-note figures of the piano interludes in the first two stanzas now occupy every measure. At first, the compass is restricted and the tone rather cold, but both are no longer so by the end. With the action of engraving the ice comes the tension and disquiet of weak-beat accents and sixteenth-note upbeats throughout the second half of each measure. In the autograph manuscript, one can see where Schubert at stage 2 altered the original duple and quadruplet sixteenths in stanza 4 to triplet sixteenth notes in order to increase the rhythmic motion that bespeaks mounting agitation (Illus. 7). Schubert also writes a more active bass line throughout the stanzas in E major, as well as chromatic neighboring harmonies that embellish the basic chords of the key—greater color and motion, after the gray, quiet chill of stanzas 1 and 2. Perhaps the most poignant detail of all is the imperfect "broken circle" depicted in the melodic line for mm. 37–38 and the half-cadence that does not resolve but stops abruptly, leaving only silence where the downbeat of resolution should be.

With stanza 5, the chilly minor mode and restricted motion of the right-hand chordal patterns used earlier return in the accompaniment. Schubert also brings back the vocal line of the "hard, stiff crust," but this time placed in the bass. The submergence of the previous melodic

7. Autograph manuscript of "Auf dem Fluße," stanza 4 (folio 13v). Courtesy
The Pierpont Morgan Library, New York, Cary 90.

line for stanzas 1 and 2 seems doubly significant. The wanderer will
not accept the proposed return to glacial immobility and refuses to
join in, but at the same time the melodic activity in the bass suggests
motion below the surface, the first hint of the rushing torrent beneath
the frozen crust. The wanderer refuses as well what starts as the
conventional return of the A section in a three-part song form. Rather
than bringing back E minor after the semitone shift to D-sharp minor,
that cadence on a distant key is the start of an extended development
of the previous music. When the sudden deflection to D-sharp minor
recurs (significantly abbreviated), the bass plunges an octave lower

than before, the widened compass another of the indices of increasing emotional turbulence throughout this song, and the motion increases still more, from the triplet sixteenth notes in stanza 4 to thirty-second notes here. No longer is the radical shift of tonality stated within small, tight boundaries; now it is expressed in a way that finally makes overt the innate violence of the gesture and asserts heated, rushing motion and overflowing boundaries as truer to the heart's inmost self than frozen passivity.

The setting of stanza 5 cost Schubert considerable effort; eventually he had to make a fair copy of the last page of the song, folio 14 recto (mm. 51–74) which he tipped into the autograph manuscript. The struggle with the final verse of Müller's poem actually begins on folio 13 verso (mm. 32–50), one of the most heavily revised pages in Part I. There, the harmony arpeggiated in thirty-second notes in the bass of m. 47 is a dominant seventh chord, embellished by the minor ninth-degree E, above the bass D-sharp, thus creating a cross-relation between F-double-sharp and the F-sharp chord tone of the D-sharp-minor triad in the right hand on the first beat. Schubert elides the cadential resolution of the new tonal realm with violent motion away from that key and toward its subdominant G-sharp minor (Ex. 25).

Example 25.   "Auf dem Fluße," m. 47, autograph ms.

In the engraver's fair copy and in the first edition, Schubert altered the arpeggiated bass figure to a D-sharp-minor chord with the accented neighbor-note figure E–D-sharp at its apex, therefore shortening the approach to G-sharp minor (Ex. 26). The revision apparently occurred during the process of collaboration between copyist and

Example 26.   "Auf dem Fluße," m. 47, engraver's copy

composer on the engraver's fair copy; one can see that accidentals were erased in that measure and that the fourth pitch of the left-hand arpeggio, probably a C-sharp, was erased and replaced by a D that lacks the necessary sharp sign, added finally in the first edition. Schubert apparently also had difficulties with the vocal line of mm. 48–49 at the words "Ob's unter seiner Rinde / Wohl auch so reißend schwillt?" Evidently, he planned at first to delay the singer's entrance until the movement to G-sharp minor had already been effected by the piano. The superiority of the stage 2 revision—in which the voice and the bass line double one another at the interval of a tenth, joined in agreement to unleash the floodgates of passion—is obvious.

According to Newcomb, one can perceive the voice and the piano in stanza 5 as now conflicting, now conjoined personae within the wanderer. For example, the piano at the beginning of the stanza pulls back from the increased emotion of stanza 4 and returns to the E-minor chill of the first stanza, while the voice refuses to cooperate and insists on the higher tessitura and ascending motion that spells greater passion. In m. 52, the frightened self represented by the piano pulls away from the G-sharp-minor sphere and insists on a return to E minor and the cautious, restricted motion of m. 41f. The tritone dissonance between the continued D-sharp in the voice and the trilled A-natural in the bass of m. 52 makes the conflict powerfully explicit. Even though the voice acquiesces in the momentary return to E minor, it overreaches its previous ceiling once again, rising to G-natural after the previous peaks on E and F-sharp and straining away from the Bs in the topmost voice of the piano.

When the return to E minor is achieved, the conflict from m. 41f assumes an even more extreme form. Instead of the previous motion to G-sharp minor, Schubert moves upward for the first time in the song to the mediant G major, and then sinks downward a semitone to F-sharp minor. Here, change happens at a more rapid rate than before. The return to E minor is permitted only two measures, rather than four, before the mediant rise, while F-sharp minor states only a single cadence before the bass ascends twice by fourths F-sharp–B–E, rather than the single ascent from D-sharp to G-sharp in mm. 47–48. Furthermore, the arrival at E minor in m. 54 is elided with the recurrence once again of the bass melody from m. 41, now in the lower octave—the compass of the song has widened in both directions from its previous narrow boundaries. The wanderer almost immediately begins to ask the same questions again, the sense of urgency now too great to permit any longer pause. Schubert altered the shift from E minor to G major in the engraver's fair copy to soften a formerly more abrupt transition. The autograph manuscript shows a root-position B-major triad, the dominant of E minor, on the weak half of the second beat of m. 55, with the low bass pitch marked staccato and isolated from the slurred melodic lines on either side. The subsequent turn to G is therefore disconcertingly abrupt. In the engraver's copy, Schubert changed the low B to the A a seventh higher, the new pitch functioning as a passing tone in the bass line (Ex. 27). Julian

Example 27.   "Auf dem Fluße," m. 55

Armitage-Smith aptly describes the revised line as a softer, "more inward" transition, the transformation of "a good bar of music into a great one."[5]

This change then necessitated a series of revisions to the corresponding passage in mm. 62–63. In the autograph manuscript, Schubert had sought to intensify the return to E minor in those two measures by double-dotting the bass melody in the piano. In m. 63, he had at first duplicated the same descending bass octave B–B that appeared in m. 55, but changed the figure in the engraver's fair copy to the same scalewise descent and passing tone one finds seven measures earlier. Because the double-dotting would then produce a clash between the thirty-second-note A in the bass and the B in the right-hand part, he removes the double-dotting altogether from the entire passage in mm. 62–65 (Ex. 28). But this created a new dilemma. The eighth-note pitch B in the vocal line of m. 63 at the word "wohl" was not at all problematic in the autograph manuscript, but in the engraver's copy Schubert changed that pitch to a sixteenth-note D-natural, thus producing a cross-relation with the D-sharps in the right-hand part. Armitage-Smith has suggested that Schubert, finding each successive alteration produced a new problem, simply walked away from the passage without correcting the cross-relation, and he proposes a return to the eighth-note B in the vocal line from the autograph manuscript to avoid that dissonant cross-relation. There are worse things, however, than such short-lived dissonances, and Schubert's

Example 28.   "Auf dem Fluße," mm. 63–65, A. autograph ms.; B. engraver's copy

A.

B.

final solution has much to recommend it. As emended, it is the voice that impels yet another deflection away from E minor in graphic depiction of the conflict between inner selves represented by the piano and the vocal line. Far from being a compositional problem abandoned in exasperation, m. 63 in the first edition is a brilliant solution to an earlier dilemma, a solution that belongs within the crescendo of rising passion traced throughout the setting of stanza 5.

The intensification continues to the end of the text, then snaps off abruptly at the postlude. The previous motion from E-minor to G-major chords becomes movement from E minor to yet another harmonic shock, the G *minor* in mm. 62–65. The darker minor mode is another index of the swelling emotion, and the deceptive deflection in m. 68 then impels another cadential statement in which the voice reaches up to high A. With that massive cadence, all force of passionate expression is spent. The instrumental part cannot even summon up the energy to extend the E-minor bass melody beyond the compass of a minor third. The thirty-second-note tremolandi are emptied of all harmonic fullness and substance, and the neutral pulse of the beginning is all that remains at the end.

The vocal cadence in mm. 69–70—the bursting point of the wanderer's proclaimed passion—reaches up to the high A presumably proscribed by the publisher, and yet Schubert neither altered it downward nor transposed the entire song. He could not: the compositional design depends in part upon the ascent traced from D-sharp through E to F-sharp, G-natural, and finally A in the vocal line, while the references to G-major and G-minor harmonies pave the way for "Rückblick." The eighth song even begins with an obvious restatement of the octave tremolandi from the postlude of "Auf dem Fluße." One need not understand the recurrence in the postlude of the original chilled or frozen motion, the restricted compass and glacial atmosphere of the beginning, as the composer's concurrence with psychological failure, with the truth of alienation reasserting itself. Passion expressed and momentarily spent usually concludes in pained calm and the saving grace of repression restored. The postlude bespeaks the exhaustion that follows on the heels of grief at its most intense.

8. Rückblick

Es brennt mir unter beiden Sohlen,
Tret' ich auch schon auf Eis and Schnee.
Ich möcht' nicht wieder Atem holen,
Bis ich nicht mehr die Türme seh'.

Hab' mich an jedem Stein gestoßen
So eilt' ich zu der Stadt hinaus;
Die Krähen warfen Bäll' und Schloßen
Auf meinen Hut von jedem Haus.

Wie anders hast du mich empfangen,
Du Stadt der Unbeständigkeit!
An deinen blanken Fenstern sangen
Die Lerch' und Nachtigall im Streit.

Die runden Lindenbäume blühten,
Die klaren Rinnen rauschten hell,
Und ach, zwei Mädchenaugen glühten!—
Da war's geschehn um dich, Gesell!

Kommt mir der Tag in die Gedanken,
Möcht' ich noch einmal rückwärts sehn,
Möcht' ich zurücke wieder wanken,
Vor ihrem Hause stille stehn.

Backward Glance

(The soles of my feet burn, though I walk on ice and snow. I do not want to draw breath again until I can no longer see the towers.

I tripped on every stone in my haste to leave the town; the crows threw snowballs and hailstones onto my hat from every house.

How differently you once received me, town of Inconstancy! At your gleaming windows, the lark and nightingale contested in song.

The round linden trees blossomed, the clear fountains splashed brightly, and ah! a maiden's eyes glowed!—then, my friend, you were done for!

When I think of that day, I long to look back once again, long to stumble back there and stand before her house.)

Immersed in memory once more, the wanderer relives his frantic flight from the sweetheart's town as if it were the present moment. With the lines "The soles of my feet burn, though I walk on ice and snow," Müller recalls the fire/ice antinomy of "Gefror'ne Tränen," "Erstarrung," and "Wasserflut" for the last time in Part I, but no longer as a principal motif. In his breathless haste to leave, the wanderer did not look where he was going and stumbled over each stone in his path, the difficulties of his escape heightened by the flock of crows who "threw snowballs and hailstones of snow onto my hat from every house." Capell and others concerned with narrative consistency have complained that the wanderer either retrieves the hat lost in "Der Lindenbaum" or mysteriously acquires another one elsewhere, but this is a memory of the earlier departure and the hat is the same one later lost in the winter storm. The psychological hardships of his leavetaking are evoked as physical difficulties, as an exaggerated interpretation of a commonplace natural phenomenon. The birds roosting on the pointed eaves of houses shift position and move about, dislodging pieces of ice ("Schloßen," or "hailstones") and snowballs. The wanderer, acutely conscious of his alienation from society, sees hostile intentions where none exist.

In the paired third and fourth verses, the impression that the wanderer sings of experiences in the present is dispelled when he addresses in memory the "town of Inconstancy" at a happier time. Stanzas 1 and 2 are thus one "Rückblick," stanzas 3 and 4 another, extending farther back in time. The "glance back" at his flight from the town is then followed by another "glance back" to the springtime love story preceding the misery of his departure. The twin memories are a miniature meditation on change. The same place that he left in such haste, even the birds on the rooftops inimical to him, once seemed an idyllic place where larks and nightingales vied with each other in song, where the round, leafy linden trees were in blossom and the streams ran clear and bright. (The line "Die klaren Rinnen rauschten hell" is reminiscent of the beginning of "Auf dem Fluße"— "Der du so lustig rauschtest, / Du heller, wilder Fluß.") Everything in the lyrical scene is either plural or paired or both; nothing is solitary. The catalyst for the transformation from springtime beauty to wintry hostility is the sweetheart herself, metonymically invoked by her glowing eyes. At the thought of her, the wanderer breaks off the recollection with a rueful colloquialism, a touch of self-deprecating but pained irony addressed to the younger self who fell in love that spring. The difference between past and present is heightened all the more by the third-person address in the words "Then, my friend, you were done for!" To mitigate the pain of remembrance, he divides himself into observer and observed, the one commenting ironically on the other.

The memories in the first four stanzas impel a single culminating stanza in which memories give birth to a wish. Whenever the wanderer recalls "the day" (the day when he first saw her, the memory he evokes in the fourth stanza), he imagines staggering back to the town and standing still in front of her house, no more.[1] Realist that he is, he says nothing of seeing *her*, only the house where she used to live. After the fears expressed in the songs from "Erstarrung" on, the purpose of the imagined return is clear. If he could only go back and see the house, his memories would be revived and his sorrow could continue to speak of her. Even so, the thought is clearly a wish beyond the bounds of action since he does not say, "I will go back" or "I must go back," but only "I would like to look back one more time. . . . I would like to return."

Although Müller criticized other poets for their exaggerated concern with sound at the expense of meaning, he knew that the sonorous properties of words are the bearers of poetic meaning, and his concern for the union of sound and sense in verse is particularly evident in "Rückblick." The tongue stumbles over the accumulation of clotted /cht/, /ch/, and /sch/ sounds in the first verse—"Tret' ich auch schon auf Eis und Schnee"—as the wanderer stumbles over the stones, the frantic flight difficult both in speech and actuality. The liquid /l/ 's and /r/'s of of the birdsong, rustling brooks, and blossoming trees in the third and fourth verses

> Die *L*e*r*ch' und Nachtiga*ll* im Streit
> $\cdot\;\cdot\;\cdot\;\cdot\;\cdot$
> Die *r*unden *L*indenbäume b*l*ühten,
> Die k*l*a*r*en *R*innen *r*auschten he*ll* . . .

are a marked change from the percussive /st/, /ts/, /t/, and /z/ sounds in the second verse:

> Hab' mich an jeden S*t*ein ges*t*oßen
> So eil*t*' ich zu der S*t*ad*t* hinaus . . .

---

[1] There is no ghostly double haunting the wanderer and the scene he envisages is peaceful, not horrifying, but the thematic kinship between "Rückblick" and Heine's "Der Doppelgänger" from the *Buch der Lieder* is nonetheless striking. In both poems, the poetic persona stands in front of his lost sweetheart's house, or wishes he could stand there, and is haunted by the shade of his younger self in love. Heine's masterpiece is more complex than Müller's poem, however. Müller ruefully decries the downfall of the fellow he once was, but in Heine's poem the poetic persona is mocked by a spectral self who mimics his former lovelorn mannerisms. Three incarnations of the poet appear on the same nocturnal scene.

Those harsh /st/ and /t/ consonants still sound at the start of the third verse when the wanderer "speaks" to his sweetheart's town in memory, "Du Stadt der Unbeständigkeit," but disappear as the bitter reference to inconstancy is followed by an evocation of the town's beauty that fateful spring. The /au/ diphthongs that darken the first and second stanzas ("auch schon auf") and the rhyming "hinaus" and "Haus" in the second stanza are found only once in the fourth stanza in the word "rauschten," the single occurrence softened and modified by the /l/ 's and /r/'s surrounding it on either side. "Rückblick" furthermore contains more alliterative word pairs than any other poem in the cycle: "Stein gestoßen," "Lindenbäume blühten," "Rinnen rauschten," "Mädchenaugen glühten," "wieder wanken," "stille stehn," the latter followed by a line with the words "geschehn" and "Gesell." The staggered internal rhyme and the repetition of the subject-verb "Möcht' ich" in the parallel lines from stanza 5

> Möcht' ich noch einmal *rück*wärts sehn,
> Möcht' ich *zurücke* wieder wanken . . .

are simple but effective ways of conveying the fervor of the wanderer's wish to return. This is verbal music not for its own sake but as an instrument of heightened poetic meaning.

The composition of "Rückblick" evidently cost Schubert considerable difficulty. The entire song appears in the autograph manuscript in fair copy, a copy almost certainly made when Schubert was already at work on the songs of Part II. He writes "Voce" and "Pianoforte" in front of the appropriate staff systems at the beginning of "Rückblick" just as he does for each song of Part II (unlike his practice for every other song in Part I), while the paper for the inserted page is of a type Schubert began using only in the summer of 1827. "Rückblick" is the culmination of a dramatic progression that stretches from "Gute Nacht" through "Rückblick," and therefore its composition may well have required extra effort. The wanderer remembers the panic-stricken flight in the piano introduction before he recounts it in words, the beginning of stanza 1 joining music already in full hue and cry. The sound is constant, the right hand echoing the left hand like pounding feet, the direct ascent and crescendo expressive of panic. There is no break in the motion when the singer enters, or at any other time, until the words "stille stehn" at the end of the entire song. Even at the fermata in m. 27, the transition between stanzas 3 and 4 (the A and B sections), Schubert indicates no cessation in sound.

The progression from diatonicism to chromatic ascent by semitones
in the initial motivic figure of the introduction, culminating in an
entire bar filled with a single unharmonized pitch, is a register of
increasing tension within the figure. The later appearance of the parallel major mode is foreshadowed in the succession of B-flat and B-
natural in mm. 1 and 3; the measured tremolando octave Ds in the
B section are foretold in mm. 2 and 4; and the textural contrast between
the two bars of each figure prefigures the contrast between the full
texture of the A and A¹ sections and the transparent clarity of the B
section. It is a remarkably evocative beginning to a remarkable song.

There is nothing rhythmically or metrically irregular about the introduction, but the same is not true of the extraordinary setting of
stanzas 1 and 2. The syllabic declamation, largely in successive eighth
notes, is reminiscent of "Der Jäger" from *Die schöne Müllerin*, one of
whose accompanimental motives is an exact inversion of the first
measure of "Rückblick." The jealousy in "Der Jäger" and the panic-
stricken recollections of "Rückblick" each inspired the sacrifice of
rhythmically inflected melody to the driven quality produced by prosody in equal note values. Where the unaccented syllable of a line
with a feminine ending (the even-numbered lines) is followed by the
unaccented syllable at the beginning of the next line, Schubert sets
those two syllables as two sixteenth notes in the interior of a compressed phrase, the elision and therefore the lack of any articulation
or breathing room between the lines of the poetic text resulting in
the asymmetrical three-bar phrases at the beginning and end of the
A section. The panic expressed in the words becomes the rhythmic
opposition of the notated $\frac{3}{4}$ meter against the actual $\frac{2}{4}$ metrical divisions
of the vocal line, as Arnold Feil has demonstrated.[2] The regular tactus
established by the quarter-note beats in the introduction is disturbed
by the rhythmic unrest engendered by the vocal line, a disturbance
that gives a vivid impression of panic-stricken flight. In the first vocal
phrase, the melodic peaks, enforced by the crescendo markings and
the unusual accent mark in the voice part, show the true rhythmic
downbeats as occurring on the words "beiden" and "Eis" ("Es brennt
mir unter *bei* - den Sohlen, / Tret' ich auch schon auf *Eis* und Schnee").
The metrical cross-currents are further complicated by the canonic
imitation at the distance of one beat between the vocal line and the
accompaniment, in graphic depiction of pursuit. The wanderer who
feared being driven out of town by a society hostile to him ("Gute
Nacht") now re-creates in imagination the sounds of a chase. The

²Feil, *Franz Schubert*, 38–44.

metrical alignment of the imitating line in the accompaniment is differently disposed within the barlines than the vocal line it follows, and this compounds the metrical turbulence. The tactus may be steady and constant, but it is fraught with conflicting emphases. The canonic imitation ceases momentarily at the words "Hab'mich an jedem Stein gestoßen / So eilt' ich zu der Stadt hinaus" (the two interior phrases of the A section), and the concurrence of the accompaniment and vocal line is regularized. Even the phrasing is briefly rendered symmetrical, those two lines of text occupying four bars rather than the asymmetrical three bars of the preceding vocal phrases. But the level of tension is hardly lessened, given the darkness of the dominant minor tonality (there is no major mode, nothing of imagination's brightness, in these two stanzas), and the cross-rhythms, conflicting accents, and fragmentary canonic imitation all recur with the return to tonic for the shower of ice and snow "hurled" at the wanderer by his avian ill-wishers. Schubert's repeated descending-"pelting" figures for the crows' projectiles and the aggrieved shift of emphasis from the noun to its adjective upon repetition of the phrase, "The crows threw snowballs and hailstones on to my *hat* . . . on to *my* hat," are typically ingenious details of text setting.

In Schubert's reading, the word "Haus" at the end of stanza 2 is the key that unlocks the second *Rückblick*. When the wanderer sings this word (a potent symbol throughout the cycle for the love, home, and happiness he does not have), his thoughts turn to the sweetheart's house in earlier, happier times. The wanderer is clearly taken by surprise, ambushed by recollection, as the change to the parallel major mode occurs on the second and third beats of the last measure of the A section. It stops the wanderer in his tracks: the major chord sustained by the fermata at the end of m. 27 is an instant of stillness in which memory crystallizes and takes shape. Like the "city of inconstancy" in its different guises, the B section is both "anders" (different) and yet linked to the A section, since the panic-stricken tempo is unchanged throughout the song and much of the music is closely related to the desperate flight. The vignette of the town in happier times is set in a G major so diatonic as to rival in clarity the "clear streams" of the wanderer's remembrances. The conflicting meters, multiple accents, and canonic pursuit are all banished. The texture thins and becomes translucent, while the unharmonized octave Ds from mm. 2 and 4 are transformed into a constant, lulling pedal point in the right hand. The bass line and the vocal line are paired, often doubling one another at the tenth and never dissonant or metrically at odds. Each line of text is set as an individual, symmetrical

melodic phrase, without the extra impetus of the sixteenth-note elisions, although the declamatory stream of eighth notes remains. The
cadences, both the half-cadence in mm.30–31 ("Du Stadt der Unbeständigkeit") and the tonic cadence at mm. 34–35 ("Die Lerch' und
Nachtigall im Streit"), are marked by momentarily thickened chord
doublings: this "Streit" prompts, not dissonance and conflict, but a
fuller, sweeter euphony.

   The first hint of the trouble that will transform this place into a
"City of Inconstancy" receives from Schubert tonal recognition of
disturbance. At the words "Und ach, zwei Mädchenaugen glühten"
in mm. 40–41 and 44–45, Schubert swerves briefly away from the
diatonic G major of the idyllic recollection and brings back the accompaniment figures divided between the left and the right hands
as in the A section. The maiden's glowing eyes are the culmination
of the town's beautiful attributes in prior days, so the melodic line is
a transposed variant in *Terzensteigerung* of the preceding phrase, "Die
klaren Rinnen rauschten hell," but in the minor mode of later tragedy
not the major mode of the wanderer's happier memories. The phrase
on the submediant (the D-sharps will soon become the enharmonic
E-flat in m. 48 for the sudden transition back to G minor) is placed
in a higher register of its own, distinct from what surrounds it. It is
tempting to hear the ground snatched from beneath the wanderer's
feet, or the ethereal quality of new love literally registered in the
higher tessitura. At the return to diatonicism and the rueful words
"Da war's geschehn um dich, Gesell!" Schubert places a weak-beat
accent on the diminished seventh chord at the word "da" in unmistakable rueful emphasis—"*Then*, my friend, you were done for." The
figuration in the piano (m. 43) returns to the limpid two-part clarity,
but after the wanderer repeats those same words, a return to memories that precede her appearance is no longer possible. Instead, the
piano repeats "war's geschehn, war's geschehn" wordlessly, the second time in minor. This time, there is no reflective pause, no fermata.
The thought that he was "done for" that day when he first saw her
leads seamlessly to the final stanza.

   The final stanza is a variant of the music for stanzas 1 and 2, without
the darkness of dominant minor and with a return to G major. Schubert has his wanderer repeat over and over again the wish to "stumble
back there and stand before her house"; when he does so, in G major,
the underlying poignant desire to restore the tranquillity and happiness of the idyll remembered in the B section is evident. The cross-
metrical rhythmic counterplay of the crows who threw snow and ice
at him in the A section is varied as a representation of staggering

("wanken"), each time with the adjective "vor *ihrem* Hause," "before *her* house" triply emphasized by the high G, the prolongation across the bar line in mm. 63–64, and the intensification of the subdominant. When the wanderer for the last time repeats "Vor ihrem Hause stille stehn," his triplet eighth figures "drag" against the continued sixteenth notes in the accompaniment in an apt rhythmic representation of slowed motion. The singer at the end "stands still" on a sustained G in the lower register, but before the piano accompaniment does likewise, there is a final flurry of sixteenth-note agitation on plagal cadential harmonies whose traditional connotations of prayer or plea no one could mistake.

9. [Das] Irrlicht

In die tiefsten Felsengründe
Lockte mich ein Irrlicht hin:
Wie ich einen Ausgang finde
Liegt nicht schwer mir in dem Sinn.

Bin gewohnt das Irregehen,
'S führt ja jeder Weg zum Ziel:
Unsre Freuden, unsre Leiden [Wehen],
Alles eines Irrlichts Spiel!

Durch des Bergstroms trockne Rinnen
Wind' ich ruhig mich hinab—
Jeder Strom wird's Meer gewinnen,
Jedes Leiden auch sein [ein] Grab.

Will-o'-the-Wisp

(A will-o'-the-wisp lured me into the deepest rocky abysses. How I am to find my way out does not trouble my mind.

I am used to straying—every path leads to one goal. Our joys, our sorrows, are all a will-o'-the-wisp's game!

I calmly wend my way downward through the dry gullies of the mountain stream. Every river will reach the sea, every sorrow too will reach its grave.)

Along the course of his inward journey, the wanderer now follows a will-o'-the-wisp, a delusory train of thought that leads him into the depths of depression. Such is the wanderer's melancholy that he declares himself unconcerned with finding a way out of the abyss, although Müller's careful choice of words indicates both the bravado of denial and its opposite. This is a classic instance of ambivalence in which the proclamation "I don't care" is proof that one cares very much indeed. But melancholy resignation rules over bravado. "My way out" implies knowledge of a goal and the energy and resolve to make his way there, and the wanderer believes himself possessed of neither one. "I am used to straying," he says drearily, resigned for the moment to the formless void that is his present and future. The only surcease he can imagine is in death; as every stream sooner or later flows into the ocean, so every sorrow is eventually obliterated in the grave. Ultimately, all joys and sorrows are as fleeting as the will-o'-the-wisp, a brief play of illusory light. If the tone is meditative and calm, the sense is not. The atmosphere is thick with the aimlessness of despair, and the peacefulness he invokes in the final verse is resignation to sorrow and a barely veiled longing for death.

And yet the wanderer's earlier recognition in "Erstarrung" that the sorrows of love and loss *do* end ("Wenn meine Schmerzen schweigen . . .") reappears in "Irrlicht" as a universal principle: everything, joy and sorrow alike, culminates in death. This is hardly optimism, but rather the expectation of ultimate surcease and the bleak place-

ment of his own misery within the larger context of countless lives
that come and go. It is cold comfort, this denial of meaning in individual experience, but comfort it is, for the moment, and the fact that
the solitary wanderer seeks in thought an alliance with the rest of
humanity ("*our* joys, *our* woes") is among the most striking aspects
of the poem. One detail of the landscape at the end seems multiply
significant. The *mise-en-scène* changes in stanza 3 (confirmation, if any
were needed, of an interior soulscape) to an image of the dry gulches
of a mountain stream bed by which the wanderer traces a descending
course. A protagonist who used to walk along the river bank with
his sweetheart and whose thoughts of her have flowed in watery
paths from the beginning now invokes "trock'ne Rinnen," as if ac-
knowledging that the wellsprings of passion are now dry. In "Gefror'ne Tränen" and "Auf dem Fluße," he feared emotional death
and therefore asserted fiery cauldrons and rushing torrents beneath
the frozen surface, but now, further withdrawn into alienation and
despair, he invokes dried-up river beds without even the possibility
of movement.

Schubert set "Irrlicht" in the B-minor tonality he had used before
for such desolate poems as the duet "Mignon und der Harfner," D.
877 ("Nur wer die Sehnsucht kennt"); "Die liebe Farbe" from *Die
schöne Müllerin*; "Der Leidende," D. 432 and D. 512; "Der Unglück-
liche," D. 713; "Grablied für die Mutter," D. 794; and, later, Ludwig
Rellstab's "In der Ferne," one of the *Schwanengesang* lieder. Beyond
the choice of the B-minor tonality, Schubert filled the lied with musical
symbols both obvious and not-so-obvious. Because the wanderer
meditates on ultimate endings in "Irrlicht," it seems only appropriate
that Schubert should set this text as a series of four-bar and two-bar
phrases each of which closes with a strong cadence. The wanderer's
desire for the journey's end is given musical representation in the
way he insists on endings. In particular, Arnold Feil suggests that
the entire song is stated *in nuce* in the introduction, its course of events
summed up in the cadential figures first presented there and then
elaborated throughout the body of the song. The "irre Gehen," or
straying motion, is represented in mm. 1–2—instead of the customary
progression I IV V I, Schubert reverses the interior pitches I V IV I,
while the more usual rhythmic succession of long-short durations in
$\frac{3}{8}$ meter is reversed, short-long, both compositional elements representative of staggering motion. The weary stumbling is followed by
a restitution of balance, a resolute cadence, in mm. 3–4 in which the
unharmonized final gesture in m. 4 reverses the descending motion
of those same pitches in m. 1. Uncertainty, life, pessimistic descent,

and staggering motion are symbolized by the musical gestures in mm. 1–2 and lead to certainty, ending, the grave, in mm. 3–4.[1] The directional symbolism of the vocal line is readily detectable, as when the initial phrase of stanza 1 falls to the lowest register of the cycle—Müller's abyss. At the beginning of stanza 2, the wanderer's statement that he is used to going astray is set to a varied version of mm. 5–6 in which dramatic ascending motion embellished with passing tones is juxtaposed with equally dramatic descending octaves. The line mimics "going astray," exaggerating direction both up and down within a single two-bar phrase spanning the range of a twelfth, virtually the entire vocal compass of the song. The phrase that follows ends with a miniature musical symbol of paths that each lead to the same goal ("'S'führt ja jeder Weg zum Ziel"): contrary motion between the vocal line and the soprano voice in the accompaniment, the two lines converging on the tonic pitch. In stanza 3, the descent along a dry stream bed wends its melodic way back down to tonic in the low register and the short-lived peacefulness ("'Wind' ich *ruhig* mich hinab") of a Picardy third cadence. One can also hear the alternation between unharmonized and harmonized phrases throughout the Stollen of this Bar form (stanzas 1 and 2) as a representation of the will-o'-the-wisp's flickering light.

On many occasions in this cycle, Schubert freely exercises the composer's perogative to make explicit in music the multiple interpretive possibilities the poet must leave implicit. In the twofold settings of the final lines of stanzas 1 and 2, Schubert translates the wanderer's ambiguity—his denial of concern and what lies beneath that denial—into successive cadences on different tonalities and with sharply contrasting rhythmic and melodic profiles, as he had done earlier in "Wasserflut." The first ending tells of bravado, the devil-may-care words that "doth protest too much" couched in the brightness of relative major, in a vaulting leap upward of a tenth and bold dotted rhythms, but the exaggerated assertiveness does not last long. Schubert then has the wanderer repeat the words "Liegt nicht schwer mir in dem Sinn" and "Alles eines Irrlichts Spiel" in the melancholy coloration of tonic B minor. The second time, it is the words "nicht schwer" (not heavily) that come to life in the anticipation tones, neighbor notes, and appoggiaturas that fill the vocal line, reminiscent of "Auf dem Wasser zu singen," D. 774, composed in 1823 to a text by Graf Leopold von Stollberg-Stollberg. The light impulsion of the thirty-second notes in the melodic line over a foundation of repeated

[1]Feil, *Franz Schubert*, 101–2.

chords occupies only eight bars (mm. 13–16, 25–28) of "Irrlicht,"
which is furthermore in a slow tempo, and fills the entire song in
"Auf dem Wasser zu singen," but in both instances Schubert associated this particular melodic manner with lightness, with the buoy-
ancy of a boat on the waves (in "Auf dem Wasser zu singen," a
metaphor for Time bearing each frail human bark to timeless realms
beyond life) or the wanderer's supposed lightness of mind. The same
cadential figure repeated in *Terzensteigerung* by the piano (mm. 15–
16, 27–28) confirms the reestablishment of B minor, the tonality be-
lying the assertion of uncaring and reinforcing the melancholy implicit
in the words. In the next song, "Rast," Schubert uses similar melodic
figuration for the words "Der Rücken fühlte keine Last" (My back
felt no burden) when the wanderer once again asserts an easy burden
and a light yoke.

  With the Abgesang (stanza 3), the composer introduces a new element of contrast, one not foretold in the Stollen: C major as the musical
symbol of the Protean struggle to achieve the destined goals of the
sea and the grave. Here, the Neapolitan tonality is given an epic
quality, the "journey to the sea" a heroic endeavor of vaulting lines
and full harmonies. There is only minimal peacefulness, or *Ruhigkeit*,
in the bass-soprano dissonances against the B–pedal point in mm.
29–32, before the turn to C major, but rather the tensions appropriate
to someone formulating such gloomy, grand conclusions. At the beginning of stanza 3, Schubert lays as heavy and shocking a stress on
the new chromatic pitch as he can, in preparation for the fuller revelation of its meaning to come in the following phrase. The contrast
between the Neapolitan key in major mode and tonic B minor, a
contrast rendered in the strongest cadential terms possible, is a revision of the poetry. Where Müller implies an analogy, Schubert states
a contrast between rivers that reach the sea in grand epic fashion and
sorrows that reach the grave, the wanderer's own B-minor sorrows.
In the end, the music lapses in defeat back into B minor. When the
wanderer reaches upward to G ("*auch* sein Grab") in m. 39, he attempts the epic vaulting grandeur of the C-major streams and tries
to assert that he too belongs to the greater world of Nature, but cannot
sustain the effort and slips back to B minor. And yet, although the
B-minor cadence from the previous stanzas returns (like a traditional
Abgesang, elements of the Stollen recur), the non-legato repeated
chords from the Stollen—the journeying figure—do not recur. The
wanderer, after all, sings of a future time when his journey will end.
The sense of defeat conveyed in the last vocal cadence, especially the
lapse from G to F-sharp, is confirmed all the more deeply by the lack

Text within the illustration: LOCK-TE MICH EIN IRR-LICHT HIN:

KOLO MOSER

8. Koloman Moser's *Lockte mich ein Irrlicht hin* as a *femme fatale*, 1897.
Courtesy Historisches Museum der Stadt Wien.

of separation between the end of stanza 3 and the beginning of the postlude, a repetition of the introduction. The last word, "Grab," is thus elided with the music that precedes verses about heedless straying. The implied contradiction is deliberate, and it says, "No grave, no rest yet, only more sorrow to come."

In a booklet presented to women at a municipal ball held in Vienna for the Schubert centenary in 1897, the Viennese artist Koloman Moser represented the *Irrlicht* as a *femme fatale* of the era, a flower-crowned rhapsode whose presumed nudity is swathed in snaky, flowing masses of hair—the *fin-de-siècle* visual emblem par excellence of dangerous female sexuality (Illus. 8). For Moser, the delusory thought that leads the wanderer into the abyss of melancholy is the thought of his lost sweetheart, mythologized as a seductive nixie complete with water lilies in her hair, silhouetted against the black background of Müller's crags and ravines. Even the stylized music staff that forms the caption metamorphoses at the right margin into still more decorative tendrils swirling about the *Irrlicht* in close kinship with the strongly corded locks of hair.[2] The image is neither Müller nor Schubert, but it *is* a fascinating demonstration of each generation's capacity to see and hear its own concerns, artistic and otherwise, mirrored in past works.

[2]The drawing is also reproduced in Robert Waissenberger, ed., *Vienna, 1890–1920* (New York, 1984), 124.

10. Rast

Nun merk' ich erst, wie müd' ich bin,
Da ich zur Ruh' mich lege;
Das Wandern hielt mich munter hin
Auf unwirtbarem Wege

Die Füße frugen nicht nach Rast,
Es war zu kalt zum Stehen,
Der Rücken fühlte keine Last,
Der Sturm half fort mich wehen.

In eines Köhlers engem Haus
Hab' Obdach ich gefunden;

[203]

Doch meine Glieder ruhn nicht aus:
So brennen ihre Wunden.

Auch du, mein Herz, im Kampf und Sturm
So wild und so verwegen,
Fühlst in der Still' erst deinen Wurm
Mit heißem Stich sich regen!

Rest

(Only now do I notice for the first time, as I lie down to rest, how tired I am; walking kept my spirits merry on the inhospitable road.

My feet did not seek rest; it was too cold to stand still. My back felt no burden: the storm helped blow me onward.

In a charcoal burner's cramped hut, I found shelter, but my limbs cannot rest, their wounds burn so.

You too, my heart, so wild and daring in storm and battle, for the first time in the calm feel your serpent sting you fiercely!)

As long as he continues on his way, the wanderer does not notice how tired he is because the act of wandering draws him along, occupying his entire awareness. Later, in "Das Wirtshaus," he will say that his "path" leads him on, but here he still experiences the journey as directionless wandering. As in "Der Wegweiser," he recognizes the inhospitable nature of the roads along which he travels, but he does not yet question why this should be. It is too cold to stand still, and the storm winds lighten the weight on his back, the wintry elements aiding and abetting his compulsion to journey on. The word "munter" in stanza 1 is a particularly striking detail of the poem, as desolate roads do not usually engender cheer in the travelers who find themselves there, but the sense of cheer—a word with bitterly sarcastic overtones—is relative to the gnawing misery he experiences when he attempts to rest. Then the motion of the journey is no longer a distraction from psychological torment, and the serpent within his heart, a vivid metaphor for pain, gives him no peace. Müller knew a much happier version of the compulsion to travel: the pleasure of going to different places, visiting the Webers and Mendelssohns, attending operas, and seeing the sights of Nature (he tells his wife, Adelheid, in one letter that a day spent outside enjoying the sights of Nature followed by an evening at the theater has afforded him the perfect delights of travel). In another letter, written in July 1826, he writes, "I love travel so much that no sooner am I seated in the coach, with the last of the city behind me, than I feel as free and fresh as a young lad."[1] The wanderer Müller created a few years earlier was not so fortunate, and yet the cheer he asserts when traveling ("Das Wandern hielt mich munter hin / Auf unwirtbarem Wege"), however relative, is a recognizable echo of the poet's own Wanderlust.

Schubert sets the four stanzas of Müller's poem as two musical strophes, the second slightly varied for reasons both of prosody and textual nuance. The strophic form may at first appear to be at odds with the poetic content, since "Rast" is divided into halves contrasting the journey outside in the winter storm with the shelter and stillness inside the charcoal burner's hut, yet Schubert sets each of the two halves to the same music. The repetition, however, reflects the underlying unity beneath the contrasts of motion/stillness, external/internal, cheer/pain. Whether he is inside or out in the storm, the wanderer is not at rest, and the change of place only underscores the unchanging spiritual malaise throughout. The wounds in his heart were there all along, even though he becomes aware of them only when he stops to rest.

In the introduction, Schubert represents trudging footsteps that continue nonstop, the motion of "feet that did not seek rest" and are not given respite anywhere in the song. Throughout each musical strophe, through the momentary references to relative major, through the deceptive cadences, through the singer's phrases, the footsteps plod onward inexorably, in a manner far from merry. The trudging left-foot–right-foot division between the two hands in the accompaniment, the mid-measure accents, and the reiterated rhythmic pattern, the staccato eighth note at the end of the measure an upbeat to impel continuation to the next measure, all speak of journeying without rest. The arch-shaped phrase, almost entirely over a tonic pedal in the bass, extends over a seamless six measures rather than the conventional four or eight bars, its nonmelodic character strongly marked. The small ascent in the soprano voice is hardly lyricism in flight, and neither is the restricted chromatic voice-leading in the inner voices. This irregularly shaped piano introduction ends inconclusively, hanging in mid-air on a dominant chord prolonged by a fermata, and finds tonic resolution only in m. 7 at the singer's verb "merk," to notice. The mood of dispirited exhaustion is already apparent before the singer enters.

[1] Wilhelm Müller, *Diary and Letters of Wilhelm Müller*, 137, 147.

To the vivid sound picture of a constant, muffled, heavy tread in
the introduction and stanza 1, Schubert adds more details as the
wanderer recounts reasons for his journeying compulsion: it was too
cold to stand still, and the storm lightened his load and drove him
along. Schubert retains the near-omnipresent rhythmic pattern in the
accompaniment to mm. 17–20 ("Die Füße frugen nicht nacht Rast, /
Es war zu kalt zum Stehen"), but the rising octave figures must have
seemed too static for the verbal emphasis on motion, and he therefore
substitutes dissonant appoggiaturas as a piercing goad to keep going.
The words too "did not seek rest," the composer compressing four
iambs into little more than a measure, while the harmonic progression
likewise refuses to settle anywhere but rather moves through a parallel
six-three sequence embellished with seventh chords. The reach upward to C at the apex of the vocal phrase for the word "nicht" to
emphasize the negation and the chilling touch of minor at the word
"kalt" are other refinements of Schubert's text-setting art, by a happy
coincidence, equally expressive in stanza 4. There, the ascent to the
tonic degree heightens the word "Kampf" ("Auch du, mein Herz, in
Kampf und Sturm") and the enharmonic leading tone underscores
the adjective "so" in telling emphasis: "So wild und *so* verwegen."
    As the wanderer continues his account of the storm winds pushing
him along, Schubert continues to avoid a resting place. At the words
"Die Rücken fühlte keine Last" (mm. 21–22), the music correspond-
ingly lightens, relieved of some of its weight by means of pianissimo
dynamics, the leap into a higher vocal tessitura, and a momentary
suspension of harmonic forward progress. The passage is poised for
almost three measures on a single diminished seventh chord, the
effect one of remarkable unease. The appoggiaturas, passing tones,
anticipation tones, and sixteenth-note rhythms associated in "Irrlicht"
with the light motion of the will-o'-the-wisp and the wanderer's as-
sumption of uncaring nonchalance recur here in a different context
and a different melodic profile. But with the last line of stanzas 2 and
4, lightness suddenly becomes force. Of all Schubert's many means
in this song of conveying the dogged, painful nature of the journey
at this point, one of the most powerful is the deceptive movement in
mm. 24–25, 54–55, especially as the deceptive submediant harmony
in mm. 25 and 55 is followed in each instance, not by resolution, but
by a recurrence of the eerie diminished seventh chord. The full A-
flat-major triad in the bass is vitiated of its third and becomes a hollow
fifth, joined by the remaining pitches of the prolonged dissonance.
The avoidance of tonic closure propels the music farther ahead, as
the wind pushes the wanderer along—and with similar force. It seems

only appropriate that Schubert elides the end of the vocal part with the final recurrence of the introduction in yet another musical representation of the continuing journey, like the similar elision with which "Irrlicht" ends.

11. Frühlingstraum

Ich träumte von bunten Blumen,
So wie sie wohl blühen im Mai,
Ich träumte von grünen Wiesen,
Von lustigem Vogelgeschrei.

Und als die Hähne krähten,
Da ward mein Auge wach;
Da war es kalt und finster,
Es schrieen die Raben vom Dach.

Doch an den Fensterscheiben
Wer malte die Blätter da?

[208]

Ihr lacht wohl über den Träumer,
Der Blumen im Winter sah?

Ich träumte von Lieb' um Liebe,
Von einer schönen Maid,
Von Herzen und von Küssen,
Von Wonne und Seligkeit.

Und als die Hähne krähten,
Da ward mein Herze wach;
Nun sitz' ich hier alleine
Und denke dem Traume nach.

Die Augen schließ' ich wieder,
Noch schlägt das Herz so warm.
Wann grünt ihr Blätter am Fenster?
Wann halt' ich mein Liebchen im Arm?
[Wann halt' ich dich, Liebchen, im Arm?]

Dream of Spring

(I dreamed of bright flowers that blossom in May. I dreamed of
green meadows, of merry bird calls.
    And when the cocks crowed, my eyes awoke: it was cold and dark,
and the ravens screeched from the rooftop.
    But who painted the leaves there on the window panes? Are you
laughing at the dreamer who saw flowers in winter?
    I dreamed of mutual love, of a beautiful maiden, of embraces and
kisses, joy and rapture.
    And when the cocks crowed, my heart awoke: now I sit here all
alone and reflect upon the dream.
    I close my eyes again; my heart still beats so warmly. When will
you turn green, leaves on the window? When shall I hold my love
in my arms?)

    The wanderer at last falls asleep and dreams of a springtime vista
that closely resembles the idyllic memories in "Rückblick," with Maytime flowers, green meadows, and birdsong. Twice he is awakened,
startled out of sleep by the cocks' crowing and the screeching of ravens
outside on the roof. The first time, he is able to go back to sleep and
recapture his dream, but when he is once more awakened in the same
way, it is irretrievably gone. He is left desolate, the cold, darkness,

and isolation all the more painful in comparison with the Arcadian loveliness of his dream vision.

Müller is adept at suggesting what causes or influences the mysterious passage from present awareness to memory, from dreams to wakefulness or the reverse. The description of the dream landscape in the first verse ends with the joyful sounds of birds singing (reminiscent of the lark and nightingale in contention from "Rückblick"); at that instant, the dream is abruptly interrupted by bird cries of a different sort, the harsh cawing of ravens and roosters. (The lilting combination of anapests and iambs in the first stanza gives way in the second stanza to three lines of unrelieved iambs, the poetic pace notably quicker than in the first verse.) When the wanderer's eyes open ("Da ward mein Auge wach"), Müller implies that the wanderer's *senses* have been brought back to the real world, that he is once again aware of the cold, the darkness, the harsh sounds, but that his heart is still engaged in the dream world, to which he then returns. The wanderer dreams of sights, sounds, and scents in the first verse, and, in exact parallel, it is his senses alone that are roused to reality when the cocks crow for the first time.

Having just dreamed of green fields and flowers, the awakened wanderer in stanza 3 looks about him, sees what appear to be leaves on the window panes, the winter frost mimicking the patterns and forms of living Nature, and asks who painted them. Before he goes back to sleep, rejoining his dream, he wonders if the artist (Nature? God the creator of inherently fickle love in "Gute Nacht"?) who made ice crystals as simulacra of greenery mocks him for his Maytime visions out of season—another hint of the wanderer's disbelief in a divine order, except as a cruel entity disposed to mockery. Significantly, the wanderer speaks of his imaginative inner self, that which has conjured up his dreams of love and springtime, as "the dreamer." Once again, the third-person address bespeaks the wanderer's awareness of different selves long before the final self-division at the end of the cycle. The later renunciation of dreams in "Im Dorfe" has its roots in the uneasy sense expressed here that dreaming can only arouse the scorn of whatever malevolent force exists beyond human knowledge.

There is no answer to his questions, and the frost patterns on the window are his avenue back to Arcadia. Since he dreams this time of hearts, reciprocal love, blessedness, and "a beautiful maiden," it is no longer just his senses, but his heart, the inner emotional being that distilled the dream vision from his own past experience, that is roused when the cocks crow yet again. A return to the dream is no longer possible, although he closes his eyes once more in a vain attempt to recapture it while its aftermath still lingers on, perceptible in the warmth of his heartbeat. The vision gone beyond recall, the wanderer once again asks himself questions, wondering when and if unreality might become real: when will the leaves truly deck the window frames in green, and when will he hold his beloved in his arms? The first question is metaphorical, not meteorological, a way of asking when his wintry misery will give way to renewed life and hope, but there are no answers, not even any expectation of an answer. In their impossibility, the questions put an end to the poem.

It is rare in *Winterreise* to find a passage of any length that is almost entirely diatonic, and the first fourteen measures of "Frühlingstraum" are a privileged moment in the cycle. The wanderer's dream of springtime and love becomes perfect musical symmetry, grace, and tonal clarity, the only chromaticism the E-sharp neighbor notes in mm. 3 and 11 ("lustigem Vogelgeschrei") that will shortly be enharmonically reinterpreted as bird cries of another sort and as waking reality; the first F-natural appears in m. 18 beneath the word "wach." The wide-ranging melodic lines, weak-beat accents, and complex harmonies throughout most of the winter journey are banished entirely from this dream. Instead, a simple broken-chordal accompaniment in the right hand (the dream is restricted to a narrow middle register, without extremes of height or depth) flows without interruption, an Arcadian stream, beneath a melody whose poignancy is only partly definable. One can point to the motivic unity created by the neighbor-note cell figures, to the expressive ascending sixths in the vocal line (E–C-sharp, F-sharp–D) that frame the stanza on either side, to the tonic-submediant progression in mm. 5–6 that Schubert earlier used with such telling effect in "Im Frühling," but perhaps the essence of the passage has to do with the Schubertian dialectic between Classicism and Romanticism. Here, traits of the classical language appear in a distillate form in which the ambiguities and tensions of the style are expunged, to be followed and displaced by more contemporary stresses and strains, by the chromaticism of the "Schnell" sections. The eighteenth-century gestures in "Frühlingstraum" are, literally, a dream set apart, one whose perfection cannot last.

"Frühlingstraum" is a study in contrasts and disjunctions, the silences between sections dramatizing the shocking changes of tempo, voicing, motion, tonal direction, and mood. These are among the most striking instances in *Winterreise* of what one might call "sounding silences," filled with expectation or suspense about what is to follow. (Only the transition from stanza 3 to stanza 4, the resumption of the dream, is bridged by sound rather than silence, by an arpeggio that lifts the music up from the lowest depths of the *Langsam* section back to the register of the dream. At the end of the entire song, the final A-minor chord can be heard as a barrier against the recurrence of that gesture, against the now-impossible extension of the dream into a third episode.) The dream in stanza 1 is self-enclosed but too short to constitute an entire song; a listener who did not know the poetry and whose expectations were dependent on the unfolding musical structure might expect to hear another strophe to the same music or the continuation of the dream setting in a second tonal area. Instead, the lucid diatonic strains are replaced by tense, rising chromatic sequences in the vocal line (reminiscent of the rising tension in stanza 2 of "Die Wetterfahne," similarly expressed), and the serene broken-chordal figuration by accompaniment as explosive punctuation. The dissonances so violently displaced into the upper register are onomatopoeia for the harsh sounds of the screeching birds, but they are expressive as well of the ugliness of waking reality and the shock of the rude awakening. The riccocheting two-bar fragments immediately overthrow the A major of the dream and replace it with rapid, unstable motion and insistent minor mode, culminating in parallel minor to the dream. Everywhere there is dissonance; no sooner does one tone cluster resolve than another, equally abrasive, succeeds it. The dark side of the idyll is a reality so entirely different that the cause-and-effect relationship between them becomes paradoxically clear and their shared tonic all too appropriate. Dreadful reality produces the need for such a dream, although the vision is too fragile to resist reality's greater force for long. Furthermore, despite the fast tempo and chromaticism of stanza 2, the meter and motivic material are those of the dream. Not yet fully awake, Schubert's wanderer clings to disintegrating fragments of the springtime reverie until it is utterly swept away in the measured tremolos and piercing dissonances of the final four bars of the stanza.

In this song, the major mode of imagination's bright realm is doomed always to be displaced by minor, and the wanderer's musings in the third and sixth stanzas meet with the same fate. The A-major tonality of the dream can no longer sound in its former diatonic purity but returns slightly destabilized, shifting as the wanderer "reflects upon the dream." In the autograph manuscript, Schubert at first wrote a different key signature for the *Langsam* sections, but whatever it was, he scored through it too thoroughly for us to decipher now. Instead, he chose to retain the key signature of the dream to call it into question, to make it a slightly uncertain quantity as the monologist wonders about his reverie. Is he mocked for his dreams? Will the dream ever become reality? I have elsewhere proposed that Schubert's accompaniments mimic wordless motion within the wanderer's mind (in the introduction to "Der Lindenbaum," for example), and the relationship between the ends of stanzas 2 and 5 and the beginnings of stanzas 3 and 6 is another example. The piano introduction to the *langsam* verses recasts figures from the preceding cadence in another meter, tempo, and key; that is, the slow A-major arpeggiation in the bass (mm. 27–28) begins with the exact pitches that conclude the fortissimo A-minor harmony (m. 26) at the end of stanzas 2 and 4.[1] After waking abruptly from his dream, the wanderer stops as if frozen in shock; from shock, he drifts wearily into thought. Those thoughts begin from the point where the flurry of turbulent motion stopped and rise from within to reach articulation in words.

By the ends of stanzas 3 and 6, major mode is entirely vanquished by minor. Despite the tonic closure in the vocal line, the articulation in A major at mm. 35–36 is weak, with C-sharp rather than the root in the bass, and minor mode follows on its heels, a melancholy certainty to the end of the stanza. One of the most painful details in the third stanza is the appearance of minor for the first time in the verse at the verb "lacht," or "laugh" ("Ihr lacht wohl über den Träumer . . . "), all the more moving for its quietness and lack of bluster. When the wanderer notices the ice leaves on the window, he can still cling to the tonality of the dream, but when he reflects on the creator of such mockery, he lapses into the minor mode of tragedy and waking reality. In yet another example of strophic serendipity in this cycle, the division of this stanza into major- and minor-mode passages is equally appropriate for stanza 6, where the wanderer attempts to hold onto his dream ("Die Augen schließ ich wieder, / Noch schlägt das Herz so warm") in its major tonality, then asks pained questions in minor, "Wann grünt ihr Blätter am Fenster? / Wann halt' ich mein Liebchen im Arm?" The first invocation of the last line of these stanzas—"Der Blumen im Winter sah?" and "Wann halt' ich mein Liebchen im Arm?"—stretches back up to the higher register in perceptible yearning, another painful detail among so many in this song.

Placing Schubert's setting of "Frühlingstraum" side by side with Kreutzer's setting from the *Ländliche Lieder von Wilhelm Müller*, Op. 80 (see the chapter on "Der Lindenbaum"), one realizes yet again the

---

[1]Those two measures of piano introduction were an addition at stage 2 in the autograph manuscript. Schubert clearly saw the need for a transition to the briefly tonicized subdominant at the beginning of the *langsam* stanzas and created one that is a direct outgrowth of what comes before it.

dramatic difference between Kreutzer's strategy of suppression in strophic songs such as this, typical of so much of the Biedermeier song repertoire, and Schubert's more profound and detailed reading of the text. Composers often—perhaps always—ignore aspects of the poetry they appropriate for musical setting, but Kreutzer has to suppress far more than Schubert did to unify his twenty-eight-bar musical strophe by means of a single conventional broken-chordal pattern in the accompaniment (Ex. 29). Recognizing, like Schubert, the paral-

Example 29.   Kreutzer's "Frühlingstraum," from *Ländliche Lieder*, Op. 80

lelism between the two halves of the poem, he repeats the music of stanzas 1–3 for stanzas 4–6, but there are none of the bone-jarring contrasts between the different states of wakefulness and dreaming which one finds in Schubert. In his typical fashion, Kreutzer selects certain images for modest text-painting—the ravens screech to heavier chordal harmonies accented on the offbeats, and the fantasy of scornful laughter ("Ihr lacht wohl über den Träumer, / Der Blumen im Winter sah?") at the end of stanza 3 inspired the climactic rise to the peak of the musical strophe—but the sense of shock, the drift back into dream, the fluidity of newly awakened consciousness, all of this and more of Müller's depths remain unplumbed . . . until Schubert.

Throughout *Winterreise*, especially in Part I, Schubert contrasts parallel or relative major and minor modes as musical symbols of the polarity between memory and the present moment, imagination and outward perception, happy past and tragic present, what one scholar has called "Schubert's tragic perspective."[2] In "Frühlingstraum," that tragic dichotomy is presented in the starkest terms. The vision of earthly paradise conjured up by the imagination exists only to be destroyed by a battering ram compounded of dissonance, tonal instability, and the darkness of minor. The disjunctions are not and cannot be resolved into a unity that will fully embrace and then dissolve the contrasts. Synthesis is not possible, and therefore the ending of "Frühlingstraum" has a particular dreary melancholy that comes from awareness of an ideal but illusory world vanished beyond recall.

[2]William Kinderman, "Schubert's Tragic Perspective," in Frisch, *Schubert: Critical and Analytical Studies*, 65–83. Kinderman cites Hans Heinrich Eggebrecht's statement in "Prinzipien des Schubert-Liedes" (*Archiv für Musikwissenschaft* 27 [1970], 96) that "in Schubert's songs, major and minor are often juxtaposed with one another as the illusory world of beautiful, bright dreams to the real world of banal, wretched, naked reality."

12. Einsamkeit

Wie eine trübe Wolke
Durch heitre Lüfte geht,
Wenn [Wann] in der Tanne Wipfel
Ein mattes Lüftchen weht:

[216]

So zieh' ich meine Straße
Dahin mit trägem Fuß,
Durch helles, frohes Leben,
Einsam und ohne Gruß.

Ach, daß die Luft so ruhig!
Ach, daß die Welt so licht!
Als noch die Stürme tobten,
War ich so elend nicht.

Loneliness

(As a dark cloud drifts through clear skies, when a faint breeze
blows through the fir branches—
Thus I go on my way with dragging feet, through bright, happy
life alone and without greeting.
Alas, that the air is so calm! Alas, that the world is so bright! While
the storms still raged, I was not so miserable.)

The wanderer, his scant sleep broken by interrupted dreams, continues saddened and exhausted, "with dragging feet," on his journey.
In the aftermath of "Frühlingstraum," he is obsessed with his loneliness and sense of difference from others, and he imagines analogies
in Nature both for his slow, tired motion and the marks of his separation from others. (It is a disturbing measure of his alienation that
the standard of comparison, here as elsewhere, is not to be found in
living beings, but in nonhuman Nature.) He is, he says, like a dismal
cloud, barely propelled through the treetops by a small and weary
puff of air. Other people, more vital and energetic than he, are "heitre
Lüfte," while the wanderer himself is a "mattes Lüftchen," smaller
than the other breezes. Although diminutives abound in *Die schöne
Müllerin*—"Sternlein," "Bächlein," "Waldvögelein," "Blüm'lein" (little star, little stream, little forest bird, little flower)—and tell of Nature
as a friend and companion to the miller lad, they are rare in *Die
Winterreise*. The word "Lüftchen" conveys, not a sense of kinship
with his surroundings but rather weakness and diminished size, a
self shrunken and clouded by melancholy, unlike other, more fortunate inhabitants of the "world so bright."
At the center of the poem is the bright/dark polarity of the "dark
cloud" and the "bright, happy life" through which the wanderer
passes. Once again, one realizes how precise and powerful Müller's
unassuming language so often is in this cycle: the wanderer does not

speak of "people," but of "life" in implicit recognition that his own deadened, alienated existence is not truly living. He is so separated from others that they do not even acknowledge his presence; for all his difference, he is invisible to others. In "Gute Nacht," he feared the hostility of other people, but matters have worsened since that time, and he now sees himself as eliciting no response at all. When Schubert prolongs the stressed syllable of the first iamb in "Ein-samkeit"—"Wie *ei* - ne trübe Wolke"—in seeming contradiction of its syntactical unimportance, he underscores the wanderer's acute sense of loneliness, interpreting the words "as a dark cloud" to read "as a *single, lonely* dark cloud." When the same melodic phrase is repeated to the words "Wenn *in* der Tanne Wipfel," the small over-emphasis on the preposition "in" can no longer be considered an expressive prolongation for interpretive reasons, but the repetition has other purposes that justify the atypically faulty prosody. The second half of the simile in stanza 1 sounds to the same music as the first half, as if the wanderer is too depressed and lethargic to change his tune.

Although there are no obvious thematic connections between the two poems, Müller allows us to suppose that the wanderer's renewed awareness of his solitary state in "Frühlingstraum" ("Nun sitz' ich hier alleine"—"Now I sit here all alone") has given rise to the meditation on loneliness that follows. "Einsamkeit" is the consequence of "Frühlingstraum" in another sense as well, a repudiation of the spring vision in his dream. Now the wanderer asserts that he prefers winter storms to sunshine and peaceful breezes, despite his earlier wistful memories of spring. He feels less wretched—not happy, merely less miserable—in a blizzard than in benevolent weather. He consciously allies himself with everything in Nature that is inimical to others because there he finds the analogues to his own turmoil and isolation. Beauty and brightness are for other people, not for him; rejecting illusion for reality (*his* reality), he wishes for ice, snow, and storm. In another instance of Müller's poetic economy, his choice of minimal words for maximum effect, the syntax of the paired lamentations "Ach, daß die Luft so ruhig! / Ach, daß die Welt so licht!" reveals by omission. The wanderer does not say "Oh, that the breeze *is* so peaceful! Oh, that the world *is* so light!" because for him, they are not.[1]

---

[1]Müller had earlier written similar exclamations in the fifth stanza of "Erster Schmerz, letzter Scherz" (First sorrow, last jest), the seventeenth poem of *Die schöne Müllerin* and the second of the three poems Schubert omitted from his setting of the cycle. In "Erster Schmerz, letzter Scherz," the miller imagines the hunter and miller maid making

The setting of the first verse is diatonic and harmonically limited, a graphic demonstration in sound of a protagonist too weary and dispirited to summon the strength for anything beyond those few harmonies in B minor. Everything about the setting of the first stanza bespeaks minimal, mechanical motion. The B pedal point throughout the introduction and first stanza (mm. 1–14); the unchanged repetition of the first vocal phrase; the narrow, middle register, without heights or depths; the constant, slow, eighth-note tactus, without pause or break; and even the lack of a pause separating the introduction from the texted body of the song (the wanderer's words join the weary motion already in progress) are all musical metaphors for the way-farer's exhausted, plodding progress. The vocal line too seems de-pleted of energy, barely able to raise itself to the C-sharps at "Wol - ke" and "Wip - fel" and then falling away from that peak, the ex-hausted confinement to a semitone at the beginning a gesture that confirms how tired he is. It is only with stanza 2 and the completion of the analogy to the wanderer's own bleak situation that the bass finally moves, if not very far, and the melodic line widens in a var-iation of the first phrase. The endings of the vocal phrases in stanza 2 were originally diatonic, culminating on the tonic pitch, but Schubert revised those phrases in the autograph manuscript such that the pass-ing tone E-sharp leads to the dominant and foreshadows the accented F-naturals of stanza 3. The half-cadence is unharmonized, Schubert's infrequent and therefore all the more powerful way of heightening moments of especially austere inwardness in this cycle. Here, the wanderer's bitter reflection that he is "alone and without greeting" leads to the outburst of lamentation in the final stanza, lamentation that unleashes motion and chromatic turbulence beyond his capacity in stanzas 1 and 2. Active despair suddenly wells up and overwhelms the leaden bleakness of the first two verses.

Schubert divides the song into contrasting zones of static diatoni-cism and chromatic turbulence, and the latter caused him considerable difficulty. Of all the visible signs of struggle in Part I of the autograph manuscript, those evident on folio 20 verso (the setting of stanza 3) are among the most dramatic. It is no wonder that he wrote the word "Fine" at the end of Part I with such a bravado flourish, after struggles as intense as those apparent in "Einsamkeit," the end of the cycle—

---

making love and cries out in anguish: "Ein Jäger, ein grüner Jäger, / Der liegt in ihrem Arm— / Ei, Bach, wie lustig du rauschest! / Ei, Sonne, wie scheinst du so warm!" (A hunter, a green-clad hunter lies in her arms—O brook, how merrily you babble! O sun, how warmly you shine!). In "Einsamkeit," Nature once again is at odds with the protagonist's misery.

or so he thought at the time. On folio 20 verso, Schubert wrote the vocal line for the initial version of mm. 21–39, filling in the accompaniment for mm. 24–30 in the brown ink of stage 1 before crossing out everything on the page with impatient, slashing strokes of the pen, his frustration clearly visible. Because of the need to revise everything on folio 20 verso, Schubert did not bother with his usual crosshatching marks of deletion over single pitches and chords, resorting instead to large X's, and therefore the initial version is plain to see. Much of what is sketched on this page was kept when he made a fair copy of the last half of his song to complete the manuscript—the tremolando diminished seventh chords, the "sighing figure" in the upper register of m. 25 whose accented A-flat prefigures the G-sharp and A-flats of the crucial dominant seventh and German sixth chords to follow, and the triplet chords for the rising storm ("als noch die Stürme tobten"), but the jagged, tritone-laden vocal line is remarkably awkward.[2] If one needed further evidence of Schubert's willingness to dispense with conventional lyricism in this cycle and replace it with a harsher, deeper beauty, it is here. Schubert initially set the last line of text exactly as one finds it in Müller, "War ich so elend nicht," without the inspired masterstroke of the internal text repetition, "War ich so elend, so elend nicht" in the final version. The difference between "misery" and "less misery" may not be much, but the wanderer wishes for the latter anyway; Schubert's side-by-side polarization dramatizes the difference between the two states.

In the transition to stanza 3, Schubert once again suggests mental or emotional stirrings in the wanderer's mind between stanzas of Müller's text, finds instrumental symbols for the process that leads to words. It is the painful words "einsam und ohne Gruß" (alone and without greeting) at the end of stanza 2 that impel the outburst of lamentation, "Ach, daß die Luft so ruhig!" and Schubert makes the connection apparent musically. The ascent in the piano in mm. 22–23, which proceeds seamlessly from the cadence "und ohne Gruß" just before it, takes the intervals of the cadential motive in mm. 21–22—a minor third and successive semitones—and extends them, registrally displaced, until the voice joins in with the first lamenting

---

[2]Schubert had earlier associated an emphatically outlined tritone in the vocal line with a poetic motif of isolation so profound as to be almost unbearable. In his September 1816 setting of Goethe's "Lied der Mignon" ("Nur wer die Sehnsucht kennt," or "Mignon's Song—Only he who knows longing"), D. 481, Schubert sets the word "Allein [und abgetrennt von aller Freude]" (Alone and cut off from all joy) in m. 5 to a blatant descending leap of a tritone.

phrase (that is, the G–E–E-sharp–F-sharp pitches of the words "und ohne Gruß" flow into the F-sharp G-natural semitone and the outlined diminished seventh chord G–A-sharp–C-sharp–E of the piano transition). After the restricted motion and the few weary diatonic chords of stanzas 1 and 2, the lamentations are tonally unsettled and unstable, beginning with a series of semitone-related diminished seventh chords which resolve on the distant harmony of the lowered VII, A major. In the transposition of "Einsamkeit" from its original D minor to B minor, the A-major harmony of clear skies and peaceful breezes is additionally the smallest of references to the A major of the "Frühlingstraum" dreams. Just when the triplet sixteenth chords of the rising storm seem headed back to the wanderer's own B-minor climate in m. 28, there is a deflection that culminates on the dominant of C major. If one accepts C major as the key of Nature in its most grandiose manifestations, then "Irrlicht" and "Einsamkeit" have more than their principal tonality in common. In each, the Neapolitan tonal contrast in the last section of the form epitomizes the contrast between sublimity in Nature—streams that reach the ocean in "Irrlicht," raging tempests in "Einsamkeit"—and the wanderer's black misery. In both, C major does not last, but is displaced by the B minor emblematic of desolation. At the invocation of the wanderer's misery ("War ich so elend") in mm. 31–32, the "dragging feet" figures from the introduction (mm. 3–5) recur, but in a C major still unresolved over its dominant pedal. At the word "elend," the effort to bring about the storminess he longs for cannot be sustained, and the dominant seventh of C is respelled as its enharmonic equivalent, the German sixth of B minor. With that harmonic gesture, the wanderer lapses back into the tonality of stanzas 1 and 2. Sinking back to B minor in this fashion is defeat translated into tonal terms.

The wanderer does not accept defeat without a struggle, however, and repeats the entire third stanza. This time, the transition in the piano and the two-bar vocal phrase that follows ("Ach! daß die Luft so ruhig!") are varied to foreshadow the dominant of C major before the attempt to establish that key as the new tonal realm, to displace B minor with a key more to his liking. Now the wanderer knows the goal he wishes and bends the passage in that direction earlier than he had done before. But the remainder of the passage is an almost literal reenactment of the same defeat he had suffered before, the repetition implying the wanderer's incapacity to imagine some other way that might successfully oust his B-minor desolation and replace it with the new, brighter, distant key. The final measure of his defeat is apparent in the postlude, only minimally deserving of the name. Schubert simply repeats the final tonic chord in the trudging rhythms of the introduction. The outbursts of lamentation have left the wanderer even wearier and more miserable than he was at the beginning of the song.

13. Die Post

Von der Straße her ein Posthorn klingt.
Was hat es, daß es so hoch aufspringt,
    Mein Herz?

Die Post bringt keinen Brief für dich.
Was drängst du denn so wunderlich,
    Mein Herz?

Nun ja, die Post kommt aus der Stadt,
Wo ich ein liebes Liebchen hatt',
Mein Herz!

Willst wohl einmal hinübersehn,
Und fragen, wie es dort mag gehn,
Mein Herz?

The Post

(A posthorn sounds from the road. Why do you leap so high, my heart?
The post brings you no letter: why then do you surge so strangely, my heart?
But yes, the post comes from the town where I once had a beloved sweetheart, my heart!
Do you want to peer out and ask how things are there, my heart?)

Capell calls "Die Post" the "problem of the *Winterreise*" and writes that, although it "does well enough" in Müller's sequence, "its lightness is out of keeping with the tragic wanderer who is soon to say, 'Ich bin zu Ende mit allen Träumen' " in "Im Dorfe.'"[1] According to Capell, Schubert in October 1827 ("Die Post" was composed before that date) might not have recalled right away the "passion and significance with which he had charged [the songs] composed earlier in the year," or perhaps, he proposed, the song was conceived as inappropriate comic relief from the bleakness on either side. A closer look at Müller's poem and Schubert's setting, however, reveals more than a quaint genre picture of bygone times and a purpose beyond comic relief. In Schubert's placement, the song acts to revitalize the journey at a point of low ebb after "Einsamkeit" and shows the wanderer once again probing his heart, questioning the mystery of an unexpected strong reaction to a sound he hears. The sounds are not inner voices this time, as in "Der Lindenbaum," but come from the outside world and jolt the wanderer out of the leaden apathy one hears at the end of "Einsamkeit." I have already discussed the significance of the moment in the second chapter: the poem is an essential clue to the meaning of the journey.

---

[1]Capell, *Schubert's Songs*, 242.

Müller often borrowed themes from other poets and poems for use in his own works, including the Romantic image of the posthorn as emblematic of Wanderlust. The unhappy persona of Ludwig Tieck's "Der Posthornschall" (The posthorn fanfare) hears the postilion's signals as an invitation to escape his sorrow ("Weit weg, weit weg, / Von allen Schmerzen weg"—"Far away, far away, distant from all sorrow") by fleeing to distant and exotic lands, only to find that his loneliness and grief follow him wherever he goes,[2] and Schubert's friend Moritz von Schwind fashioned an engraving titled *Der Postillon bläst sein Abschiedslied* (The postilion blows his call to departure),[3] to cite only two examples. Müller, who had elsewhere borrowed from Joseph von Eichendorff's verse,[4] possibly found in one of Eichendorff's most famous poems, "Sehnsucht,"[5] a springboard for his own imagination. Like Müller's wanderer, the poetic persona in "Sehnsucht" hears a posthorn in the distance ("aus weiter Ferne / Ein Posthorn im stillen Land") and his heart flames in response ("Das Herz mir im Leib entbrennte"), the mysterious heart-felt agitation the essence of Romantic longing for something unknown and faraway. The posthorn fanfares are the goad to awaken longing and to impel journeys in search of whatever fresh experiences might appease the restless, indefinable desire. Müller, however, adapts the theme to his own quite different ends. His wanderer, already en route to an unknown goal, cares only to question why he has felt this inexplicable emotional surge in response to the sound. What he feels is not *Sehnsucht*, or Romantic yearning, but issues from some other source. Müller had earlier written an unusually lengthy poem (fourteen quatrains) titled "Des Postillons Morgenlied vor der Bergschenke" (The postilion's morning song before the mountain inn, printed in the

---

[2] Ludwig Tieck, *Gedichte* (Berlin, 1841), 41–43.
[3] Reproduced in Günter Böhmer, *Die Welt des Biedermeier* (Munich, 1977), 219.
[4] See Joachim Schulze, "O Bächlein meiner Liebe: Zu einem unheimlichen Motiv bei Eichendorff und Wilhelm Müller," *Poetica* 4 (April 1971), 215–23. Cecilia Baumann, in *Wilhelm Müller*, discusses Müller's borrowings from Goethe, Schiller, Tieck, Friedrich de la Motte-Fouqué, August Bürger, Ludwig Uhland, Thomas Moore, and others as "springboards for his imagination" (44). She also points out the strong parallel between Müller's "Ungeduld" in *Die schöne Müllerin* and Edmund Spenser's "Colin Clouts Come Home Again": "Her name in every tree I will enbosse, / That as the trees do grow, her name may grow; / And in the ground each where will it engrosse, / And fill with stones that men may it know."
[5] Joseph von Eichendorff, *Werke I* (Stuttgart, 1953), 35. See also the third of his *Wandersprüche*, ibid., 45: "Was willst auf dieser Station / So breit dich niederlassen? / Wie bald nicht bläst der Postillon, / Du müßt doch alles lassen" (Why do you settle down at this roadside station? As soon as the coachman blows his horn, you will have to leave it all behind).

Waldhornisten I), in which the coachman's horn calls are a greeting to his sweetheart, a sound with the power to enliven and arouse. That poem, however, is a lighter, brighter, more stereotypical treatment of the familiar theme than its enigmatic and original transformation in "Die Post."

In "Die Post," Müller departs from the quatrain form that prevails throughout the cycle and writes stanzas that consist of a single rhyming couplet in iambic tetrameters followed by the brief refrain "Mein Herz." In two of the four stanzas, a short, declarative statement is then followed by a longer question, while the final stanza is a single question, the wanderer once again probing his inner emotional being for knowledge of its mysteries. The refrain is a folkish touch of a kind not found anywhere else in the cycle; by means of its rhythmic recurrence, Müller underscores the fact that the wanderer's heart is an entity distinct from the rational, questioning self. In an attempt to explore the mysterious rush of feeling logically, the wanderer first explains to his heart/himself that there can be no letter for him and then asks again what the "odd" emotion is. With the third stanza, he believes he has the answer to his questions in stanzas 1 and 2 and concludes with a different sort of question, an afterthought to the "answer" in stanza 3. Müller's words belie the seeming certainty, however, and cast doubt on the wanderer's proposed solution to the mystery. The folk-song-like alliteration of "ein liebes Liebchen" sounds rather like a jingle, and "to peer out and ask how things are there" has little emotional content beyond an ill-defined, almost disinterested, momentary curiosity. When Schubert sets the supposed answer "Nun ja, die Post kommt aus der Stadt" to the music of stanza 1, with its question "Was hat es, daß es so hoch aufspringt?" he makes explicit the fact that the "answer" is no answer at all. The question still resounds musically throughout the proposed explanation, contradicting it.

Conradin Kreutzer set "Die Post" as the sixth song in his *12 Lieder und Romanzen* of Op. 76, published by Kistner in Leipzig. "Die Post. Aus Wilhelm Müller's Winterliedern" was also printed in the *Wiener Zeitschrift* for 1826, and there is every likelihood that Schubert could have known the song, which precedes his own setting. The Viennese publication date gives rise to yet another question about the genesis of Schubert's cycle: if Schubert had found Kreutzer's song in the *Wiener Zeitschrift*, a song clearly labeled "Aus Wilhelm Müller's Winterliedern," might he not have wondered, as he was composing Part I, about the existence of other winter songs by Müller not included in his *Urania* source? "Die Post" is vintage Kreutzer, harmonically

more conservative than Schubert's lied but with an occasional colorful
detail and ample evidence of the composer's concern for text expression. Looking at the two settings side by side, it seems possible that
the earlier work could have provided a model for Schubert's later,
more radical treatment of the same or similar elements in D. 911. For
example, Kreutzer's piano introduction, with the right-hand part na-
ively and unnecessarily marked "Posthorn," merges directly into the
texted body of the song without a separation or cadence of any kind
(Ex. 30). Schubert does likewise but changes the instrumental figu-

Example 30.   Kreutzer's "Die Post," mm. 1–6

ration just before the singer enters, reserving the postilion fanfares
for the introduction and the interlude between stanzas 2 and 3. Both
composers use triplet eighth-note broken-chordal patterns in the bass,
but Kreutzer's up-and-down arpeggiation is conventional, whereas
Schubert's more original "clip-clop" voicing transforms the classical
Alberti bass figuration into word-painting. Even though Schubert
does not leave the single E-flat-major chord (the fact that E-flat major
is a horn tonality provides another touch of word-painting verisimi-
litude) for six entire measures, the counterplay of rhythms and triadic
motives prevents monotony. The two composers, however, read the
poem differently. Kreutzer, who marks his setting "Agitato," represents that agitation by means of two-against-three patterns in the
texted portions of the song and postilion fanfares that pit duplet
figures against the continuing triplet eighths in the bass. Schubert's
wanderer, more revitalized and mystified than agitated, searches for
answers harmonically; after listening to the fanfares, he ranges afield

tonally in quest of an explanation. It is a more profound reading of the poem by far.

Kreutzer's wanderer hears the postilion fanfares throughout the lied and is consequently bound more closely to their tonal limitations, with one striking exception: the mediant shift emblematic of surprise and agitation at the words "Was hat es, daß es so hoch aufspringt" in stanza 1 (Ex. 31). Schubert's wanderer, however, does not hear

Example 31.   Kreutzer's "Die Post," mm. 7–14

omnipresent fanfares. The composer limits the obvious reference to the external world and instead depicts a wanderer more preoccupied with his reactions to the sound than with the sound itself, an almost immediate progression from external observation to inward mental processes. Given the classical framework of Kreutzer's style, it is difficult to know whether the repetitious fanfares are merely genre painting or whether Kreutzer was attempting the portrayal of obsessive fixation. But where Kreutzer's influence on Schubert seems most

probable is in the repetitions of the words "mein Herz" (Ex. 32).
Kreutzer's expressive variations of those figures, especially the chro-

Example 32.   Kreutzer's "Die Post," mm. 44–55

matic inflection that follows the words "Wo ich ein liebes Liebchen
hatt' " and the expansive variant at the end of the song, may have
provided Schubert with a model for his own setting.

For the introduction to "Die Post," Schubert writes a postilion fanfare that never leaves the notes of the tonic triad, in imitation of actual
fanfares such as "Postillons Signal" from Erk and Böhme's collection

lection of German folk songs (Ex. 33).[6] The incomplete outlines of the
dominant seventh are confined to the broken-chordal patterns in the

Example 33.   "Postillions Lied," from Erk and Böhme's collection

bass of mm. 7–8, just before the accompanimental figuration shifts to
dotted patterns that can be construed pictorially as the hoofbeats and
the sounds of the coach in motion, but also as the excited rhythms
of the wanderer's heart. The harmonies remain anchored to tonic and
dominant only until the middle of m. 12, when the wanderer asks,
"Was hat es, daß es so hoch aufspringt, / Mein Herz?"; with the first
question of the poem, Schubert moves rapidly away from E-flat
through the circle of fifths, arriving at the key of D-flat major, significantly distant from the E-flat major of the mail coach and its fanfares. The question is given added expressive urgency by the upward
leap of a sixth in the vocal line (m. 15) at the first invocation of the
words "Mein Herz?" a leap to nontonic closure. With no answer
forthcoming, he returns to the tonic, again quite swiftly, to begin the
musical search anew and asks the same question, this time investing
the twofold statement of "Mein Herz" with harmonically reinterpreted reminiscences of the chromatic motion earlier in the stanza.

The end of the first and third stanzas are among the most quietly
dramatic moments in the cycle as the unharmonized dominant pitches
stop with a jolt just short of the first beat of m. 26, followed by a
measure of complete silence. One imagines a mental drama in which
the wanderer awaits an answer from his heart, listening with such
concentration that all sounds from the outside world are blotted out.
There is no answer to fill the expectant questioning silence in which
he waits, and therefore in stanza 2 he tries to discover the cause for
his inexplicable emotion by other means, by negative induction: first,
he says what could *not* be the source of his strange reaction and then
asks the question again in different words, more intense than before,
even slightly frustrated ("Was drängst du denn so wunderlich, / Mein

[6]Ludwig Erk and Franz Böhme, *Deutscher Liederhort* (Leipzig, 1925), no. 615, 462.

Herz?"). When the music resumes, the jaunty energy of the dotted rhythms is gone, and a more subdued "heartbeat" rhythmic ostinato takes its place, the darker parallel minor emblematic of a somber inner realm. The fanfares are of less import to the wanderer now than answering the mystery of that sudden heartfelt leap of undesignated emotion.

Composers, like actors, can choose from different possible readings of a text, and the individual words they stress or leave unaccented affect, even determine, the listener's understanding of the song. For example, "The post brings *you* no letter," The post brings you *no* letter," The post brings you no *letter*," or "The post brings you *no letter*" are among the various interpretations a reader or composer might select. Schubert has the wanderer pause between the initial words "Die Post" and the remainder of the line, as if the protagonist had to take an extra breath or stop for an instant to muster courage before he can bring himself to state an unpleasant truth, that there is no hope of communication from the outside world for him. It is an eloquent pause—quietly tragic. When the same music recurs to the words of stanza 4, Schubert no longer breaks the vocal phrase with this poignant rest, but instead prolongs the word "wohl" in the line "Willst *wohl* einmal hinüber sehn?" thus creating durational emphasis on the element of uncertainty and also of longing. "Do you want to peer out and ask how things are there?" Is this, he asks his heart, what you truly desire? Schubert can make his wanderer ask questions more insistently than the poet could. In both stanzas 2 and 4 when the words of the verse are repeated, the affective nuances—the rests, the yearning prolongations of "drängst," "wohl," "fragen"—are no longer present because the emotion is no longer fresh. Instead, the phrase drives toward the refrain "Mein *Herz*," no longer separated from the preceding melodic line but joined with it in greater urgency than before.

Schubert performs harmonic sleight-of-hand when the silence stops. The E-flat-minor chords seem at first the beginning of another of Schubert's major-minor mode contrasts, the delayed resolution of the unharmonized dominant pitches that precede the measure of silence. But this is no resolution, no answer, rather the start of another progression in a different tonality (the flatted mediant G-flat major), retroactively understood. The wanderer changes focus in this stanza, withdrawing his attention from the outside world in order to query his heart, and the removal to a different place is heralded by the change of tonal place and rhythmic ostinato. The wanderer still searches harmonically for an answer to the mystery and this time looks farther, going one step beyond the D-flat-major stopping point of his first question in stanza 1. The new key—distant from the postilion fanfares—does not lead to an answer, so the wanderer repeats the entire stanza, statement-and-question both, returning to tonic E-flat major. Like the repetition of the question in stanza 1, this occurs over an extended dominant pedal (mm. 38–45), culminating in the dramatic gesture of a dissonant high A-flat in the vocal line against the continuing B-flats in the bass. *Pace* Capell, the moment is not light. It is after all, in Part II that the wanderer discovers his fate, and Part II begins with his persistent efforts to make his heart yield its secrets. His efforts are unsuccessful here, but they foreshadow the revelation to come.

In Schubert's reading, the wanderer hears the posthorn fanfares a second time, and the sound prompts further speculation and a tentative answer to the mystery. Müller does not say that a renewed burst of sound from the coachman impels the words "Nun ja, die Post kommt aus der Stadt"; this was the composer's brilliant intuition. So too was the insight that set the supposed explanation and its aftermath to a near-literal repetition of the music for stanzas 1 and 2. The wanderer in stanza 3 makes what seems to be a declarative statement (But yes, the post comes from the town where I once had a beloved sweetheart), but the supposed declaration culminates in the same questioning, listening silence as before, followed by the significantly diffident question in stanza 4 about returning one day. This time, the unharmonized dominant pitches do not lead to silence, as before. The wanderer no longer searches for an answer, and the song simply ends, with two curiously laconic tonic chords. The tepid nature of the last question in this questioning poem is registered in the perfunctory conclusion.

The echoes of the postilion's fanfares in poetry retained an evocative charge as sounding symbols of nineteenth-century quests even after railroads had begun to replace the horse-and-coach as a principal means of transportation over long distances. A Viennese *Taschenbuch* from 1840 titled *Orpheus* contains, among much else, a poetic cycle of "Posthornklänge" (Posthorn melodies) by the Austrian poet Johann Nepomuk Vogl (1802–1866), who devises eight variations on a single theme: the sounds of the posthorn as irresistible goads that compel, first, a journey out into the world and then a return home.[7] Vogl, a prolific minor poet in a belatedly Romantic style, was not the equal

---

[7]The "Posthornklänge" were published in *Orpheus: Musikalisches Taschenbuch für das Jahr 1840*, ed. August Schmidt (Vienna, 1840), 49–54.

of Eichendorff or Tieck or Müller, but the final poem from his cycle can serve to demonstrate the enduring attraction of poetic journeys that begin and end with the rousing sound of the postilion's fanfares.

> Nun, Schwager, blas' dein letztes Stück,
> Das schönste, das du kannst,
> Denn wieder naht sich mir das Glück,
> Ein Glück, das du nicht ahn'st.
>
> Stoß' jetzt in's Horn mit aller Kraft,
> Mit deiner ganzen Kunst,
> Denn mit dem Schluß der Pilgerschaft
> Zerfließt mein Leid wie Dunst.
>
> D'rum tön' das Horn, d'rum schall' sein Klang
> So hell, als wie noch nie,
> Wie Harfenton, wie Elfensang,
> Wie Sphärenharmonie.
>
> Daß man's vernehm' allüberall,
> Die Fahrt ist nun gemacht,
> Und zur Geliebten hat dein Schall
> Für immer mich gebracht.

(Now, coachman, blow your last melody, the most beautiful one that you can. For once more good fortune draws near, good fortune you do not even suspect.

Now blow your horn with all your might, with all your art, for at the end of my pilgrimage, my sorrow blows away like mist.

Therefore blow the horn, let the music resound brightly as never before, like heavenly harps, like elfin song, like the music of the spheres.

All hearken to it everywhere: the journey is over, and your music has brought me back to my beloved forever.)

Vogl's wanderer, whose circular quest leads him back home to his sweetheart, is more conventional and happier by far than Müller's. The monologist in *Winterreise* does not even know what the sounds mean to him; when he finds out, the coach is long gone, and the news is not occasion for rejoicing.

14. Der greise Kopf

Der Reif hat einen weißen Schein
Mir über's Haar gestreuet.
Da glaubt' [meint'] ich schon ein Greis zu sein,
Und hab' mich sehr gefreuet.

Doch bald ist er hinweggetaut,
Hab' wieder schwarze Haare,
Daß mir's vor meiner Jugend graut—
Wie weit noch bis zur Bahre!

[234]

Vom Abendrot zum Morgenlicht
Ward mancher Kopf zum Greise.
Wer glaubt's? Und meiner ward es nicht
Auf dieser ganzen Reise!

The Gray Head

(The frost has strewn a white sheen upon my hair; I thought I had already become an old man and I was overjoyed.
But soon it melted away; I have black hair once again, so that I shudder at my youth—how far away the grave still is!
Between dusk and dawn, many a head has turned gray. Who can believe it? Mine has not, on this whole long journey!)

The wanderer has slept out in the open, and frost has formed on his hair during the night. When he awakens, he believes for a moment that his hair has turned white overnight, and therefore he rejoices in his proximity to death. This is the only time in the entire cycle that Müller uses the verb "sich freuen," even modifying it with the adverb "sehr" to indicate great rejoicing. The frost soon melts, however, the wanderer's hair is black once again, and he shudders in horror. Surely his travails deserve, he implies, the reward of age and imminent death granted to other, more fortunate sufferers. The reversal of the more usual human condition—the wanderer grieves over youth and life, rejoices in the illusion of age and the approach of death—permeates the poem.

"Der greise Kopf" is, typically for this cycle, tightly organized, a compression of the classical schema thesis-antithesis-synthesis (the illusion of old age-disillusionment-summation) into a mere three quatrains. Wolfgang Stechow has pointed out how beautifully Müller reinforces this structure by means of word sound, that is, the brightness or darkness of the prevailing vowels in each stanza.[1] In the first stanza, bright diphthongs predominate, the wanderer welcoming the miraculous gift of old age vouchsafed overnight: "Reif," "weiß," "Schein," "gestreuet," "Greis," "sein," "gefreuet," and—in Müller's text—"meint'." In the second stanza, when the illusion is dispelled, the sound darkens in grief, with words such as "bald," "hinweggge-taut," "schwarze," "Haare," "Jugend," "graut," and "Bahre" (the liquid consonant /r/ acts to darken those vowels nearest to it). How-

---

[1] Wolfgang Stechow, " 'Der greise Kopf': Eine Analyse," in *Fides: Festschrift für Werner Neuse*, ed. Herbert Lederer and Joachim Seyppel (Berlin, 1967), 66.

ever, two of the key words in the stanza, "wieder" in the second line and "weit" in the fourth line, are heightened by the recurrence of the bright diphthongs amid the darker colors (Schubert subsequently emphasizes those words still more by means of prolongation and repetition). In the third stanza, with its bitterly sarcastic commentary on the paradoxes of time and fortune, Müller mixes bright and dark, the darker colors predominating once again. This time, the few iron-ically bright sounds are not buried within the lines but are the rhyming end words of the second and fourth lines: "Greise" and "Reise." The diphthong /ei/, echoing throughout the first stanza as the sounding symbol of rejoicing, now recurs when there is no longer any cause for joy.

Throughout the *Urania* poems of Part I, Müller creates a sense of great tension between the forward motion of the journey and the gravitational pull of the past. "Die Post" is among the last manifes-tations of those opposing directional forces in the cycle, no longer equal, since the momentary thought of returning to the sweetheart's town is an experiment by which to test his answer to the mystery of heartfelt emotion at the sound of the postilion's fanfares. With "Der greise Kopf," however, the tension changes to a struggle between the forces of life and death, between the wanderer's desire for an end to his journey and whatever force denies him the death wish repeated throughout Part II. He was tempted by death earlier in "Der Linden-baum" when the prospect of death in the winter storm beckoned him and in "Irrlicht" when he consoled himself with the thought of even-tual death, but in Part II, beginning with "Der greise Kopf," the desire for death becomes an obsession.

Rolf Vollmann, in his essay "Wilhelm Müller und die Romantik," writes of the childlike quality (*Kindlichkeit*) of Müller's images and turns of phrase in *Die Winterreise*, the naive, child's-eye view evident in images such as "die runden Lindenbäume" (the round linden trees) in "Rückblick." A child might look at a tree in full leaf and see it as a round object, could speak of the river as covering itself with a cold and hard crust, and could invoke these images and others like them with a childlike matter-of-fact quality. The wanderer also speaks of death as a child might do, without considering, either here or later, the means by which it occurs. To Vollmann, it is an "unnatural child-ishness" and one made chilling by the objectivity of tone in which dire things are said.[2] The wanderer may indeed "speak as a child," but he does not think of childish things.

[2]Rolf Vollmann, "Wilhelm Müller und die Romantik," in Feil, *Franz Schubert*, 183.

Schubert's introduction is a graph of the poem in microcosm, a broadly arching, symmetrical phrase that seems a musical metaphor for awakening, ascending to heights of joy, and then descending to disillusionment, all over a tonic pedal point. The entire experience of "Der greise Kopf" is stated in capsule form at the beginning and then expanded in the texted body of the song. When the latter half only of the introduction recurs as a piano interlude in the setting of stanzas 1 and 3 and as the postlude (mm. 9–10, 34–35, and 43–44), it is downfall and disappointment that are echoed in the piano part. The obvious musical justification for that choice is the instrumental echo of the preceding texted cadences, but the repetitions of descent have as well a grim dramatic signification. One can also think of the introduction as a tightly encapsulated initial harmony that expands outward and then contracts back to its original restricted compass, symbolic of expanding hopes and the subsequent contraction that comes with disillusionment, lapsing in the end back to the tonic harmony he never really left. Whatever poetic reading one might impose on the phrase, with whatever justification from Müller and Schubert alike, the phrase is a marvelous construction in increasing intensity. With each attempted move away from the tonic harmony, the melody ascends, straining farther away from the bass (the double-dotted pitches in mm. 1–2 seem as if gathering strength for the next vault upward), and the harmonies become richer, culminating in the dominant ninth against the tonic bass of m. 3. Only here, at the beginning of downfall is the first beat of the measure prolonged, the struggle against the continuing tonic bass at its strongest. The turning-figure motion around the mediant pitch E-flat in m. 4 seems a last-ditch effort to stave off final relapse back to middle C.

Schubert repeats the introduction in its entirety as the first vocal phrase, without the unvocal double-dotting and with the apex modified downward a third for the singer. The result is a rare example in the cycle of an introductory musical idea—the kernel from which the entire song then grows—producing slight distortions in the prosody. Schubert's reading of the poem inspired the creation of the introductory phrase from which the remainder of the lied is subsequently derived, that phrase then somewhat at odds with the iambic tetrameters and trimeters of Müller's first two lines of text. The durational emphasis on the second beat of mm. 1 and 2 and the first beat of m. 3 at the midpoint of the introductory phrase in the piano subsequently becomes durational emphasis on the words "ei - nen," "Schein," and "ü - ber's" ("Der Reif hat ei - nen weißen Schein / Mir ü - bers Haar gestreuet"), neither correct declamation nor expressive warping of the text for purposes of interpretation. When the same music returns at the beginning of the last verse, however, the prosodic accents more accurately and expressively emphasize the last light of dusk and the first light of morning, the nocturnal span in which others grow old but not the unfortunate wanderer: "Vom *A*-bend - *rot* zum *Mor*-gen - *licht* / Ward *man* - cher Kopf zum Greise."

Schubert sets the wanderer's short-lived joy in illusion (mm. 11–14) in the dominant, freed briefly from its prior anchorage to the tonic bass and with the A-flats from earlier reinterpreted in the dominant realm. The instrumental echo of the cadence asserts the turn to the dominant even more strongly, but the wanderer hints that his great delight is doomed to disappointment by bringing back the triplet eighth-note rhythms of m. 3—the fall from the heights—and a smoothly conjunct variation of its descending profile, less precipitous than before. Impending disillusionment is already foreshadowed in the very phrase with which the wanderer expresses his rejoicing, the voice exchange in contrary motion a way of emphasizing the magnitude of his delight ("sehr gefreuet"). The wanderer sings of his experience after it has occurred, and the account of his joy is therefore tinged with knowledge of the unhappy ending. Later, similar contrary motion between the voice and the accompaniment recurs in expanded form in m. 38 at the words "dieser ganzen Reise," and one hears the simultaneous directions both up and down as symbolic of the long, weary journey.

When the wanderer recounts the melting of the hoar frost and the discovery that his hair is once again black, Schubert conveys the shock of the moment in a style akin to recitative, with rapid harmonic motion and minimal punctuating chords. Even more extraordinary is the lengthy unison passage that follows, Schubert setting apart the twofold invocation of Müller's last line of stanza 2 as too stark for harmonization.[3] The tonality for these two sequential phrases is unclear, all the more so as Schubert stresses crucial pitches from earlier in the

---

[3] In his song "Totengräbers Heimweh" (Gravedigger's homesickness), D.842, composed in April 1825 to a poem by Jacob Nicolaus Craigher, Schubert composed a passage in C minor entirely in unison writing, a passage that strongly resembles mm. 24–29 of "Der greise Kopf." Even the grace-note figure is the same. The text for mm. 41–48 of "Totengräbers Heimweh" is: "Von allen verlassen, dem Tod nur verwandt, / Verweil' ich am Rande, das Kreuz in der Hand, / Und starre mit sehnendem Blick hinab / Ins tiefe, ins tiefe Grab!" (Forsaken by all, kin to death alone, I linger on the brink, cross in hand, and stare yearningly down into the deep, deep grave!). The kinship between the two texts in which the poetic speakers long for death is obvious.

lied but without their full tonal context. The passage begins from the E-flat of the cadence just preceding, accents the C that is the root of C minor, refers prominently to the F-sharp–G of the deluded rejoicing, and retraces the leap in mm. 2–3 from D–A-flat in reverse. The motivic relationship to what has come before is evident, but the mystery of the unknown, horrifying distance from the grave is expressed in the tonal ambiguity of the passage.[4]

Because the final stanza has no reminiscence of hope and short-lived joy, there can be no excursion to the dominant region emblematic of the short-lived joy. Only the initial phrase of the last verse is unchanged musically, the arch-shaped line from stanza 1 representative as well of the span of time from dusk to dawn in which other, more fortunate people turn old overnight. When Schubert changed Müller's verb "Da *meint'* ich schon ein Greis zu sein" in stanza 1 to "glaubt' " (I thought I had already become an old man), he must already have had in mind the tragic-ironic parallel between his setting of that line and its varied recurrence to the words "Wer glaubt's? Und meiner ward es nicht" (Who can believe it? Mine has not). The melodic line of mm. 11–14 is reinterpreted in C major, and the contrary motion that formerly called attention to the magnitude of the wanderer's joy is now extended as a musical symbol of "this whole long journey." Schubert had earlier invoked "straying" in "Irrlicht" as melodic lines that ascend and descend simultaneously, and he would shortly thereafter use a much longer and more chromatic instance of voice exchange in contrary motion as "the road from which no one has returned" in "Der Wegweiser." The disillusionment of "Der greise Kopf" ends with the return of tonic minor mode ("Auf dieser ganzen Reise") and descending melodic fifths in the vocal part, significantly the inverse of the ascending motion of mm. 1–2. "This whole long journey" now on repetition appears as a descent, the unknown and dreadful future extent of the journey bitterly emphasized in the prolongation of the dominant ("*Rei* - se").

[4]I wonder whether Hugo Wolf might have recalled this passage from "Der greise Kopf" when he composed the second of his *Drei Gedichte von Michelangelo*, "Alles endet, was entstehet" in March 1897 (Mannheim, 1898). Where the spirit voices in this poem say, "Und nun sind wir leblos hier, / Sind nur Erde, wie ihr sehet" (And now we are lifeless here, / Are only dust, as you see), Wolf set those words as two unharmonized sequential phrases whose tonal ambiguity, motivic relationship with what precedes them, and scalewise descending motion are reminiscent of Schubert's song, composed seventy years earlier. Much is different in the later song, and the resemblance may be no more than coincidence, but it is intriguing to reflect that Schubert's living protagonist who longs for the distant grave later becomes Wolf's voices of the dead speaking to those still alive.

15. Die Krähe

Eine Krähe war mit mir
Aus der Stadt gezogen,
Ist bis heute für und für
Um mein Haupt geflogen.

Krähe, wunderliches Tier,
Willst mich nicht verlassen?
Meinst wohl bald als Beute hier
Meinen Leib zu fassen?

Nun, es wird nicht weit mehr gehn
An dem Wanderstabe.
Krähe, laß mich endlich sehn
Treue bis zum Grabe!

The Crow

(A crow has come with me from the town; to this day, it has been steadily flying about my head.

Crow, you strange creature, will you not leave me? Do you intend soon to seize my body as your prey here?

Now, I will not have to journey much farther with my walking staff. Crow, let me at last see faithfulness unto the grave!)

The wanderer hopes that the crow that has followed him since he left the town is an omen of death, circling overhead like a vulture waiting for its intended prey to die. The words "wohl bald," and "hier" (soon, here), clustered together in one anxious question, are registers of his mounting desperation: "Do you intend soon to seize my body as your prey here?" In the last stanza, he tries to assure himself that he will no longer have to continue his journey, that it will end here in death, and he therefore speaks as if wish were fact, declaring, "Well, I will not have to journey much farther with my walking staff." The word "soon," the emblem of imminence, is succeeded by the word "now" as the wanderer's desire for death becomes more urgent. Knowing, however, that his wish is not reality, he then pleads with the crow for constancy to the purpose he has imputed to it. His last words in the poem, "Treue bis zum Grabe," are taken from the marriage service and the traditional vow to be faithful "til death do us part." Since he was not vouchsafed fidelity in love, he would at last find it in death, the plea especially bitter because "fidelity" will not, he hopes, have to endure for long. The limits of inherently inconstant love should not be strained in granting his wish. With that plea, the poem ends, and the wanderer looks in the next scene for yet another omen.

The death the wanderer envisions in "Die Krähe" is further evidence of Müller's originality, not in the imagery, but in the tone. There is no self-pity or sentimentality in the bleak scene the wanderer paints in two lines, the brief, unembellished image of his own corpse with the avian predator claiming it as booty. The realistic wanderer does not name the agent of death because there is no present danger or circumstance that might promise his demise, no tempest in which he might freeze and die. Instead, he moves in imagination beyond the act of dying itself to the fate of his body as the prey of wild animals (one remembers the "wild animals' tracks" that the wanderer says he will seek out and follow in "Gute Nacht").

Schubert retains the C-minor tonality of "Der greise Kopf" for "Die Krähe," a tonal link between these two songs about the disappointment of death wishes. The elements in the introduction by which the composer suggests the crow's constant circling motion overhead—the high tessitura, with the bass in the treble register; the broken-chordal figuration that rises and falls within restricted confines; and the ceaseless motion with no pause or break—are strongly colored by Schubert's distinctive use of the chord on the Phrygian flatted second degree in the second phrase (he will later use the flatted second degree to unforgettable effect as a cadential chord in "Der Wegweiser"). This harmony always has a peculiarly dark quality, the result of tension between the flatted second's melodic gravitation toward the tonic pitch and its harmonic position in a chromatic supertonic harmony that goes to the dominant before proceeding to tonic. Schubert introduces the harmony at the beginning of a two-bar phrase in root position, less common than its appearance in first inversion, and then restates the harmony in the next measure in the more usual first inversion as dominant preparation with the flatted second degree in the melody. In this introduction, the inherent dramatic darkness of the flatted supertonic is quietly at odds with the limpid texture, placid motion, and soft dynamic level. Furthermore, the melodic line of the introduction, with its asymmetrical 2 + 3–measure phrase structure, begins and ends with the same semitone interval an octave apart and descending motion between, reminiscent of the initial vocal phrase of "Gute Nacht." When the introduction is restated as the vocal line and accompaniment of stanza 1 and the beginning of stanza 3, the Phrygian second is significantly absent, replaced by the diatonic supertonic seventh, and the cadence is therefore notably lighter, no longer weighed down by the whole-step descent.

Not until the climax of stanza 3 does the flatted second degree return, first within the tonicized subdominant, or F minor (mm. 30 and 35) and then as a chord tone in one of the most emphatic diminished seventh harmonies in the cycle (m. 33). There could be no more telling signal of the wanderer's despairing disbelief in "Treue bis zum Grabe" and his doubt that the grave truly awaits him than the deceptive motion, the refusal of resolution which impels another statement of the pleading command, but in a lower register. Even before that point, Schubert does not sustain the C-minor root position tonic chord on the word "[Wandersta] - be" in m. 28 but passes immediately through it and on to the plea for constancy. The wanderer cannot really believe that he "will not journey much farther with my walking staff." It is tempting to hear the lowered registers at the end of the song and throughout the postlude as a sign of lowered expectations and ultimate disillusionment. The final conjunction of the journeying motive in the right hand and the continued descent in the bass down to the low C reserved only for the last measure tell simultaneously of the death of hope and the resumption of the journey.

Although less overtly dramatic than the climax of stanza 3, Schubert's setting of stanza 2 is fraught with quieter but considerable tensions. The wanderer turns from narrative self-address to direct address ("Crow, you strange creature, will you not leave me? Do you intend soon to seize my body as your prey here?"). Therefore, the prosody changes from the unimpassioned stream of eighth notes in stanza 2 to a more inflected declamation, each question broken into anxious fragments. Even more remarkable is the rising chromatic sequence traced throughout the stanza, beginning with the E-flat of the relative major tonality on which stanza 1 ended and rising from there through F to G in the bass, the entire sequence recapitulated in the bass of m. 24. It is at the words "Willst mich nicht verlassen?" that the music begins to inch its way upward, the tension all the greater for the confinement to such narrow boundaries. The neighbor-note chromatic motion in the bass and inner voice produces in mm. 20–21 ("Meinst wohl bald als Beute hier") not only the outlined augmented triad as the neighbor harmony, but an enharmonic foreshadowing of the A-flat pitches in the F-minor harmonies of stanza 3. Most telling of all are the cross-relation between the bass and soprano produced by the voice-leading in mm. 22–23, graphic expression of the verb "fassen" (to grip, as with talons), and the shifting, unstable bass phrasing across the bar lines, evocative of uncertainty and disquiet. The plea in stanza 3, however, stays within the bar lines, the force of the wanderer's desire for death evident in the emphatic downbeats. The neighbor-note semitone progressions of stanza 2 continue but intensified in a five-bar phrase, like the five-bar phrase of the introduction. The questions to the crow now impel an outburst of desperation at the end, reminiscent of the similar outcry in "Wasserflut": a steep rise to a dissonant diminished seventh chord, followed by a balancing phrase leading to resolution and cadence.

16. Letzte Hoffnung

Hie [Hier] und da ist an den Bäumen
Manches bunte Blatt [Noch ein buntes Blatt] zu sehn,
Und ich bleibe vor den Bäumen
Oftmals in Gedanken stehn.

Schaue nach dem einen Blatte,
Hänge meine Hoffnung dran;
Spielt der Wind mit meinem Blatte,
Zittr' ich, was ich zittern kann.

Ach, und fällt das Blatt zu Boden,
Fällt mit ihm die Hoffnung ab,
Fall' ich selber mit zu Boden,
Wein' auf meiner Hoffnung Grab.

[245]

Last Hope

(Here and there on the trees, many a colored leaf can still be seen,
and I often stand lost in thought before those trees.
I gaze at a single leaf and hang my hopes on it; if the wind plays
with my leaf, I tremble violently.
Ah, and should the leaf fall to the ground, my hope would fall with
it. I too fall to the ground and weep on the grave of my hopes.)

The wanderer once more finds the symbol of his own condition in
an image from Nature: a leaf falling from a tree. The fate of the leaf,
blown from its branch by the wind, represents for the wanderer the
death of hope. An extraordinary range of emotions is compressed
into these twelve lines. He often stands lost in thought, he tells us,
before the trees that have long represented comfort, shelter, and love
to him ("Der Lindenbaum," stanzas 1 and 2), trees now with their
last autumnal leaves clinging tenuously to the branches. What those
thoughts are, he does not say, but he chooses one leaf among them,
emblematic of all his hope. As the leaf trembles in the wind, the
wanderer also quakes in mounting fear until "hope" falls to the
ground, followed by the wanderer himself. There he weeps, the only
time in Part II that he does so and the last time in all of *Winterreise*.
Within a single short poem, Müller travels from somber reflection
through anxiety and terror to profound grief at the end. There are
other psychologically rich poems in the cycle, but none with this
emotional range.

Müller uses a limited vocabulary of words with one or two syllables,
with more word and phrase repetition than one finds anywhere else
in the cycle. The word "leaf" or "leaves" appears four times in three
quatrains, "trees" twice in the first verse, "hope" three times, "tremble" twice in one line, "fall" three times, and the phrase "to the
ground" twice in the last verse. The repetitions shape the internal
structure of the stanzas, such that the first and third lines of each
quatrain end with the same word, each beginning with the letter *b*
("Bäumen," "Blatte," "Boden"—a different vowel each time), and
the word "Hoffnung" is the third trochee of the second line of stanza
2 and of the second and fourth lines of stanza 3. Details vary with
each repetition, however. *A* leaf at the beginning of the second verse
becomes *my* leaf two lines later as the wanderer claims it for his own.
In the final stanza, a chain reaction occurs in which "all fall down,"
first the leaf, then hope, then the wanderer himself. The first two
times, the verbs are conditional, a cause-and-effect statement: "Ah,

and *should* the leaf fall to the ground, / My hope *would* fall with it." As soon as he says so, the anticipated catastrophe actually happens, and the wanderer falls to the ground—present tense. Not until the last line of the poem does one find a new action (weeping) and a new word (grave). The emphasis on the verb "to fall" in the last stanza is especially remarkable because each line of the preceding verse (stanza 2) contains a different verb, heightened by the omission of the subject "ich" and by the placement of the verbs as the initial trochee of each line: "gaze," "hang," "play," and "tremble." The latter verb is repeated and inverted in a way that evades translation into English and is wonderfully expressive of obsessional fear ("*Zittr'* ich, was ich *zittern* kann"). This clustering of repeated words throughout "Letzte Hoffnung," the restriction of thought and therefore of language to a very small compass, is a psychologically accurate portrayal of what happens in a state of panic and obsession. The mind harps on the same images over and over, and the world shrinks to a single symbolically charged object.

Schubert once again edits the poetic text, and one of those changes is particularly notable for what it suggests about the composition of this song. The first editorial alteration is straightforward. Müller's "Hier und da" becomes Schubert's "Hie und da," surely a change made for improved phonetic sound in music. Müller's word "hier" ends with a liquid consonant that darkens the vowel and transforms it into a diphthong. By changing to the pure /ee/ of "Hie," the composer provides for the uninterrupted flow of vowels until the rhythmic downbeat on the word "da" and begins the vocal line with a notably tense, bright sound. But the alteration of the second line of the poem perhaps originated with the conception of the piano introduction, once again, the kernel from which the song is derived. The introduction alternates between fragmented arpeggiations of dominant harmonies, without a single tonic chord (already a harmonic index of tense expectation), and establishes the rhythmic dislocations of the song. The intervallic cells from which the song is fashioned (descending major and minor seconds and thirds, with the minor third and minor second predominating) are onomatopoeia for the falling leaves, drifting downward singly and in clusters. By altering Müller's phrase "noch ein buntes Blatt" (yet a colored leaf), with its emphasis on the singular, to "manches bunte Blatt" (many a colored leaf), Schubert reinforces the word-painting in the accompaniment. Could Schubert, reading the poem, have conceived the musical figures representative of *many* falling leaves and then altered the poetic text in accord with his inspiration?

Müller's poem epitomizes *Angst* at its most acute, barely this side
of a psychotic break and so intense that even catastrophe is better
because certain. The wanderer's extreme instability is evident in every
aspect of the music at the beginning. The listener has no way to verify
the indicated $\frac{3}{4}$ meter in the introduction. The disposition of the motivic figures does not help locate the passage metrically, while the
insistent diminished seventh harmony and the refusal of resolution
keep the hearer suspended in mid-air tonally as well. Reducing the
passage to its fundamentals, one notices the descending pattern of
the semitone motives and the dominant pathway downward F–B-
flat–F. The fermata on the dominant in m. 4—as yet lacking a context
in which to assert a dominant function—seems to promise imminent
clarification of the tonality, but instead Schubert starts the whole
Angst-ridden roundelay all over again in the piano and adds to it a
vocal line that begins with the same intervallic figure C-flat–A-flat,
juxtaposed an eighth note later. To compound the rhythmic turbulence and metrical confusion, the accented initial syllable of the second
and fourth trochees in lines 1 and 3 of stanza 1 is prolonged on the
second beat of $\frac{3}{4}$: "Hie und *da* ist an den *Bäu* - men . . . ," "Und ich
blei - be vor den *Bäu* - men," literally staying (bleiben) on the key
words and syllables an instant longer at still further cross-purposes
with the indicated meter. This music is an astonishingly apt representation of a mind disordered. The sense of being literally "up in
the air" is heightened by harmonies that seldom alight and then do
so only briefly, by the splintering of harmonies into intervallic segments and by the tension-fraught relationship of the vocal line and
the piano accompaniment for much of stanzas 1 and 2.

The symbolism becomes all the more expressive when the wanderer
momentarily reassures himself with the statement that many leaves
can still be seen. Not until that point does the wanderer wrench tonal
and rhythmic order from the multiple dislocations and we hear E-flat
major for the first time—in m. 8. No sooner does the resolution take
place than the hint of stability vanishes immediately, without even a
single full beat to allow the tonic chord time to establish itself in the
listener's ear. Schubert repeats the first phrase (lines 1 and 2) for the
second phrase, but with the cadence altered in accord with the nuances of the final line of the stanza. The quickened harmonic rhythms
(a representation of the word "oftmals" or "often"?) culminate in the
wanderer and his music both standing lost in thought, "in Gedanken
stehn," on the mediant pitch G, the dominant of the implied C-minor
sphere already strongly suggested in m. 11. The prolongation of that
pitch and the lack of harmonization are the concomitants to stark,

fearful thoughts. What those thoughts are, we do not know, and the brief patch of unison writing suggests dire knowledge withheld.

"Letzte Hoffnung" is a virtual compendium of variation techniques, a radical refashioning of the intervallic cells stated in the introduction. At the beginning of stanza 2, Schubert repeats the same intervallic cells throughout the first two lines of the quatrain (mm. 13–18) in an uncannily apt representation both of staring fixedly at the chosen leaf ("Schaue nach dem einen Blatte") and the incessant tension, the nervous motion of acute *Angst*. As the wanderer invests all his hope in the one fragile leaf ("Hänge meine Hoffnung dran"), Schubert prolongs the dominant of C minor without ever resolving it; the harmony does not "fall" to its resolution. As the wind plays with the leaf, the B-naturals are respelled enharmonically in order to turn back to the dominant of E-flat, the harmonic goal of the wanderer's attack of trembling at the end of the stanza. There, one notices as well the passing tone D-flat that so expressively darkens the words "zittr'ich" (I tremble). This entire stanza (mm. 13–24) has no tonic resolution, however momentary. The wanderer's leaf has not yet fallen, there is no reassurance to be found in the other remaining leaves, and everything hangs in mid-air, unresolved and trembling, until it does.

At the end of the piano introduction, the dominant does not resolve but is prolonged for two more measures before the tonic first appears. Schubert does something similar, and even more intense, at the midpoint of the song: the "trembling figure" on B-flat is followed by an instant of silence, after which the C-flat–A-flat cell from the diminished seventh chord of the introduction sounds three times in succession, in different registers and reinforced by octave doubling. It is as if the wanderer in his terror cannot go beyond those initial pitches, as if the leaf remains suspended there for this last moment before it falls. The wanderer's knowledge at some level that what he fears will inevitably come to pass is apparent when Schubert arrives at the darkened parallel minor of tonic while the wanderer is still speaking in subjunctive possibilities: "And should the leaf fall to the ground, my hope would fall with it." The separation of the two clauses in the vocal line is yet another wonderful detail: the wanderer must pause for more than a measure before he can bring himself to state the consequences of the leaf's fall. The setting of the words "Fällt mit ihm die Hoffnung ab," with its echo in the piano, is reminiscent of a similar rhythmic and melodic manner in "Wasserflut" at the words "ist gefallen in den Schnee," another motif of falling motion and grief. When the disaster *does* happen, it is just as he had anticipated, except that he falls from a higher point than before (*Terzensteigerung*) and continues the descent to the ground in the piano part, arriving finally at tonic in the major mode indicated in the key signature. After the instability and darkness of so many diminished-seventh harmonies, so many prolongations of the dominant, and parallel minor mode, E-flat major embodies the clarity of resolution, even if that resolution is catastrophic.

When the wanderer weeps in the final lines of stanza 3, the falling-leaf figures cease and the familiar intervallic cells assume chordal shapes in the accompaniment; Schubert would again resort to the solemnity of this block-chordal texture at the end of the next song, "Im Dorfe," for another statement of great emotional gravity. The details of the large I–VI–IV–V–I progression traced throughout the final section of this through-composed form are beautifully expressive: (1) the ascending passing motion in the inner voice of mm. 35–36, which creates another of the rare, intense augmented triads in the cycle, balanced by the *descending* passing motion of mm. 41–42, which momentarily darkens tonic to minor; (2) the *Terzensteigerung* by which B-flat–E-flat at the first statement of the word "Wein'" (Weep) becomes B-flat–high G in the second, parallel to the rising elevation of the twofold falls; and (3) the powerful effect of the subdominant that has been avoided until this climactic final section. The postlude cannot in this instance restate the introduction literally, since what was anxious suspense there is now tragic certainty. Schubert therefore re-models the principal intervallic figures of the song as a prolongation of plagal cadence, rendered darker and more intense by the flatted-second and seventh degrees. The chromatic tensions persist to the end of one of the most harrowing songs in the entire cycle.

17. Im Dorfe

Es bellen die Hunde, es rasseln die Ketten.
Es schlafen die Menschen in ihren Betten,
  [Die Menschen schnarchen in ihren Betten,]
Träumen sich Manches, was sie nicht haben,
Tun sich im Guten und Argen erlaben:
Und morgen früh ist Alles zerflossen.—
Je nun, sie haben ihr Teil genossen,
Und hoffen, was sie noch übrig ließen,
Doch wieder zu finden auf ihren Kissen.

Bellt mich nur fort, ihr wachen Hunde,
Laßt mich nicht ruhn in der Schlummerstunde!
Ich bin zu Ende mit allen Träumen—
Was will ich unter den Schläfern säumen?

In the Village

(The dogs bark, their chains rattle, people sleep [snore] in their beds, dreaming of many things they do not have, consoling themselves with the good and bad: and with early morning, it is all vanished. Well, they have enjoyed their share, yet they hope to find on their pillows what they still have left to enjoy.

Drive me away, you barking, watchful dogs, don't let me rest in this hour of sleep! I am through with all dreams—why should I linger among the sleepers?)

The nocturnal scene is reminiscent of "Gute Nacht," not only in the images of sleeping townspeople and wakeful dogs but in the distinction between two separate worlds: that of the wanderer and that of the sleeping villagers, by extension, the rest of humanity. The wanderer is acutely aware that others (his sweetheart in "Gute Nacht," the villagers of "Im Dorfe") can sleep undisturbed by biting torment within, the serpent of pain he has invoked in "Rast." They have dream fantasies of desires both good and bad which vanish with the dawn, leaving no trace behind, unlike the wanderer, who "reflects upon the dream" in "Frühlingstraum" and is grief-stricken at the loss. Although here he emphasizes difference rather than his similitude to dreaming humanity, his reflections in "Im Dorfe," the dispassion more apparent than real, are born of that common bond. He too has dreamed of what he does not have, only to suffer upon awakening with the dream still intact in his mind. In the gap between Müller's eight-line initial stanza and the closing quatrain lies the memory of illusions dispelled and the grief occasioned by their dissolution. The implicit complaint that he has not had his allotted portion of happiness in life is the import both of the line "Je nun, sie haben ihr Teil genoßen" and the entire poem. The ages-old lament "Why me? Why am I so unfortunate, beyond the common lot?" resounds throughout "Im Dorfe."

Schubert altered the second line of the poem. Müller's text reads "Die Menschen schnarchen in ihren Betten" (People snore in their beds), while Schubert's line "Es schlafen die Menschen in ihren Betten" (People sleep in their beds) continues the parallel clauses ("Es bellen . . . es rasseln") from the first line. This implies a kinship between the chained dogs and their owners which goes beyond Müller's assertion of difference—the "snorers" must be truly oblivious to sleep through the barking, rattling noises outside—to emphasize the similitude of men and beasts. (The wanderer had invoked dogs as emblems of the world's hostility in "Gute Nacht" at the beginning of the cycle, and he does so again both here and in "Der Leiermann" at the end.) The composer's awareness of the poet's text is evident in the see-saw minor sevenths in the vocal line, the "stretched" intervals evocative both of snoring and the wanderer's scorn. Müller's word "schnarchen" is a wonderful one, the doubled /ch/ and /sch/ sounds and the complex, darkened /a/ vowel apt word music for the uncouth action they signify, but Schubert chose instead the more singable pure /a/ of "schlafen."

The nonstanzaic formal structure is unusual in this cycle and so too are the poetic rhythms, a mixture of iambic, anapestic, trochaic, and dactylic meters whose changing stresses correspond to the progression of events in the poem. The first two lines, or the description of the dogs and the villagers, are a mixture of iambic and anapestic feet, with more anapests than anywhere else except "Frühlingstraum"; the rhythmic effect of these anapests is different, however, less light and graceful, more marchlike. At the word "Träumen" and the third line, the meters change to dactyls and a few trochees, as the wanderer imagines what the townspeople might be dreaming. This third line is symmetrically divided by a caesura into one dactyl and one trochee in each half, while the fourth line is an undivided succession of three dactyls and a concluding trochee. Earnestness, grief, profundity are difficult to achieve in predominantly dactylic verse because the inherent tripping quality of the meter undermines any seriousness of purpose,¹ and the clustered dactyls here have a certain scornful ring. The fifth line, the wanderer's assertion that the dreams will vanish with the first morning light, is nominally a return to the iambs and anapests of lines one and two. When he set that line to music, Schubert, however, placed an extra durational emphasis on the word "Und" that both provides a rhythmic transition from the dactyls and trochees to the iambs and stresses the inevitability of the dreams' disappearance—"*and* with early morning, it is all vanished."

In the last three lines of Müller's eight-line stanza (Schubert's B section), the wanderer is still absorbed in his speculations about the villagers' nocturnal dream fantasies. His scornful tone does not succeed in concealing its origins in pained jealousy: "They have enjoyed their share [I have not], yet they hope to find on their pillows what they still have left to enjoy [and I, to my sorrow, know better]." Müller arranges those lines once again in iambic and anapestic feet, but the disposition is different in each line:

Jĕ nun,   siĕ ha - bĕn ihr Teil gĕ - nos - sĕn
iamb   [caesura] iamb   anapest   iamb

Und hof - fĕn, wăs sie nŏch ü - brig lie - ßĕn,
iamb   anapest   iamb   iamb

Dŏch wie - dĕr zŭ fin - dĕn auf ih - rĕn Kis - sĕn.
iamb   anapest   anapest   iamb

The anapaest in line seven is broken syntactically by the comma separating the two clauses. For the quatrain at the end of the poem, Müller at first turns to trochees and dactyls in which the accented first syllable of the dactyls emphasizes the verbs in the imperative and the alliterative / sch / sounds and lulling /u/'s that denote rest and sleep. Only the final couplet maintains the same metrical pattern in two successive lines, thereby rhythmically connecting the declaration "Ich bin zu Ende mit allen Träumen" (I am through with dreams)

¹Goethe knew this when he wrote the "Cophtisches Lied I" (Coptic song I), later set to music by Hugo Wolf. In this poem, a self-styled magician based on the eighteenth-century charlatan Cagliostro declaims windy nonsense in a stream of dactyls, each verse ending with an adage whose obviousness is comic: "Töricht, auf Beßrung der Toren zu harren! / Kinder der Klugheit, o habet die Narren / Eben zum Narren auch, wie sich's gehört!" (It is foolish to expect wisdom from fools! / Children of wisdom, leave fools to their own devices, as is proper!). Wolf, tongue firmly in cheek, preserves the dactylic rhythms throughout his setting.

with the subsequent question "Was will ich unter den Schläfern säumen?" (Why should I linger among the sleepers?). The rhythmic changeability of this poem is Müller's measure of the wanderer's bitter compound of scorn, envy, anger, and puzzlement, and the complexity of these shifting accents and stresses makes extraordinary demands on a composer's prosodic invention. The unusual $\frac{12}{8}$ meter Schubert uses here, and only here, both accommodates the various poetic meters and invests the song with a distinctive breadth.

"Im Dorfe" is set in D major—quite a shock, after the E-flat minor/ major of "Letzte Hoffnung." The wanderer speaks in this poem as someone who has willfully placed as much distance as possible between the trauma of "Letzte Hoffnung" and the meditations in the village, and Schubert accordingly distances the two songs tonally from one another. The fact that the opening D-major chord of "Im Dorfe" is placed in the same register as the final chord of "Letzte Hoffnung" both heightens the shock of tonal distance from the previous scene and yet conveys the closeness of the two root pitches. It is not, after all, that far to fall from the grief at the end of "Letzte Hoffnung" to these bitter reflections by night. The atmosphere and motion of the work are established in the first six measures of a remarkably independent piano part, far more than mere depiction of the nocturnal scene. To be sure, we hear the rattling of chains in the measured bass trills and the dogs' barking in the repeated chords, the nocturnal vignette embellished by further details of Schubert's invention. In his imagined scenario, the dogs periodically rattle their chains and bark with extra vigor, then fall tensely silent for a moment, listening to determine whether the intruder in their midst has gone away. When he remains, they resume their restless activity. The measured trills in the bass seem a particularly apt device since a trill is both stasis, the music chained to two pitches a semitone apart, and motion. The nonmodulatory chromaticism of the introduction likewise rattles chains without going anywhere, a "disturbance of the peace" but without any change of place. (However, the B-flats in the topmost voice of mm. 3, 9, and 10 foreshadow the flatted submediant tonality that is such a powerful element at the end.) But the trills and repeated chords, the chromatic harmonies, the silences of almost half a measure in $\frac{12}{8}$ have meaning beyond pictorialism. Arnold Feil has pointed to the contrast within each measure of downbeat/regular pulsation and the tense, accented chord on the upbeat, followed by the prolonged uneasy silence that fills the remainder of the measure, as a first instance of the marked contrasts on several levels throughout the song.

Schubert's powerful use of silence at structural points in other compositions here becomes silence as an integral part of the principal musical material of the song.

The wanderer does not want to be numbered among the deluded dreamers and their wakeful, hostile dogs, and therefore he refuses to accord his part with the instrumental sounds depicting a milieu he scorns. His phrases and the piano phrases conflict with each other from the beginning, when the wanderer enters "early:" the harmonic progression I–II$_5^6$–V–I traced throughout the introduction is not yet concluded when the singer enters. After his entrance, the wanderer fills the tense silences in the accompaniment with his remarkably unlyrical reflections—the "chanting" on a minor third in the vocal line of mm. 6–8 ("Es bellen die Hunde, es rasseln die Ketten") seems like a mimicry of children's taunting songs. Only at two places do the piano and voice accord in perfect unanimity: when the wanderer in lines 6–8 sings of the villagers who hope to find in dreams whatever life has failed to give them and when he asks "Why should I linger among the sleepers?" at the end of the song. In the first instance, the lyricism of m. 20f approaches the parodistic. The villagers, according to the wanderer, have it all: they have their allotted share, and dreams supply the rest. In their world, everything is sweetness and light, without conflict and in total concord. Here, the piano and voice can even double one another at the tenth. At the beginning and again in mm. 29–37 and mm. 39–42, however, the disjunctions between the voice and the accompaniment are sounding symbols of the wanderer's alienation from what he conceives the villagers' world to be.

Unable to find surcease in dreams, the wanderer insists in "Im Dorfe" that they are vain substitutes for reality. Schubert's principal musical metaphor for dreams as useless figments of the imagination, accomplishing nothing, is an extended pedal point—flurries of motion in the upper voices over a bass that remains fixed in place. The first mention of dreams ("Träumen sich manches, was sie nicht haben") begins a passage fixated on the dominant pitch A, the background thus extraordinarily static (mm. 12–17) and yet increasingly tense because of the delayed resolution to tonic. None of the great deeds concocted in a dreamer's fantasy is actually enacted, and therefore there can be no tonal conclusion, no "coming down to earth" until the dream vanishes. In this passage, Schubert reverses the left- and right-hand parts so that the trill figure is in the right hand and the repeated chords in the bass; had he maintained the previous disposition, the trill figures in the bass, stuck on A, would rapidly become intolerable. Rather, the bass lies chained to its pedal point like sleepers motionless in their beds while the right-hand trill figures rise in symbolic mimicry of the flights of fancy the dreaming mind creates. With morning and wakefulness, everything in the dream vanishes irrevocably. In the plunge downward two and one-half octaves from the apex of the trill to tonic resolution (the end of the dream) in the low bass of m. 17, we hear a reminiscence of the wanderer's earlier shock and disillusionment when his own dreams ended and he was jolted back to waking reality.

The dreaming villagers inhabit, for a time, a sphere other than reality, so the wanderer leaves D major (but not the pitch D, which sounds as a pedal point throughout mm. 19–26) and the music of the restless dogs behind in the setting of lines 6–8, the B section of Schubert's form. This middle section is reminiscent of the central section of "Rückblick" in the G-major tonality (although the tonal context is different), the pedal point D, the feeling of $\frac{6}{8}$ meter (even though the time signature $\frac{12}{8}$ remains), and the lyricism, in contrast with what precedes and follows it. (Schubert uses subdominant substitutes in the A section and reserves G major for this interior meditation on dreams.) Unlike the setting of the first five lines, the B section is filled with fragmentary text repetitions characteristic of songlike lyricism but conspicuously missing from the A section. Here, the wanderer twice insists that the sleepers have their allotted portion *now* ("Je nun, je nun") and twice repeats the verb "to hope" ("Und hoffen, und hoffen"). The villagers can still hope for visionary joys in sleep, but the wanderer has just lost what he believes to be his last vestige of hope in "Letzte Hoffnung," and that loss echoes in his reflections here. The appoggiaturas on the verbs "ge - *nos*-sen" and "*lie - ßen*"[2] are mocking emphasis on that which the villagers already have ("genossen") and that which remains to be supplied in dreams ("ließen"), the two almost exactly alike. In the wanderer's pained, envious account, there is no difference between the townspeople's good fortune awake and asleep. Having enacted the words "wieder zu finden" by "finding them again" in a descending sequence that is almost parodistically light, he is unable to bear any further thought of the vil-

---

[2]The A-sharps of the appoggiaturas in mm. 21 and 23 are an enharmonic respelling of the B-flats from m. 3 in the introduction and the A section, which become all the more important in the setting of the quatrain at the end.

lagers' refuge in dreams and returns abruptly to D major. The return
in m. 26 is rendered all the more emphatic for the tritone leap to a
C-sharp in the vocal line and the prolonged dissonant clash of C-
sharp against D (the piercing sound of the /ee/ v owel in "*ih* - ren
Kissen" adds to the effect). In Schubert's reading, the wanderer is
suddenly sickened by his speculations and wrenches his thoughts
away from such profitless avenues with a force palpable in the awkwardness of the voice-leading and the dissonant insistence on C-
sharp. Reality is D major, and the wanderer wrests the music back
to it, back to terra firma, with disconcerting suddenness.

From the higher register of the townspeople's dreams, the wanderer, once more aware of the nocturnal scene around him, descends
back down to the bass trills and repeated chords from the beginning
of the song, back to the unresolved conflict between the voice and
the piano. The descent, unharmonized to parallel the transition to
the B section, includes significant chromatic pitches from earlier in
the song and foreshadows their recurrence in the final section, including E-sharp (subsequently respelled as F-natural) and B-flat in
the first bass trill figure (m. 29). For the wanderer's references to the
wakeful dogs and the "hour of sleep," Schubert brings back the beginning of the A section (mm. 7–11 return as mm. 31–35), the wanderer's wish that he not sleep ironically set to the previous "snoring"
figure, but at the word "Ende" in m. 36 the literal recurrence of
previous music ceases.

Whether or not the question at the end is rhetorical, that is, an
angry verbal goad with which to impel the wanderer's flight from
humankind, is itself a question. The ending can certainly be read in
that way, but Schubert seems to have understood it as genuine self-
inquiry, more thoughtful than contemptuous in tone. His wanderer
seems truly to wonder why he lingers in a village peopled by those
he professes to find contemptible; whether he senses the barely
cloaked envy, born of despair, that has led him to stay and speculate
about the surcease others enjoy is an ambiguity left unresolved. For
the duration of the question, the wanderer speaks with such solemn
intensity that he blocks out the sounds of the external world. The
rattling trills and barking repeated chords cease and are replaced by
the neutrality of a block-chordal accompaniment. The underlying urgency of the query is expressed in a rate of harmonic change more
rapid than that of the figures compounded of trills, repeated chords,
and potent silences. Even the way in which Schubert begins the ques-

tion tells the listener that it is neither angry nor rhetorical: the wanderer breaks with the previous rhythmic conflict, joins the piano with
the voice in perfect unanimity, and prolongs the initial word "Was"
slightly but noticeably beyond what one would expect from an upbeat.
"Why should I linger among the sleepers? What am I doing that I
remain here?" he asks in real perplexity, and Schubert accordingly
dwells on "Was" in interpretive emphasis. Each time, the chord at
the word "Was" is the harmonic transition back to the D major chord.
The transition from one kind of accompanimental figuration to another and from one rhythmic pulse to another—it has the disposition
of the block-chordal texture to follow and yet is set as an eighth note,
like the end of the barking/rattling figure. Furthermore, the wanderer
leaps to the topmost pitch D of the question at the word "ich" (I) in
mm. 38 and 43: "Why should I (who am so different from these
people) remain here among them?"

The question is set apart from the nocturnal sounds on either side
by rhythmic-metrical means as well. Measures 38–39 are actually a
single hyper-measure in triple meter, each "beat" consisting of a
dotted half note; the crescendo indications make the actual rhythmic
structure apparent. The crucial word "säumen" thus actually occurs
on a downbeat, and its stressed initial syllable constitutes a single bar
unto itself, an emphasis readily audible when one listens to the passages. The old conflicts return, however, in m. 39, and the wanderer
must repeat the question before he can at last leave the village. When
he does so, "säu-men" is prolonged throughout an entire hyper-
measure of its own, the wanderer lingering over the verb "to linger"
(mm. 44–45) in a manner at significant cross-purposes with the very
intent he avows. The archaizing cadential formula, in which the
penultimate dominant harmony is embellished with suspensions in
the manner of a Baroque chorale, invests the question's ending with
great gravity. The longing to be like the sleepers he derides, to find
comfort in dreams, has kept him there despite his recognition of
difference.

Every compositional choice Schubert made in setting this passage
conveys the wanderer's longing for precisely that which he condemns
and renounces in "Im Dorfe," in sum, the human condition. It is
against human nature and beyond the power of human will to fore-
swear dreams, and the wanderer is shortly thereafter unable to carry
out his tragic declaration. But here he both asserts that he will do so
and yet is strangely reluctant to leave surroundings in which others

do not live by his newly proclaimed law. That reluctance produces a necessarily exaggerated reaction in the next song, "Der stürmische Morgen." Only by mustering the fiercest resolve can he overcome the mysterious compulsion (paraphrasing "Rückblick") "to stand still before these houses."

18. Der stürmische Morgen

Wie hat der Sturm zerrissen
Des Himmels graues Kleid!
Die Wolkenfetzen flattern
Umher in mattem Streit.

Und rote Feuerflammen
Ziehn zwischen ihnen hin.
Das nenn' ich einen Morgen
So recht nach meinem Sinn!

Mein Herz sieht an dem Himmel
Gemalt sein eignes Bild—
Es ist nichts als der Winter,
Der Winter kalt und wild!

The Stormy Morning

(How the storm has torn the heavens' gray robe! Tattered clouds
flutter about in weary strife.
And red flames flash between them—this is what I call a morning
after my own heart!
My heart sees its own image painted in the sky; it is nothing but
winter—cold, wild winter!)

The somber meditation in "Im Dorfe" is followed by an outburst
of furious energy in "Der stürmische Morgen." Rejecting futile
dreams, the wanderer finds a climate more to his liking—the tempest
he had earlier longed for in "Einsamkeit"—and declares himself revitalized by the turmoil. Müller's scene is painterly in its details (the
verb "gemalt," or "painted" in stanza 3 is indeed appropriate): the
gray robe of the sky rent by the storm; the spent fragments of tattered
storm clouds which drift into one another, at the mercy of the wind;
and the red flare of the lightning, a rare touch of color in the cycle.
The flashes of red that light up the monochromatic landscape are
given sonorous life in the percussive /ts/ and /z/ consonants and the
piercing /ee/ sounds of "Ziehn zwischen ihnen hin," and Müller similarly punctuates the emphatic iambs of the wanderer's final proclamation "Es ist nichts als der Winter, / Der Winter kalt und wild!"
with percussive consonants. The wanderer had earlier in "Frühlingstraum" mused on the artist who painted leaves of frost on the window; now he finds a Turneresque tempest painted on the heavens
and asserts its likeness to the stormy passions in his heart.

Müller repeats motifs from earlier in the journey, but the tone is
uncharacteristic, an exercise in denial and bravado. Schubert accordingly devises a musical setting full of displacing tensions that belie
the wanderer's fierce proclamations. As in "Auf dem Fluße," the
wanderer proposes an analogy between his heart and turbulence in
Nature; his heart can see its image mirrored in the strife that fills the
skies. "This is what I call a morning after my own heart [the idiom
"after my own heart" is indeed the apposite phrase]," he says, not,
"This is a morning after my own heart." If he proclaims it to be so,
if he asserts the analogy with atypical force, perhaps he can believe

it, but Müller's choice of words hints at the wanderer's underlying disbelief. The emotional turmoil is certainly real; whether this is truly the "climate of choice" is not. The grim, wild energy of the moment briefly revitalizes the journey, but it does not and cannot last. This is the shortest song in the cycle.

Those tensions are fully apparent in the introduction, which begins on the D *major* of "Im Dorfe" just before it, not the D minor indicated in the key signature. The bitter nocturnal reflections in the village have unleashed a storm of feeling the next morning, and Schubert underscores the chronology of emotional events by means of the "tonal corridor" that links the two songs. The unison writing in much of "Der stürmische Morgen," the rhythmic acceleration throughout mm. 1–2, the increasing number of accents on the strong beats (m. 1) and on the even subdivisions of the measure (m. 2), the sequential ascent in the first measure and the juxtaposition in m. 2 of a rising chromatic "inner voice" and hammered repetitions of the tonic pitch in the upper register, the chromaticism that so thoroughly disturbs the D major of the first measure—these are all musical indices both of power and rising tension. But the placement of higher pitches on the weaker half of the beat in mm. 1–2 adds an element of conflict to the strong accents, especially as the motion accelerates. The more forceful the music, the more insistent the gesture becomes. The progression from a diatonic ascent to a chromatic continuation is reminiscent of the principal motive of "Rückblick" and produces the same sense of increasing urgency throughout the phrase. The ascent reaches a climax of tension with the diminished seventh chord on the raised fourth degree in the middle of the second bar, the D major of m. 1 now thoroughly in doubt. The wanderer resorts to naked force to resolve the matter: yet another rhythmic acceleration to dramatize the descent from B natural to B-flat and then to the dominant pitch A, culminating in the violent registral contrast that sends the right hand catapulting upward more than two octaves at the end. The wanderer will shortly use the pitch-rhythm tensions of mm. 1–2 to characterize the "tired strife" that fills the heavens, but there is nothing weak about the conflicts that pervade the introduction.

After this initial violence, Schubert has the singer charge right through the stanza without a pause or break. The wanderer's first vocal phrase asserts the D minor that has "won out" by the end of the introduction and does so in strict conformity with the meter. The steep ascent and the melodic fourths and fifths are closely related motivically to the introduction, however, and the turbulence that so fascinates the wanderer floods back in the setting of the third and fourth lines. The strife that fills the lied is expressed in part by means of an unusual emphasis on the tense, unstable sound of diminished seventh harmonies—in this brief song, we hear all three of them. The piano interlude between stanzas 1 and 2, which recurs as the postlude, pits the rising left hand against the precipitously falling right hand until the "clouds" almost collide, both storm-driven parts outlining a diminished seventh on the raised fourth degree. The chromatic B-natural pitches so furiously asserted in that interlude are then followed in strongest contrast by a setting of the second stanza in the key of B-flat, the modulation accomplished without transition or fanfare. Schubert's wanderer simply jumps to B-flat for the proclamation "I call this a morning after my own heart."

The rhythmic disturbances that spell strife in stanza 1 disappear from the wanderer's defiant assertion in the second stanza, proclaimed after the manner of a military march complete with fanfares. The full chordal texture, the relative diatonic clarity of mm. 10–13, the unharmonized B-flat fanfares between phrases, and the metrical regularity are all distinct from the tensions that pervade the first stanza, tearing at the tonal and rhythmic fabric the way the storm has torn the gray garb of the heavens. The brightness of major mode heightens the wanderer's atypical assertion of rightness and may indicate as well that he only imagines matters to be "right" for the moment—they are not truly so. Additionally, Schubert's use of a dominant substitute for the proclamation "Das nenn' ich einen Morgen / So recht nach meinem Sinn!" is perhaps especially appropriate because the statement is so unconventional. Most people prefer springtime beauty rather than winter storms, and the choice of flatted submediant rather than the dominant key seems the perfect tonal concomitant to such perversity.

Following the B-flat fanfares in m. 11, the B-flat remains and becomes the seventh degree of a diminished seventh chord, resolving downward and thus revealing itself to be the upper neighbor to A. In this varied recurrence of the music of stanza 1, strife returns full force and pervades the remainder of the song, the greater balance of the initial vocal phrase no longer possible in the exultation of cold, wild winter. Omitting that first phrase, Schubert restates mm. 6–7 ("Die Wolkenfetzen flattern / Umher in mattem Streit") to the words "Mein Herz sieht an dem Himmel / Gemalt sein eignes Bild" in mm. 14–15 to establish the analogy between storminess in the heavens and storminess in the wanderer's heart. The diminished seventh harmony A–C–E-flat–G-flat that is a neighboring chord to the tonicized B-flat in mm. 10 and 12 (stanza 2) recurs here respelled at the climax of the

song, when the "Feuerflammen" blaze forth even more wildly—
the savagery of the end is unequaled anywhere else in the cycle.
The grim, wild energy of the moment revitalizes the journey, but it
is short-lived and uncharacteristic. For a brief time, the wanderer
exclaims, "Blow, winds, and crack your cheeks! rage! blow!" but he
is no Lear and the defiant mood does not last.

19. Täuschung

Etwas geschwind

Licht____ tanzt freund-lich vor __ mir her ____ ;

simile

Ein Licht tanzt freundlich vor mir her;
Ich folg' ihm nach die Kreuz und Quer;
Ich folg' ihm gern, und seh's ihm an,
Daß es verlockt den Wandersmann.
Ach, wer wie ich so elend ist,
Gibt gern sich hin der bunten List,
Die hinter Eis und Nacht und Graus
Ihm weist ein helles, warmes Haus,
Und eine liebe Seele drin—
Nur Täuschung ist für mich Gewinn!

[266]

Delusion

(A light dances cheerfully before me; I follow it to and fro. I follow it gladly, knowing that it deceives the wanderer. Ah, one as wretched as I am gladly surrenders to the beguiling gleam that reveals to him, beyond ice and night and terror, a bright, warm house and a beloved soul within—even mere delusion is a prize to me!)

As in "Irrlicht," the wanderer follows another illusory light without caring where it leads him. The near-frenzy of "Der stürmische Morgen" has dissipated, and the dreams renounced in "Im Dorfe" are not so easily banished when nothing exists to take their place. Anyone as wretched as he is gladly—Müller twice in close proximity uses the word "gern," found nowhere else in the cycle—surrenders to the bright guile that promises refuge and love somewhere beyond the night and cold. The wanderer's fantasies never change. Once again, he yearns for the reciprocated love of "Frühlingstraum" and longs to come in from the cold, to find shelter from his wintry desolation of the spirit. Even as he follows the will-o'-the-wisp in a feigned lightheartedness more tragic than overt grief, he knows its promises are only deception.

"Täuschung" is another of the formal oddities of the cycle, a single ten-line stanza in rhyming couplets. The absence of stanzaic divisions is significant: the feigned lightness and underlying misery are all of a piece, and the near-insane wanderer is momentarily incapable of articulation in discrete poetic units. The tensions that have the wanderer literally dancing on the edge of insanity are manifest when the regularity of the rhyming couplets is increasingly contradicted by syntax that cuts across and through the arrangement in paired lines. For the brief duration of the pretense at gaiety (lines 1–4), form and content exist in equipoise; Müller even links the first two couplets by means of the repeated words "Ich folg' ihm / Ich folg' ihm." But with the admission of misery and the outbreak of lamentation, his thoughts can no longer be contained within couplet boundaries and spill over into the subsequent lines in an almost uncontrolled fashion. The dichotomies of wretchedness/gladness, ice-night-horror/the bright, warm house, and reality/fantasy that begin with the fifth line continue unchecked through the ninth line and clearly could have gone on longer, had the wanderer not checked his self-lacerating impulses in midstream. The final couplet is riven in two by the wanderer's refusal to continue indulging hopeless fantasies.

"Täuschung" is a rare example of *contrafactum* in Schubert's music, its source an aria from Act II of his opera *Alfonso und Estrella*, D.732, to a libretto by his friend Franz Schober. The aria likewise is a tale of illusion, of supernatural love similar to the Lorelei story and to other legends of enchantresses who lure mortal men to their deaths. The tale is inserted into the opera on the slightest of pretexts when Alfonso begs his father Troila to sing to him once again "the beautiful song of the cloud-maiden." The father replies that surely by now Alfonso could sing the story himself, but his son dutifully responds, "You know well that I haven't your skill or your soulful melodies." Troila gives in—"Now listen!"—and launches into the tale, set as an extended through-composed aria. The legend begins with a hunter at rest in a green field; at evening, a lovely maiden lures him away with her beautiful singing ("Will you be my friend, my servant? The greatest of good fortune has come your way"). She points to her golden castle in the clouds and promises him that the stars will greet him and the storms will do his bidding. Müller's poem evidently recalled Schober's words describing the doomed hunter's journey as he follows the siren into the clouds:

> Er folgte ihrer Stimme Rufen
> Und stieg den rauhen Pfad hinan,
> Sie tanzte über Felsenstufen
> Durch dunkle Schlünde leicht ihm vor.

(He followed the sound of her voice and climbed up the rugged path. She danced lightly in front of him, over the rocky steps, through dark gorges.)

Both the "friendly light" and the cloud-maiden dance in front of those whom they lure along rock-strewn or icy pathways, and both are seductive creatures who promise love's fulfillment. In both, beauty masks horror, and both are agents of death. But the differences are just as instructive as the similarities and necessitated alteration of the aria model when transformed into song. The wanderer knows from the beginning that the will-o'-the-wisp is an illusion, while the more naive huntsman is entirely deluded. Not until the cloud-castle vanishes beneath him and he topples to his death does he realize that his "great good fortune" was nothing of the kind. The "death" that threatens the wanderer is the dissolution of his sanity under the burden of despair, but unlike Schober's huntsman, he wrenches himself away from danger at the last minute by sheer force of will. Schubert's melodic parallels linking the friendly light and the fantasied house, deception and the "beloved soul," underscore the awareness of illusion. So too does the prolongation of certain single-syllable words throughout five beats in $\frac{6}{8}$ meter ("Licht," "folg'," "es," and so on), a prolongation that results in the asymmetrical juxtaposition of three-bar vocal phrases with different phrasing in the accompaniment. Those prolongations, accentuating by contrast the melodic motion that follows, culminate in the durational emphasis on the keyword "*Täu* - schung"—"Nur Täuschung ist für mich Gewinn." The melodic leap to E at the word "mich" (previously, "*Wan* - dersmann") is another kind of emphasis, equally telling.

Schubert borrows only the music of the cloud-maiden's dance along the rocky paths, ten measures of the B-major third section of the aria. The broken-chordal figuration in sixteenth-note patterns for the harp is not transferred to "Täuschung," but the remainder reappears largely intact, including the mid-measure accents. One might, somewhat fancifully, find poetic significance in the fact that the right-hand part consists primarily of repeated pitches followed by an ascending figure toward the end of each phrase: the light remains in place for a moment, then dances on and lures the wanderer after it. As Feil observes, there is already something expressive of abnormality, a first taint of lunacy, in the contrast between the short eighth-note upbeat at the beginning of the first vocal phrase and the prolonged downbeat on "Licht."[1] Furthermore, the disposition of the phrasing in the accompaniment and its relationship to the phrase structure of the vocal part is quite remarkable. This light does not flicker and change like the will-o'-the-wisp in "Irrlicht," but remains constantly, alluringly in view, and its invitation to follow ever onward becomes in music an entire series of elided phrases. The end of the introduction is simultaneously the beginning of the phrase the wanderer joins; where the wanderer's words "vor mir her" at the end of that first phrase reach their end, the accompaniment is in mid-phrase on a dominant-seventh chord in first inversion and echoes the wanderer's cadential tag as a further enticement to go forward. The ceaseless iteration in the accompaniment is indeed insane, a *moto perpetuo* dance of despair. The final tonic chord of the song has an almost arbitrary sound, the wanderer putting a halt to figuration that would otherwise go on and on and on. The fermata over that last chord seems much more than the conventional prolongation of the final tonic; rather, it is a bar to keep the dance at bay and prevent it from starting up again. It is a

[1]Feil, *Franz Schubert*, 115.

brilliant, terrifying conception by which Schubert transforms the Viennese *élan* of the dance into something so grimly obsessive, in utter contradiction of the surface gaiety. Were there ever a ball in Bedlam, the *danse macabre* that is "Täuschung" would have been fitting music for it.

"Täuschung" is music of fixation, and it goes nowhere—the zigzag motion "nach die Kreuz und Quer" is actually fixed in place. In a foreshadowing of the greater harmonic fixity of "Der Leiermann," this song is monomanaically rooted to A major throughout, the bass line a study in unrelieved diatonicism. The tonal obsession with A, the renunciation of any modulation to other keys, is such that the unprepared C-natural on the first beat on m. 22, the outbreak of overt lamentation, "Ach," comes as a jolt. The lack of preparation for this sudden injection of minor mode into the continued blithe but relentless dance rhythms is disconcerting, all the more as the C-sharp returns just as abruptly two measures later at the words "gibt gern"— but not as a constituent of an A-major chord. Not until the return of the A section and the word "weist [ein helles, warmes Haus]" does an A-major harmony reappear after the extended dominant throughout mm. 24–30, a musical demarcation that occurs in mid-sentence of the poetry. The progressively more acerbic soprano-bass dissonances in mm. 25–26 and the separation of the words "gibt gern" from the remainder of that line by a rest are still more ways of heightening the tension of this passage. Everywhere else in "Täuschung," the melodic motion in the right-hand part echoes the singer's cadence with which it is elided in mocking echo. Only in the B section is the instrumental mockery extended to such length as one finds in mm. 24–27, and only here does it assume the character of a true countermelody, as if bodying out the "bright lie."

When the wanderer names aloud the ice, night, and terror that are his lot, the artificial gaiety cannot go on as before. The mad, incessant quarter-note–eighth-note figures in the right hand never stop throughout the entire song, but now that rhythmic pattern resounds in the parts for the left hand and the voice as well (mm. 28–30)— Schubert had earlier used similar "heartbeat" figures in "Die Post" when the wanderer speaks to his heart. The three-measure phrases for the voice are no longer extended to conventional four-measure length by the piano, as in the A section, and we understand in this way the suffocating sense of misery grown so great that breathing room between phrases is no longer possible. With each terrifying reality the wanderer invokes, another intensifying element is added to the music. "Nacht" is sustained throughout almost an entire measure, while "Graus" is both similarly sustained and intensified by the passing motion that produces an augmented triad, an infrequent and therefore special register of tension in the cycle. The B-sharp of the dominant augmented triad is an enharmonic recurrence of the C-naturals at the beginning of the B section, the lamenting words "Ach," "elend," and "Graus" thus linked by their common pitch relationship.

The extended dominant of the B section merges by elision into the return of the A section, an abbreviated return. Here, the wanderer wrenches himself away from continued masochistic indulgence in the fantasy of a "bright, warm house." The refusal to continue imagining what he cannot have is signified by the dash at the end of Müller's ninth line, a dash that becomes in the musical form omission of the expected third vocal phrase (mm. 13–16), and the isolation of the final vocal phrase. Unlike the last lines of every other song, the last line of this poem is not repeated. Measures 31–37 repeat mm. 6–12; where the dash appears, Schubert makes the listener aware that music heard previously has been omitted. (The durational emphasis on "*ei* - ne" in m. 35 is a means by which to emphasize the wanderer's desire for *one* beloved, a single soul with whom to share his lot.) Because we hear the return of the A section as a recapitulation, we expect the piano to extend the three-measure phrase in mm. 35–37 ("und eine liebe Seele drin—") into a fourth measure; when this does not happen, we hear the words "Nur Täuschung" as beginning too early and know that the suffocating misery of the B section has reappeared. Even more, we know that the form of the A section is a deception, that its elements have broken down and are revealed as a lie at the end. The "beloved soul and bright house" are mad illusions; the light is deception; and the dance is a claustrophobic entrapment within the narrowest of boundaries.

20. Der Wegweiser

Was vermeid' ich denn die Wege,
Wo die andern Wandrer gehn,
Suche mir versteckte Stege
Durch verschneite Felsenhöhn?

Habe ja doch nichts begangen,
Daß ich Menschen sollte scheun—
Welch ein törichtes Verlangen
Treibt mich in die Wüstenei'n?

[272]

Weiser stehen auf den Wegen [Straßen],[1]
Weisen auf die Städte zu,
Und ich wandre sonder Maßen,
Ohne Ruh', und suche Ruh'.

Einen Weiser seh' ich stehen
Unverrückt vor meinem Blick;
Eine Straße muß ich gehen,
Die noch keiner ging zurück.

The Signpost

(Why do I shun the paths that other travelers take, and seek hidden paths through snowy, rocky heights?

Yet I have done no wrong that I should shun people—what foolish desire drives me into the wilderness?

Signposts stand on the roads, signposts pointing toward the towns, and I wander on, relentlessly, restless, yet seeking rest.

I see a signpost standing immovably before my eyes: I must travel a road from which no one has returned.)

For the first time, the wanderer asks himself why his journey is so different from that of others, what compulsion drives him to continue, and why he chooses to be so isolated. It is not a matter of chance that he takes hidden, difficult paths (the percussive /t/ and /st/ consonants of "versteckte Stege" the embodiment in sound of the craggy pathways): he seeks them out, without knowing why. Signposts point the way to towns, but he will have nothing to do with other human beings, even though he is guiltless of any crime. When he asks himself what "foolish desire" drives him out into the wilderness, the adjective "törichtes" (foolish, crazy) speaks volumes about his frustration and the need to know what compulsion governs his every action and condemns him to exile. The repetition of the word "Ruh'"—the poetic semblance of a long sigh—in the last line of stanza 3, like the repeated words in close proximity in "Letzte Hoffnung," conveys the intensity of his desire for an end to his journey.

The kinship between "Gute Nacht" and "Der Wegweiser" constitutes a bridge spanning much of the cycle. In both, the principal

[1]Schubert set lines 1 and 2 of this stanza as a single four-bar (2 + 2) phrase and therefore may have altered Müller's word "Straßen" in order to create the alliteration of "Wegen" and "Weisen" in close succession.

subject is the journey itself, its nature and cause, and the journeying figure therefore appears throughout both works, in the same *mässig* tempo and eighth-note tactus. The differences, however, are even more telling. In "Gute Nacht," the eighth-note motion in the accompaniment is constant, without pause and without rhythmic alteration, and the journeying figure seldom invades the vocal line. The journey has only just begun. By the twentieth song, matters are much bleaker. Here, the wanderer questions the journey, probes it as something he must finally understand, and therefore the figure from so long ago is subjected to prolongation, new harmonizations, rhythmic permutations, shifting registers, and interruption, as if by turning the figure inside out he could at last see and know it fully—and he does. The journeying figure pervades both the vocal line and the piano part as the primary musical idea of the song, subject to many of the variation techniques at Schubert's considerable disposal. The variety of changes wrought on the motive, culminating in the solemnity of its rhythmic augmentation at the end, are emblematic of the progression from bewilderment at the beginning to comprehension at the close.

Before the wanderer begins to sing, Schubert already establishes a contrast in the introduction between the smoother, diatonic roads the "other travelers" take (mm. 1–2) and the wanderer's hidden, chromatic pathways (mm. 3–4). That same contrast is extended into the setting of the first stanza, in which other people travel along diatonic paths in mm. 6–10 (paths plural, the journeying figure in the voice and right-hand part echoed by its transposition in the bass), while the wanderer's more jagged route in mm. 11–19 is a matter of motion away from tonic, of chromatic descent in the bass, of weak-beat accents, and grace-noted turning figures that produce brief but clashing cross-relations between the bass and the inner voice—multiple indices of conflict. When the wanderer repeats the words "seek hidden paths," he has descended one whole step to the flatted seventh harmony of F minor, indeed "hidden" from those who travel along G-minor pathways. The contrast between his own life and that of everyone else is here drawn in tonal terms that recur in the next song. Near the end of "Das Wirtshaus" when he takes up his walking staff to resume his journey, F minor sounds once more.

The parallel major of mm. 22–27 is a protestation of innocence set in the brighter major mode. Like the beginning of the first verse, the passage is almost completely diatonic, the chord voicing fuller and sweeter, rhythmically unitary and without the distinction between different voices as different "Wegen" or "paths" in stanza 1. Schubert's wanderer is so mystified by his own actions that he repeats the words "Daß ich Menschen sollte scheun" a step higher, on the way to the climactic E in m. 28. There the tonality and texture change radically, the wanderer turning away from the brighter sounds that accompany his protest of innocence in order to fragment, vary, and reharmonize the journeying figure. The swift motion away from G major and the twofold deceptive progression to an accented C-major chord heighten the desperate intensity of the question "Welch ein törichtes Verlangen / Treibt mich in die Wüstenei'n?"

Throughout "Der Wegweiser," the journeying figure is given an added impetus by means of an upbeat, at first carefully separated from the non-legato figure by slurs. When the motion stagnates in m. 2, the upbeat that follows is a spur to start it up once more. The initial trochees of Müller's lines in trochaic tetrameters become the upbeats in the vocal line, the sixteenth-note anacruses leading to the strong syllable of the second trochees. The only poetic line distorted prosodically by the repeated rhythmic pattern is the eighth line, "Treibt mich in die Wüstenei'n," which Schubert then repeats in order to complete the cadence and emphasize still more strongly the verb "treibt" (drives, compels, forces). The anacruses' disappearance from the piano transition at the end of the B section is only one hint among several of the revelation to come. That passage in the piano foreshadows the final stanza, but the wanderer does not yet recognize it for what it is. The brief silence following the half-cadence in m. 39, significantly unresolved, is the silence of incomprehension, a pause in which the wanderer fails to understand what he has just heard and therefore returns to the beginning of the song.

The "Wüstenei'n" (wilderness, desert places) of B minor lead back to G minor and the music of the first stanza, to statements that repeat the same questions he has asked in the first two verses. The wanderer who speaks in stanza 3 of the signposts that point the way to towns will shortly see his own signpost and his own road; the image of the signposts is the key to unlock the mystery of his self-exile and alienation. The only variations to the recurrent music from stanza 1 are impelled by the cry "Ohne Ruh', und suche Ruh' " in the last line, words Müller's wanderer says only once. Not so Schubert, whose wanderer repeats the phrase over and over in massive desperation. The first time he sings those words, he doubles the inner voice in m. 48, with the first syllable of the verb "*su - che*" prolonged against the moving inner line. But the second time, passion wrenches syntax and declamation out of their accustomed channels. The connective "und" would not, in other contexts, receive such emphasis, but here, the prosodic distortion, the furious weak-beat accents on "und," is a

masterful detail of interpretation. The connective signifies continuation, and the wanderer, who has lamented "all this long journey,"
can no longer bear its continuation.

When the journeying figure appears in its starkest guise, alone in
the piano at mm. 55–56, the wanderer sees the signpost, fixed and
unmoving from its unharmonized pitch, and at last understands the
nature of his journey. For this moment of revelation, Schubert creates
powerful musical symbols for something so awesome as a vision of
destiny within the mind, tonal disorientation whose rising chromatic
bass line conveys rising horror within the mind. A series of voice
exchanges within a diminished seventh harmony brings the exchang-
ing voices closer and closer together in mm. 57–67, the danger of
collision obviated by the downward leap in the bass at m. 62 and the
ascending motion in the vocal line, which shifts inner chord tones
into the topmost voice. Because of the leap in the vocal line and the
prominent placement of the B-flat-minor and C-sharp-minor chords
(mm. 61 and 63, at the words "eine Straße muß ich gehen"), those
harmonies are emphasized rhythmically beyond their harmonic function as passing chords, and the listener is thus led to expect a shift
in tonality. That this does not happen increases the already considerable tension of this remarkable passage. Carl Schachter and Edward
Aldwell have written of the "breathtaking original quirk of notation"
here: the D-flats in the vocal line of mm. 63–64 are in seeming contradiction to the C-sharp in the accompaniment and the drive to dominant. The vocal line is an arpeggiation of a diminished seventh
consisting entirely of minor thirds, without the augmented second
interval that would return the arpeggiation to the initial scale degree
at the octave. Arpeggiation in minor thirds never comes back to its
origin, no matter how long it continues—G–B-flat–D-flat–F-flat–A-
double-flat–C-double-flat, and so on. "Schubert's strange notation,
therefore, embodies a musical symbol for 'a road from which no one
has ever returned.' "[2] It is a powerful and moving symbol, especially
when the G-sharp of the C-sharp-minor chord returns respelled as
the Neapolitan sixth near the end of the long, fraught passage. The
dark, intense sound of that chord comes at the culmination of the
drive-to-cadence beneath the sustained word "*kei* - ner," the horror
of realization quickening at the end.

It was Müller's feint throughout much of the cycle to write as if the

[2]Carl Schachter and Edward Aldwell, *Harmony and Voice-Leading*, vol. 2 (New York,
1979), 220–21.

wanderer sings of thoughts and emotions as he experiences them. The voice exchange and the uncertainty of tonal orientation beautifully reflect, not only the phenomenon of the road with no possible return, but the chaos of a mind stunned by the sight. The initial realization over, the wanderer repeats the entire quatrain, this time with his eyes fixed on the immutable signpost. The repeated Gs in the inner voice, like a tolling bell, sound on and on, while the boundaries of the road narrow in a slow, inexorable convergence surrounding the fixed point.

21. Das Wirtshaus

Auf ei - nen To-ten - a - cker hat mich mein Weg ge - bracht, all -
hier will ich ein-keh-ren, hab ich bei mir ge-dacht.

Auf einen Totenacker
Hat mich mein Weg gebracht.
Allhier will ich einkehren:
Hab' ich bei mir gedacht.

Ihr grünen Totenkränze
Könnt wohl die Zeichen sein,
Die müde Wandrer laden
In's kühle Wirtshaus ein.

Sind denn in diesem Hause
Die Kammern all' besetzt?
Bin matt zum Niedersinken,
Bin [Und] tödlich schwer verletzt.

O unbarmherz'ge Schenke,
Doch weisest du mich ab?
Nun weiter denn, nur weiter,
Mein treuer Wanderstab!

The Inn

(My journey has brought me to a cemetery. I'll take lodgings here,
I thought to myself.

Green funeral wreaths, you must be the signs that invite weary
wanderers into the cool inn.

Are all the rooms in this house already taken? I am tired and ready
to collapse, I am fatally wounded.

O unmerciful inn, do you nonetheless turn me away? On then,
ever onward, my trusty walking staff!)

Müller took his images in "Das Wirtshaus" from life. In nineteenth-
century Austria and Germany, it was the custom for innkeepers to
put evergreen wreaths on the doors of inns and country houses as a
sign to customers that the new wine, or *Heurige*, was available. Schubert, whose friends told of his liking for an occasional glass of *Heurige*
at the cafés in nearby Grinzing, would surely have recognized the
reference. Here, the wanderer sees the funeral garlands in a cemetery
and associates them with the hospitality and shelter of an inn. Once
again, he looks for signs and portents that the death he desires is
close at hand. The metaphor of the cemetery as an inn where tired
wanderers may rest was not Müller's invention, but he embellishes

the metaphor with a uniquely German symbol of welcome, an example of his belief that the best verse grew from home soil and was
rooted in the language, images, and customs of the poet's native
region.

Two elements of "Das Wirtshaus" have a poignance that stems
from Müller's invocations of the same images earlier in the cycle.
Throughout the journey, the wanderer has remembered, dreamed
of, even sought in vain the greenery of springtime past, green traditionally symbolic of hope and life. Yet the green in Part I is always
a memory or a dream. Not until "Das Wirtshaus" does he see real
greenery, and then it is the emblem of death, not life. (The wanderer
who does not believe in God passes over any symbolic reference of
evergreen branches to the soul's life after death.) The scene in the
cemetery is furthermore the last time in the cycle that the wanderer
speaks of houses, similarly one of the poetic leitmotifs of the cycle.
His awareness of exclusion from the world of others is represented
from the beginning in images of the wanderer standing outside his
sweetheart's house, or longing to return and do so again, dreaming
of shelter and a "bright, warm house," and finally seeking the one
house that seems to promise him refuge: the grave.

"Das Wirtshaus" is the only song in the cycle in F major; major
mode is a principal factor in the peaceful, almost emotionless (until
the end) atmosphere of this song. Wrapped in thoughts of death and
walking as if carrying a bier, as if walking in a dream, the wanderer
sings of last things in tones purged of rebellion against fate. Schubert
sets the graveyard vignette tonally apart from "Der Wegweiser" in
G minor just before it and "Mut" in G minor just after—here is another
example of his use of tonality to separate certain songs from each
other rather than draw them together. (The relationship between "Der
Wegweiser" and "Mut" thus has to be perceived across the distancing
gap created by the F-major episode between them.) Schubert inherited
eighteenth-century and earlier associations of F major with pastoral
scenes (as in his earlier songs "An die Natur," D. 283, and "Erlafsee,"
D. 586) and with lullabies, that is, with the essence of peacefulness
and calm. He had earlier set the lovely "Schlaflied," D. 527, to a text
by his friend Johann Mayrhofer in F major, and Mahler would later
compose the lullaby-farewell "In diesem Wetter!" at the end of the
Kindertotenlieder in that same key, a continuation of the traditional
associations. Thrasybulos Georgiades finds a close kinship between
the melody of "Das Wirtshaus" and the F-centered Kyrie from the
Requiem Mass, which Schubert would have known from his days as
parish organist of Liechtental and his Stadtkonvikt schooldays; in-

deed, Georgiades writes that the Requiem Kyrie is the *cantus firmus* from which the vocal part of "Das Wirtshaus" is derived. In particular, he sees resemblances between the plainchant melody for the initial word "Kyrie" and Schubert's first vocal phrase, between the subsequent melody for the word "eleison" and Schubert's second vocal phrase, and between the phrase for the final invocation of the words "Kyrie eleison" and Schubert's initial phrase for stanza 3, at the words "Sind denn in diesem Hause / Die Kammern all' besetzt?"[1] It is an appealing supposition: the wanderer sings of what he hopes will be the appointed time and place of his death to a melody derived from the Requiem Mass, but whether Schubert intended the listener to hear the plainchant paraphrased in his song is unclear. It might seem inappropriate that an unbelieving wanderer would turn to plainchant at the end, but the anticlerical Schubert himself was shocked into pleading with God for death and transcendence during one of the crises of his venereal disease in May 1823.[2] His wanderer, believing himself on the threshold between life and death, may likewise revert to remnants of the faith he has renounced. Schubert *did* paraphrase the Requiem Kyrie in the first movement, "Wohin soll ich mich wenden" in F major, of his *Deutsche Messe*, D. 872, his only other large vocal composition from 1827 and one possibly composed at the same time as Part II, so the plainchant Requiem was not only a reminiscence from youthful days but a present concern. "Wohin soll ich mich wenden," however, is simpler than "Das Wirtshaus" in every way, the secular lied a more complex meditation on death than the religious work.

The harmonic rhythm of the introduction establishes in microcosm a pattern reflected on a larger scale in the texted body of the song: a progressive quickening of the rate of harmonic change which becomes

[1]Thrasybulos Georgiades, " 'Das Wirtshaus' von Schubert und das Kyrie aus dem Gregorianischen Requiem," in *Gegenwart im Geiste: Festschrift für Richard Benz*, ed. Walther Bulst and Arthur von Schneider (Hamburg, 1954), 126–35.

[2]In the entry for 8 May 1823 of his (now lost) diary, Schubert wrote a poem titled "Mein Gebet" (My prayer), one of his few attempts at writing poetry. Desperation sounds in every line of the poem.

Mein Gebet

Tiefer Sehnsucht heil'ges Bangen
Will in schön're Welten langen;
Möchte füllen dunklen Raum
Mit allmächt'gem Liebestraum.

Großer Vater! reich' dem Sohne,
Tiefer Schmerzen nun zum Lohne,
Endlich als Erlösungsmahl
Deiner Liebe ew'gen Strahl.

a mirror of rising tension in the words. Notably, it is the latter, more intense half of the introduction which recurs between stanzas 1 and 2, stanzas 2 and 3, and at the end, as the postlude. In a similar crescendo of intensity, the mild chromaticism of stanzas 1 and 2 is intensified in stanza 3 and becomes still more pervasive in the final stanza, with its densely compacted passage through F minor, A-flat major, C minor, and F major. It is tempting to hear the C minor of mm. 25 and 27 ("Nun weiter denn, nur weiter . . . ") as an allusion to the paired songs "Der greise Kopf" and "Die Krähe," especially the wanderer's plea at the end of "Die Krähe" not to continue further with his walking staff.

A similar gradual intensification characterizes the vocal line, hymn-like in its narrow range in stanzas 1 and 2. The setting is also hymnlike in the instrumental doubling of the melody and the disposition of the chord voicing, especially in stanzas 1 and 4 with the closely grouped treble chords over a bass doubled at the octave—an organ pedal. Arnold Feil notes a resemblance between the higher obbligato soprano voice in the accompaniment to stanza 2 and solemn brass music (*Blaskapelle*) to accompany burial, the "trumpet" melody especially effective where Schubert has the higher voice branch off from the doubled vocal line in mid-phrase at the words "Totenkränze könnt wohl die Zeichen sein." As in stanza 1 of "Einsamkeit," the wanderer's utter weariness and despair are evident in the medium-low vocal register and limited melodic range. Only with the third and fourth verses does the vocal range expand to its full compass of a minor ninth E–F.

Sieh, vernichtet liegt im Staube,
Unerhörtem Gram zum Raube,
Meines Lebens Martergang
Nahend ew'gem Untergang.

Tödt' es und mich selber tödte,
Sturz' nun Alles in die Lethe,
Und ein reines kräft'ges Sein
Lass, o Großer, dann gedeihn.

(In deep longing, holy fearfulness, I would reach out to more beautiful worlds, would fill this dark realm with love's all-powerful dream.
Almighty Father! grant Your son, whose lot now is great sorrow, the eternal ray of Your love as redemption.
On the road to martyrdom, nearing eternal ruin, my life lies annihilated in the dust, a prey to unheard-of grief.
Kill it, and then kill me myself; hurl everything now into Lethe and then, O Mighty One, grant me a pure and powerful existence.)

See Deutsch, *Schubert: A Documentary Biography*, 270.

Within each stanza, particular details stand out as especially expressive. The mediant progression that bridges the first and second texted phrases (mm. 7–8), from the brief cadence on G minor to the IV/F harmony—"All*hier* will ich einkehren"—both invests the designation of place ("right here") with a poignance out of all proportion to the economy of the gesture and prepares the way for a more strongly stressed subdominant at the beginning of stanza 3 ("Sind denn in diesem Hause"). Similarly, the C-major–C-minor chords in m. 6 and the B-flat-major–B-flat-minor chords in m. 8 anticipate the parallel modes of the fourth stanza. In stanza 2, however, Schubert varies what had been the B-flat-major–minor progression in stanza 1 by altering the second chord, the dissonance of G–A–B-flat in simultaneity a beautifully expressive rendering of the tired wanderer's pain. In the third stanza, Schubert conveys the desperation behind the words "Bin matt zum Niedersinken" by introducing F in the higher register of the vocal line for the first time and only then "sinking down" in exhaustion. The flatted-sixth-degree D-flat in mm. 20–21 at the words "Bin *töd* - lich schwer verletzt" and the dissonance in m. 20 are also telling details—dissonance and minor-mode coloration for deathly oppression.

In the transition to the last stanza, Schubert turns to parallel minor for the wanderer's reproach to the "unmerciful inn." The voice leading of a diminished fourth in the tenor produces a rare augmented triad ("Doch weisest du mich ab?"), and the asperity on the word "mich" is a powerful and economical expression of the wanderer's sense of being singled out for especially harsh treatment—"Do you nonetheless turn *me* away?" The turn from F minor to a cadence on the relative major A-flat can be heard additionally as the tonal enactment of "being turned away." The entire stanza, with its shifts among F minor, relative major, C minor, and F major, is music that travels, if slowly and not very far. The wanderer already envisages the motion that must follow his rejection at the inn. Finally, the twofold setting of the last two lines of text, the resigned-bitter-poignant address to the walking staff, is remarkable for its division each time into contrasting halves. The words "Nun weiter denn, nur weiter," with Müller's beautifully effective darkening of alliterative sound from "nun" to "nur," is set as a tension-filled phrase momentarily on C minor, the vocal line in its upper compass and the dissonant appoggiatura accenting the key word "nur." (The unanimity of the voice and bass Fs in m. 27 is even stronger emphasis than the dissonance of E-flat against F in the bass and D in the soprano voice of m. 25). The final words, "Mein treuer Wanderstab," return each time to tonic major and the lower compass for the voice. The impression that the wanderer's mood and voice soften, the resignation less bitter in tone, as he designates the walking staff his "faithful" companion makes of the reestablishment of tonic in those bars something very moving.

22. Mut

Fliegt der Schnee mir in's Gesicht,
Schüttl' ich ihn herunter.
Wenn mein Herz im Busen spricht,
Sing' ich hell und munter.

Höre nicht, was es mir sagt,
Habe keine Ohren.
Fühle nicht, was es mir klagt,
Klagen ist für Toren.

Lustig in die Welt hinein
Gegen Wind und Wetter!

[285]

Will kein Gott auf Erden sein,
Sind wir selber Götter!

Courage

(When snow flies in my face, I shake it off. When my heart in my
breast speaks to me, I sing loudly and merrily.
I do not hear what it says to me; I have no ears. I do not feel what
it laments—lamenting is for fools.
Cheerfully out into the world, against the wind and storm! If there
is no God on earth, then we ourselves are gods!)

In "Mut," the wanderer attempts a bravado exercise in denial. There
is nothing "bright and merry" about this song, in which both text
and music have the compression of a clenched fist. The omission of
the subject "ich" from the three parallel statements of negation in the
second stanza, "höre nicht," "habe keine," "fühle nicht," is both
Müller's characteristic economy and a register of unconscious revelation, of poetic truth telling. Once the wanderer identifies the op-
ponents in his internal struggle, "I" and "my heart," in stanza 1, he
omits the subject "ich" and thereby places the verb—the action—
first. The emphasis on the acts of denial is obvious; less obvious is
the implication that it is not his true self who acts to deny what he
feels and hears, and therefore he cannot honestly invoke a false "I."
In Schubert's setting, the compression takes the form of terse cadential
phrases, while the tensions are enacted rhythmically. The desperately
Promethean song is an admission of precisely that which the wanderer
tries to deny.

"Mut" is one of only two songs in Part II for which sketches (more
accurately, first versions) are extant. "Mut" is presently in a private
collection in Vienna, although a facsimile and description were published in an article by Alexander Weinmann. The sketch in the original
A-minor tonality is actually the fully realized conception of the first
two stanzas and the first twelve measures of Stanza 3, without a single
revision. In October 1827, Schubert added an additional twelve measures to the autograph fair copy—another and varied setting of the
final stanza—and a repetition of the piano introduction as the postlude. The chief fascination of the sketch, apart from its surety, is the
lack of a classically balanced closing section. With the varied repetition
of stanza 3, Schubert made further capital of the traditional contrast
of parallel minor and major modes, already invoked in the setting of
stanzas 1 and 2, and extends the tonal range of the song by means

of a brief foray into the relative major tonality. The wanderer's proclamation about going forth into the world ("Lustig in die Welt hinein") is thus symbolized by the excursion abroad into another key,
the B-flat-major "tempest" key of "Der stürmische Morgen" prepared
in this instance by the accented and prolonged B-flats in stanzas 1
and 2.

The fierce energy and brevity—no wasted words or sounds here—
are apparent in the piano introduction, and so too is the conflict born
of inner psychic war. The indicated meter is $\frac{2}{4}$, but the first two measures already transgress duple meter, with three contenders for the
role of downbeat and figures that span the bar line as if that bar line
were a pictograph for the obstacles that must be forcibly brushed
aside, broken through, drowned out, and ignored. The separation of
mm. 1–2 into two terraced levels in two different actual meters at
cross-purposes, the two registers then brought together and metrically regularized in mm. 3–4, seems the analogue to conflicts recognized, then forcefully dealt with and brought under control.

The same pattern of rhythmic tension, followed by assertive, brisk,
metrical order then prevails in the texted body of the song, with the
added factor of contrasting asymmetrical and symmetrical phrasing.
Schubert dwells on the key words indicating an obstacle in stanza 1
("der *Schnee*" and "mein *Herz*"), prolonging them over the bar line
to signify the great obstruction they represent and therefore extending
the phrase to three measures. Feil points out that the melodic line
makes a bounding start upward, only to be pulled down by a rhythmic
counterweight in mm. 6–7.[1] The instrumental echo of the three-note
motive to which the wanderer sings the words "der Schnee" (the
snow) and "mein Herz" (my heart) also acts to emphasize the weight
of the obstacle. This asymmetry subsequently requires not one but
two cadential phrases in strict $\frac{2}{4}$ meter to restore the musical-metrical-
structural order the wanderer insists *must* replace the imbalances created by foolish grief. Nor is asymmetry-symmetry of phrasing the
only contrast in the setting of stanzas 1 and 2. The three-measure
statements of adversity are half-cadences dominated by the melodic
extension of the tonic G-minor harmony. The melodic line is largely
unharmonized, framed on either side by full chordal harmonies
but with the interior in unison writing. In contrast, the two-measure
brusque assertions of "action done, completed, obstacle vanquished"
which follow are marked by the brightness of major chords, their
dotted rhythms and full texture in contrast to the austerity of the

[1]Feil, *Franz Schubert*, 122.

phrases in minor. The phrases in major end with the full trochee and feminine ending of Müller's even-numbered lines, one syllable shorter than the incomplete trochee and masculine ending of the odd-numbered lines; however, Schubert emphasizes what would otherwise be an unstressed syllable in a rhythmically weak place in the bar by setting that syllable or word each time (1) as a full quarter note, (2) as a strong intervallic leap of an octave or a fifth, and (3) as the tonic resolution. These cadences, in which the normally weak second beats are strengthened and charged with conflict, are followed immediately by the next phrase—the song, like the wanderer, rushing forward without tolerating any such weakness as a break. Articulations abound in this song composed entirely of cadential formulas, but some of the combative force of the song comes from the nonstop accompaniment.

The change of key signature to parallel major at the beginning of the last verse follows the words "Klagen ist für Toren" as if to indicate that the wanderer will no longer permit himself any impulse to minor-mode lamentation. He also bans any more three-measure phrases, cross-metrical complications, or unison austerity, until the words and their instrumental echoes end. Then, once again without pause or break, the introduction returns, and with it, minor mode and metrical tension. But even within stanza 3 the wanderer, for all his determination, is not able to banish his grief entirely. The trumpet fanfare in the topmost voice, above the vocal line of mm. 37–40, seems the clarion call to his purpose in "Mut," but when he repeats those same words, "Lustig in die Welt hinein," again, the pitch B-flat and the G-minor chord return, a reminder that neither the wanderer nor his world is "merry." Schubert then has the wanderer reject the returned G minor immediately and transform B-flat into tonic and bright major mode. Because the single hint of tonic minor in m. 50 must be counteracted so energetically, the accompaniment to the B-flat major passage (mm. 51–54) is marked by fuller chordal harmonies than before, while the embellished echo of the texted cadence is the most emphatic of all of the piano interludes in its wide range and the distance of more than two octaves between the left- and right-hand parts. The return of the introduction as postlude, beyond classical closure, signifies that the imperatives of the lamenting heart cannot be denied, for all the wanderer's efforts.

23. Die Nebensonnen

Drei Sonnen sah' ich am Himmel stehn,
Hab' lang und fest sie angesehn [angeschaut];

[289]

Und sie auch standen da so stier,
Als wollten [könnten] sie nicht weg von mir.
Ach, meine Sonnen seid ihr nicht!
Schaut Andern [Andren] doch in's Angesicht!
Ja [Ach], neulich hatt' ich auch wohl drei:
Nun sind hinab die besten zwei.
Ging' nur die dritt' erst hinterdrein!
Im Dunkeln [Dunkel] wird mir wohler sein.

The Mock Suns

(I saw three suns in the sky; I looked at them long and hard. And they stood there as steadfastly as if unwilling to leave me. Alas, you are not my suns! Look in other people's faces! Yes, not long ago I too had three suns: now the two best have set. If only the third would follow them—I would feel better in the dark.)

The three suns have been variously interpreted (one writer proposed a Pauline exegesis as Faith, Hope, and Love),[1] but the most obvious reading is the right one: the two illusory suns are symbols of the beloved's eyes. Müller had used this metonymic image of heavenly lights and the beloved's eyes in two earlier poems, most notably "The Two Stars" from 1817.

Die zweie Sterne

Ich weiß zwei Sterne stehen,
Den Namen weiß ich nicht,
Die waren am ganzen Himmel
Mein allerliebstes Licht.

Sie schienen immer und immer
So traut zum Fenster herein,
Vier selige Augen schauten
So immer und immer hinein.

Da sanken sie wieder zur Erde
Und nieder an meine Brust:
Ein Himmel war unten und oben,
Das haben die Sterne gewußt.

Der Himmel ist ausgezogen
Aus meinem Busen so weit,

[1]Cited in Capell, *Schubert's Songs*, 228.

Die Sterne stehen da oben
In kalter Herrlichkeit.

Das Fenster ist verschlossen,
Nach den Augen fragt mich nicht.
Ich wollt', es ging' erst unter,
Das liebe Sternenlicht![2]

(I know two stars—I do not know their names—that were the lights
I loved best in the whole sky.
They shone, ever and always, so intimately in the window, four blessed
eyes always looking inside.
Then they sank again to earth and still lower, to my breast. A heaven
was above and below—the stars had wished it so.
Heaven has gone and is so distant from my heart. The stars are up
above in cold majesty.
The window is closed; I do not look for those eyes. I wish the beloved
starlight had vanished first!)

The metaphor of heavenly light as the beloved's eyes is much the
same, and the two poems end similarly with the wish for darkness.
In both, the poet relies entirely on the central metonym, without ever
invoking the words "she," "her," "beloved," or "sweetheart." The
twofold implication is both that she has become pure poetry and that
the matter is too painful for direct reference. In "Die Nebensonnen,"
Müller alters the cliché by substituting mock suns or illusions of light,
for stars. According to one interpretation, the wanderer speaks of
two sets of *Nebensonnen* in the poem, the first in lines 1–4 an optical
illusion produced by the tears in the wanderer's own eyes as he looks
up at the heavens, the tears refracting the image of the sun into
multiple replications, and the second a poetic analogy between his
sweetheart's eyes and heavenly light. The wanderer does not say that
he weeps, but the grief he can no longer banish in song ("Mut") has
returned full force; the oblique reference is in character for a figure
who seldom mentions weeping. In another interpretation, the mock
suns are produced by an atmospheric illusion known as parhelia, in
which light is refracted by ice crystals in the clouds to form neighboring images of the sun on either side, images that disappear when
the atmospheric conditions change. The sympathetic feature of this
interpretation is that parhelia is both reality and illusion, a recurrent

[2]"Die zweie Sterne" is included in the "Vermischte Gedichte" in Wilhelm Müller,
Gedichte, ed. James Taft Hatfield (Berlin, 1906), 379.

leitmotif of the cycle. The sight of parhelia is both real and an illusion, and it beautifully symbolizes the reality and illusion that was his sweetheart. The first reading, however, is not dependent on an infrequent atmospheric phenomenon and may be preferable for that reason.

Looking at the mock suns, the wanderer believed for a time that they were steadfast and would never leave him. (The changes of verb tense in the poem, from past to present imperative to conditional, reveal that the wanderer sings this song shortly after the two illusory suns have vanished.) When they disappear, he realizes that they were an illusion and could not have remained with him, just as his sweetheart's love was also an illusion that disappeared from sight. He had earlier invoked her memory with the metonymic image of her eyes in "Rückblick" ("Und ach, zwei Mädchenaugen glühten"—"And ah, a maiden's eyes glowed"), and now he does so again in a more final way. At last, he understands fully that she was not meant for him and says so, even though the admission saddens him so much that he wishes for utter darkness. Müller establishes the importance of the wanderer's past love—it was, after all, the goad for the journey—in the adjective "best" ("die besten zwei"). The entire poem is an admission that such sorrow cannot be denied, despite the wanderer's efforts in "Mut."

Once again, Schubert altered words in Müller's text, an unusually large number of textual changes. All five of the alterations result in improved melodic sonority, but two are additionally refinements of meaning. When Schubert changes Müller's "Ach, neulich hatt' ich auch wohl drei" to "Ja, neulich hatt' ich...," he does more than remove the unvocalized and guttural /ch/ sound from the phrase and replace it with the pure vowel of the word "Ja," he also intensifies the lament by means of affirmation: "Yes, this recently was mine, and now it is gone," the contrast between past and present all the more bitter. When Schubert turns to the unexpected brightness of C major chords at those words in mm. 19–21, he confirms the reading apparent in the change of a single monosyllabic word. Similarly, the voiced consonant /w [v]/ and /o/ vowel of Schubert's verb "wollten" is more singable than Müller's "könnten," but the two words also impute a different state of mind to the sweetheart. More than Müller, Schubert grants a measure of autonomy and will to the sweetheart: she seemed as if *wanting* constancy.

Schubert's music, both instrumental and vocal, is permeated with Viennese dance strains, and "Die Nebensonnen" is another of the songs derived from dance in this cycle. Arnold Feil has described it as a stately ceremonial dance, a sarabande,[3] and I have earlier pointed to the second-beat durational emphases as premonitory of the hurdy-gurdy tune in the final song. The dotted rhythms on the first beat and the narrow melodic compass are other indices of kinship to the German dances on which Schubert had earlier lavished all the resources of high art, as in the twelve *Ländler* of Op. 171, D. 790.[4] Throughout the cycle, in such songs as "Frühlingstraum," "Täuschung," "Die Nebensonnen," and "Der Leiermann," the evocations of dance—one of the most convivial, physically joyful activities of humankind—assumes a particularly potent significance in this context of loneliness and alienation.

The introduction and stanza 1 are more complex than their seeming diatonic simplicity might suggest. Schubert creates a series of poetic-musical alliances between neighboring harmonies and the *Nebensonnen*, between the repetition of the pitches A B C-sharp D throughout mm. 1–15 and the fixity of the wanderer's gaze, between the subtle instability of tonic and the fact of an unstable illusion that subsequently vanishes. The "dominants" in m. 1 are not so much structural dominants as anticipations of a neighboring harmony and the prolongation of that neighbor. The "dissonant" note or chord is longer than the resolution; if one wished to be a bit fanciful, one could see in the subsequent texted occurrence of that neighboring harmony on the words "[Drei Sonnen] *sah*" the musical embodiment of the inner dissonance produced by thus staring at the illusory suns. Schubert's dynamic marking for m. 1, that is, the crescendo through the second and third beats, underscores the fact that the C-sharp at the end of m. 1 is more than a passing tone—it is also a return back to the opening C-sharp. The questions of hearing become the musical symbols at a structural level for the wanderer's questions of sight and belief. Is what he sees real? Is the strength and simplicity apparent on the surface actual, or is it fundamentally unstable and destined to

---

[3]Feil, *Franz Schubert*, 143. Feil also points out that the eighth note before the first measure has a different function than the one before the second measure, the latter bound to the preceding dotted quarter note by a slur. Schubert thereby prevents the reinterpretation of that latter eighth note as an upbeat to m. 2. Furthermore, the downbeat is subdivided, with both tonic and dominant harmonies appearing in the first beat, and the normally unstressed second beat is prolonged—these are all elements that make the rhythmic structure unstable. The motion stagnates within each two-measure phrase in a manner that makes the wanderer's weariness and depression evident on the rhythmic level.

[4]See David Brodbeck, "Dance Music as High Art: Schubert's Twelve Ländler, Op. 171 (D. 790)," in *Schubert: Critical and Analytical Studies*, ed. Walter Frisch (Lincoln, Nebr., 1986), 31–47.

disappear? Certainly when Schubert repeats the introduction as stanza 1 and sets the word "fest" (strong) to a tonic that is not structurally a tonic but a dominant extension, the singer moving away from A to the motivically and harmonically important B, the impression of strength is significantly undermined. Even more so, when he reinterprets the same melodic phrase as an extension of the submediant and supertonic in mm. 10–15, he virtually announces the suns' fidelity as only an illusion, even though the cadences in mm. 13 and 15 return briefly to A.

The instabilities and the Ländler patterns that contain them vanish with the first four measures of the third stanza, an expression of tragic certainty. The lowered third degree of parallel minor mode in mm. 16–18 becomes the pivot for Schubert's transposition of the initial phrase—really the only phrase in this monothematic song—a minor third higher. Schubert places past and present in contrasting harmonic realms, the recent past ("Ja, neulich hatt' ich auch wohl drei") clothed in the brightness of C major chords and the present in tonic minor. Perhaps the most affecting detail of this passage is its ending. The cadence in m. 23 ("besten zwei") resolves deceptively to the F-major harmony that was emphasized so strongly at the peak of m. 21 just before. Even though the wanderer here admits his loss ("Nun sind hinab die besten zwei"), the longing to hold on to past happiness, to retain that time when "neulich hatt' ich auch wohl drei" is symbolized in the deceptive motion to a chord accompanying those words of past possession. Even the transition to a half-cadence which follows is strongly colored by that same harmony, requiring that Schubert reestablish the prior diatonic VI on F-sharp in the setting of the last two lines of text when the wanderer longs for darkness—death once again? Perhaps since the experience in the cemetery he dare not wish for death openly, and the desire for darkness is a covert expression of the same longing.

24. Der Leiermann

Etwas langsam

Drü-ben hin-term Dor-fe steht ein Lei - er- mann,

Drüben hinter'm Dorfe
Steht ein Leiermann,
Und mit starren Fingern
Dreht er was er kann.

Barfuß auf dem Eise
Wankt [Schwankt] er hin und her;
Und sein kleiner Teller
Bleibt ihm immer leer.

Keiner mag ihn hören,
Keiner sieht ihn an;
Und die Hunde knurren [brummen]
Um den alten Mann.

[295]

Und er läßt es gehen
Alles, wie es will,
Dreht, und seine Leier
Steht ihm nimmer still.

Wunderlicher Alter,
Soll ich mit dir gehn?
Willst zu meinen Liedern
Deine Leier drehn?

The Hurdy-gurdy Man

(There, beyond the village, stands a hurdy-gurdy man, and with
numbed fingers he grinds away as best he can.

Barefoot on the ice, he totters to and fro, and his little plate remains
always empty.

No one wants to listen, no one looks at him, and the dogs snarl
around the old man.

And he lets everything go on, as it will—turns, and his hurdy-
gurdy never stops.

Strange old man, shall I go with you? Will you grind your hurdy-
gurdy to my songs?)

Even those who find little good to say about Müller's poetry admit
that the last poem in the cycle goes far toward redeeming its author.
Capell, no admirer of the poet, writes that "Müller must be given his
due. 'Der Leiermann' was an inspired ending.'"[1] In this powerful
work, utmost economy of means produces the maximum emotional
effect, all the greater for the objectivity of tone. Schubert took his cue
from the poet when he pared the musical materials for this song to
the bare minimum, appropriating the text so thoroughly into music
that it is impossible to read the words without hearing the song in
one's mind. But the poem is a self-sufficient work of art in its own
right. W. H. Auden once wrote that a few good poems in a lifetime
are perhaps all that even a great poet can expect, and Müller did
indeed write "a few good poems."

Even in this poem, Schubert changed two words, surely for reasons
of sound, not sense. "Schwanken" and "wanken" are synonyms, but
the voiced consonant /w (v)/ of "wanken" does not impede the vocal
phrase as do the multiple consonants of the poet's word "schwan-

[1]Capell, *Schubert's Songs*, 239.

ken." Similarly, "brummen" and "knurren" are synonyms. Müller's word "brummen" is part of the alliterative phrase that enjambs the third and fourth lines of stanza 3 ("Und die Hunde brummen / Um den alten Mann") and perhaps alludes as well to a *Brummenbaß*, or organ bourdon. The drone bass of the hurdy-gurdy has its counterpart in the drone bass of the growling dogs. It is a felicitous choice of wording on several counts, "musical" in a poetic sense, but Schubert possibly did not want the interruption of the flow of vowels created by the multiple /m/ sounds and therefore substituted a word in which liquid /r/'s replace the /m /'s of "brummen." Once again, Schubert's care for every detail of the poem-as-melody is apparent.

Much has been made of the fact that the title character plays a hurdy-gurdy, the drone sounds and mechanized action of this beggar's instrument a very limited kind of music.[2] The musical limitations are undeniable, but the hurdy-gurdy is only partly mechanical. The sound box resembles that of a modified lute or guitar with drone strings that are set into vibration by a wooden wheel revolving inside the sound box and turned by a crank at its tail end, like an endless bow, while the melody strings or *chanterelles* are operated by a primitive keyboard mechanism or a set of stopping rods. The rosined wheel is turned by the right hand, and the keyboard mechanism that stops the melody strings is played by the left hand. Once the wheel has been set in motion, the drone bass does not change, but the melody, although its range is restricted, must be played, a humble variety of musicianship a necessity. In Illustration 9, a photograph of a Napoleonic-era hurdy-gurdy, one can see the characteristic shape and mechanism of the archetypal beggar's instrument. Although the elderly musician seems a *Doppelgänger* phantom, a projection of the wanderer's mind rather than a physical being playing upon a physical object, the choice of instrument is nonetheless significant. It is easy enough to imitate a drone bass and write a single-line melody within a narrow range, but Schubert characteristically does much more. The grace notes in mm. 1–2, for example, can be heard as a stylized representation of what happens when a hurdy-gurdy player first begins to turn the wooden wheel that operates the drone of the bourdon strings. At first, the sound is slightly under the pitch and becomes constant when the motion of the wheel is regular. The rhythmic pattern in mm. 4–5, 7–8 and thereafter could be a representation of

---

[2]Feil, *Franz Schubert*, 192, points out that the instrument is not the *Drehorgel*, but the *Dreh-* or *Radleier*, a beggar's instrument since the Middle Ages. See Marianne Bröcker, *Die Drehleier: Ihr Bau und ihre Geschichte* (Düsseldorf, 1973).

9. A hurdy-gurdy of the Napleonic era. Courtesy Sammlung Alter
Musikinstrumente, Kunsthistorisches Museum, Vienna.

the necessary break in the hurdy-gurdy melody due to the technical
adjustment from a single-line succession of pitches to a chord sounded
on the *chanterelles*. Instead of pressing one rod or key at a time in a
more legato fashion, the player has to let go of the last single-rod
note in order to prepare to press down three at once, a movement
all the more awkward if the player's fingers are numb from cold.[3]

How even Schubert could have created so much from so little remains a marvel. Even though "Der Leiermann" is only sixty-one
measures long and much of the song consists of stanzaic repetition
(the hypnotic power is due in part to the effect of the unusual exact
repetition), it was still extremely daring to limit the tonal material in

[3]John Reed points out that one can also hear something of the old man's "dot-and-
carry-one" wavering gait in that rhythmic figure. I am indebted to John Reed for this
suggestion in a letter.

so drastic a fashion. "Der Leiermann" is, in its utmost economy of means, as radical a departure from the conventions of early nineteenth-century lieder as Schubert's foreshadowings of Wagnerian chromaticism in songs such as "Daß sie hier gewesen" or the explorations of tonal indeterminacy in "Die Stadt." "Der Leiermann" is completely "diatonic" in A minor, the D-sharp grace notes in mm. 1–2 the only touches of "chromaticism." Schubert restricts the song essentially to a single harmony, nothing else. The melody that joins the drone bass in m. 3f only bodies out the initial hollow fifths, while the "dominant" chords seem more like neighbor notes than structural dominants. I have qualified such designations as "dominant," "diatonic," and "chromaticism" by means of quotation marks because this music, while unmistakably moored to A minor, does not exist to define a tonality, either within its own boundaries or by means of excursions to other keys, followed by a return to and reestablishment of the principal tonality. There are "cadences," to be sure, but they are cadences within a context so restricted as to defy classical definitions. Instead, they are inflections that feign endings within a context of endless continuation, an exercise in ceaseless turning. The relationship between the vocal line and accompaniment makes this clear where the resolution of the "dominant" chords over the drone is elided with the beginning of the vocal phrase. By the end of the song, not even the sustained full tonic chord on the strong first beat and the tonic pitch in the topmost voice can convince the ear of termination. Rather, the last chord seems like a blind or a bar, shutting us out from implied continuance beyond the fermata. This music is the symbol for what the wanderer fears and foretells his future to be: sounding nothingness, and, horrifyingly, it has the potential to go on and on, beyond bearing.

The four stanzas of narration, in which the wanderer describes the scene and the elderly man, are set as two musical strophes (the music of stanzas 1 and 2 repeated to the words of stanzas 3 and 4), while the last stanza with its direct address, the wanderer speaking to the hurdy-gurdy player, is a variation of the same musical material. Within the apparent simplicity of the larger formal structure, however, is a complex design of motivic variations and repetitions. The beggar-musician is the refracted image of the wanderer himself, his own fears given independent life and form, and Schubert accordingly defines the two figures musically as separate but like beings. The hurdy-gurdy tune and the wanderer's vocal part are fashioned from the same minimal materials, and yet the two are distinct from each other rhythmically and melodically. The wanderer's creation of a *Dop-*

pelgänger from within his wounded and alienated soul prefigures Rimbaud's haunting phrase "Je est un autre" (I am an Other), and Schubert both creates the "Other" as a distinct entity and makes apparent a kinship uncannily close. Until the last verse, only the drone bass or the drone plus a "sighing figure" on A–G-sharp accompanies the wanderer's words, as if he were taking care to sing only in the pauses between the old man's melodic phrases. Most powerfully of all, when the wanderer asks at the end, "Shall I go with you? Will you grind your hurdy-gurdy to my songs?" the tension of the moment when Self speaks to Self in such grim colloquy is apparent in the metrical disjunctions between the voice and piano.

The hurdy-gurdy melody exemplifies what one scholar calls "gigantic simplicity."[4] The hurdy-gurdy player has a total of three phrases at his disposal, no more, and the second and third phrases are variants of the first. The initial phrase is both symmetrical and asymmetrical at the same time: the ascending interlocking thirds A–C–B–D of the first beat are symmetrically balanced by the descending interlocking thirds C–A—B–G-sharp, while the figure repeated in mm. 2 and 3 slightly rearranges those same intervallic cells, and yet the phrase is an asymmetrical three-bar construction (1 + [1 + 1]). Four times in close proximity one hears the melodic interval A–C, the rhythmic pattern and direction of the cell altered each time but the last. The repeated, accented dominant chords over the drone bass do not truly resolve, although their twofold statement (as if the hurdy-gurdy player were momentarily too numbed, too unthinking, to remember what comes next and therefore repeats himself) heightens the tension productive of a need for resolution. Instead, the resolution is simultaneously the beginning of yet another phrase (mm. 6–8) in which the original minor third A–C of m. 3 is widened to a perfect fifth, duplicating the bass, and the intervallic cell of the third is transposed upward. The entire range of the vocal part, a minor ninth from E to F, is thus established in the introduction, the wanderer taking his cue from the hurdy-gurdy player and adapting his song to its restrictions. The final variation of the hurdy-gurdy melody occurs only at the end of each musical stanza, at the points where the words reach a momentary stopping point before resuming. This last variant widens the initial interval still further. Its extension of an additional bar produces a full-octave statement of the A-minor scale, but the

<hr />

[4]Joseph Kerman, "A Romantic Detail in Schubert's *Schwanengesang*," in *Schubert: Critical and Analytical Studies*, ed. Walter Frisch (Lincoln, Nebr., 1986), 48. Kerman was referring to "Ihr Bild," but the phrase aptly describes "Der Leiermann" as well.

placement of the tonic chords on weak beats (mm. 28–30) and the "stammering" repeated motives from mm. 7–8 are contradictions of closure. Placing the three phrases side by side, one can trace the progressive widening of the initial figure (Ex. 34), without, however, any escape from the anchorage to a single harmony.

Example 34.   "Der Leiermann." A. mm. 3–4; B. mm. 19–20; C. mm. 27–29

Like the piano part, the singer is given to exact repetition, hypnotic in effect, but of two-bar phrases rather than one-bar figures, those phrases separated by recurrences of the hurdy-gurdy tune. When one juxtaposes the first instrumental phrase with the first vocal phrase and the widened instrumental variant from mm. 6–8 with the singer's second phrase, one can see both the relationships and the differences, especially the greater number of perfect fourths and fifths for the singer. That preponderance of perfect intervals and their placement within the melodic phrase produce what is in effect a sequence of changing meters in the vocal line against the unchanging metrical structure of the accompaniment.[5] The disjunctions of the final stanza are especially remarkable, a succession of three bars in $\frac{2}{4}$, one in $\frac{3}{4}$, then $\frac{2}{4}$, $\frac{1}{4}$, $\frac{2}{4}$, and $\frac{3}{4}$ drawn across the bar line at palpable cross-purposes with the drone bass (Ex. 35). A mind disordered finds no secure metrical foothold. One notices in particular the emphasis on the word "Liedern," given a "measure" of its own and the melodic "turning" (*drehen*) about the octave leap in unforgettable emphasis.

The syllabic stream of eighth notes one finds in the vocal line of stanzas 1–4 are not declamatory in the usual sense, as there is little allowance made for longer and shorter, stressed and unstressed syl-

[5]See Feil, *Franz Schubert*, 148.

Example 35.   "Der Leiermann," mm. 53–61

lables. What distinguishes the prosodic manner of stanzas 1–4 from "Die Krähe," in which the wanderer also observes, then speaks to an "odd" creature in an even succession of eighth notes, is a melodic contour frequently at odds with normal speech inflections. The rise and fall of the melodic line is often counter to the stresses of "correct" declamation in music. Weak or unstressed syllables are set to weaker beats but on higher pitches than the stressed syllables, not at all unusual when the rise in pitch is part of an ascending melodic progression but unusual when that is not the case. Where "er" is placed higher than "dreht" (m. 14) and the weaker second syllable of "barfuß" higher than the first syllable (m. 17), where words that a less gifted composer would have set as upbeats ("*und die* Hunde knurren") appear as strong first beats, the normal laws of prosody are upset. Melodic speech from some other realm takes their place, all the more striking because the contravening of conventional prosody is not consistent. Phrases and segments within phrases ("mit starren Fingern") exemplify correct prosody, even when the actual metrical disposition is not the $\frac{3}{4}$ meter of the instrumental part. It is easy enough to discern the $\frac{2}{4}$ meter in the vocal line of mm. 47–48, but how does one metrically interpret a phrase such as mm. 35–36 ("Und die Hunde knurren / Um den alten Mann")? Müller uses the connective "und" five times in stanzas 1–4, the better to convey the immediacy of the scene—the wanderer enumerates each detail as it strikes his eye without stopping for more considered or periodic utterance. Schubert, recognizing their significance beyond the commonplace function of linkage between clauses, sets those connectives

on the first beat of the measure where the word occurs at the beginning of the line and on a high pitch where it does not ("dreht, *und
seine Leier . . . "*). He also disregards syntactical divisions in the poetry. The stream of successive eighth notes flows through commas
and adjacent clauses without a break of any kind. The triadic descent
at "knurren um" goes through the notated bar-line division, the me-
ters for the entire phrase perhaps definable as $\frac{2}{4}$, $\frac{3}{4}$, and—$\frac{1}{4}$? In every
detail of deliberately abnormal prosody, Schubert tells the listener of
conflicts within a mind divided.

The combination of monumental simplicity and complexity in "Der
Leiermann" is cause for marvel, its perfection of form and expression
acknowledged in later homages to the cycle and in echoes of its last
song. The most haunting of those echoes is Brahms's intricate six-
voice canonic setting of Friedrich Rückert's "Einförmig ist der Liebe
Gram, / Ein Lied eintöniger Weise" (Love's sorrow is monotonous, a
song with only one tone), the thirteenth and last work in Brahms's
Kanons für Frauenstimmen, Op. 113, published seven years before the
composer's death.[6] The double canon—a two-part canon for the altos
and a four-part canon above it for the sopranos—is an undisguised
rearrangement and variation of Schubert's hurdy-gurdy song (Ex. 36),
one in which the open fifth and the semitone F–E figure are the
principal constituents of the alto canon and phrases from both Schubert's piano accompaniment and vocal line appear in the soprano
canon. As Malcolm MacDonald points out, this late work (the other
twelve canons date mostly from the 1850s and 1860s, but his appro-
priation of "Der Leiermann" is the exception) encapsulates within a
single small composition many crucial aspects of Brahms's musical
personality: his reverence for the past, his bonds with his predecessors, his personal interpretation of previous masterpieces, his belief
that musical meanings and ideas have continuity, even a bit of self-
directed ironic commentary on the composer's own personal life,
evident in his choice of this particular text about someone who "hums
along" with songs of love's sorrow but does not sing them himself.[7]

---

[6] The text is the sixteenth in a series of individual quatrains—the smallest of small
songs—titled "Stellen aus Hafisens Liedern" (Places from Hafis's songs) in the *Östliche
Rosen*; Müller, one remembers, disapproved of this poetic collection. Lines 3 and 4 are
"Und immer noch, wo ich's vernahm, / Mitsummen mußt' ich's leise" (And yet always
whenever I heard it, I had to hum along with it softly). See Friedrich Rückert, *Werke*,
vol. 4, ed. Elsa Hertzer (Leipzig, n.d.), 146. Brahms's first biographer, Max Kalbeck,
quotes the composer as saying in 1887, "It is unbelievable, the musical riches in Schubert's songs" and then citing the beginning of "Gute Nacht" as an example of his
predecessor's mastery of text declamation. See Max Kalbeck, *Johannes Brahms, 1833–
1856*, 1st half-volume, 3d ed. (Berlin, 1912,), 220.
[7] Malcolm MacDonald, *Brahms* (New York, 1990), 1–2.

Example 36. Brahms's "Einförmig ist der Liebe Gram," Op. 113, no. 13, mm. 1–10

A younger contemporary of Brahms's, the Viennese composer Wilhelm Kienzl (1857–1941), was less successful when he extracted "Der Leiermann" from the complete poetic cycle and set it as an individual song, but then he was only fifteen years old at the time, a fact either he or his publishers are careful to point out in the anthologies of his songs.[8] From the perfect fifth in the bass to the sixteenth-note figures in the piano (the hurdy-gurdy, as in Schubert, plays between vocal phrases), from the dominant harmonies over the continuing tonic drone bass to the contours of the vocal line, Kienzl is deeply indebted to Schubert's entire cycle, not just to "Der Leiermann"—even the dogs growl to trill figures adapted from "Im Dorfe." His song, however, is however, permeated with the sentimentality, the obvious pathos, his predecessor avoided (Ex. 37). For both Kienzl and Brahms,

Example 37.   Kienzl's "Der Leiermann," mm. 5–18

Schubert himself, as well as his creation *Winterreise*, was an object of mingled nostalgia and reverence, but only Brahms could subsume the nostalgia in contrapuntal mastery.

Before Kienzl and Brahms, another composer paid "Der Leiermann" perhaps the most perceptive homage of all. When Franz Liszt, who was one of the most influential proponents of Schubert's music in the decades just after the composer's death, transcribed twelve of the *Winterreise* songs for piano solo, he used the music of stanzas 1–2 of "Der Leiermann" almost entirely unaltered as the prelude to "Täuschung," the latter a typically Lisztian étude in registral contrasts and a virtuosic sprinkling of grace notes, far more than Schubert had

[8]Wilhelm Kienzl, *Kienzl-Album: Eine Auswahl von Liedern & Gesängen* (Vienna, ca. 1904), 12–13.

used.[9] Liszt evidently understood the hallucination in "Der Leiermann" as apt for pairing with the illusion in "Täuschung," the two
poems similar in their extremity of psychic pain. Uncharacteristically,
he does not embellish the music of "Der Leiermann" beyond a few
extra D-sharp grace notes in the bass and the occasional arpeggiation
of the hurdy-gurdy drone—he accords this song a relative "touch me
not" respect unwonted in his virtuosic transcriptions. The song does
not invite lavish encrustations, both because its music is reduced to
such stark minimalism and because the metrical and melodic complexities would only have been obscured by added keyboard figuration, hardly a service to a composer Liszt venerated.

In a curious fashion, Liszt's minimal transcription of "Der Leiermann" leads us at the end of this book back to Müller and the point
from which we began. Playing the version for piano alone, one realizes that (*pace* the advocates of absolute music) the lied does not
fully make sense without the words to clarify its few stark elements.
Such restriction would be unbearable in a purely instrumental work;
in conscious or unconscious recognition that this is so, Müller's words
are printed parenthetically in the Liszt transcription. In the lied itself,
the center of the structure is neither that of verbal meaning nor that
of musical notation but a compound of the two. Music dominates,
but does not rule in solitary splendor. One reads the poem and hears
Schubert's music involuntarily; listening to Liszt's transcription, one
supplies the words out of a similar desire to complete what is otherwise incomplete.

[9]According to Alan Walker, *Franz Liszt: The Virtuoso Years 1811–1847* (New York,
1983), 136–38, Liszt was influenced by the Belgian-born musician Chrétien Urhan, one
of the earliest European champions of Schubert's music. Liszt's 1838 concerts in Vienna
were a major stimulus for the numerous song transcriptions published by Diabelli and
Haslinger.

Postlude

One cannot leave *Winterreise* without addressing the vexed question of words and music in nineteenth-century lieder. Müller thought of the two arts as necessary complements of each other, as halves of a whole, although within limits—he knew the difference between *poesia per musica* and *poesia* definitely not *per musica*, and he knew also the limits of his own musical understanding. However, other writers in his own century, Nietzsche among them,[1] spelled out the truism that words and music are combatants that battle it out in an arena where music always has the superior arsenal and always subjugates whatever victimized verse the composer appropriates. Poets who recognized and resented their inevitable defeat were wont to snarl something akin to Victor Hugo's words "It is forbidden to place music alongside this poetry,"[2] but neither those words nor any others have stopped marauding musicians in their quest for poetry-for-music or, worse yet from the poet's point of view, poetry that could be edited and altered to suit the composer's desires. Would Müller have sanctioned Schubert's textual revisions as the tone poet's perogative, had he known of them, or would outrage over music's vandalism have sprung into being? The inoffensive settings of his verse by the likes

---

[1]"A necessary relation between poem and music . . . makes no sense, for the two worlds of tone and image are too remote from each other to enter into more than an external relationship. The poem is only a symbol and related to the music like the Egyptian hieroglyph of courage to a courageous soldier" (Friedrich Nietzsche, "On Music and Words," trans. Walter Kaufmann, cited in Carl Dahlhaus, *Between Romanticism and Modernism: Four Studies in the Music of the Later Nineteenth Century*, trans. Mary Whittall [Berkeley, Calif., 1980], 112). This passage is also cited in Lawrence Kramer, *Music and Poetry: The Nineteenth Century and After* (Berkeley, Calif., 1984), 128. See also Edward T. Cone, "Words into Music: The Composer's Approach to the Text," in *Sound and Poetry*, ed. Northrop Frye (New York, 1957), and Susanne Langer, *Feeling and Form* (New York, 1953), 149–68, for other arguments on the subject.

[2]Cited in René Berthelot, "Défense de la poésie chantée," *Revue musicale* 186 (1938), 90.

[307]

of Albert Methfessel, Bernhard Klein, and Ludwig Berger[3] which
Müller knew and lauded posed no great challenge to poetic sensibil-
ities, especially a poet as receptive to music as was Müller. Not so
Schubert. Implicit in Hugo's words *"alongside* this poetry [italics mine]" is the
poet's denial that text and music can ever fuse together and his defensive claim that poetry is not destroyed by music. But of course it
is, and fundamentally so. Poetic meaning derives in part from the
disposition of line, rhyme, meter, and stanza, from verse's many
devices, such as enjambment, that are obliterated by music. When
Müller chooses a single ten-line stanza in rhyming couplets for "Täuschung" and then breaks down the order of those terse couplets in
the last half of the stanza, those two compositional decisions, and all
the others belonging to the linguistic realm, are fundamental to the
meaning of the poem as such. Music, however, rides roughshod over
the very structures that constitute poetry. One cannot tell a sonnet
from a quatrain from a prose poem in musical setting, and neither
Schubert nor any other composer can gainsay the violence, or wants
to. Indeed, they exploit it. For example, the singing voice itself, especially at the high and low ends of the voice, makes individual words
and syllables difficult to distinguish, and the veiling or virtual obliteration of the poetry becomes an expressive instrument beyond the ken
of language. Schubert only seldom makes use of melisma, a readily
apparent means of dissolving text into music, in this cycle, and where
he does, the instances are brief—the outbreaks of florid fury in "Die
Wetterfahne" or melodies floated on air and driven by storm winds
in "Rast." But there are other ways in which the voice can overwhelm
the text and wrest the listener's attention from verbal cognition to

[3]Ludwig Berger's ten *Die schöne Müllerin* songs of 1818 ("Des Müllers Wanderlied,"
later titled "Wohin?" in the complete poetic cycle; "Müllers Blumen," later "Des Müllers
Blumen"; "Der Müller," later "Die böse Farbe"; "Müllers trockne Blumen," later
"Trockne Blumen"; and "Des Baches Lied," later "Des Baches Wiegenlied," are the
five Müller texts) include two songs in which the piano accompaniment steals the show
from the vocal part: the setting of Hedwig Stägemann's "Vogelgesang vor der Müllerin
Fenster," with its modified riot of birdsong onomatopoeia in the piano, and "Des
Baches Lied," with its thirty-second- and sixty-fourth-note chordal pulsations and
arpeggiation for the piano. In the latter song, the "water music" in the piano outweighs
the singer's funereal chanting on repeated pitches within the range of a perfect fourth.
Could Berger have known of Beethoven's *An die ferne Geliebte*, Op. 98, published shortly
before Berger's songs? The second song in Beethoven's cycle, "Wo die Berge so blau,"
contains as its middle section recitational chanting paired with a more eloquent piano
part. What is perhaps most noteworthy about Berger's strategy in his *Die schöne Müllerin*
songs is the tacit proposition that this is the most arresting way to end the set: with
melodic declamation that actually underscores the differences between song and speech
and with the assignment of greatest expressivity to the instrumental part.

musical experience. When Schubert sets the wanderer's last question, "Willst zu meinen Liedern / Deine Leier drehn?" to octave leaps whose upper limit lies squarely on the *passagio* or "break" in the voice (the transitional pitches between the middle and high registers, requiring well-honed vocal technique to traverse), he makes the vocal stress of this phrase emblematic of the sundering strains of despair. When the final prolonged E of "drehn"—it is easier to sustain a high G or even A than an E or F in the *passagio*—encounters the downbeat that follows just after in the piano, we sense both in the rhythmic conflict and in the tension of that exaggerated melodic profile the corollary tensions of a mind strained to the breaking point. Indeed, the text of the last phrase is barely intelligible, attacked as it is by the near-grotesque repeated leaps from one register to another, as if the singer were musically strangling on the words in his anxiety. Where fear is most acute, as in the similarly constituted cry "Es schrieen die Raben vom Dach" in "Frühlingstraum" or the desperate disjunctions of the phrase "und suche Ruh' " in "Der Wegweiser," Schubert devised melodic symbols for the panic-induced loss of civilized controls on register and range.

Nor is it only the singer's voice that competes with the poetry from the vantage point of superior strength. The richer the instrumental part, the more one is enjoined to pay attention to the piano and therefore less heed to words and linguistic meaning. Schubert's piano accompaniments tend to be thicker and more complex by far than the writing for piano in lieder by the likes of Eberwein, Kreutzer, or even von Weber; the contemporary critics, both approving and disapproving, often comment on the fact. As the piano "so reißend schwillt" (so raging swells) in the setting of the last stanza of "Auf dem Fluße," those same words in the vocal line are in increasing danger of inundation, even as the raised vocal tessitura warps the text in its own way. The eighteenth-century presumption that the instrumental part should be the humble servitor of the vocal melody in songs is literally overturned in "Die Krähe" when Schubert lifts the accompanimental figuration high above the vocal line in stanza 3 and has it far outdo the singer in insistent stridency. In Müller's poem, the crow who accompanies the wanderer—the wordless companion to the voice— becomes, for the moment, the most important object in the world. As the creature's significance increases, the piano part comes close to blotting out the vocal line but without any change in the "subordinate" instrumental figuration. "The revenge of the accompanist" might be one possible caption for this passage in which music asserts its primacy over text in vocal music. The piano and voice join forces

in the unison passages of "Der stürmische Morgen" and yet the pian-
o's timbre on the same pitches assigned the voice contends with the
intelligibility of the words. Once released from bondage to the vocal
part, the piano goes on a rampage in the interlude between stanzas
1 and 2 and in the postlude, while the pounding *ffz* seventh chords
near the end wrest the ear from all but the fiercest delivery of Müller's
words. One recalls as well the loud outbursts from the piano in the
interstices between phrases in the A section (stanzas 1 and 2) of
"Rückblick." Terrors partially tamped down by the vocal line, by the
attempt to restrain fear in verbal expression, immediately flood to the
surface whenever the musicalized words cease. Finally, where Schubert makes use in "Mut" of music's traditional power to state or imply
what the text tries unsuccessfully to suppress, he calls on the power
of loud instrumental sound to defend against and drown out that
which the words would deny. The more the wanderer attempts lying
to himself, the more powerful the truth becomes and the more conscious he is of the utter contradiction in what he does.

Schubert's reliance on the instrumental part is also, and perhaps
most problematically, evident in those places where I have suggested
a narrative interpretation of an entire passage or even a brief gesture
for the piano, such as the journeying figure. To do so is at times
openly to flout the poet, to fill in the omissions and empty spaces
that are an integral part of the poetic form with music. For example,
Müller, who willfully adopted and adapted certain traits from folk
poetry, invests "Der Lindenbaum" with the reticences, the omitted
information, characteristic of folk or folklike verse, but Schubert con-
travenes that strategy with a piano introduction that I have proposed
can be heard as an inner scenario, an untexted mental drama complete
with a "listening" silence in m. 2 before the rustling figuration resumes. Even the fact that the *pianississimo* half-cadence at the end of
the introduction merges without a pause or rest into the texted body
of the song suggests the seamless slippage into memory. But one can
only interpret the passage programmatically, as narrative, in retro-
spect: it is music first and narrative second. In another example, the
sudden turn from G minor to G major in "Rückblick" happens in the
instrumental interlude between the A and B sections, or between
the setting of stanzas 2 and 3, Schubert enacting in the piano the
exact moment at which the wanderer is ambushed by the second
recollection of the song, the second "glance back." Similar instances
occur over and over again in *Winterreise*, music filling the white spaces
between, before, and after stanzas with instrumental music whose

design suggests thought processes, mental turns and twists from one
bend in the poetry to another. And this brings me to my final point
and the end of the journey.

It may seem inconsistent or even perverse to point out the multiple
ways in which Schubert's music overrides Müller's text after arguing
throughout this entire book that Müller is worthier of praise for his
poetic craftsmanship—including those elements music defaces or
obliterates—than some have supposed, but the inconsistency is more
apparent than real. The ways in which Schubert dramatizes, contradicts, obscures, ignores, drowns out, alters, edits, mimics, repeats,
warps, and subordinates poetry to music are all responses to poetry,
complex and multifarious responses. If I have attempted to point out
features of the poetry *as poetry*, the exercise is not irrelevant to a
consideration of Schubert's cycle, in part because one is thereby more
aware of the essential differences between the two arts and of the
transformation, at times brutally executed, wrought by music on
verse. But there is more to the matter than a general demonstration
of music's tyranny over words. Schubert, I believe, took the poetry
seriously, not merely as verbal fodder to be mashed to a pulp by
music—although that is the way many musicians see this work—but
as a richly allusive psychodrama of mythic dimension. When he sets
the line "Why should I linger among the sleepers?" at the end of "Im
Dorfe" as a genuine question, not rhetorical self-reproach; when he
brings back the music of the panic-stricken search in "Erstarrung"
beyond its cessation in fact; and when he constructs his hurdy-gurdy
player and wanderer from the same musical components but gives
each figure its own identity, he pays homage to Müller's words as,
literally, meaningful.

The particular mythic dimension of this work is one peculiarly attractive to modern and postmodern inheritors of the nineteenth century. Müller tells of those dissonances that are the inescapable
condition of consciousness, a *Bildungsbiographie* or spiritual history in
which a spirit sets out in search for its lost and sundered self. When
the quest culminates in partial understanding, the seeker wants only
to reject what he finds, and the self is rent asunder all the more.
Rejection is impossible; neither an alternative self nor death is within
his grasp. "Das Wirtshaus" is a disillusioned and secularized version
of the plea "Let this cup pass from me"; the silence following his plea
(silence that Schubert fills with music) is a decree to continue the
prolonged crucifixion that is existence. In Romantic literature, the
division, conflict, and suffering of the wayfaring spirit are customarily

seen as leading ultimately to a greater good, to reintegration on a higher plane, but not so here—except in the paradox with which the work ends. Out of the denial that art transcends misery comes art and transcendence. If this is a final betrayal of the poetry, I doubt anyone would wish it otherwise.

Ludwig Uhland's *Wander-Lieder*

1. Lebewohl

Lebe wohl, lebe wohl, mein Lieb!
Muß noch heute scheiden.
Einen Kuß, einen Kuß mir gib!
Muß doch ewig meiden.

Eine Blüt', eine Blüt' mir brich
Von dem Baum im Garten!
Keine Frucht, keine Frucht für mich!
Darf sie nicht erwarten.

Farewell

(Farewell, farewell, my love! Today I must leave you. Give me a kiss, a kiss! I must forever depart.
Break off a flower, a flower for me from the tree in the garden! No fruit, no fruit for me! I will long since have gone away.)

2. Scheiden und Meiden

So soll ich nun dich meiden,
Du meines Lebens Lust!
Du küssest mich zum Scheiden,
Ich drücke dich an die Brust.

Ach Liebchen! heißt das Meiden,
Wenn man sich herzt und küßt?

[313]

Ach Liebchen! heißt das Scheiden,
Wenn man sich fest umschließt?

Parting and absence

(So now I should leave you, my life's happiness! You kissed me in parting; I pressed you to my breast.
Oh beloved! is this parting when one kisses and caresses? Oh beloved! is it separation when one clasps so closely?)

3. In der Ferne

Will ruhen unter den Bäumen hier,
Die Vöglein hör' ich so gerne.
Wie singet ihr so zum Herzen mir!
Von unsrer Liebe was wisset ihr
In dieser weiten Ferne?

Will ruhen hier an des Baches Rand,
Wo duftige Blümlein sprießen.
Wer hat euch, Blümlein, hieher gesandt?
Seid ihr ein herzliches Liebespfand
Aus der Ferne von meiner Süßen?

In the distance

(I'll rest here under the trees and gladly hear the little birds. Your singing goes straight to my heart! What do you know of my love in this far-off distant land?
I'll rest here on the banks of the stream where sweetly perfumed little flowers bud and grow. Who sent you here, little flowers, to bloom for me? Are you a sweet token of love that my beloved sent me from so far away?)

4. Morgenlied

Noch ahnt man kaum der Sonne Licht,
Noch sind die Morgenglocken nicht
Im finstern Tal erklungen.

Wie still des Waldes weiter Raum!
Die Vöglein zwitschern nur im Traum,

Kein Sang hat sich erschwungen.
Ich hab' mich längst ins Feld gemacht,
Und habe schon dies Lied erdacht,
Und hab' es laut gesungen.

Morning song

(Dawn has not yet come; the morning bells have not yet rung down in the dark valley.

How still the wide realm of the forest! The little birds twitter in their dreams; no song can yet be heard.

For a long time, I have been up and walking in the field and have created this song and have sung it loudly.)

5. Nachtreise

Ich reit' ins finstre Land hinein,
Nicht Mond noch Sterne geben Schein,
Die kalten Winde tosen.
Oft hab' ich diesen Weg gemacht,
Wann goldner Sonnenschein gelacht,
Bei lauer Lüfte Kosen.

Ich reit' am finstern Garten hin,
Die dürren Bäume sausen drin,
Die welken Blätter fallen.
Hier pflegt' ich in der Rosenzeit,
Wann alles sich der Liebe weiht,
Mit meinem Lieb zu wallen.

Erloschen ist der Sonne Strahl,
Verwelkt die Rosen allzumal,
Mein Lieb zu Grab' getragen.
Ich reit' ins finstre Land hinein
Im Wintersturm, ohn' allen Schein,
Den Mantel umgeschlagen.

Night journey

(I ride forth into the dark land. Neither moon nor stars are shining; the cold winds rage. I have often been this way when golden sunshine laughed, when mild, caressing breezes were blowing.

I go to the dark garden. The withered trees rustle; the dead leaves fall. Here, when the roses bloomed, when everything was consecrated to Love, I used to walk with my beloved.

The sun has gone down; the roses are all wilted. My love was carried to her grave. I ride forth into the dark land, through winter storms, bereft of all light, wrapped in my cloak.)

6. Winterreise

Bei diesem kalten Wehen
Sind alle Straßen leer,
Die Wasser stille stehen,
Ich aber schweif' umher.

Die Sonne scheint so trübe,
Muß früh hinuntergehn,
Erloschen ist die Liebe,
Die Lust kann nicht bestehn.

Nun geht der Wald zu Ende,
Im Dorfe mach' ich halt,
Da wärm' ich mir die Hände,
Bleibt auch das Herze kalt.

Winter journey

(All the streets are empty in this cold wind. The river is frozen and still, but I wander about.

The sun seems so pale and cold and soon will disappear. Love is gone, joy cannot endure.

I go through the forest; I'll stop at the village. There, though I warm my hands, my heart still stays cold.)

7. Abreise

So hab' ich nun die Stadt verlassen,
Wo ich gelebet lange Zeit;
Ich ziehe rüstig meiner Straßen,
Es gibt mir niemand das Geleit.

Man hat mir nicht den Rock zerrissen,
Es wär' auch schade für das Kleid!

Noch in die Wange mich gebissen
Vor übergroßem Herzeleid.

Auch keinem hat's den Schlaf vertrieben,
Daß ich am Morgen weitergeh';
Sie konnten halten nach Belieben,
Von *Einer* aber tut mir's weh.

Departure

(So now I have left the city where I lived for a long time. I briskly traverse the streets; no one wants to go with me.

They haven't torn my coat to shreds—that would be a shame for the garment!—or bitten my cheek with excessive sorrow.

Nobody lost sleep lamenting because I depart in the morning. That doesn't matter, but there is one person who makes me suffer.)

8. Einkehr

Bei einem Wirte wundermild,
Da war ich jüngst zu Gaste;
Ein goldner Apfel war sein Schild
An einem langen Aste.

Es war der gute Apfelbaum,
Bei dem ich eingekehret;
Mit süßer Kost und frischer Schaum
Hat er mich wohl genähret.

Es kamen in sein grünes Haus
Viel leichtbeschwingte Gäste;
Sie sprangen frei und hielten Schmaus
Und sangen auf das beste.

Ich fand ein Bett zu süßer Ruh'
Auf weichen, grünen Matten;
Der Wirt, er deckte selbst mich zu
Mit seinem kühlen Schatten.

Nun fragt' ich nach der Schuldigkeit,
Da schüttelt' er den Wipfel.

Gesegnet sei er allezeit
Von der Wurzel bis zum Gipfel!

At the inn

(A wonderfully friendly host recently asked me to be his guest; a golden apple on a long branch was the sign board at the inn.

My host was the good apple tree; it nourished me with sweet fare and the freshest water.

Many lightly winging guests came to its greenhouse; they leaped about and feasted and were the best singers.

I found a bed for sweet rest on the soft, green mat. The inn itself covered me with its cooling shade.

Now when I asked about payment, it shook its branches. May it be blessed to eternity from its roots to its peak!)

9. Heimkehr

O brich nicht, Steg, du zitterst sehr!
O stürz nicht, Fels, du dräuest schwer!
Welt, geh nicht unter, Himmel, fall nicht ein
Eh' ich mag bei der Liebsten sein!

Returning home

(Oh, do not break, bridge, you tremble too much! Oh, do not quake, rocky ridge you menace me so much! World, don't end; sky, do not fall before I am with my beloved again!)

Selected Bibliography

Sources for the Poems

Müller, Wilhelm. "Wanderlieder von Wilhelm Müller. Die Winterreise. In 12 Liedern." In *Urania. Taschenbuch auf das Jahr 1823*. New Series, 5. Leipzig and Berlin: F. A. Brockhaus, 1823, 207–22.

———. *Gedichte aus den hinterlassenen Papieren eines reisenden Waldhornisten II. Lieder des Lebens und der Liebe*. Herausgegeben von Wilhelm Müller. Dessau: Christian G. Ackermann, 1824, 75–108. 2d ed. 1826.

Sources for the Music of *Winterreise*

Schubert, Franz. [Autograph manuscript] "Winterreise von Wilh. Müller." Part I. 21 folios. [Dated at the beginning] "Febr. 1827 Frz. Schubert mpia [manu propria]." In the Mary Flagler Cary Music Collection of the Pierpont Morgan Library, New York City.

———. [Autograph fair copy] "Fortsetzung der Winterreise." 16 folios. [Or Part II; the "O" of "Oct." corrected on the first page, perhaps from "S" for "September"]. 1827. Bound with autograph copy, Part I.

———. [Engraver's fair copy] "Winterreise / von Wilh. Müller / in Musik gesetzt / von / Franz Schubert / A[nn]o 1827." Part I. 32 folios. In the Vienna Stadt- und Landesbibliothek, Musiksammlung, MH 5391/c.

———. [First edition of Part I] *WINTERREISE. / Von / WILHELM MÜLLER. / In Musik gesetzt / für eine Singstimme mit Begleitung des Pianoforte / von / Franz Schubert. / 89stes Werk. / I.ᵗᵉ Abteilung.* Vienna: Tobias Haslinger, January 1828.

———. *Neue Ausgabe sämtlicher Werke*. 4th ser.: Lieder. Vols. 4a and 4b, 242–5, 260–78. Ed. Walther Dürr. Kassel: Bärenreiter, 1979.

———. *Die Winterreise: Faksimile-Wiedergabe nach der Original-Handschrift*. Kassel: Bärenreiter, 1955.

———. *Winterreise: The Autograph Score*. New York: The Pierpont Morgan Library in association with Dover Publications, 1989.

Sources for Some Individual Songs

Schubert, Franz. [Autograph first version] "Muth." One folio (verso side empty), unsigned and undated. In the collection of Hans Kann, Vienna.
——. [Autograph first version] "Die Nebensonnen." In the Vienna Gesellschaft der Musikfreunde, A 235.
—— [Manuscript copy] "Die Post." In a song album from the Peterskirche Archiv in Vienna, f26r–29v. Österreichische Nationalbibliothek, Vienna.
——. [Manuscript copy] "Die Post. Aus der Winterreise von Wilhelm Müller." In the Liederalbum Anton Schindler, f50v–52v, in an unknown hand. Universitätsbibliothek Lund.

Works by Müller, Schubert, and Their Contemporaries

Allen, Philip Schuyler. "Unpublished Sonnets of Wilhelm Müller." *Journal of English and Germanic Philology* 4, no. 1 (1902), 1–9.
Bauernfeld, Eduard. *Aus Alt-und Neu-Wien*. With an Afterword by Rudolf Latzke. Vienna: Österreichische Schulbücherverlag, 1923.
——. *Aus Bauernfelds Tagebüchern*, ed. Carl Glossy. Vienna: C. Konegen, 1895–96.
——. *Erinnerungen aus Alt-Wien*, ed. Josef Bindtner. Vienna: Wiener Drucke, 1923.
Deutsch, Otto Erich. *Franz Schubert: Thematisches Verzeichnis seiner Werke in chronologischer Folge*. Kassel: Bärenreiter, 1978. Abbreviated as *Franz Schubert: Werkverzeichnis*. *Der kleine Deutsch*, ed. Werner Aderhold, Walther Dürr, and Arnold Feil. Kassel: Bärenreiter, 1983.
——, ed. *Schubert: A Documentary Biography*, trans. Eric Blom. London: J. M. Dent, 1946, and New York: Da Capo Press, 1977. A revised version of *Schubert: Die Dokumente seines Lebens und Schaffens*. Munich: Müller, 1914, and Kassel: Bärenreiter, 1964.
——, ed. *Schubert: Memoirs by His Friends*, trans. Rosamond Ley and John Nowell. London: Adam and Charles Black, 1958. First pub.: *Die Erinnerungen seiner Freunde*. Leipzig: Breitkopf & Härtel, 1957.
——, ed. *The Schubert Reader*, trans. Eric Blom. New York: W. W. Norton, 1947.
Hatfield, James Taft. "Another Unpublished Sonnet of Wilhelm Müller." *Journal of English and German Philology* 4, no. 4 (1902), 9.
——. "Earliest Poems of Wilhelm Müller." *Publications of the Modern Language Association* 13 (1898), 250–85.
——. "Newly-discovered Political Poems of Wilhelm Müller." *American Journal of Philology* 24 (1903), 121–48.
——. "Wilhelm Müllers unveröffentlichtes Tagebuch und seine ungedruckten Briefe." *Deutsche Rundschau* 110 (March 1902), 362–80.
Hensel, Luise. *Aufzeichnungen und Briefe von Luise Hensel*, ed. Hermann Cardauns. Hamm: Breer and Thiemann, 1916.

——. *Aus Luise Hensels Jugendzeit, neue Briefe und Gedichte zum Jahrhunderttag ihrer Konversion (8. Dez. 1818)*, ed. Hermann Cardauns. Freiburg im Breisgau: Herder, 1918.

——. *Lieder von Luise Hensel*, ed. Joseph Reinkens. Paderborn: F. Schöningh, 1870.

Kreutzer, Conradin. *Conradin Kreutzer's Frühlingslieder and Wanderlieder: A Facsimile Edition with New Translations*, trans. and ed. Luise Eitel Peake. Stuyvesant, N.Y.: Pendragon Press, 1989.

Lohre, Heinrich, ed. *Wilhelm Müller als Kritiker und Erzähler: Ein Lebensbild mit Briefen an F. A. Brockhaus und anderen Schriftstücken*. Leipzig: F. A. Brockhaus, 1927.

Müller, Wilhelm. *Debora*. In *Deutscher Novellenschatz*, ed. Paul Heyse and Hermann Kurz, 3d ser., vol. 6. Munich: Rudolf Oldenbourg, 1876.

——. *Diary and Letters of Wilhelm Müller*, ed. Philip Schuyler Allen and James Taft Hatfield. Chicago: University of Chicago Press, 1903.

——. *Gedichte*, ed. F. Max Müller. Leipzig: F. A. Brockhaus, 1868.

——. *Gedichte*, ed. E. Hermann. Berlin: Grote, 1874.

——. *Gedichte*, ed. Paul Wahl and Otto Hachtmann. Leipzig: Feuer-Verlag, 1927.

——. *Gedichte: Gesamt-Ausgabe*, ed. Curt Müller. Leipzig: Philipp Reclam, 1894.

——. *Gedichte: Vollständige kritische Ausgabe mit Einleitung und Anmerkungen*, ed. James Taft Hatfield. Berlin: B. Behr, 1906, and Nendeln, Liechtenstein and New York: Kraus Reprint, 1973.

——. *Griechenlieder. Neue vollständige Ausgabe*. Leipzig: F. A. Brockhaus, 1844.

——. "Herr Peter Sequenz: Oder die Komödie zu Rumpelskirch, Posse in zwei Abtheilungen, nach Gryphius und Shakespeare frei bearbeitet." In *Jahrbuch deutscher Nachspiele* 2 (1823), 37–98.

——. *Homerische Vorschule: Eine Einleitung in das Studium der Ilias und Odyssee*. Leipzig: F. A. Brockhaus, 1824.

——. *Homerische Vorschule: Eine Einleitung in das Studium der Ilias und Odyssee*, ed. Detlev Carl Wilhelm Baumgarten-Crusius. 2d ed. Leipzig: F. A. Brockhaus, 1836.

——. *Lieder der Griechens*, 2 vols. Dessau: Christian Georg Ackermann, 1821–1822.

——. *Lyrische Reisen und epigrammatische Spaziergänge*. Leipzig: Leopold Voss, 1827.

——. *Missolunghi*. Dessau: J. C. Fritsche, 1826.

——. *Rom, Römer und Römerinnen*, ed. Wulf Kirsten. Berlin: Rütten and Loening, 1978.

——. *Rom, Römer und Römerinnen: Eines deutschen Dichters Italienbuch aus den Tagen der Romantik*, ed. Christel Matthias Schröder. Bremen: Carl Schünemann, 1956.

——. *Rom, Römer und Römerinnen: Eine Sammlung vertrauter Briefe aus Rom und Albano mit einigen späteren Zusätzen und Belegen*. 2 vols. Berlin: Duncker and Humblot, 1820.

——. *Siebenundsiebzig Gedichte aus den hinterlassenen Papieren eines reisenden Waldhornisten*. Dessau: Christian G. Ackermann, 1821. [Cited as *Waldhornisten I.*]

———. *Vermischte Schriften,* ed. Gustav Schwab. 5 vols. Leipzig: F. A. Brockhaus, 1830.

———. *Wilhelm Müllers Rheinreise von 1827 sowie Gedichte und Briefe,* ed. Paul Wahl. Dessau: Walther Schwalbe, 1931.

———. *Die Winterreise und andere Gedichte,* ed. Hans-Rüdiger Schwab. Frankfurt am Main: Insel Verlag, 1986.

———, trans. *Blumenlese aus den Minnesingern: Erste Sammlung.* Berlin: Maurer, 1816.

———, trans. *Doktor Faustus: Tragödie von Christoph Marlowe.* With a Foreword by Ludwig Achim von Arnim. Berlin: Maurer, 1818.

———. trans. *Doktor Faustus: Tragödie von Christoph Marlowe.* In *Faust: Theater der Jahrhunderte,* ed. Margret Dietrich, 57–111. Munich: Georg Müller, 1970.

———, and Wolff, Oskar Ludwig Bernhard, eds. *Egeria: Raccolta di poesie Italiane populari.* Leipzig: Ernst Fleischer, 1829.

Secondary Sources

Abraham, Gerald, ed. *The Music of Schubert.* New York: Norton, 1947.

Allen, Philip Schuyler. "Wilhelm Müller and the German Volkslied." Ph.D. diss. University of Chicago, 1899. Reprinted in *Journal of English and Germanic Philology* 2, 3 (1901).

———, and K. M. Klier. "Wilhelm Müller und das deutsche Volkslied." *Das deutsche Volkslied: Zeitschrift für seine Kenntnis und Pflege* 28 (May 1926), 57–61, 73–77.

Armitage-Smith, Julian. "Notes on *Winterreise.*" *Musical Times* 113 (1972), 766–67.

———. "Schubert's *Winterreise,* Part I: The Sources of the Musical Text." *Musical Quarterly* 60 (January 1974), 20–36.

Arnold, Robert Franz. "Der deutsche Philhellenismus: Kultur und literarhistorische Untersuchen," chap. 4: "Wilhelm Müller und seine Freunde." *Euphorion,* 3 (1896), 71–181.

Badura-Skoda, Eva, and Peter Branscombe, eds. *Schubert Studies: Problems of Style and Chronology.* Cambridge: Cambridge University Press, 1982.

Baum, Günther. "Das Problem der *Winterreise.*" *Neue Zeitschrift für Musik* 111 (December 1950), 643–44.

———. "Schubert-Müllers '*Winterreise*' neu gesehen." *Neue Zeitschrift für Musik* 128 (1967), 285–96.

Baumann, Cecilia. *Wilhelm Müller—The Poet of the Schubert Song Cycles: His Life and Works.* University Park: Pennsylvania State University Press, 1981.

Becker, Aloys Joseph. *Die Kunstanschauung Wilhelm Müllers: Ein Beitrag zum Verständnis und zur Würdigung seiner künstlerischen Persönlichkeit.* Borna-Leipzig: Robert Noske, 1908.

Bell, A. Craig. *The Songs of Schubert.* London: Alston, 1964.

Biba, Otto. "Schubert's Position in Viennese Musical Life." *19th-Century Music,* 3 (November 1979), 106–13.

Biehle, Herbert. *Schuberts Lieder in Kritik und Literatur*. Berlin: Wölbing Verlag, 1928.

Brandenburg, Hans. "*Die Winterreise* als Dichtung: Eine Ehrenrettung für Wilhelm Müller." *Aurora* 18 (1958), 57–62.

Bretscher, Paul Martin. "The History and Cultural Significance of the *Taschenbuch Urania*." Ph.D. diss., University of Chicago, 1936.

Brown, Maurice. *Schubert: A Critical Biography*. London: Macmillan, 1958.

——. "Schubert's *Winterreise*, Part I." *Musical Quarterly* 39 (1953), 39–57.

Brües, Otto. "Der Griechen-Müller." *Das innere Reich: Zeitschrift für Dichtung, Kunst und deutsches Leben* 8 (February 1942), 602–7.

Caminade, Gaston. *Les chants des Grecs et le philhellenisme de Wilhelm Müller*. Paris: Félix Alcan, 1913.

Capell, Richard. *Schubert's Songs*, 2d ed. New York: Macmillan, 1957.

Carlton, Stephen. "Sketching and Schubert's Working Method." *Current Musicology* 37–38 (1984), 75–88.

Chailley, Jacques. *Le Voyage d'hiver de Schubert*. Paris: Leduc, 1975.

Cottrell, Alan P. *Wilhelm Müller's Lyrical Song-Cycles: Interpretations and Texts*. University of North Carolina Studies in the Germanic Languages and Literatures 66. Chapel Hill: University of North Carolina Press, 1970.

Dürr, Walther. "Schubert and Johann Michael Vogl: A Reappraisal." *19th-Century Music* 3 (November 1979), 126–40.

Einstein, Alfred. *Schubert: A Musical Portrait*. New York: Oxford University Press, 1951.

Eisenhardt, Günther. "Vertonungen von Gedichten Wilhelm Müllers." *Zwischen Worlitz und Mosigkau, Schriftenreihe zur Geschichte der Stadt Dessau und Umgebung* 21 (1977), 7–14.

Erk, Ludwig, and F. N. Böhme, eds. *Deutscher Liederhort: Auswahl der vorzüglicheren deutschen Volkslieder, nach Wort und Weise aus der Vorzeit und Gegenwart gesammelt und erläutert*. 3 vols. Leipzig: Breitkopf & Härtel, 1893–1894.

Feil, Arnold. *Franz Schubert—Die schöne Müllerin, Die Winterreise*, trans. Ann C. Sherwin. Portland, Ore.: Amadeus Press, 1988. First pub.: *Franz Schubert—"Die schöne Müllerin" und "Die Winterreise": Mit einem Essay "Wilhelm Müller und die Romantik."* Stuttgart: Philipp Reclam, 1975.

Feuchtmüller, Rupert. *Leopold Kupelwieser und die Kunst der österreichischen Spätromantik*. Vienna: Österreichische Bundesverlag, 1970.

Fischer-Dieskau, Dietrich. *Auf den Spuren der Schubert-Lieder: Werden, Wesen und Wirkung*. Wiesbaden: F. A. Brockhaus, 1971.

——. *The Fischer-Dieskau Book of Lieder: The Original Texts of over Seven Hundred and Fifty Songs*, trans. George Bird and Richard Stokes. New York: Knopf, 1977.

——. *Schubert's Songs: A Biographical Study*, trans. Kenneth S. Whitton. New York: Knopf, 1977.

Fröhlich, Hans J. *Schubert*. Munich: Hanser Verlag, 1978.

——. "Wilhelm Müller: 'Im Dorfe.' " *Frankfurter Anthologie* 3 (1978), 59–62.

Gal, Hans. *Franz Schubert and the Essence of Melody*. London: Victor Gollancz Ltd., 1974.

Georgiades, Thrasybulos. *Schubert: Musik und Lyrik*. Göttingen: Vandenhoeck & Ruprecht, 1967.

———. " 'Das Wirtshaus' von Schubert und das Kyrie aus dem Gregorianischen Requiem." In *Gegenwart im Geiste: Festschrift für Richard Benz*, ed. Walther Bulst and Arthur von Schneider. Hamburg: C. Wegner, 1954.

Grasberger, Franz, and Othmar Wessely, eds. *Schubert-Studien: Festgabe der Österreichischen Akademie der Wissenschaften zum Schubert-Jahr 1978*. Vienna: Verlag der Österreichischen Akademie der Wissenschaften, 1978.

Greene, David B. "Schubert's *Winterreise*: A Study in the Aesthetics of Mixed Media." *Journal of Aesthetics of Art Criticism*, 29 (Winter 1970), 181–93.

Hake, Bruno. *Wilhelm Müller: Sein Leben und Dichten*. Berlin: Mayer und Müller, 1908.

Hartung, Günter. " 'Am Brunnen vor dem Tore.' Über ein Lied von Wilhelm Müller und Franz Schubert." In *Reden und Vorträge*, ed. Dietrich Löffler and Dieter Bähtz. Halle: Saale, 1978, 23–38.

Hatfield, James Taft. "The Poetry of Wilhelm Müller." *Methodist Review* 77 (July 1895), 581–94.

———. "Wilhelm Müllers Dichtungen." *Der Westen* (Chicago) 44 (6 February 1898), 2.

Heine, Heinrich. *Briefe*, ed. Friedrich Hirth. 6 vols. Mainz: Florian Kupferberg, 1950.

Hentschel, Cedric. *The Byronic Teuton: Aspects of German Pessimism, 1800–1933*. London: Methuen, 1940.

Hilmar, Ernst. *Franz Schubert in His Time*, trans. Reinhard G. Pauly. Portland, Ore.: Amadeus Press, 1988. First pub.: *Franz Schubert in seiner Zeit*. Vienna, Cologne, Graz: Hermann Böhlaus, 1985.

Just, Klaus Günther. "Wilhelm Müllers Liederzyklen *Die schöne Müllerin* und *Die Winterreise*." *Zeitschrift für deutsche Philologie* 83 (1964), 452–71. Reprinted in *Übergänge: Probleme und Gestalten der Literatur*. Bern: Francke Verlag, 1966.

Khokhlov, Jurii. *O poslednem periode tvorcestva Shuberta* [On the final period of Schubert's creativity]. Moscow: Muzyka, 1968.

Koepke, Richard Paul. "Wilhelm Müllers Dichtung und ihre musikalische Komposition." Ph.D. diss., Northwestern University, 1924.

Kralik, Heinrich. *Schuberts Liederzyklen "Die schöne Müllerin," "Winterreise," und "Schwanengesang." In verkleinerter Nachbildung der Original-Ausgaben*. Vienna: Steyermuhl, 1900.

Kramer, Richard. "Schubert's Heine." *19th-Century Music* 8 (Spring 1985), 213–25.

Kreißle von Hellborn, Heinrich. *Franz Schubert*. Vienna: Carl Gerold's Sohn, 1865.

Landau, Anneliese. *Das einstimmige Kunstlied Conradin Kreutzers und seine Stellung zum zeitgenössischen Lied in Schwaben*. Leipzig: Breitkopf & Härtel, 1930.

Lewin, David. "Schubert, 'Auf dem Fluße.' " *19th-Century Music* 6 (Summer 1982), 47–59.

Marshall, H. Lowen. "Symbolism in Schubert's *Winterreise*." *Studies in Romanticism* 12 (1973), 607–32.

Moore, Gerald. *The Schubert Song Cycles.* London: Hamilton, 1975.
Müller, Friedrich Max. *Auld Lang Syne.* New York: Scribner, 1898.
——. *My Autobiography: A Fragment.* New York: Scribner, 1901.
Mustard, Helen Meredith. *The Lyric Cycle in German Literature.* Columbia University Germanic Studies 17. New York: King's Crown Press, 1946.
Nollen, John. "Heine and Wilhelm Müller." *Modern Language Notes* 17 (April–May 1902), 103–10, 131–38.
Peake, Luise Eitel. "The Song Cycle: A Preliminary Inquiry into the Beginnings of the Romantic Song Cycle." Ph.D. diss., Columbia University, 1968.
Reed, John. *Schubert: The Final Years.* London and New York: St. Martin's Press, 1972.
——. *The Schubert Song Companion.* Manchester, U.K.: Manchester University Press, 1985.
Reeves, Nigel. "The Art of Simplicity: Heinrich Heine and Wilhelm Müller." *Oxford German Studies* 5 (1970), 48–66.
Reininghaus, Frieder. *Schubert und das Wirtshaus: Musik unter Metternich.* 2d ed. Berlin: Oberbaumverlag, 1980.
Reinkens, Joseph Hubert. *Luise Hensel und ihre Lieder.* Bonn: P. Neusser, 1877.
Rissé, Joseph. *Franz Schubert und seine Lieder: Studien.* 2 vols. Erfurt: Bartholomäus, 1873.
Robinson, Paul. *Opera and Ideas: From Mozart to Strauss,* chap. 2: "The Self and Nature: Franz Schubert's *Die schöne Müllerin* and *Winterreise,*" 58–102. New York: Harper and Row, 1985.
Rupprich, Hans. *Brentano, Luise Hensel und Ludwig von Gerlach.* Vienna: Österreichischer Bundesverlag für Unterricht, Wissenschaft und Kunst, 1927.
Sams, Eric. "Schubert's Illness Re-examined." *Musical Times* 121 (1980), 15–22.
Schaeffer, Erwin. "Schubert's 'Winterreise.' " *Musical Quarterly* 24 (1938), 39–57.
Schoolfield, George C. *The Figure of the Musician in German Literature.* University of North Carolina Studies in the Germanic Languages and Literatures 19. Chapel Hill: University of North Carolina Press, 1956.
Schroeder, David P. "Schubert the Singer." *Music Review* 49 (November 1988), 254–66.
Schulze, Joachim. "O Bächlein meiner Liebe: Zu einem unheimlichen Motiv bei Eichendorff und Wilhelm Müller." *Poetica* 4 (April 1971), 215–23.
Schwabe, Friedrich. "Über Tonmalerei in Schuberts 'Winterreise.' " Ph.D. diss., University of Zurich, 1920.
Schwarmath, Erdmute. *Musikalischer Bau und Sprachvertonung in Schuberts Liedern.* Tutzing: Schneider, 1969.
Seidel, Elmar. "Ein chromatisches Harmonisierungsmodell in Schuberts 'Winterreise.' " *Archiv für Musikwissenschaft* 26 (1969), 285–96.
Solomon, Maynard. "Franz Schubert and the Peacocks of Benvenuto Cellini." *19th-Century Music* 12 (Spring 1989), 193–206.
——. "Schubert and Beethoven." *19th-Century Music* 3 (November 1979), 114–25.

Souchay, Marc-André. "Zu Schuberts 'Winterreise.' " *Zeitschrift für Musikwissenschaft* 13 (1930–1931), 266–85.

Spiecker, Frank. *Luise Hensel als Dichterin: Eine psychologische Studie ihres Werdens auf Grund des handschriftlichen Nachlasses*. Evanston, Ill.: Northwestern University Press, 1936.

———. "Luise Hensel und Wilhelm Müller." *Germanic Review* 8 (October, 1933), 265–77.

Stechow, Wolfgang. " 'Der greise Kopf': Eine Analyse." In *Festschrift für Werner Neuse*, ed. Herbert Lederer and Joachim Seyppel. Berlin: Die Diagonale, 1967, 65–67.

Stockel, Rudolf. "Die musikalische Gestaltung von Sprachform und Gehalt in Schuberts 'Winterreise.' " Ph.D. diss., University of Erlangen, 1949.

Uthmann, Jörg von. "Wilhelm Müller, 'Der Lindenbaum.' " *Frankfurter Anthologie* 4 (1979), 53–57.

Volkmann, Hans. "Schuberts Leiermann." *Zeitschrift für Musik* 46 (1929), 137–39.

Weinmann, Alexander. "Zwei neue Schubert-Funde." *Österreichische Musikzeitschrift* 27 (1972), 75–78.

Winter, Robert. "Paper Studies and the Future of Schubert Research." In *Schubert Studies: Problems of Style and Chronology*, ed. Peter Branscombe and Eva Badura-Skoda, 209–75. Cambridge: Cambridge University Press, 1982.

Wirsing, Sibylle. "Wilhelm Müller, 'Rückblick,' " *Frankfurter Anthologie* 3 (1978), 63–66.

Youens, Susan. "Poetic Rhythm and Musical Metre in Schubert's *Winterreise*." *Music & Letters* 65 (January 1984), 28–40.

———. "Retracing a Winter Journey: Reflections on Schubert's *Winterreise*, D. 911." *19th-Century Music* 8 (Summer 1985), 36–54.

———. "Schubert, Mahler, and the Weight of the Past: *Lieder eines fahrenden Gesellen* and *Winterreise*." *Music & Letters* 67 (Winter 1986), 48–61.

———. "Wegweiser in *Winterreise*." *Journal of Musicology* 5 (Summer 1987), 357–79.

———. "*Winterreise*: In the Right Order." *Soundings* 13 (Summer 1985), 41–50.

Index

Library of Congress Cataloging-in-Publication Data

Youens, Susan.
  Retracing a winter's journey : Schubert's Winterreise / Susan Youens.
    p. cm.
  Includes bibliographical references and index.
  ISBN 0-8014-2599-9 (alk. paper)
  1. Schubert, Franz, 1797–1828. Winterreise.   I. Title.
  MT115.S37Y7   1991
  782.4'7—dc20   91–55234

[331]